JAPAN'S ROAD
to the PACIFIC WAR

Deterrent Diplomacy

Studies of the East Asian Institute · Columbia University

JAPAN'S ROAD
to the PACIFIC WAR

Deterrent Diplomacy

JAPAN, GERMANY, *and the* USSR

1935-1940

Selected translations from

Taiheiyō sensō e no michi:

kaisen gaikō shi

Edited by JAMES WILLIAM MORLEY

Columbia University Press · New York · 1976

The Japan Foundation, through a special grant, has assisted the Press in publishing this volume.

Library of Congress Cataloging in Publication Data
Main entry under title:

Deterrent diplomacy.

(Japan's road to the Pacific war)
Translation of 3 selected essays which originally appeared in Taiheiyō sensō e no michi, prepared by Nihon Kokusai Seiji Gakkai, Taiheiyō Sensō Gen'in Kenkyūbu.
CONTENTS: Ōhata, T. The Anti-Comintern pact, 1935–1939.—Hata, I. The Japanese-Soviet confrontation, 1935–1939—Hosoya, C. The Tripartite pact, 1939–1940.
1. Japan—Foreign relations—Germany—Addresses, essays, lectures. 2. Germany—Foreign relations—Japan—Addresses, essays, lectures. 3. Japan—Foreign relations—Russia—Addresses, essays, lectures. 4. Russia—Foreign relations—Japan, Addresses, essays, lectures. 5. World War, 1939–1945—Diplomatic history—Addresses, essays, lectures. I. Morley, James William, 1921–   II. Nihon Kokusai Seiji Gakkai. Taiheiyō Sensō Gen'in Kenkyūbu. Taiheiyō sensō e no michi. III. Title.   IV. Series.
DS849.G4D47   327.52   75-25524
ISBN 0-231-08969-4

Columbia University Press
New York   Guildford, Surrey

The East Asian Institute of Columbia University

The East Asian Institute of Columbia University was established in 1949 to prepare graduate students for careers dealing with East Asia, and to aid research and publication on East Asia during the modern period. The faculty of the Institute are grateful to the Ford Foundation and the Rockefeller Foundation for their financial assistance.

The Studies of the East Asian Institute were inaugurated in 1962 to bring to a wider public the results of significant new research on modern and contemporary East Asia.

Editor's Foreword

A few years ago the Japan Association on International Relations (Nihon Kokusai Seiji Gakkai), which embraces Japan's leading scholars of international affairs, undertook an ambitious collaborative research project on the origins of the Pacific War from the 1920s to 1941. Under the leadership first of Kamikawa Hikomatsu,* professor emeritus of international politics at Tokyo University, and then of Tsunoda Jun, professor of diplomatic history at Kokugakuin University and head of the Shidehara Peace Collection of the National Diet Library, an impressive number of objective diplomatic and military historians were assembled. They were given access to a wide range of primary materials, including not only those of the International Military Tribunal for the Far East but also a mass of others hitherto unavailable from the former imperial army and navy, the Justice Ministry, and the Foreign Ministry. The private papers of Prime Ministers Konoe Fumimaro and Okada Keisuke, Ugaki Kazushige (who served as both army and foreign minister), Colonel Ishiwara Kanji, and others were now available. In addition, a number of leading participants in the events made themselves available for interview. Each scholar in the project was given personal responsibility to present the facts on a given subject as he saw them.

The result was a collection of remarkably objective essays, designed not to fit an overall interpretation of events, an approach that was consciously rejected, but, as one researcher put it, "to provide clues and materials for future historians." Published in 1962–63 in seven volumes by the press of Japan's largest newspaper, the *Asahi shimbun*, under the title *Taiheiyō*

* In accord with Japanese usage, Japanese names are given throughout this volume with the surname first.

sensō e no michi: kaisen gaikō shi (The Road to the Pacific War: A Diplomatic History of the Origins of the War), the series was immediately acclaimed as the most informative, factually based account of Japan's road to war.

Japan's Road to the Pacific War is a translation of selected parts of that work. The principle of selection has been to include those essays or portions of essays that focus primarily on the policy of Japan rather than other countries and draw on materials of an unusual character. While each essay stands on its own authority, its value has been greatly enhanced by a brief introduction by its scholar-translator.

In each case as faithful a translation as possible has been rendered, but translation is not a mechanical process. With languages and cultures as different as the Japanese and the American, minor omissions, revisions, or insertions have occasionally been made, with the approval of the author, to make the translated version more readily intelligible. In addition, for the convenience of researchers, footnotes have been clarified and occasionally changed to indicate subsequently published sources that were originally used in archival form. An effort also has been made to standardize the spellings and identifications of the names of persons and institutions and the titles of documents. Many have contributed to this painstaking translation and editorial work, but for this and all volumes in the series, the contributions of Shumpei Okamoto and Dale K. A. Finlayson should be particularly noted.

In addition, for help on individual essays, Hans Baerwald would like to express his thanks to Elizabeth Keith Thurley, Steven Young, Tominaga Jun'ichi, and Diane Baerwald; Alvin Coox would like to thank Imaoka Yutaka and Yano Mitsuji; and James Morley would like to thank Shumpei Okamoto and Michael K. Blaker.

Deterrent Diplomacy recounts Japan's negotiations with Germany and the Soviet Union in the period from 1935 to 1940, when it explored the uses of alliance diplomacy to try to clear its opponents from the field. This volume is one of five in the series *Japan's Road to the Pacific War*. A list of the five volumes in the series is as follows:

J.W.M.

Contents

ONE

The Anti-Comintern Pact
1935-1939
by
Ōhata Tokushirō

Translated
with an Introduction by

HANS H. BAERWALD

Introduction
by
HANS H. BAERWALD

"Yes, you could say that Ribbentrop and I were very good friends," said former Ambassador Ōshima Hiroshi, recalling events of thirty years before. "In fact, we often saw each other in the evening. You might say that we were good companions, enjoying good wine and kirsch. Indeed, it is possible that the original Anti-Comintern Pact would never have been concluded had it not been for the close relationship that existed between Ribbentrop and myself." [1]

Professor Ōhata's essay on the origins of the Japanese-German Anti-Comintern Pact and its subsequent enlargement to include Italy—both steppingstones to the Tripartite Pact which formed the basis of the "Axis partnership"—amply confirms Ōshima's comment. There is a growing body of literature on the enigma of Japanese-German relations during the 1930s and World War II.[2] Ōhata's contribution, included here, is primarily an intensive examination of the maneuvering that took place within the Japanese government itself. What emerges is a story of incredible infighting, faulty communication, deliberate deception, and boundless ambiguity in the relationships between the Japanese Foreign Ministry, the navy, and the army, as well as between them and the representatives of the German government.

There were elements within both the Japanese and German governments that were never really convinced that a close relationship between the two nations was a good idea. At the time a Japanese-German pact (initially very vague in conception) first became the subject of discussions between Ōshima and Ribbentrop in the spring of 1935, neither was in a truly authoritative position. Ribbentrop was the Nazi Party's foreign policy adviser, close to Hitler and deriving his power from that relationship. Ōshima was military attaché in the Japanese embassy, a career army officer known for his strongly pro-German sympathies and viewed with varying degrees of suspicion by the Japanese Foreign Ministry.

One of the most fascinating subsidiary themes in Professor Ōhata's work is the manner in which Ōshima manipulated the policy of his own government and was subsequently maneuvered into becoming Japan's ambassador. Ōshima himself was not at all certain, he later asserted, that he actually desired the ambassadorial assignment. "Ever since I was fourteen I had been associated with the Japanese army, as a student and as a career officer. I was not convinced that I could handle a diplomatic assignment and agreed only after serious self-reflection and much encouragement from my associates and my superiors." [3]

One point emerges with crystal clarity from Ōhata's narrative: it was Ōshima who was the prime instigator of the Anti-Comintern Pact. On this issue all previous commentaries concerning the origins of the pact, particularly those that rely on the affidavits filed by Ōshima with the International Military Tribunal for the Far East, have now been superseded. Ōshima was the first to suggest to Ribbentrop that Japan and Germany conclude an alliance. According to Ōshima, the alliance was to be aimed at the Soviet Union. Ribbentrop countered this suggestion with the idea that a pact against the Comintern be used as a "cover" and that Ōshima's proposal for a German-Japanese alliance against the Soviet Union be placed in a secret protocol. As is well known, it was the latter combination that was ultimately adopted. Hence, the affidavit submitted by Ōshima to the International Military Tribunal, and scholarship based on it, is not really incorrect; it is incomplete. For this reason alone, Ōhata's contribution carries considerable weight. [4]

As Ōhata points out, Ōshima and Ribbentrop desired a German-Japanese alliance. Such an alliance was also promoted by some elements in the Japanese military and by the so-called Shiratori faction within the Foreign Ministry; and it was supported by a growing body of ultranationalist writers, who helped to create a national mood of dissatisfaction with the international status quo. Nonetheless, unanimity within the Japanese government was never really achieved. The alliance, from its very inception, had feet of clay.

Both the Japanese Foreign Ministry and the navy were by no means convinced that an alliance with Nazi Germany was possible or desirable. Of course, within the Foreign Ministry there was the Shiratori faction; but as Ōhata's research indicates, Shiratori's ambitions were largely neutralized when he was sent to Sweden. In fact, Shiratori's letter to Arita is a classic example of that of a bureaucrat manqué with a grand design. Ōshima's *modus operandi* of bypassing the Foreign Ministry also did not endear him to the officials of that ministry, who were trained in the conduct of traditional diplomacy and were, it would appear, somewhat appalled by Ōshima's and Ribbentrop's backstairs maneuvering. The atmosphere in the Japanese embassy in Berlin was not exactly conducive to mutual trust. Those officials who were not favorably disposed to the alliance with the Nazis were spied upon and harassed, often by their subordinates, to insure their loyalty.[5]

Furthermore, as is well known but as Ōhata documents in great detail, many officials in the Japanese government wanted Anglo-Japanese relations to remain the cornerstone of Japanese diplomacy and were therefore ideologically opposed to any steps that might undermine that relationship. A careful reading of the materials related to the seemingly endless sessions of the Five Ministers Conference reveals the kind of braking power that was available within the Japanese government against those who questioned the wisdom of a particular policy, for example, the quiet question; the telegram that was drafted and redrafted until no one was really certain what its contents meant, least of all the representatives of the imperial Japanese government abroad; the misplacement of key documents; messages that never reached their proper destinations; and more. Even thirty years later our author appears frustrated with the process and comments laconically that there was a breakdown in decision-making within the government.

In the sections translated here Ōhata concentrates on the inner workings of the Japanese government. However, one has only to read any of the already available European and American works to realize the questioning responses of Japan's allies in the Anti-Comintern Pact enterprise. Initially, did the Japanese really want the pact? Obviously some of them did, but how many? And were they really in power? Did the Japanese subsequently want the pact to be strengthened? Again, only the most tentative conclusion emerges. Against whom was the pact to be directed? Was it the Comintern or the Soviet Union, and to what extent was this distinction a convenient fiction? When expanded, should France, Britain, and the United States also be included as targets? Carefully and in great detail, Ōhata explains all the possible combinations and permutations in elaborating the answers to these questions.

The picture that emerges is that of a group of decision-makers who were far from certain of their own convictions. Especially fascinating in this regard is the enigmatic Arita Hachirō, buffeted from all sides during his tenures as foreign minister, who in one of his memoirs refers to himself as "Bakahachi" (Hachi the fool). Viewed from abroad, the Japanese were all too easily seen as playing a game of duplicity and double-dealing—of promises made but not really kept. However, a fairer, and possibly more accurate, description would be that there was all too little unanimity within the Japanese government.

It is really Ōshima who emerges as the main actor in this particular episode in Japanese foreign policy-making. Without him and a few ultranationalist ideologues the Anti-Comintern Pact would probably never have been concluded. For on the German side, while Ribbentrop was receptive, it would appear reactions were lukewarm within the Foreign Office, the military, and the business community that had stakes in China.[6]

Ōhata is extremely careful in drawing any large-scale conclusions. He is primarily concerned with the inner workings of the Japanese government—with the varying responses to Ōshima's proposals or to the proposals made by the Germans (and later the Italians), and with the decision-making apparatus, especially the function of the Five Ministers Conference. He is less concerned with such questions as whether or not the Anti-

Comintern Pact served Japan's national interest at the time. His data do permit one to conclude, however, that the Anti-Comintern Pact certainly did point Japan in the direction of the partnership with the Axis and ultimately confirmed the worst fears of its opponents within Japan, namely, that it would lead to the alienation of Britain and the United States. It is also obvious that while proponents of the project proved to be more powerful than its opponents, the margin of decision was rarely overwhelming.

Essay
by
ŌHATA TOKUSHIRŌ

Japan's willingness to join in an alliance with Germany can be understood in the context of two interrelated domestic developments. The first of these was the turbulent political situation in Japan during the early 1930s. The second was the growth of extremist ideological tendencies in influential private, army, and bureaucratic circles.

Renovationism and Anticommunism

While both Japan and Germany were severely afflicted by the world depression of 1929, the crisis in Japan had actually begun two years earlier with the financial panic of 1927, when many small and medium-sized banks were forced into bankruptcy and the first Wakatsuki cabinet was driven from office by intrigue within the Privy Council. Tanaka Giichi, the new prime minister, and Takahashi Korekiyo, the new finance minister, both of the Seiyūkai, tried to save the situation by more active foreign and financial policies. Tanaka notably replaced the "Shidehara diplomacy" with a more positive policy toward China, exemplified by the Shantung Expedition and the calling of the Eastern Conference. Concurrently with these moves, on May 18, 1928, he issued a "Declaration for the Maintenance of Public Peace in Manchuria," in which he announced that "the maintenance of public peace in Manchuria" was of such "utmost importance to Japan" that, should the disorders in China proper spread to Manchuria, "the imperial government [of Ja-

This is a translation by Hans H. Baerwald of Ōhata Tokushirō, "Nichi-Doku bōkyō kyōtei: dōkyōka mondai (1935–1939)," in *Taiheiyō sensō e no michi*, Vol. 5, Part I, Sec. 1, 2, and 3, pp. 3–155, together with footnotes.

pan] will be forced to take suitable and effective measures." He thus made clear that the basic foreign policy of the Tanaka cabinet was to convert Manchuria into a special zone under Chang Tso-lin.[1] On July 2 these policies were interrupted when Tanaka resigned to take responsibility for Chang's assassination by the Kwantung Army. The succeeding cabinet, led by Hamaguchi Osachi of the Minseitō, favored a sound policy of fiscal austerity. It enforced a 10 percent reduction in the salaries of civil servants and lifted the gold embargo. However, the worldwide depression of 1929 threw masses of workers into unemployment, and two consecutive bad crops reduced the farmers to desperation.

The national anxiety in these years encouraged the left wing movement. The Communist Party challenged the government openly and, in spite of mass arrests in the March 15 (1928) and April 16 (1929) incidents, continued to carry out an active program. In the 1928 general election the Labor-Farmer Party elected two candidates, and the several proletarian parties together succeeded in electing eight candidates. As the depression continued, wages declined further and unemployment spread. Labor and tenancy disputes increased in number and were often accompanied by bloody riots. The government was unable to deal effectively with the basic social and political causes of the riots; the political parties were deadlocked; much corruption was exposed; and people increasingly lost faith in their government.[2]

In conjunction with these developments the right wing movement rapidly mushroomed. An investigation by the Home Ministry Police Bureau revealed that 634 right wing groups with 122,000 members were organized in the period between 1927 and 1937. In Tokyo alone there were 172 such societies with over 34,000 members, three times the number that had existed in the Taishō era (1912–25).[3] Developing close ties with the military, they greatly exacerbated the domestic crisis and secured great influence over the government in the years before the signing of the Anti-Comintern Pact by creating a series of incidents involving the assassination or attempted assassination of prime ministers and other influential politicians. This culminated in the Minobe case in 1935 and the attempted military coup on February 26, 1936.[4]

These numerous civilian right wing organizations differed in their ideologies and policies, especially concerning foreign affairs. Many did not have specific foreign policies; however, nearly all advocated "renovationist diplomacy" (kakushin gaikō) and rejected "cooperative diplomacy" (kyōchō gaikō). Moreover, nearly all called for an ultranationalistic exaltation of the emperor, capitalizing particularly on the Minobe case to consolidate their ideological ascendancy. For many years Tokyo Imperial University Professor Minobe Tatsukichi had been interpreting the Japanese constitution to mean that the emperor was not sovereign, that he was only one of the organs of the sovereign state and therefore limited by the constitution as were other organs of the state. This had seemed reasonable to a more liberal generation, but by the 1930s numerous right wing groups, anxious to unify the nation around the Throne, seized on this "organ theory" as a particularly pernicious doctrine and denounced it in order to exalt their own views of imperial sovereignty. In February 1935 Baron Kikuchi Takeo, a lieutenant-general in the Reserves, attacked this theory and assailed Minobe as an "academic rebel." Although the charges against Minobe were dismissed by a plenary session of the House of Peers, Kikuchi pressed Prime Minister Okada Keisuke and others to express their objections to the organ theory. The Seiyūkai, the Minseitō, and the Kokumin Dōmei passed resolutions demanding that "the government make a greater effort to clarify the fundamental concept of the national polity and exalt its essence." The army published a pamphlet entitled "Views on Great Japan's Imperial Constitution" that also demanded the constitution be interpreted in conformity with the unique Japanese national spirit. Bending to these demands, on August 3 and October 15, 1935, the government issued a so-called "Declaration to Clarify the Nature of the National Polity" in which the organ theory was rejected.

Army extremists, like the middle-grade officers who formed the Evening Society (Issekikai), the Comrades Society (Dōjinkai), the Cherry Blossom Society (Sakurakai), and the Little

Cherry Blossom Society (Kozakurakai), and reservist general officers in the more politically oriented renovationist groups like the Imperial Way Society (Kōdōkai), the Society of Enlightened Ethics (Meirinkai), and the Thirty-Six Club (Sanroku Kurabu) worked in close collaboration with civilian extremists to establish the supremacy of their views over the nation's strategic policy as well. In this they championed the concept of a "national defense state." In October 1934, for example, the army published a pamphlet entitled "The Essence of National Defense and Proposals to Strengthen It," [5] which set forth in concrete form some of the ideas that had been germinating since the Manchurian Incident. The concluding argument was that all aspects of policy, domestic and foreign, should be subordinated to the requirements of "national defense," so that the country would be prepared for total war.

The army pamphlet took a stand in direct contradiction to Shidehara diplomacy, which emphasized peace and cooperation with other nations. Noting the demise of the world order envisioned by the Versailles peace treaty, it discussed the international situation of 1935 and warned of crisis in 1936 and 1937 as a result of America's naval rivalry and the completion of the Soviet Union's five-year plan. It concluded with the demand that Japan embark on a more positive diplomacy:

> Cooperative diplomacy will not solve the present emergency, which is not an isolated incident but represents a world emergency that has come about despite the great efforts that have been made by all countries since the World War. Japan must take advantage of the glorious challenge posed by the Manchurian Incident and our withdrawal from the League of Nations. We must accept our fate, firmly refusing to be weakened by avoiding the challenge, and must have the courage to use this opportunity to formulate a great plan for our country's next hundred years.

These views were echoed in another army pamphlet, published about the time the Anti-Comintern Pact was concluded in November 1936. Entitled "Perfecting the Army's Preparedness and the Spirit Required," it advocated strengthening the army and called for "the reform of civil government and the renovation of the state."

New groups of civilian bureaucrats also attempted to further the cause of "political renovation." They were in some ways different from other rightist groups and on occasion even opposed them; on the other hand, they were critical of the older bureaucrats for deferring to the wishes of the party politicians and like the other rightists advocated a "renovation of the state." One organization that included many of these bureaucrats was the National Foundation Society (Kokuhonsha), organized in 1924 by Hiranuma Kiichirō, Takeuchi Kakuji, and Ōta Kōzō. It embraced a large membership of military servicemen on active duty as well as civilian bureaucrats. Another was the Society for the Maintenance of the National Prestige (Kokuikai). Organized in 1932 around such prominent leaders as Prince Konoe Fumimaro, Viscount Okabe Nagakage, Count Sakai Tadamasa, and Gotō Fumio, it appealed particularly to promising officials in middle-level and junior positions, many of whom were to rise to high wartime posts.

These bureaucratic renovationist influences were brought into focus in 1934 with the establishment by the Okada cabinet of the Cabinet Deliberative Council and the Cabinet Research Bureau. These bodies, removed from Diet influence, were designed to assist the cabinet in formulating national policies that would meet the army's wishes. The Cabinet Deliberative Council consisted of individuals at the very heart of the government, such as Prime Minister Okada and Finance Minister Takahashi Korekiyo, as well as senior members of the Minseitō (other parties having refused to participate) and representatives from the financial world, including Ikeda Seihin of the Mitsui Bank and Kagami Kenkichi of Mitsubishi. The Cabinet Research Bureau was made up of some junior, renovationist-minded officials from various ministries under the direction of the Home Ministry administrator Yoshida Shigeru (not to be confused with the diplomat and later prime minister of the same name). Although not then able to control the policies of the government, a number of these young renovationist bureaucrats were later to attain such prominence that a brief roster of the most important is of some interest. In the Home Ministry, besides Yoshida Shigeru, there were Karasawa Toshiki, Aikawa Katsuroku, Masuda Kaneshichi, Nakamura Keinoshin, Yasui Eiji, and Abe Genki; in the Agriculture and Forestry Ministry, there were Ishiguro Tadaatsu, Ino Sekiya, and Shigemasa Seishi; in the Ministry of Colonial Affairs, there were Kawada Isao and Tomita Kenji; in the Ministry of Commerce and Industry, there were Yoshino Shinji, Takeuchi Kakichi, and Kishi Nobusuke; in the Finance Ministry, there were Kaya Okinori, Aoki Kazuo, and Yamada Tatsuo; in the Postal Ministry, there were Okumura Kiwao, Sengoku Kōtarō, and Wada Hiroo.

The Foreign Ministry, too, had its renovationist bureaucrats, led by individuals such as Shiratori Toshio and Tani Masayuki. Indeed, Shiratori ultimately became the principal spokesman for "renovationist diplomacy." He was appointed director of the ministry's Public Information Division in October 1930. The following year, at the time of the Manchurian Incident, he became the Foreign Ministry's liaison official with the Army Ministry. During the course of almost daily meetings with Lieutenant-Colonel Suzuki Teiichi of the Army Ministry's Military Affairs Bureau and Mori Kaku of the Seiyūkai, he came to share the army's desires and to advocate Japan's withdrawal from the League of Nations and its adoption of "renovationist" policies. His young supporters, particularly the junior (section chiefs and below) renovationist officials who formed the Association of Colleagues (Ryōyūkai) shortly after the Manchurian Incident, began a movement to place the senior Asia specialist Obata Yūkichi in the minister's chair and make Shiratori vice minister.[6] These activities soon embroiled Shiratori in a controversy relating to the establishment of a Policy Research Division in the Foreign Ministry. This division was conceived of as a kind of Foreign Ministry general staff, in the sense that it would investigate diplomatic problems and formulate policy. Shiratori's intention was to establish a nationwide network for the Policy Research Division and to use it as a vehicle for popularizing renovationist diplomacy. Responsibility for Asia policy was normally the province of the First Section of the Asia Bureau, then headed by Tani Masayuki. Since the Policy Research Division proposal was advanced by critics of the Asia Bureau (especially by Shiratori) and threatened its prerogatives, relations between Shiratori and Tani and their supporters grew strained.

Vice Foreign Minister Arita Hachirō sought to resolve the dispute by sending Shiratori abroad as minister to Sweden but for a time was stymied. As he explained: "At that time Mori Kaku, Shiratori Toshio, and Suzuki Teiichi were working closely together, Mori being in charge of domestic affairs, Shiratori in charge of diplomacy, and Suzuki in charge of the military. They were upset by the plan to send Shiratori abroad, as they hoped to bring the government's and the military's policies in line with their own point of view. In addition, Shiratori simply refused to leave." Foreign Minister Uchida Yasuya also did not favor Shiratori's departure, but to avoid trouble he officially announced Shiratori's appointment as minister to Sweden without specifying a date, thus permitting Shiratori to remain in Japan. The argument dragged on until August 1933, when Arita resigned as vice minister to become minister to Belgium and Tani became counselor to the government of Manchukuo. Shigemitsu Mamoru was given the vice minister's post rather than Shiratori and promptly threatened to force Shiratori's resignation if he did not depart. Shiratori finally left for Sweden in December.

The remaining renovationists continued to maneuver within the Foreign Ministry. In 1934 they engineered the transformation of the Foreign Ministry's Policy Research Division into what became the Research Division and arranged for its chief, Kurihara Tadashi, to appoint to it an increasing number of those officials who advocated renovationist diplomacy. As a consequence, individuals handling diplomatic relations with the Axis powers came to be selected principally from the Public Information Division, which Shiratori had headed, or from the Research Division, which he had created.

Representative of the thinking of the renovationist group in the Foreign Ministry is a pamphlet entitled "The Unique Principles Guiding Japanese Diplomacy" by Nimiya Takeo, an official in the Research Division. This 152-page pamphlet is reported as having influenced the youth of the day, especially students. It was officially published in December 1936, the month after the ratification of the Anti-Comintern Pact, and the views it presented paralleled those of partisans of the pact within the Foreign Ministry. In the introduction Nimiya set forth the belief that clarification of Japan's *kokutai* or national polity should be the basis both for the reform of domestic politics and for a revolution in Japan's foreign policy. Part I, "Unity on a Broadly Conceived Principle of Development," described Japan's diplomacy as faced with a choice between (1) a broadly conceived "development" or expansionism based on the ideal of race and capable of satisfying the interests of the nation for the next hundred years, and (2) a policy of timidity, classically exemplified by the Shidehara policy, which aimed only at the interests of the moment. While Japan seemed to be pursuing the latter path, Nimiya argued, in actuality ever since the Sino-Japanese War it had been pursuing the former; but not being clear about this, it was now inviting its own defeat, as exemplified in the policies adopted to deal with the Manchurian Incident.

Part II, "The Asian Racial Movement and the Principle of Asia for the Asians," emphasized that an expansionist policy was defensible only on the basis of racial nationalism, which Japan's diplomacy must take into account. Part III, "The Japanese Racial Spirit as the Guiding Principle of Diplomacy," asserted that traditional Japanese morality, not western imperialism, must be the guide. Material gain, Nimiya contended, was not an acceptable reason for war; rather, justice and idealism must be the basis. Hence, an aggressive diplomacy that might lead to war was tenable only if based on idealism. "Clarification of the nation's *kokutai*, which has risen like a flood tide to revitalize domestic politics, must also become the basis for improving Japan's foreign policy." These ideals, he went on, could be summed up in the concept of "Japanism," which he defined by such mystical slogans as "eight corners of the world under one roof," "emperor-centrism," and "cooperative familism," all of which implied the denial of traditional "power politics" and "imperialism" and called for the building of a "new order" in which Japan would assume leadership. In discussing concrete diplomatic issues Nimiya repeatedly referred to Japan's problems with China and the Soviet Union which, he said, presented "the greatest challenges that confront Japanese diplomacy." The Soviets had to be expelled from China, where their "Red ideas" were creating the possibility that Asia would be torn asunder. To avoid this and to establish a society based on permanent mutual cooperation among Japan, Manchuria, and China, warned Nimiya, would require sacrifices and possibly even war with the Soviet Union. But such a war, like the Manchurian Incident, would have nothing to do with European-style imperialism. It would be justified and indeed should be welcomed as the price for realizing such Oriental ideals as "the harmony of the five races" and "peaceful economic cooperation."

Commitment to the kind of "Japanist" diplomacy set forth by Nimiya in his pamphlet was weak in the Nazi-minded Axis faction of the Foreign Ministry, but such thinking did parallel certain lines of thought that were developing within army and civilian right wing movements. It had its counterpart also in the Ministry of Education, which in 1937 published *Kokutai no hongi* (The Essence of the National Polity). While this textbook did not advocate an alliance with Germany, pointing out the undesirability of emancipating and reviving Oriental society, only to subject it to a German- or Italian-style dictatorship, it did promote anti-Sovietism and anticommunism and thus helped to lay the groundwork for a Japanese-German coalition as envisaged by Nimiya's pamphlet.

Japan created Manchukuo after the Manchurian Incident of 1931 and temporarily stationed its forces inside the Great Wall of China in 1933, thereby exerting pressure on the Chinese government. Foreign Minister Hirota Kōki tried to counteract Japan's resultant international isolation by pursuing a more cooperative policy in the midst of these developments. Nonetheless, this isolation was further deepened when Japan withdrew from the League of Nations on March 27, 1933 (effective two years later), abrogated the Washington Naval Disarmament Treaty in 1934, and withdrew from the London Disarmament Conference in 1936. In addition, the Amō declaration of 1934, which warned other states not to engage in joint action against Japan, caused a further deterioration in Japan's relations with other nations, especially the United States, during 1935 and 1936. The Japanese army, meanwhile, accelerated its efforts to separate north China from China proper, creating the East Hopei Anticommunist Autonomous Council in November 1935 and the Hopei-Chahar Political Council in December. On January 21, 1936, Foreign Minister Hirota propounded to the Diet the so-called "Three Principles," (in reality, demands), which he felt should guide Japan's policy toward China:

1. The [Chinese] Nationalist government should be prohibited from condoning any anti-Japanese activities and should be encouraged to promote Sino-Japanese cooperation.
2. The Nationalist government should recognize the existence of Manchukuo and promote cooperation between China and Manchukuo in north China.
3. Japan and China should cooperate to oppose communism in Outer Mongolia.

Hirota hoped that these principles would stabilize Sino-Japanese relations and that the third point relating to anticommunism would help Japan to win worldwide sympathy. According to Morishima Gorō, who drafted Hirota's three principles, the anticommunist statement was inserted at the army's request and was the result of a Foreign Ministry compromise with the army. Nonetheless, in a certain sense Hirota's diplomacy was from the outset motivated by anticommunism.

It was a stance that he and his colleagues often justified by reference to the announced policies of the Comintern. In July 1935 the Comintern had held its seventh congress, which had adopted a resolution to carry on the fight against fascism; and pointing with urgent concern to Japan's, Germany's, and Poland's "imperialistic ambitions of world redivision," it instructed communists throughout the world that "the most important goal of all communist parties is to oppose this ambition with all their united power." This resolution advocated collaboration with democratic socialism and capitalism and the establishment of a broadly based "united front" with those who agreed with the stated goal. Accordingly, in the same year, the Comintern published a separate manifesto calling on the Japan Communist Party to heal its factionalism and build such a united front in Japan.

These resolutions of the Seventh Comintern Congress made a major impact on the Japanese government, the military being consumed by concern over possible moves by the Red Army. Needless to say, the Comintern and the Soviet Union were one and the same: a previous Comintern resolution had required that the fight against imperialism should be carried on "solely from the point of view of protecting the Soviet Union" and had stated that "the people who are working to support peace" were those most deeply and positively concerned with strengthening, replenishing, and supporting the Red Army. If the counter-revolution were to begin, it continued, communists must do their best "to give help to the Red Army so that it may triumph over the armies of imperialism." As a consequence, Japan felt threatened by the buildup of the Soviet army. The army pamphlet on "The Essence of National Defense and Proposals to Strengthen It," mentioned earlier, described the Soviets' stockpiling of armaments in the USSR and arming of troops in the Far East and called attention to the fact that Japanese forces in Manchukuo were numerically inferior. After assuming his new post as chief of the Operations Section of the General Staff in August 1935, Ishiwara Kanji tried to strengthen the army in Manchukuo and Korea to meet the Soviet challenge. During this period the frequent disputes on the border between the Soviet Union and Manchuria gave urgency to the army's demands for an increase in weapons production.

The resolutions of the Comintern Congress had not only opposed Japan's, Germany's, and Poland's "ambitions of world redivision" but had also criticized the attitudes of Italy and Britain. Thus communist activities were arousing general hostility among the world powers. In view of these developments, an anti-Comintern policy seemed to provide a possibility for drawing together the army and the Foreign Ministry and perhaps avoiding Japan's further isolation from the powers.

Shiratori, of course, was a strong advocate of this view. Although not directly involved in Hirota's diplomacy, Shiratori was observing the state of the world from his vantage point in Sweden. Late in 1935 he set forth his views in a wide-ranging letter to Arita, who apparently remained on good terms with him despite their former disagreement. Arita's generally favorable response takes on special significance in view of his appointment the following year to the Hirota cabinet as foreign minister, a post that placed him in charge of the Anti-Comintern Pact negotiations.

Shiratori initiated the correspondence in a letter dated November 4, in which he argued that Japan's most critical need was the removal of external influences from China and Manchukuo. "If we leave them as they are," he wrote, "these countries will automatically enter the circle of our imperial power and we will be able to exploit them, but that is not enough. We must actively intervene so as to be able to compete with forces from the outside. It is not sufficient for China to have superficially close relations with Japan; rather, China must be brought to cooperate actively with Japan in the expulsion of external influences that are hostile to China and Japan." Among such threatening external influences, Shiratori went on, "it is the power of Red Russia that is the most important and will become the principal problem of our imperial diplomacy." To solve this problem, "we must secure the collaboration of China as well as the cooperation of Britain and the United States."

At the same time, Japan should concern itself with the European political situation, for if the European countries went communist, this would have particularly dangerous repercussions on India and China, and through them on Japan. "If we are merely bystanders and communist power increases," he warned, "we may be faced with the choice of ourselves going communist or being invaded, either of which would be disastrous. In the present situation it is only Russia that poses a threat to Japan."

Shiratori advocated also that negotiations be undertaken with the USSR directly. He set forth the following minimal demands: cessation of Red activities in various parts of Asia, disarmament of Vladivostok, and complete Russian withdrawal from Outer Mongolia and Sinkiang with no troops to be stationed east of Lake Baikal. He also suggested that the fishing and forestry problems and the north Sakhalin reversion issue be resolved and recommended that the purchase of the Maritime Province be considered in the future. If these demands were not met, Japan should be prepared for war.

This in turn meant that Japan should launch an "appropriate diplomacy" as quickly as possible. He proceeded to sketch what such a diplomacy required. "We do not need a specific understanding with Germany and Poland because they share our anti-Russian views. In case of need, we will stand together. Britain is the only problem." Adjustment of Anglo-Japanese relations, in his view, meant reconciling other policies toward China. Here caution would have to be exercised, for the only acceptable basis for such a reconciliation would be Britain's acknowledgment of certain basic Japanese policies toward China, namely, the establishment of a Sino-Japanese alliance as the foundation of Japan's China policy vis-a-vis Russia, China's recovery of its sovereignty over Outer Mongolia and Sinkiang, joint Sino-Japanese suppression of the communist rebellion, and the strengthening and reorganizing of the Chinese military.

Shiratori concluded his plea with the argument that war with the Soviet Union was inevitable and Japan in fact need not fear it. "So far as I can determine, the army believes that war with Russia is unavoidable. Border incidents and activities in Outer Mongolia support the validity of this threat." Therefore the Foreign Ministry should stop temporizing on Soviet policy, heal the split with the army, and join it willingly and convincingly. So-called cooperative diplomacy, after all, is one that cringes before power and in the contemporary situation becomes passive and insignificant. The present goal of Japanese diplomacy should be the clarification of Soviet-Japanese relations before the foundation of Soviet political power can be built within the country as well as abroad. In brief, Shiratori's plea called for war against the USSR. "We cannot stand too much of a sacrifice," he acknowledged, but not much would be required. "It is not too painful to contemplate the war's development once our crack troops confront their revolutionary army;

not too much effort will be necessary to bring their nation to collapse."

Arita replied that he did not agree with Shiratori's analysis of Britain's role in China, nor with the supposition that Poland and Germany would stick by Japan under all circumstances. He did not believe that the Japanese and the Slavs were fated to fight each other or that the Soviet Union would collapse if it were to fight a major power. Nor did he think that all the points Shiratori suggested should be raised with the Russians; he did not go along with the demand, for example, that all Soviet troops should be withdrawn from east of Lake Baikal. Arita did agree with Shiratori on such significant propositions as the need for excluding external, especially Soviet, influences from China, the deceptive nature of the Soviet peace policy, and the danger of communization of China and India. "Japan should not be lax in protecting itself and China from Red propaganda," he agreed, conceding that it would be necessary "to complete the armament program so that propaganda and other challenges could be met with military force."

After the announcement that Arita would become foreign minister, Shiratori sent him a letter indicating that he too wanted to be posted home. "But no money for my fare being available, I have been asked to postpone my return. I have even offered to pay my own fare. I know mine is an unpopular position, but I want to be able to discuss it in various circles. I shall try to avoid upsetting senior officials in the Foreign Ministry, who no doubt would prefer a nuisance like me to remain abroad." Shiratori must have known at the time that some of the young renovationists in the Foreign Ministry were working for his appointment as vice minister. However, he was not permitted to return.

Meanwhile, Japan and Germany seemed to be drawing closer together in their domestic and foreign policies. Although a fascist revolution had occurred in Italy some ten years earlier, the Nazis' rise to power in 1933 was a development of more significance to Japan because from that time on Germany began systematically to rebel against the international order established at Versailles, creating a convergence of German and

Japanese interests. Rumors began to circulate about close contacts between Germany and Japan, rumors that were reported by the American ambassadors in both countries.[7]

There was as yet no truth to these rumors about a German-Japanese entente, although Hirota in his Three Principles had advocated Sino-Japanese collaboration against communism. Nonetheless, it is worth noting that Obata Yūkichi, the Japanese ambassador to Germany in the immediate pre-Nazi period, was worried about the consequences of growing Nazi influence over certain Japanese. He was particularly concerned lest the Japanese military be "hoodwinked by the Nazis and drawn closer to them," so that if the Japanese military came to power, "they would begin to emulate the Germans." The problem was becoming grave, since "there are already so many pro-German Japanese soldiers that any increase in their numbers will only make the situation worse. We must stop this nonsense and if possible exclude soldiers who belong to the German faction from service in our German embassy as military attachés or their assistants. Contacts with the Nazis should not be the sole province of the army but should be broadened as much as possible." As a consequence of Obata's recommendation, close contacts were developed between the embassy and the Nazis, including even the head of the party's Foreign Affairs Department, Alfred Rosenberg. This did not, however, weaken relations between the Japanese army and the Nazis; in fact, they grew even closer and eventuated in the arrival of the pro-German military attaché Colonel Ōshima Hiroshi.[8]

The Negotiations

Colonel Ōshima became military attaché in Germany in March 1934. A year later he was promoted to major-general and in 1938 to lieutenant-general. He spoke German fluently, reportedly better than any other Japanese official in Germany at the time. His duties were to study Soviet-German relations with emphasis on German intentions in the event of a Soviet-Japanese war.[9] Prior to Ōshima's departure from Japan, Colonel

Iimura Yuzuru, head of the Europe-America Section of the General Staff's Intelligence Division, instructed Ōshima also to sound out the possibilities of Japanese-German cooperation in obtaining intelligence about the USSR.

Ōshima's activities in 1935 are difficult to ascertain because there are several versions. All versions agree, however, that some kind of German-Japanese alliance began to be the subject of discussions between Ōshima and Joachim von Ribbentrop, the chief diplomat of the Nazi party. In his affidavit to the International Military Tribunal for the Far East, Ōshima stated that Ribbentrop had approached him in May or June of 1935 about the possibility of concluding a defensive alliance between Japan and Germany. Ribbentrop was said to have conducted this probe through an intermediary, Friedrich Hack, who was serving as a broker for the Heinkel Aircraft Company in dealings with the Japanese army and navy.

This version is in general accord with, and indeed may be based on, a memorandum prepared by Ōshima and dated December 14, 1945, which affirms that it was Hack who initially inquired about the possibility of a German-Japanese defensive alliance in late spring or early summer of 1935. According to the 1945 memorandum, Ōshima first responded by pointing out the difficulties involved but later did approach Ribbentrop (through Hack) with the suggestion that a treaty designed to restrict the Soviet Union's activities in the event of a war with either Germany or Japan might be advantageous. He also met Ribbentrop at Hack's residence about October 4 or 5 (after the Seventh Comintern Congress), at which time Ribbentrop indicated his own agreement with the project and inquired as to whether the Japanese army was in accord with such a proposal.

Years later Ōshima offered a slightly different version, claiming that he had met Ribbentrop in the spring of 1935 and had himself proposed the conclusion of an agreement between Germany and Japan that would commit each to refrain from assisting the USSR in any way should the USSR make war on the other.[10] Ōshima stated that he had made his suggestion after he became aware of Ribbentrop's strong anticommunist bias, Hack again figuring as the intermediary.

During the course of these meetings Ribbentrop periodically inquired about the intentions of the Japanese army. In response to a cable sent in June 1935 to the General Staff, Ōshima was informed that there was agreement with his proposals but that Lieutenant-Colonel Wakamatsu Tadaichi, head of the German desk in the Intelligence Division's Europe-America Section, was being sent to Germany to ascertain the intentions and degree of commitment of the German army.

Specifically, Prince Kan'in Kotohito, chief of the Army General Staff, ordered Wakamatsu to investigate the following points: 1) the intent of the German army and government concerning "the treaty Ribbentrop wants"; 2) the possibility of concluding an anticommunist agreement between Japan and Germany; and 3) Ribbentrop's personality and outlook as well as his status within the German government. Vice Chief of Staff Sugiyama Gen submitted the following reasons in support of Japan's need for such a treaty: Japan's international isolation after the Manchurian Incident; the military threat posed by the Soviet Union; the need for further protection against communism, the enemy of Japan's polity; and Japan's desire to cooperate with all countries, particularly China and Germany (which were strategically important), but also with Britain and the United States. As a first step Japan was desirous of cooperating with Germany in these anticommunist efforts.[11] Questions can be raised about the degree to which this reasoning actually expressed the army's intentions, but it later created difficulties for Foreign Minister Arita, who had to face the delicate problem of balancing the desire for an anti-Comintern alliance against the desire for good Anglo-Japanese relations.

During Wakamatsu's two-week stay in Berlin, he met Minister of Defense Werner von Blomberg in the company of Ribbentrop. Ribbentrop suggested that, as the Comintern threatened both Germany and Japan, an anti-Comintern agreement should be concluded between them in conjunction with a separately considered secret agreement. Wakamatsu responded that the Japanese army was in accord with these views and reported Ribbentrop's suggestion to the General Staff before returning to Tokyo at the end of January 1936.

During his negotiations with Ribbentrop, Ōshima had not consulted the Japanese embassy in Germany. Ambassador Mushakōji Kintomo in fact had been pondering separately Japan's policy toward Germany ever since his appointment to the post in December 1934. He envisaged three alternatives—a close relationship with Germany, a rather neutral posture, or a cautious stance involving the development of closer ties with Britain and the United States on the ground that Germany posed a danger to Japan—but he had not opted clearly for any one of them. He recognized that British and American attitudes toward Japan had been relatively cool since the Manchurian Incident, unfriendly in fact; the third alternative therefore seemed a bit unrealistic. However, Japan might find itself even more isolated if it adopted a neutral posture vis-à-vis Germany, in view of the latter's effort to develop and maintain close contacts with Britain with respect to the problem of naval armaments. Thus the second alternative was likewise not very promising. This left the first, that is, drawing closer to Germany, but standing in the way of this policy were the problems posed by Germany's increasing trade with China, where Germany had begun to surpass Britain and to loom as Japan's principal competitor.

Among Mushakōji's staff, opinion was divided. A meeting took place on July 4, 1935, for example, attended by Counselor of Embassy Inoue Kōjirō, Military Attaché Ōshima, and Naval Attaché Yokoi Tadao. Ōshima emphasized the need to strengthen Japan's ties with Germany, whereas Inoue proposed that Japan act in concert with Britain and the United States while simultaneously cooperating with Germany. But Mushakōji was unable to achieve concrete results in any of these directions prior to his return to Japan later in the month.

Ōshima's negotiations with Ribbentrop gradually became more concrete after Mushakōji's depature. Although he operated outside embassy channels, the Foreign Ministry was not totally uninformed about his activities; for example, Okamura Yasuji, chief of the General Staff Intelligence Division, often discussed matters relating to the anti-Comintern pact project with Tōgō Shigenori, chief of the Foreign Ministry

Europe-America Bureau. The Foreign Ministry was also briefed to some extent through meetings with army bureaucrats as well as through Morishima Gorō, chief of the First Section of the ministry's Asia Bureau. Nonetheless, doubts remain about the extent to which the Foreign Ministry was kept informed. Perhaps due to a mix-up of files, one report from Inoue (chargé d'affaires during Mushakōji's absence) containing information about Ōshima's activities that Inoue had obtained from German journalists and Nazis, was never seen by officials in the Foreign Ministry.[12]

Regardless of the extent to which the details of Ōshima's negotiations may or may not have been known to the Foreign Ministry, Foreign Minister Hirota was convinced that Japan's diplomatic policies had to be developed in harmony with the military. Mushakōji, upon his return to Japan, consulted with Vice Foreign Minister Shigemitsu and agreed with him that the army should be strengthened and its attention directed toward the Soviet Union; this policy, it was reasoned, would satisfy the army and could therefore serve as the common basis for Japanese foreign policy. It would appear that leading individuals within the Foreign Ministry, including Hirota, Shigemitsu, and Mushakōji, had agreed in principle with the proposal that Japan should pursue an anti-Comintern policy. In the meantime Ōshima had sent a draft of his proposal to the army. He was told that while the army agreed, it intended to consult the Foreign Ministry and the navy and send him word later.

Events in Japan in 1936—including the February 26 Incident, the resultant fall of the Okada cabinet, the unwillingness of Konoe to serve as prime minister, and the investiture of the Hirota cabinet—delayed the progress of German-Japanese negotiations. Toward the end of March Army Minister Terauchi Hisaichi invited Mushakōji to a meeting of about twenty Army Ministry officials. Only Military Section Chief Machijiri Kazumotō made a strong case on behalf of a German-Japanese military alliance, leading Mushakōji to believe that some differences still existed within the army.[13] However, while problems did remain, there is reason to believe that Machijiri's views reflected those of the army's mainstream.

At the same time, Arita's fears of the Soviet Union and concern over the army's views were also increasing. On his way from Europe to China, where he was posted as ambassador in February 1936, he had stopped off in various countries to gather information. In Poland Minister Itō Nobufumi and Military Attaché Yamawaki Masataka told him that Soviet power should not be underestimated and that Japan should not be too belligerent. In Germany Military Attaché Ōshima had informed him that the German General Staff was taking a serious view of Soviet manpower resources and that Germany's attitude toward the USSR was governed by caution.[14]

These opinions led Arita to feel that Japan should not adopt a belligerent posture and that consultation between Germany and Japan would be advantageous given the similarity of their interests vis-à-vis the Soviet Union and their mutual desire to take countermeasures against any growth of the Soviet army. He also believed that such contacts with Germany would ease Japan's sense of isolation in the aftermath of the Manchurian Incident. On this basis he gradually came to agree with Ōshima's ideas about Japanese-German cooperation [15] and conveyed his feelings to Mushakōji in Japan, urging the ambassador to discuss the matter fully with Foreign Ministry officials prior to his return to Berlin. Arita also advocated such a cooperative policy in conversations with Vice Foreign Minister Shigemitsu, and by the time he himself became foreign minister in the new Hirota cabinet on April 2, discussions had been initiated within the ministry regarding some kind of anti-Comintern pact that would of course be directed also against the Soviet Union. Arita seems to have had in mind what he came often to refer to as a "vague promise" written in watery ink; "an agreement in grey," he liked to call it, leaving for later the black ink of firm commitments.[16]

While Arita thus began to close the policy gap with the army, he was probably not fully informed about the details of the Ōshima-Ribbentrop negotiations; nor did he in any event want the ministry to be bound by the army's thinking or activities. He reached an agreement with Mushakōji that the Foreign Ministry should consider the whole matter afresh, and that it should not be influenced by the army's informal conversations. On May 8 Arita cabled Mushakōji, with Prime Minister Hirota's consent, instructions to the effect that the government's policy in this initial stage was to make no firm commitments. Mushakōji was not to present a proposal but simply to assess the intentions of the German Foreign Office and the Nazi Party concerning the proposed pact in an effort to find out how important they believed such an agreement to be and what kind of pact they desired.

In the interim the army had instructed Ōshima that the negotiations would henceforth be conducted by the Foreign Ministry with Mushakōji as its agent, but that Mushakōji had the option of taking charge immediately or asking Ōshima to continue the negotiations he had begun. Only then did Ōshima inform Mushakōji concerning the complexity of the negotiations (some reports indicate that he had done so prior to Arita's May 8 telegram), and in the light of this information Mushakōji asked Ōshima to continue in charge until Hitler had arrived at a decision.

After responsibility for the conduct of the negotiations had been transferred to the Foreign Ministry, Mushakōji informed Germany of Japan's firm intention of concluding an agreement and requested that a concrete draft be presented. Germany did so at the beginning of July, although it is possible that the drafts of the Anti-Comintern Pact and attached protocols were those previously negotiated by Ōshima and Ribbentrop. After the war Ōshima related that he had requested Furuuchi Hiroo, a secretary in the embassy, to assist him in the preparation of a draft. He also stated that in July, while attending the Wagner Festival, he had received a German draft from Dr. Hans von Raumer, chief of the Far Eastern Section of Ribbentrop's *Büro*, and that upon meeting Hitler there he was told the draft had not satisfied the führer, who had made some amendments to it.

A full text of the German proposal, which included a draft anti-Comintern pact with an attached secret protocol, apparently did not survive the destruction of archives in both countries at the end of the war; but from the diary of Baron Harada Kumao, the IMTFE testimony of Yamaji Akira (chief of the Second Section of the Foreign Ministry's Europe-Asia Bureau), and particularly the ministry's unpublished account of these negotiations, one can surmise that the German draft was generally welcomed by Japan's leaders although they took some issue with details.

The Japanese army, Arita told Harada on July 18, wanted the treaty to provide for: (1) German neutrality in the event Japan encountered difficulties with the Soviet Union, and (2) German participation in joint defensive measures against the Comintern. The Japanese Foreign Ministry was prepared to agree but did not want the second provision to be publicized.[17] In addition, the Foreign Ministry had two reservations: first, that Japan should be careful not to antagonize the USSR excessively and thus bring about a war, Soviet-Japanese relations being very delicate when compared with German-Japanese relations; second, that Japanese-German cooperation should not become the cause of unnecessarily antagonizing other countries, especially Britain, with which it was essential to keep in contact so that discussion of various problems important to both countries could continue.

Initially the Army Ministry strongly opposed the second condition concerning relations with Britain, but finally on July 24 it conceded, joining with the Foreign Ministry in a memorandum "Concerning the Conclusion of a Political Pact between Japan and Germany." This document incorporated both the Army Ministry's desires and the Foreign Ministry's reservations and set forth a unified view on the revisions that were to be sought. It was agreed further that, "while negotiating with the Germans about the foregoing points, Japan should also open negotiations with Britain for a draft treaty that will respect Britain's vested interests in China." In short, the army agreed with the Foreign Ministry that revisions should be sought in the German draft in order to reflect both the delicacy of the current Soviet-Japanese situation and the special quality of Anglo-Japanese relations.

This understanding helped to pave the way for the incorporation of the anti-Comintern line into the overall "Fundamentals of National Policy" decision taken by the Five Ministers

Conference on August 7. The following day it was confirmed in greater detail by the prime minister, the foreign minister, and the army and navy ministers in a document entitled "The Foreign Policy of Imperial Japan," in which the four ministers pledged the government to a new "positive" foreign policy aiming at: (1) the progressive development of Manchukuo, (2) the independent adjustment of relations with the Soviet Union and China, and (3) Japan's peaceful advance to the south. The adjustment of relations with the Soviet Union was required because:

> The Soviet Union's revolutionary pressure on Asia increases as it continues to strengthen its national defense and international position through a huge rearmament program. Its goal, a Red penetration of many areas, interferes with Japan's East Asia policy and poses a grave threat to our empire's defense. Thwarting the Soviet Union's aggressive intentions therefore has become the most crucial element in our diplomacy. This goal must be achieved by diplomatic means and by completion of a defense buildup.

The main diplomatic means was to be a kind of anti-Soviet encirclement, described as follows:

> Germany has interests that closely parallel ours vis-à-vis the Soviet Union because of the special arrangement that exists between Russia and France. Hence, it is in Germany's interest to cooperate with us; and we in turn should promote close relations with Germany, leading to an alliance between Japan and Germany. This relationship must be expanded to include Poland and other friendly European countries near the Soviet Union as well as other Asian and Islamic countries, as a further restraint on the Soviet Union.

Mushakōji conducted more than ten negotiating sessions with Germany on the basis of the Army–Foreign Ministry decision of July 24. Like the German proposals themselves, the records of these sessions have not been preserved; but other sources as well as a comparison of the July 24 decision with the final texts indicate that there were difficulties with the pact itself and other more serious ones with the secret supplementary protocol.

In the draft pact there was, first of all, the problem of the preamble, which Hitler had wanted to strengthen and which the Japanese government felt was already too strong. In accord with the government's decision of July 24, Ōshima suggested that the preamble be toned down and a strongly worded statement issued separately. Initially Hitler refused, asserting that the working masses would not bother to read it if it were a separate statement; but in the end he abandoned the whole idea of amending the draft preamble, and the Japanese government presumably allowed it to stand.

In the body of the draft pact an issue seems to have arisen over its scope. Whatever the Germans may have wanted, the Japanese government was prepared for only a very limited commitment. In the words of the Japanese decision of July 24:

> The Anti-Comintern Pact itself should be limited in its phraseology and should refer only to an exchange of information and opinion concerning countermeasures to be taken against the subversive activities of the Comintern. To include more than the foregoing in the pact itself would anger and alarm the Soviet Union unnecessarily and would provide other countries with an opportunity for engaging in propaganda activities against us.

The Germans were persuaded, as Article 1 of the final pact confirms.

In the draft secret protocol, which was an undertaking directed at the eventuality of an attack or threat of attack by the Soviet Union, the Japanese decision of July 24 called for three restrictive revisions. First, the vague wording, which did not limit the kind of attack that would obligate the two countries to cooperate, should be clarified to read, "In case either country is threatened by or sustains an *unprovoked* attack. . . ." * Second, any implication that this was a general alliance should be eliminated, the operative obligation being simply that, in case of an unprovoked attack on either partner, "the governments of

* Hereafter all italics have been added by the author.

the two Treaty Powers should hold frank consultations." Third, in order to insure secrecy the Soviet Union should be referred to not by name but as a "third country." The first and second points were adopted in the final version, but the third point was not.

Article 2 of the final secret supplementary protocol provided that neither party should conclude "political treaties with the USSR contrary to the spirit of this agreement without mutual consent." The original wording of the German draft seems to have been looser. In any event, in the decision of July 24 the Japanese government found the original wording completely unacceptable, fearing that, in referring only to the future and not to the past, it permitted Germany to keep its agreements with the Soviet Union, including the 1922 Treaty of Rapallo [18] and the 1926 neutrality treaty of Berlin, while preventing Japan in future from negotiating similar agreements should it so desire. The Japanese government felt that it would be unreasonable for Germany to be permitted to continue its commitment to the Soviet-German neutrality treaty, since this would mean that only Japan's diplomacy would be restricted. Hence, Japan proposed a revision of this article that would permit it to conclude a nonaggression treaty or treaty of neutrality with the Soviet Union at some point in the future should circumstances change. Initially Ribbentrop seemed to indicate limited agreement with the Japanese proposal, but in a later telephone conversation he refused to approve it because of objections raised by Dr. Friedrich Gaus, Treaty Bureau chief in the German Foreign Office. Gaus seems to have preferred a different resolution. Apparently borrowing from the explanation used when the Franco-Soviet Treaty of Mutual Assistance was concluded on May 2, 1935, to the effect that it did not conflict with the Locarno treaties, he cited the doctrine of *rebus sic stantibus*. Accordingly, Ribbentrop wrote Mushakōji a secret note in which he pointed out that the obligations in the Soviet-German treaty were conditioned explicitly by the provision that the obligations were operative only "so long as circumstances which existed at the time that the treaty came into force" obtained. Thus, he argued, any conflict between Germany's obligation under the proposed pact or the spirit of Japanese-German cooperation and those commitments that Germany had made in the Rapallo Treaty and the Treaty of Berlin would result in the nullification of the latter treaties, because the circumstances on which they were based would no longer exist. The Japanese government accepted this explanation and secured Germany's agreement to affix it as a secret attached official note, to be known as the Third Appendix to the protocol.

One other part of this Article 2 of the secret protocol occasioned some discussion. The draft presented to the Privy Council provided that neither party would conclude any "political treaties with the USSR contrary to the *provisions* of this agreement without mutual consent." The negotiations concerning this clause seem to have aroused Germany's fear that Japan might indeed conclude a nonaggression treaty with the Soviet Union. Apparently to prevent this, at the last moment the word *Bestimmungen* (provisions) was replaced by the more flexible *Geist* (spirit).

Another troublesome issue was whether to publicize the agreements or keep them secret. In its decision of July 24 the Japanese government opted for secrecy for the entire pact and protocol. As time went by, however, the argument arose that the effect of the pact would be dissipated if the entire enterprise were kept secret. Indeed, some came to feel that the protocol as well should be released because after all the Comintern and the Soviet Union were one and the same. It was also suggested that, if the pact were to be made public, it be phrased ambiguously or, alternatively, that it be kept secret in principle but phrased in such a way as not to raise difficulties should it leak out.

In the end the Japanese government felt the protocol, which clearly named the Soviet Union, should be kept secret lest announcement adversely affect Soviet-Japanese fishery negotiations, and Germany also decided that it did not wish unnecessarily to antagonize a partner with whom it had a treaty of neutrality. The final compromise, therefore, was to publish the Anti-Comintern Pact but to keep the supplementary protocol secret.

One last point: whereas the original German draft treaty had specified a period of validity of ten years, the final treaty shortened it to five.[19]

Conclusion of the Pact

The Anti-Comintern Pact was signed on October 23.[20] Prime Minister Hirota was relieved. He told Baron Harada: "When the Anglo-Japanese alliance became a reality, it was said, 'What the navy so ardently wished, the navy has created,' and I had the feeling that the army wanted to accomplish something similar. One can now expect that, with the conclusion of the Anti-Comintern Pact, most of the army's desires have been met." There is no doubt that Ōshima and the army were most responsible for furthering the cause of the Anti-Comintern Pact. However, it would be too much to assert that the army alone was responsible. The Foreign Ministry also hoped that Japan's international isolation might be modified through cooperation with Germany. The elder statesman Saionji Kimmochi, on the other hand, did not share this view. He told Harada that he had serious reservations about the pact.

> It is useful only to Germany and contains nothing of advantage to us. I believe that the Japanese-German agreement is of benefit to Germany in virtually ten cases out of ten, but to Japan it is substantially negative. Pro-German leanings have existed among the old clan oligarchs, but the Japanese people have sentiments of friendship for Britain and the United States. Germany has supported the clan oligarchs ever since the [Meiji] Restoration, but it would be better for Japan, given its geographical position, to have Britain and the United States as its friends.[21]

Despite Saionji's vigorous criticism, the pact was referred to the Privy Council's Investigation Committee, which discussed it on November 13 and 18. In his testimony before the committee Prime Minister Hirota stressed the Soviet Union's military pressure in East Asia and the difficulties created by the Comintern, both of which constituted "a direct threat to our empire's defense and to Japan's East Asia stabilization policy." The pact would make it possible to cooperate with Germany in matters of mutual defense against the subversive activities of the Comintern and the Soviet military threat. He also stated that other countries would be invited to participate in joint action against "Red activities" and emphasized that the choice of Germany as Japan's first partner "should obviously not be considered as in any way approving Germany's domestic policies." Hirota testified further that he hoped relations with the Soviet Union would not become worse and that continuing efforts would be made to stabilize the situation on the border between Manchukuo and the Soviet Union. "The pact has made it possible to come to an understanding with Germany," he concluded, "but continuing efforts will have to be made to promote Japan's relations with Britain and the United States, especially friendship with Britain."

Foreign Minister Arita restated the challenge posed by the Soviet Union in Asia and Europe and by the Comintern's expansionist activities in Outer Mongolia, Sinkiang, and China. These threats to the defense of Japan and Manchukuo had to be removed by a combination of diplomacy and military strength. Germany too was threatened by the Soviet Union, which had concluded mutual assistance treaties with France and Czechoslovakia. Furthermore, Japan and Germany were virtually being forced into an alliance against the Soviet Union and the Comintern because of the proposal made at the Comintern's Seventh Congress to create a united front against them. He also testified that the pact was not intended to antagonize the Soviet Union, that its wording carefully avoided equating the Soviet Union with the Comintern, and that it was for this reason that the supplementary protocol was to remain secret.

The Investigation Committee concluded from their testimony that the goals of the pact served the empire's interests, that cooperation with other countries should be sought since the activities of the Comintern were worldwide, and that other nations should be persuaded to join the pact or to participate in a program of mutual defense within the framework provided by the pact.

On November 20 the pact went to the Privy Council itself,

where relations with the Soviet Union, especially the Japanese-Soviet fisheries treaty, became an issue in the deliberations. Arita reassured the councillors that, were news of the pact to become public prematurely and interfere with pending negotiations, the Soviet Union would be informed that the Japanese-German agreement was aimed only at the Comintern, whereupon it ought to be willing to sign the fisheries agreement with Japan. The council expressed its satisfaction and approved the treaty and its attachments on November 25.[22]

In his report to the Privy Council, the chairman of the Investigation Committee had expressed concern that there might be some confusion abroad and at home with respect to Japan's relationship to Nazi Germany. The government therefore decided to outline to the public the philosophy underlying the Anti-Comintern Pact. The day the pact was concluded, the Foreign Ministry announced it, affirming that it was nothing more than what it appeared to be, a defensive measure taken against the Comintern, that "no special, hidden agreement exists," and that it was "not directed against any particular country such as the Soviet Union." Germany likewise issued a statement, which bristled against the Comintern but differed from Japan's in making no reference, even in the form of a denial, to the secret protocol.[23]

The Soviet Reaction

The Japanese policy decision of July 24 had specified that care should be exercised so that the Anti-Comintern Pact would not antagonize the Soviet Union and war with Russia would not occur. This policy was reiterated during the Privy Council's discussions and was used to justify keeping the supplementary protocol secret.

News of the negotiations for the pact had early become known to the Soviet Union, however. Toward the end of 1935 a Soviet army intelligence officer had intercepted secret telegrams between the Japanese General Staff and Ōshima and had reported their contents to Moscow.[24] The American embassy in

Japan also seems to have learned that the Soviet embassy had heard of some agreement being discussed by German and Japanese military authorities. Furthermore, just when the negotiations had almost reached their climax, the *Japan Chronicle* ran an exposé and the *Asahi* of November 11 reported that the Privy Council would be discussing "a very weighty affair."

On November 16 Soviet Ambassador Constantin Yurenev asked Arita about rumors concerning a Japanese-German agreement. Arita parried his query with an explanation about Japan's anti-Comintern policy and its opposition to several resolutions of the Seventh Comintern Congress. To defend itself against them, he said, Japan was negotiating with certain countries. He emphasized that the negotiations merely concerned opposition to various activities of the Comintern and should not affect friendly relations between Japan and the Soviet Union itself. Ambassador Yurenev, not satisfied with Arita's explanation, submitted a protest on November 20 in which he asserted that the Anti-Comintern Pact was only a cover for other secret agreements. Arita did not respond.

Meanwhile, negotiations on the new Soviet-Japanese fisheries treaty were proceeding smoothly toward the target date, November 20. (The Japanese had unsuccessfully tried to hold off the Anti-Comintern Pact talks until after the fisheries treaty had been consummated.) Arita had told the Privy Council that because the Soviet negotiators had appeared eager to reach an agreement, he thought they would not refuse to sign the fisheries treaty in spite of the rumors concerning Japanese-German negotiations. But suddenly the Soviet Union decided to postpone signing the new treaty, instead renewing the old one on a year-to-year basis.

On November 28, three days after the announcement of the Anti-Comintern Pact, People's Commissar for Foreign Affairs Maxim Litvinov, in a speech to the Eighth Soviet Congress, charged that the pact was an anti-Soviet move by fascist countries. In fact, he asserted, the pact was not directed against the Comintern but was a cover for another secret agreement which had been in the process of negotiation over the past fifteen months primarily between a Japanese military attaché and a top

German diplomat. He went on to charge that by virtue of this agreement Japan had lost its independence in the conduct of its foreign policy and that, although Japan desired to have friendly relations with the Soviet Union and wished to resolve certain pending issues, and was even considering a nonaggression treaty with the Soviet Union, it would henceforth have to clear such agreements with Germany. Litvinov also stated that Italy was a partner to the agreement, although it had not yet formally signed it; and he bitterly criticized Japan, Germany, and Italy for having formed a tripartite anti-Soviet and "antidemocratic" bloc.[25]

Efforts to Expand Pact Membership

The Japanese government had hoped through the Anti-Comintern Pact to counteract the nation's international isolation, but fears had also been expressed that participation in the pact might actually worsen Japan's situation by further antagonizing other governments. For this reason the government tried to widen the pact to include several other countries.

Japanese leaders were particularly concerned about the pact's effect upon Anglo-Japanese relations, and the Army–Foreign Ministry decision of July 24 had noted:

> Japanese-German collaboration must not be a cause of anxiety to any other powers, especially Britain. Anglo-Japanese relations are not friendly at present because of the China question and certain economic issues that cannot be adjusted as yet, but one of the keynotes of our foreign policy must be to improve our relations with Britain, which has substantial influence with other world powers, and we must at the very least avoid a face-to-face confrontation with it at all costs. We must thus be careful not to allow a political pact with Germany to antagonize Britain and must take positive steps to adjust Anglo-Japanese interests by negotiating a treaty with that nation so that we are not estranged from each other and so that we can cooperate in solving various important problems.

In conformity with these aims, a draft Anglo-Japanese treaty (here paraphrased) was prepared:

The governments of Japan and Great Britain, desiring to promote their mutual friendly relations and desiring to promote world peace, agree:

1. That they should avoid estrangement from each other and should cooperate in the solution of various common problems.

2. That this treaty shall be valid for five years.[26]

When this draft was being prepared, the Foreign Ministry was optimistic about the prospect of winning additional signatories to the Anti-Comintern Pact. The Comintern's Seventh Congress had attracted the attention of Britain and the United States, and the latter especially had protested those Comintern resolutions which it interpreted as an interference in American domestic politics. Thus the Foreign Ministry hoped that other western countries could be persuaded to join an alliance against the Comintern.

It is not clear what consideration was given to or instructions issued concerning this extremely ambiguous draft treaty. Ambassador to Britain Yoshida Shigeru did not believe such a treaty would be easily concluded, and in fact negotiations with Britain made little progress despite Japan's enthusiasm and impatience. Such a treaty would have required an understanding between Japan and Britain with respect to China, and conflicts of interest there, particularly since the Manchurian Incident, rendered such an understanding unlikely. Discussions with Britain could not have proceeded without specific proposals from Japan on questions at issue between the two countries. In addition, the Soviet Union was a major element in the European balance of power, and Britain could not have dealt with it solely on the basis of an ideologically motivated anticommunism.

Time and again various agencies of the Japanese government had pledged themselves to promote friendly relations between Japan, the United States, and Britain, but especially with Britain. A memorandum prepared by the Foreign Ministry's Europe-Asia Bureau reflected such aspirations:

The government requires relations with Britain to become friendlier. To this end Ambassador Yoshida has been making

serious efforts, which in turn have had positive results in steadily improving British feelings toward Japan. However, the
Keelung Incident of October and the conclusion of the Anti-
Comintern Pact in November had an adverse effect on Britain's
attitude toward Japan. Efforts have been made to seek an amicable settlement of the incident and to obtain Britain's understanding regarding the Anti-Comintern Pact so that friendly relations would not be impaired. Finally, efforts have been made to
improve Anglo-Japanese relations by means of concrete adjust-
ments on various issues such as the China question and problems affecting trade.[27]

Contrary to Japanese expectations, Britain grew even more
wary of Germany and Japan after the consummation of the Anti-
Comintern Pact, and Anglo-Japanese "friendship," which the
Foreign Ministry so desired to improve, was thereby weakened.

Japan also explored the possibility of bringing the Netherlands into the Anti-Comintern Pact, but this effort too ended in
failure. Talks with the Dutch were opened on October 12, 1936,
when Yamaguchi Iwao, chargé d'affaires of the Japanese legation, called on the Dutch foreign minister. The Netherlands,
said Yamuguchi, was doubtless concerned about China because
of the nearness to China of its colonial possessions and the large
Chinese population of the Dutch East Indies. For its part, Japan
was equally concerned about its own position in Dutch public
opinion and in that of the Netherlands' Asian colonies. He
sought the foreign minister's understanding of Japan's China
policy and of the suffering that Red aggression in Asia had
caused. The foreign minister responded that while there was no
need for him to comment on Dutch antibolshevik sentiments,
and although he was deeply concerned that effective measures
be taken to suppress communist activities, he thought there had
been a decline in such activities in the East Indies. Yamaguchi
replied that cooperation might be advisable among all countries
that considered themselves antibolshevik, although cooperation
clearly should not imply membership in a particular bloc and,
indeed, should be confined to countering the Comintern's propaganda and exchanging information. The foreign minister
agreed that it would be useful to exchange information about
communist activities in the Dutch East Indies.

In their second conversation on October 24 the Dutch foreign minister indicated that the Netherlands intended to limit any cooperative activities to the East Indies. Yamaguchi wondered if Holland itself might also be included because the Comintern maintained in Amsterdam a powerful propaganda machine that had apparently influenced Dutch newspapers to print many articles criticizing Japan. The following day Lovink, director of the East Asia Bureau of the Dutch East Indies government, called on Yamaguchi. He hinted that his government intended to suppress not only communism but any political movements that might undermine public tranquility in the East Indies. Indeed, as negotiations progressed it became clear that the Netherlands' interest in an anti-Comintern alliance was chiefly rooted in its fears about the nationalist movement in the East Indies, whose leaders—Sukarno, Hatta, and Sastroamid-jojo—had become increasingly difficult to control. Accordingly, the director of the Political Affairs Bureau of the Dutch Foreign Ministry did express interest in exchanging intelligence, not just about communist activities but about all subversive activities in Europe and Asia. But the Dutch were hesitant about concluding a formal alliance against the Comintern because of the political overtones. In the end the Japanese decided not to press, and the negotiations came to an end.[28]

Only with Italy did Japan make any progress in recruiting new signatories to the Anti-Comintern Pact; but Italy's association, contrary to Japan's expectation, resulted in a further deterioration of Japan's international position. Italian-Japanese relations had been excellent subsequent to Mussolini's establishment of a fascist state, and Italy's own international position provided a special incentive to close ties with Japan within the framework of the Anti-Comintern Pact. Italy was being tried at the bar of the League of Nations because of its invasion of Ethiopia, and closer relations with Japan might help solidify its position in the Mediterranean, especially vis-à-vis Britain.

Italy's Foreign Minister Galeazzo Ciano told Japanese Ambassador Sugimura Yōtarō:

Italy initially erred in its foreign policy by making a distinction between the Comintern and the Soviet Union; but I have corrected this mistake since becoming foreign minister and have been pursuing a stern policy toward the Soviet Union, a posture that was agreed to and understood by Hitler. I have heard that a Japanese-German agreement concerning the Soviet Union has been reached, and I think it would be natural for a similar agreement to be made between Italy and Japan.[29]

Sugimura told Ciano that Japan was seeking the cooperation of many countries in countering the Soviet Union's communist activities, but that even if Japan were to enter into an agreement with Germany, it would not be military in character and would therefore differ from the special understanding that existed between Germany and Italy with regard to Spain. It was preferable, said Sugimura, that the present discussions be restricted to the problems involved in establishing a Japanese consulate in Ethiopia and an Italian consulate in Manchukuo, but he would be willing to discuss at a later date the possibility of a Japanese-Italian anti-Comintern pact. Sugimura communicated to his government his belief that an Italian-Japanese agreement might be considered after the establishment of the German-Japanese pact if the former were limited to the exchange of intelligence about the Soviet Union's Red activities and to the maintenance of close contact between their military officers stationed near the Soviet Union.

The day after the Japanese-German Anti-Comintern Pact was officially promulgated, Mussolini and Ciano congratulated Sugimura and told him that Italy desired a similar agreement with Japan.[30] Before discussions on such an agreement could begin, however, certain other steps had to be taken. These involved closing the Japanese legation in Ethiopia and opening a consulate in its stead, and opening an Italian consulate-general in Mukden, officially announced on December 2. Mutuality was thus achieved by an exchange involving de facto Japanese recognition of Italy's annexation of Ethiopia in return for Italy's de facto recognition of Manchukuo.[31]

Ciano continued to express interest in an Italian-Japanese

anti-Comintern agreement and inquired as to Japan's attitude. Sugimura replied, in conformity with Foreign Minister Arita's instructions, that such an agreement was not urgent but, if necessary, could be made at any time. In the meantime, consideration should be given to cultural exchanges and a commercial treaty, after which a political agreement might be considered.

Over the next six months, from February to July 1937, Italy continued to show keen interest in an anti-Comintern pact with Japan, but Japanese personnel shifts temporarily took the center of the stage. A government headed by Hayashi Senjūrō replaced the Hirota cabinet in February and Satō Naotake was appointed foreign minister in March; in April Sugimura became ambassador to France and Hotta Masaaki succeeded him as ambassador to Italy. Then in July, just before Hotta began his new duties, the first Konoe cabinet took office and Hirota once again became foreign minister.

In a speech before the Italian parliament on May 13, Ciano asserted that Italy and Japan were united in their anticommunist views. He repeated this comment the same evening at a farewell party for Sugimura and proposed that discussions regarding a political pact begin since the cultural exchange program was progressing smoothly and the commercial treaty would soon be concluded. Sugimura avoided making an immediate response; it was his view that Japan's basic anticommunist goal would be achieved through the Anti-Comintern Pact with Germany and that Italian-Japanese cooperation would be supplementary. Bringing Italy into the Japanese-German pact, he thought, would only serve to antagonize Britain, and any adjustment of relations with Italy should not interfere with Anglo-Japanese negotiations. He therefore advised the Foreign Ministry to continue normal diplomatic relations with Italy but to defer a specific agreement that might restrict Japan's and Italy's ability to act independently, particularly in view of the fact that in the past Italy had been prone to drastic and unexpected shifts in attitude.[32]

When Hirota returned to the post of foreign minister, he too felt that Britain should be given priority over Italy. He therefore instructed Hotta to subordinate to the needs of Anglo-Japanese relations any negotiations concerning an anti-Comintern pact with Italy.[33] But international developments reversed this order of priorities. Just before Hotta departed for Rome, the Marco Polo Bridge Incident occurred, and in August the Japanese army expanded its military activities from north China to Shanghai. As soon as fighting broke out, Foreign Secretary Anthony Eden told the House of Commons on July 21 that Anglo-Japanese negotiations would not be considered. On August 26 the British ambassador to China was injured when his car was fired on by a Japanese plane. Concurrently, China accused Japan of having engaged in aggression and having thereby violated the covenant of the League of Nations, the Kellogg-Briand Pact, and the Nine-Power Treaty. The case was heard, Japan was found guilty, and on October 21 the League convened in Brussels a conference of the nine powers. Even Germany expressed dissatisfaction at Japan's expansion of the war in China.

By contrast, Italy remained friendly after the China War began. In conformity with Sugimura's earlier suggestion, Hotta had brought a message from Hirota to Ciano, in which Hirota expressed the hope that both countries could cooperate on the basis of anticommunism. The Italians welcomed Hotta warmly in the expectation that his appointment indicated quick approval of an anti-Comintern pact. In view of the adverse effect of the Marco Polo Bridge Incident on Japan's international status, Hotta too was prepared to improve relations with Italy. He suggested an Italian-Japanese agreement separate from the Japanese-German treaty, reasoning that otherwise Japan might become involved in European problems through Italy's alliance with Germany, despite the secret protocol to the Anti-Comintern Pact. He basically advocated that Japan propose to Italy a rather weak agreement along the lines of an anticommunist nonaggression or neutrality pact with an agreement to consult.[34]

The Japanese army, upon learning of Hotta's proposal, expressed its concurrence and proceeded to promote cooperation with Italy. The army view, as set forth by the Army Ministry's Military Affairs Bureau, was that the most easily negotiable treaty would be an anti-Comintern neutrality and consultation agreement. This would have the advantage of imposing no specific obligations and would thus allay any fears that Japan might become involved in European problems. The army also took the position that such a treaty could not be kept secret and therefore should be publicly announced.[35]

The Foreign Ministry thereupon decided to negotiate a separate anti-Comintern pact with Italy and requested that Mushakōji seek German concurrence through Foreign Secretary Constantin von Neurath. However, Ribbentrop, who was serving as German ambassador to Britain, was informed about the Italian-Japanese negotiations and insisted that the three countries be joined together through the existing Anti-Comintern Pact—with the exception of the secret protocol, Italy simply becoming the third signatory.

On November 6, acting independently, Ribbentrop went to Rome to persuade Mussolini, Ciano, and Hotta to agree. Italy was reluctant because of the possibility of involvement in Germany's difficulties with Britain, with which Italy had signed a treaty in January. Japan also preferred a separate treaty with Italy in view of its own relations with Britain. On the other hand, Italy was anticommunist and the Anti-Comintern Pact had provided that other countries be invited to join it. In the end, therefore, Ribbentrop's view prevailed, and Italy was admitted to the Anti-Comintern Pact and its supplementary protocol as an equal partner on November 6, 1937. Thus, while Japan failed to bring about British and Dutch adherence to the Anti-Comintern Pact, the new circumstances that arose subsequent to the Marco Polo Bridge Incident did bring about Italy's participation, and later that of Manchukuo, Hungary, and Spain; and Italy's adherence to the pact opened the door for the establishment of the so-called Axis bloc.

By that time Germany had occupied the Saar, had begun to rebuild its air force and army, had withdrawn from the Locarno treaties, and had thus openly violated the international order created at Versailles; Italy had conquered Ethiopia; and Japan was continuing the military encroachment on China that had begun with the Manchurian Incident. The pact, therefore, contrary to the original intent of the Foreign Ministry, not only antagonized Britain and the Soviet Union but inevitably convinced the rest of the world that the three nations had united in a single bloc aimed at the destruction of the existing world order.

Efforts toward Strengthening the Anti-Comintern Pact

The Anti-Comintern Pact signed with such fanfare in 1936 had little immediate effect on its signatories. German-Japanese relations were polite but hardly warm. The joint committee provided for in the pact's supplementary protocol was considered but never formally set up. A joint airline was discussed by the military, but the governments never agreed.[36] The most that was achieved was a verbal agreement allegedly concluded between Japanese Military Attaché Ōshima and German Chief of Staff Wilhelm Keitel for exchange of information regarding the Soviet Union and the use of White Russians in propaganda campaigns in time of war.[37] The fundamental fact was that Germany did not like Japan's China policy,[38] and the China War intensified their differences. Germany wanted no part of it, fearing that Japan's actions would succeed only in turning the Chinese to communism and driving them into the arms of the Soviet Union.[39] But in the winter of 1937–38, as Hitler's plans for expansion in Europe matured, the German government took a new look at the value of the Japanese connection. This time it was not so much the Soviet Union as Britain and France that worried the Nazis. Accordingly, in January 1938 a diplomatic campaign was begun to persuade Japan to enter into a general defensive military alliance whose targets were understood to include the USSR, of course, but also and particularly the western democracies.

The Japanese army and the renovationist bureaucrats demanded quick acceptance of Germany's proposal while the navy, the Foreign Ministry, and other civilian ministries were opposed. The latter were prepared to strengthen the Anti-Comintern Pact against the USSR but not to risk antagonizing the British, the French, or the Americans any more than Japan was already doing in China and, in any event, not to become involved in Europe. Finally, with the backing of the emperor, the foreign minister and his allies won. The alliance project for the time was scotched and Germany turned toward the Soviet Union. But for eighteen months, from January 1938 to August 1939, the controversy raged, revealing the depth of differences among Japanese leaders over the international course Japan should follow and the power and intransigence of the renovationist bureaucrats and the army in pursuing a course of their own—a course that led eventually to the Axis alliance of 1940.

The German Proposal

Germany rearmed rapidly after 1935, marched into the demilitarized zone in the Rhineland in March 1936, renounced the Locarno treaties, and began to support Franco in the Spanish Civil War. On June 24, 1937, Defense Minister Werner von Blomberg's secret military orders were issued.[40] These contained the military plans for the year: "Operation Red" for war with France; "Operation Green" for an attack on Czechoslovakia to guard against a threat from the rear to Germany's western campaign and to prevent the establishment of Russian air bases there; "Operation Otto" for war with Austria as a special preliminary to these; "Operation Rialto" for action in the Spanish Civil War; and "Enlarged Operations Red and Green" designed for the eventuality that Britain, Poland, or Lithuania would interfere with "Operation Red." On November 10 Hitler called Defense Minister Blomberg, Army Commander-in-Chief Werner von Fritsch, Navy Commander-in-Chief Erich Raeder, Air Force Commander-in-Chief Hermann Goering, and Foreign Minister Constantin von Neurath to his official residence to give them his schedule for expansion, now known to us from the so-called Hossbach Memorandum.

At this meeting Hitler proclaimed the policy of enlarging Germany's *Lebensraum* in Europe, saying, "The goal of Germany is to protect, preserve, and expand the racial community; thus, it is a question of space." According to Hitler, Germany would have to solve this problem between 1943 and 1945 at the latest, when German strength would be at its height. The first target would be the conquest of Austria and Czechoslovakia to prevent a threat to Germany's flank in any western operations; but special consideration would have to be given to the possibility of a collision with Britain,[41] with whom relations had worsened since the signing of the Anglo-German naval agreement of 1935.[42]

Ribbentrop thought he had the answer. On January 2, 1938, he presented Hitler with a memorandum on future Anglo-German relations.[43] He recognized that a change in the central European situation could be achieved only through force. If force were applied, France could be expected to intervene. Germany could handle the French, but it would have a much more difficult time if the British were also opposed. The problem was to keep the British from joining the French. Conciliation should be tried, of course, but deterrence, he felt, was the answer, deterrence in the form of an even greater union of strength, a German-Japanese-Italian alliance that would force Britain to so disperse its military power in Europe, the Mediterranean, and Asia as to render it incapable of acting. Ribbentrop then took a preliminary sounding with Ōshima when Japan's military attaché came to pay a New Year's call. Ribbentrop proposed no concrete plan, but he did introduce the possibility of a treaty to bring Japan and Germany together. Ōshima expressed his personal agreement and made a report to the General Staff in Tokyo.

Hitler too thought the plan had possibilities and moved quickly to organize his government to carry it out. On February 4, 1938, he fired Neurath and replaced him with Ribbentrop. He also rid himself of military men such as Blomberg and Fritsch who opposed his foreign policy, and through a structural reform he assumed personal command of the army, navy, and air force. Thus Hitler and his group took over the real power in diplomacy and defense. They then replaced Germany's ambassadors overseas, appointing General Eugen Ott to Tokyo and Hans-Georg von Hackensen to Rome. The stage was now set for exploring the possibilities of an Axis alliance.

Germany's first step was to align its diplomatic policy more closely with Japan's. In February it worked unabatedly to gain Japan's good will by prohibiting the sale of arms to China and recalling its military advisers from China. On May 12 it recognized Manchukuo. The next step was to follow up on Ribbentrop's preliminary soundings. The previous November Ōshima had proposed to Keitel that the agreement to exchange military information on the Soviet Union be enlarged to include a general exchange of opinions on the situation as a whole. In the spring Keitel replied, indicating a willingness to go beyond Ōshima's proposal and to strengthen ties between the two nations.[44]

In June Lieutenant-Colonel Yoshinaka Kazutarō, chief of the Europe-America Section in the Army General Staff Intelligence Division, sent to Ōshima by courier a counterproposal representing the division's reaction to the original Ribbentrop suggestion of January. This counterproposal called for the formation of a defensive alliance between Japan and Germany against the Soviet Union to cope with the new situation in East Asia, and for the consideration of a separate agreement between Japan and Italy against Britain.

Ōshima himself thought that, inasmuch as the war with China had been prolonged and relations with Britain and the USSR had consequently become more difficult, the conclusion of such agreements would serve to strengthen Japan's international position as well as contribute to a settlement of the war with China. He wrote his own proposal based on that of Yoshinaka. While visiting Ribbentrop in early July, Ōshima, putting aside for the moment the problem of coping with Britain, sought Ribbentrop's opinion concerning the conclusion of an agreement between Japan, Germany, and Italy to hold consultations before taking any action in the event of an attack by the Soviet Union on any one of them.

A day or two later Ribbentrop told Ōshima that while he agreed with this general concept, he thought a mere consultative agreement was a halfway measure and not strong enough. He wished to conclude a treaty of mutual assistance, with a general goal rather than one limited just to the Soviet Union, explaining that if Japan, Germany, and Italy were to achieve their various aims without resorting to war, it was necessary for them to form a strong union whose target would be not only the Soviet Union but also Britain and France, the mainstays of the democratic camp.[45] To this Ōshima replied that Japan was not yet prepared militarily to consider action against powers other than the Soviet Union, so that it would be difficult to agree immediately to enlarging the proposed agreement into a mutual assistance treaty proclaiming such broad goals. Ribbentrop then said that the details of mutual assistance could be worked out separately, but for the preservation of peace it would be well for the basic treaty to be as strong as possible. With this in mind, he produced the following specific draft treaty:

> 1. In the event that one of the contracting parties is faced with diplomatic difficulties with a nonsignatory nation, the contracting parties will meet promptly to discuss common action to be taken.
> 2. In the event of a threat to one of the contracting parties by a non-signatory nation, each party will be obligated to offer all political and diplomatic assistance to eliminate the threat.
> 3. In the event that one of the contracting parties sustains an attack by a nonsignatory nation, the other parties are obligated to give military assistance.[46]

Ribbentrop also suggested that, in view of the leaks that had occurred before and during the Anti-Comintern Pact negotiations, communication by telegraph should be avoided and a special messenger sent to Tokyo. Ōshima therefore dispatched Major-General Kasahara Yukio to Japan with the German plan, on the assumption that Kasahara would be made the new military attaché in Germany.[47]

The Konoe Cabinet's Ambiguous Attitude

Meanwhile, a reorganization of the Japanese cabinet had taken place on May 26. Ugaki Kazushige became foreign minister, Ikeda Seihin entered as finance minister, and Araki Sadao was appointed minister of education. On June 3 Itagaki Seishirō replaced Sugiyama Gen as army minister.

Ugaki had demanded agreement on four conditions before accepting his appointment as foreign minister: (1) strengthened cabinet solidarity, (2) immediate concurrence upon a policy to deal with current problems, (3) unified management of Japan's China policy, and (4) not to be bound by Konoe's January 16 statement that Japan would no longer deal with the Chiang Kai-shek regime.[48] Ever since he assumed the post of cabinet councillor in 1937, Ugaki had been consistent in urging that the war with China be terminated,[49] and as foreign minister he tried to move toward this end. But his desire to concentrate on resolving the China problem was frustrated by the question of strengthening cooperation with Germany and Italy, which soon became the central issue in Japanese foreign policy.

From the beginning Ugaki was under heavy pressure from within his own ministry. After Shiratori Toshio left the Foreign Ministry for his post as ambassador to Sweden in December 1933, he maintained his influence over young diplomats stationed in Europe. In the ministry at home the renovationists or, as they were also called, the "Axis faction" continued to champion Shiratori's cause, hoping to secure his appointment as vice minister, and in cooperation with the army they tried to persuade the new foreign minister to adopt their Axis-aligned "Imperial Way" diplomacy. In an earlier meeting with Ugaki's predecessor Hirota Kōki, they had pressed for a strong policy to deal with the China War and had called for the conclusion of a tripartite alliance. On July 30, 1938, eight Foreign Ministry officials—Tōkō Takezō, Mihara Eijirō, Nakagawa Tōru, Ushiba Nobuhiko, Aoki Morio, Kai Fumihiko, Takase Jirō, and Takagi Kōichi—visited Ugaki at his private residence in Ōiso and forcefully presented their demands.[50]

Initially, they expressed their views and aspirations as loyal members of the Foreign Ministry: their analysis of the contemporary situation, their basic conception of the mission of the Japanese race, their world view, and, based on the foregoing, the foreign policy they embraced. Ugaki's criticism was then invited, but as time was limited, the discussion soon came around to specific issues, starting with personnel problems.

While Ugaki was pursuing a "truly great policy," his visitors felt it could not be successful if carried out by the existing Foreign Ministry staff. Their demand for personnel changes seems to have centered on the appointment of Shiratori as vice minister, but Ugaki said such matters were to be left to his complete discretion. They then turned to the issues of the China War and the Axis alliance, asserting that measures should be taken at once "to destroy the Chiang regime, strengthen the anticommunist axis, and remove British, French, and Soviet political power from China." They were opposed to "any attempt to reach a compromise with the Anglo-Saxon nations in East Asia" and therefore urged that the discussions then underway between Ugaki and British Ambassador Robert L. Craigie be terminated.[51] "As members of the Foreign Ministry who serve as the vanguard of the Imperial Way," they offered for Ugaki's consideration an alternative "set of basic strategies which we call Imperial Way diplomacy."

"The diplomatic strategy that would capitalize most effectively on the imminent fall of Hankow," they asserted, "would be one that strengthened the entente with Germany and Italy while maintaining firm opposition to the Chiang Kai-shek regime. Thus Britain will be forced to cooperate in order to protect its rights and interests in China." Except for certain details of the treaty with Germany and Italy, their ideas accorded with those of the army.

Ugaki made no promises concerning the meetings with Craigie, saying that the issue was to be left to him. On the question of strengthening the anti-Comintern axis, he said that his talks with Ott had made him pessimistic about the likelihood of a military alliance with Germany. But, he added, "I have ordered my subordinates to study this problem, and I would like to explore various opinions. What are your views?" They replied that it was important that everything possible be done to strengthen the alliance with Germany and Italy. This, they felt, was a feasible aim, but it depended entirely upon Japan.

Promising that another meeting would be arranged, Ugaki ended the interview by saying:

I think you realize that the reason an old man like me became foreign minister was to bring about a quick and acceptable con-

clusion to the war. This is the wish of the people of our nation.
So I ask you to wait until that policy which is the will of the
state is announced, after it has been decided in the Five Ministers Conference.

Most of the young officials who attended this meeting had
gone through their impressionable student years about the time
of the Manchurian Incident and had passed their foreign service examinations around 1932–33, when Japan had withdrawn
from the League of Nations. Normally it would have been unthinkable for officials so young to engage in frank and heated
discussions of foreign policy with the foreign minister. Doubtless their hot blood, fired by the ideals of renovationist diplomacy, explains their action. Moreover, the Axis faction advocat-
ing renovationist diplomacy had become an increasing force in
the Foreign Ministry in the years between 1933 and 1938.

It is not surprising that when senior officials in the Foreign
Ministry learned that the Army Ministry had come to regard a
strengthening of the ties between Japan, Germany, and Italy as
necessary for a solution of the China conflict, they became convinced that the view was shared by the public at large. Having
been forced to accept the Anti-Comintern Pact following army
talks with Germany two years earlier, and influenced no doubt
by the Axis faction in the ministry, they decided it would be
best, if they were not to lose control over the situation, to go
along with the trend but to concentrate on minimizing any negative aspects of the treaty. The report ultimately submitted to
Ugaki therefore stated that, as each nation had its own point of
view, it would be best to avoid linking the three nations with
one treaty; instead, Japan should conclude with Germany a
treaty of mutual assistance, extending the terms of the Anti-
Comintern Pact, and should sign a separate treaty of neutrality
and consultation with Italy.

The army, of course, took a different position. At Konoe's
request, a document entitled "On the Management of the China
Incident" was presented by Itagaki on June 17, soon after he
became army minister.[52] This proposal advocated vigorous
operations against China, arguing that if the China War were
prolonged, it "must inevitably lead from a war against China to

conflict with Soviet and British power in the Far East." For that
reason the army recommended strengthening the Anti-Comintern Pact and improving relations with the United States. In a
document of July 3 entitled "The Army's Hopes Regarding Current Foreign Policies," Itagaki expressed even more concretely
the army's views on dealing with diplomatic problems (see Appendix III for the full text). It is clear from this document that
the army's policy was not directed at the USSR alone; nor in
regard to Britain was it intended simply to check that nation.
Rather, it was increasingly seen as a way of exerting pressure on
Britain to give up its support of Chiang Kai-shek.

On July 19 the Five Ministers Conference decided to consider strengthening the Anti-Comintern Pact and approved the
following "Draft Policy for Strengthening Political Ties with
Germany and Italy," which had probably been initiated by the
army.

> The empire wishes quickly to reach separate agreements with
> Italy and Germany, making even closer our mutual ties of alli-
> ance, and desires to strengthen each nation's power to resist the
> Soviet threat and to check Britain. By this means we wish to
> contribute to a speedy and beneficial settlement of the China In-
> cident and to the advancement of our nation's leadership in East
> Asia. To this end we shall conclude a secret agreement with
> Germany to enlarge the spirit of the Anti-Comintern Pact to
> include a military alliance against the Soviet Union and a secret
> agreement with Italy to be used mainly for restraining Britain.[53]

The army and the Foreign Ministry then each set to work to
draft a detailed proposal. The document below, dated July 26
and entitled "On Strengthening the Japanese-German Anti-
Comintern Pact," is somewhat more concrete than the five ministers' draft policy of July 19. It is thought to be an army draft,
judging from its organization and content, but no decision appears to have been made on it by the Five Ministers Conference.

> With a view to strengthening the spirit of the secret supple-
> mentary protocol of the Anti-Comintern Pact, a secret treaty be-
> tween Japan and Germany alone will be concluded which will

expand the pact into an anti-Soviet offensive and defensive treaty of alliance.

The treaty will be handled separately from the Anti-Comintern Pact. The Anti-Comintern Pact and its supplementary protocol will remain in force in order to facilitate the formation of an anti-Comintern united front.

SECRET TREATY OUTLINE

1. The two allies, realizing the necessity for jointly eliminating the threat of the Soviet Union, will promptly engage in hostilities, regardless of place, should armed conflict break out between the Soviet Union and one of the contracting parties as a result of the Soviet threat. A peace treaty will be concluded only when the two allies have agreed. (Depending on the progress of negotiations with Germany, we will give consideration to the "time and method of participation in hostilities, to be decided upon after consultation between the two allies according to the existing situation." In which case, one of the allies, even before it participates in hostilities with armed forces, will offer every available assistance to the other ally.)

2. The two allies, both in war and in peace, will exchange important information concerning the Soviet Union.

3. The two allies, to stand against the Soviet threat, both in war and in peace, will cooperate in considering such propaganda and other activities against the Soviet Union and other nations as are more effective when undertaken jointly.

4. The allied military authorities concerned will coordinate their operations when necessary.

5. Neither ally may, without consulting the other ally, conclude any treaty with other nations that conflicts with the spirit of the present treaty.

6. This treaty will come into effect on the day of its signing and will be valid for a five-year period. However, if one of the two allies is involved in a war against the Soviet Union at the time of its expiration, the treaty will remain valid until a peace treaty is concluded.[54]

The Foreign Ministry saw the projected agreement as a diplomatic measure to control the Soviet Union and to make possible the prosecution of the war in China, rather than as laying the foundation for joint war against the Soviet Union. The following plan embodying Foreign Ministry proposals was formulated and presented by Ugaki at a Five Ministers Conference on August 12:

> Japanese-German political cooperation should be strengthened immediately, in view of the present situation in Soviet-Japanese relations. However, it is necessary strictly to limit the target of the treaty to the Soviet Union. If a war were to break out in Europe between Germany and countries other than the Soviet Union, so long as the Soviet Union does not intervene in the conflict Japan should be able freely to determine its own position toward the war and to deter participation by the Soviet Union. The purpose of the agreement is not an offensive and defensive alliance but rather a defensive treaty of mutual aid.

OUTLINE FOR STRENGTHENING POLITICAL COOPERATION BETWEEN JAPAN AND GERMANY

1. A mutual assistance treaty, aimed at the Soviet Union, should be concluded between Japan and Germany. This treaty should in principle be made public.

2. The general content of the treaty shall be as follows:

   1) When either of the contracting parties enters into hostilities with the Soviet Union after sustaining an unprovoked attack, the other party will offer every possible assistance.

   2) When one of the contracting parties is threatened by an unprovoked attack from the Soviet Union, both parties will immediately meet to consider measures to be taken in response to the threat.

   3) Concerning the assistance which is to be offered by one of the contracting parties to the other in the circumstances designated in this agreement, the methods by which military assistance shall be provided will be decided through prior consultation among the officials concerned. This provision to consult, however, will be stipulated in secret documents to be exchanged.

   4) The treaty shall be valid for five years.

Japanese-Italian political cooperation should be strengthened immediately, in view of the present situation in Soviet-Japanese relations on the one hand, and in German-Japanese relations on the other. So long as such cooperation remains limited, it will affect favorably our position vis-à-vis Great Britain.

It would be appropriate to limit the agreement to the level of a treaty of neutrality and consultation.

OUTLINE FOR STRENGTHENING POLITICAL COOPERATION BETWEEN JAPAN AND ITALY

1. Existing cooperation between Japan and Italy established by the Anti-Comintern Pact will be further developed by the conclusion of a treaty of neutrality and consultation. This treaty shall in principle be made public.

2. The general content of the treaty shall be as follows:

1) When either of the contracting parties sustains an unprovoked attack from a third nation, the other party will remain neutral throughout the period of hostilities.

2) When some international problem arises which is of mutual concern to the contracting parties, consultations will immediately be held upon request of either contracting party.

3) The treaty shall be valid for five years.[55]

This Foreign Ministry plan avoided making the pact an offensive-defensive alliance with Germany and emphasized Japan's relations with the Soviet Union. It was to be made public and thus was more moderate than the army plan. So, while it similarly advocated strengthening the Anti-Comintern Pact, it differed considerably in content and expression from the army draft.

Around this time an official from the Second Section of the Europe-Asia Bureau of the Foreign Ministry, Yosano Shigeru, who happened to visit the Military Affairs Bureau of the Army Ministry, received the impression that talks concerning a pact were already being conducted in Germany through Ōshima. He immediately reported to his chief, Yamada Yoshitarō, who sought further information from Kagesa Sadaaki, chief of the Military Affairs Section. Pledging Yamada to secrecy, Kagesa confirmed that meetings between Ōshima and Ribbentrop, aimed at strengthening the ties between Japan and Germany, had already begun. Yamada reported to Vice Minister Horinouchi Kensuke, who immediately cabled Ambassador Tōgō Shigenori in Berlin; Tōgō replied that he had no indication that such talks were taking place.[56] Ōshima, as in the past, was conducting negotiations with regard to the Anti-Comintern Pact without informing the embassy.

At his meeting with the young Foreign Ministry officials in July, Ugaki had expressed pessimism concerning the chances for increased cooperation with Germany and Italy. During the Five Ministers Conference on August 12 Ugaki presented the Foreign Ministry plan. When Army Minister Itagaki countered that he and the army preferred the German plan linking Japan, Italy, and Germany by a single treaty, Ugaki stressed the danger of involving Japan in complicated European problems, such as the tensions arising between Britain and Germany over Czechoslovakia, and urged caution out of regard for relations with Britain.[57] Navy Minister Yonai Mitsumasa and Finance Minister Ikeda Seihin supported Ugaki, but further discussion of the Foreign Ministry draft was postponed.

Meanwhile, on August 5 Major-General Kasahara had arrived with the German draft which, it will be remembered, was for a defensive alliance whose targets were unspecified but understood to be Britain and France as well as the USSR. Kasahara showed the draft to Ugaki and to army and navy leaders. The army immediately accepted the plan. The navy agreed with its general import but maintained that it would be better to avoid an automatic obligation to go to war, as implied in the third section. Both services agreed to work for the rapid conclusion of a pact.[58] On August 6 or 7 Kasahara, possibly because he was Ugaki's brother-in-law, passed the army and navy opinions informally to Ugaki. Ugaki, like the navy leaders, is reported to have given his personal agreement to the general purpose of the plan but accepted it merely as "information," indicating that he would need to study further the question of means.[59]

Following a meeting on the morning of August 23 between

the heads of the Military Affairs Section of the Army Ministry and the Naval Affairs Section of the Navy Ministry, a conference of Army, Navy, and Foreign Ministry officials was held that afternoon at the office of the chief of the Europe-Asia Bureau of the Foreign Ministry. As a result of these talks general agreement was reached on a revised version of the proposal Kasahara had brought. Finally, in a private conference the following evening, Ugaki and Itagaki concurred on a proposal that made the following changes in the Kasahara draft: (1) in section two "threat" was changed to "unprovoked attack" and (2) "diplomatic" to "economic"; (3) in section three "attack" became "unprovoked attack" and (4) "are obligated to give military assistance" was replaced by "will immediately enter into discussions concerning military assistance"; (5) a note was added to the effect that "clear and detailed provisions should be made by secret agreement concerning the conditions, area, extent, and methods for rendering military assistance." The next day, August 25, Ugaki presented the revised plan to Yonai. On the 26th Yonai let it be known through official channels that he agreed in principle, but he urged that Ugaki seek the opinion of Finance Minister Ikeda on the possible international economic ramifications of the treaty before its final adoption.[60]

Other versions of this episode give a slightly different sequence of events. Some sources, for example, indicate that Ugaki first showed the German plan to his subordinates on the 25th and asked for their opinion by the next day. That night Inoue Kōjirō, chief of the Europe-Asia Bureau, and Yamada Yoshitarō, chief of its Second Section, reportedly prepared a draft and added a preamble clarifying the fact that the treaty was nothing more than an extension of the Anti-Comintern Pact.[61] That evening or at some other time during these few days such a preamble was indeed prepared, but the contemporary sources do not say who cleared it.

This then was the revised draft that Ugaki presented to the Five Ministers Conference on August 26, to which approval was given. (Except for the preamble, which was entirely new, changes made in the German draft brought by Kasahara are indicated by italics.)

Draft Preamble: In view of the friendly relations between Japan, Germany, and Italy which have been advanced since the conclusion of the Anti-Comintern Pact and in view of the fact that the Comintern's activities have become a threat to world peace, particularly in various parts of Europe and Asia, and in accordance with the spirit of our common understanding on these matters, the following points have been agreed upon in order to secure the interests common to the three nations and to strengthen our defense against communist subversion:

1. In the event that one of the contracting parties is faced with diplomatic difficulties with a nonsignatory nation, the contracting parties will meet promptly to discuss common action to be taken.

2. In the event of an *unprovoked attack on* one of the contracting parties by a nonsignatory nation, each party will be obligated to offer all political and *economic* assistance to eliminate the threat.

3. In the event that one of the contracting parties sustains an *unprovoked* attack by a nonsignatory nation, the other parties *will immediately enter into discussions concerning military assistance.*

Note: Clear and detailed provisions should be made by secret agreement concerning the conditions, area, extent, and methods for rendering military assistance.[62]

After some discussion, Ugaki won his point on procedure. The ministers agreed:

1. The German draft was delivered to the imperial government through informal rather than formal diplomatic channels. Therefore, the foreign minister accepts it merely as information. However, there is no objection to the army and navy informing Germany informally of their agreement with the gist of the proposal provided certain conditions are met.

2. It is requested that the army and navy have this proposal transferred immediately to the formal negotiating level between the governments concerned through the Japanese ambassador in Germany.

Ugaki seems in general to have won also his point that the Comintern, not Britain or the United States, should remain the target and that the obligation to help Germany should clearly extend only to political and economic areas, consultation alone being required in the military field. The conference's decision continued as follows:

> 3. There is agreement with the proposal in principle. However, a number of corrections will be required after careful study, when a text is drafted. The conditions mentioned on the separate sheets are only a few such examples.
> 4. Which portions are and are not to be made public will be determined after discussions between the governments. The foreign minister thinks that the third article should not be made public, but there is no objection to having this reconsidered when negotiations are undertaken between the governments.[63]

But the approval of the Ugaki draft as containing negotiable "examples" of changes that would be needed in the German proposal left important ambiguities. With provision being made to consider unspecified revisions other than these, the army clearly had made no final concessions.[64]

Some of the more serious ambiguities are reflected in the instructions sent to Ōshima and Tōgō informing them of the August 26 decision. Both a Foreign Ministry draft and an army-navy draft of the instruction to be sent from the army and navy to their attachés in Germany were prepared. At first the Foreign Ministry objected to the army-navy draft, which merely called for a partial revision of the German plan (and this is no doubt the way Ōshima understood it). But under strong pressure from the military, the Foreign Ministry eventually agreed to the draft with only a slight change of wording. The result, a somewhat garbled version of the August 26 decision, was sent three days later as Army Telegram 235 from the vice ministers of the army and navy to Army Attaché Ōshima and Navy Attaché Kojima Hideo. The wire concluded: "We hope to conclude this treaty as soon as possible. Therefore, we hope that you will seek Germany's proposals promptly and officially."

A supplementary telegram was also sent by the vice army minister to Ōshima, as follows:

> 1. The draft preamble is intended to indicate clearly that the proposed treaty is to be an extension of the existing Anti-Comintern Pact and that it is directed principally against the Soviet

Union. Thus it avoids the use of any word or phrase that might invite any impression that countries such as Britain and the United States are regarded as direct enemies.

2. The third article of the draft treaty is designed to provide for discussion prior to the extension of military assistance, so that the responsibility for granting military aid will not be instantaneous or unconditional, and to avoid the danger of Japan's becoming involved in a purely European problem against its will.

3. This agreement is based on the principle that it is defensive, so that only unprovoked threats and attacks will be covered.

4. This treaty is still in process of being studied.[65]

Ōshima had not expected that the plan he had forwarded to Tokyo for the army's consideration would be thus adopted by the Five Ministers Conference.[66] He interpreted his instructions to mean that the German plan could be accepted with the revised wording and that, while obviously the main target of the treaty was the Soviet Union, nevertheless other nations might be included as secondary targets so long as the treaty avoided "the use of any word or phrase that might invite any impression" that other countries were "regarded as direct enemies." [67]

His conclusions were reinforced by the account of the situation in Tokyo brought him shortly thereafter by Kasahara. The Five Ministers Conference, Kasahara said, had decided that Japan's goals should be to settle the China War, strengthen Japan's international position, and facilitate the establishment of order in East Asia after the war was over; that care should be taken by means of a preamble to avoid disturbing the United States; that the duty to participate in a war should exist only in case of an unprovoked attack by another country; that the extent of cooperation should be determined in each case through special committees of the three nations after conclusion of the pact; and that the Soviet Union should be the primary target and other nations only secondary targets. What had been principally the army's demands and interpretations thus were transmitted to Ōshima as the unconditional opinion of the Five Ministers Conference itself.[68]

The source of the problem, which was to create serious confusion later, was not Ōshima but rather the uncertain domestic situation in Japan, the unclarified four-point statement amplifying the August 26 decision, and the fact that the army controlled the news it sent to Ōshima. After Ōshima received the telegram, he reported to Ambassador Tōgō on the negotiations that had taken place until then and also relayed its contents to Ribbentrop.

A somewhat different impression of the decision reached at the Five Ministers Conference was conveyed in two telegrams sent from Ugaki to Tōgō on August 31, based upon the original Foreign Ministry draft of the orders to be sent to the attachés. The first of these informed Tōgō that negotiations so far, having been conducted by the army, were considered unofficial. The official negotiations would not begin until Ribbentrop moved them out of military and into diplomatic channels. At that point Tōgō would take over from Ōshima.[69] Thus, the decisions of August 26, which were understood by Ōshima to represent conditional government acceptance of the German draft, were taken by Tōgō as guidelines for negotiations yet to come. These guidelines were given to him as follows:

1. The preamble should clearly state that the treaty is primarily to provide for defense against the subversive activities of the Soviet Union and the Comintern, and that countries such as Britain and the United States are not to be direct enemies. (Concerning the United States, this point should be made clear particularly through the addition of geographical limits.)
2. Considerable changes in phraseology in the text of the treaty are to be made after careful study. (For example, the word "unprovoked" should precede the words "threat" and "attack," because the proposed treaty is purely defensive and its principal goal is security. Also, in the expression "political and diplomatic assistance," as diplomatic assistance is included in political assistance and because Japan also considers economic assistance seriously, this wording should be altered to read "political and economic assistance." These are only one or two examples.)
3. The last part of the third clause should read "will immediately enter into discussions . . ." to avoid the danger of making automatic the obligation to render military assistance, as well as of becoming involved in a purely European problem, contrary to Japan's will. Clear and detailed provisions should be made by a

secret agreement concerning the conditions, area, extent, and
methods for rendering military assistance.[70]

The ambiguities in the phraseology of these changes thus
exacerbated the differences between Ōshima's and Tōgō's
understanding of the status of the negotiations and of the significance of the changes desired in the German proposal. Compared with the original Foreign Ministry proposal presented by
Ugaki to the Five Ministers Conference on August 12, which
had declared it essential "strictly to limit the target of the treaty
to the Soviet Union," these Foreign Ministry instructions were
notably unclear. By stating that the targets of the treaty were
"primarily" the Soviet Union and the Comintern and by stipulating that Britain and the United States were "not to be direct
enemies," room was left for the inference that the latter might
be at least secondary or indirect targets. This left Tōgō with
muddled instructions on the most sensitive point.

Much of the future confusion surrounding the problem of
strengthening the Anti-Comintern Pact was to spring from
Itagaki's and Ugaki's differing interpretations of the August 26
decision, as well as from the ambiguous position of the Foreign
Ministry, which, while agreeing to the instructions cabled to
Ōshima and Kojima by the army and navy vice ministers, sent
separate instructions to Tōgō.

On August 30 Ugaki reported to the emperor on the decision
reached at the Five Ministers Conference. At that time he stated
that Germany and Italy might not accept the treaty if its target
were limited to the Soviet Union. In any event, he added, he
wished to express Japan's views to Germany and Italy as well as
to give more consideration to the problem after observing their
reactions.[71]

The Army–Foreign Ministry Stalemate

The Foreign Ministry thereupon began to formulate a draft to be
used in formal negotiations. This draft, presented to the army
and navy for study on September 10, was as follows.

The government of Imperial Japan, the government of Italy, and the government of Germany, considering that the tripartite Anti-Comintern Pact has promoted friendly relations between the three nations, considering that the international activities of the Communist International have become a threat to world peace, particularly in Asia and Europe, on the basis of the spirit of the said pact and in order to strengthen our defense against subversive communist activities in these areas, agree to the following:

Article 1. In the event a serious conflict arises between one of the contract parties and a nonsignatory nation, the contracting parties, upon the expressed wish of the aforementioned party, will immediately begin discussions of measures to be taken.

Article 2. In the event one of the contracting parties sustains an unprovoked attack, or the threat of one, by a nonsignatory nation, the other contracting parties undertake to offer assistance necessary to stop the attack or threat. In any situation requiring such assistance, the contracting parties will immediately begin discussions concerning measures to be adopted.

Article 3. The official text of this agreement will be in the Japanese, Italian, and German languages.

This treaty shall come into force on the date it is signed and shall remain in force for a period of five years. Prior to the date of expiration, the contracting parties will meet to arrive at an understanding concerning the form of cooperation to be undertaken after the expiration of the present treaty. The undersigned, having been formally commissioned to do so by each government, hereby witness the above statements and affix their signatures to this treaty.

Signed Protocol:

On this day . . . in concluding the treaty, the undersigned plenipotentiaries have agreed to the following:

1. Concerning treaty Article 2: In view of the provisions of the protocol concluded between Japan and Manchukuo on September 15, 1932, any attack or threat of attack against Manchukuo will be considered an attack or threat of attack against Japan.

2. Concerning treaty Article 3: When assistance according to this article is being extended at the time of the expiration of this treaty, the treaty will remain valid until the situation requiring such assistance has ended.

Secret Supplementary Protocol:

On this day . . . in concluding the treaty, the undersigned plenipotentiaries have agreed to the following:

1. Assistance provided for in treaty Article 2 is understood as political and economic assistance. In the event the Soviet Union, alone or in concert with other nations, should attack one of the contracting parties, the contracting parties shall enter into discussions regarding military assistance as well. Concerned authorities of the signatory nations shall reach a prior agreement as to the actual methods of providing military aid.

2. The contracting parties will not be bound by treaty commitments with any nonsignatory nation that might conflict with this treaty.

3. This secret supplementary protocol will not be made public nor be mentioned to nonsignatory nations without prior agreement among the contracting parties.

4. This secret supplementary protocol is valid for the period during which the treaty is in force and is inseparable from it.[72]

This draft placed particular emphasis on the fourth point of the August 26 decision, in which Ugaki sought to keep the article concerning discussions of military assistance from being made public. Thus, on the basis of this earlier understanding and out of regard for relations with Britain, the Foreign Ministry draft eliminated the word "military" from Article 3 of the draft treaty approved on August 26. Reference to military assistance was placed in the secret supplementary protocol, whose terms clearly specified that such assistance would apply only against the Soviet Union in the event the USSR, alone or in concert with other nations, were to attack a signatory. Article 2 of the main treaty referred only to "necessary" assistance. In effect, no assistance was to be automatic or obligatory without prior consultation.

Both the army and navy replied that this new Foreign Ministry draft represented a complete emasculation of the policy decision of the Five Ministers Conference and declared that they could not go along with the proposed treaty on this basis. The opinion of the Navy General Staff, dated September 12, and that of the Navy Ministry, dated September 14, except for a few points, were virtually the same.[73] They stated that the draft preamble was too negative, that the phrase "in order to secure the interests common to the three nations" should be inserted as in the August 26 preamble, and that the phrase "upon the expressed wish of the aforementioned party" be removed from Article 1. The General Staff further proposed that the second sentence of Article 2 be deleted if its contents could be included in an attached secret protocol, but if this were not possible, it might be allowed to stand. The Navy Ministry was in favor of deleting this sentence altogether. It was, in fact, removed from subsequent Japanese drafts.

As for the secret supplementary protocol, the Navy General Staff asked for a complete reexamination. The Navy Ministry plan listed three alternatives concerning Article 1. The first deleted the reference to the Soviet Union, referring only to an attack by "one or more nonsignatory nations." The second added to the Foreign Ministry plan the following statement: "In case of attack or threat of attack upon one of the contracting parties by one or more nonsignatory nations other than the Soviet Union, the contracting parties will discuss whether or not to extend military aid." The third alternative called on the allied nations to provide military support in the event of an attack by the Soviet Union alone, and to discuss military support in the event of an attack by one or more nonsignatory nations including or not including the Soviet Union.

The army's revised draft, dated October 25, held firmly to the line of the August 26 decision. However, should its position not be fully sustained, the army was willing to revise the secret protocol to provide that the "assistance" stipulated in treaty Article 2 included military as well as political and economic aid and that if one of the allies were attacked by one or more nonsignatories, discussions concerning the implementation of military aid should begin immediately.[74]

In short, despite army-navy differences, both opposed any revisions that retreated substantially from the August 26 draft. At a conference with officials of the Navy and Foreign ministries and the two General Staffs on September 13, representatives of the Army Ministry strongly opposed the new Foreign Ministry draft presented three days before, and no agreement could be reached.[75] Thereafter, claiming that it was giving the draft careful consideration, the army refused to discuss it further, so that the new Foreign Ministry draft never reached the formal discussion stage.

No doubt the army was strengthened in its decision not to compromise by its knowledge of far-reaching personnel changes than going on in the Foreign Ministry. Foreign Minister Ugaki suddenly resigned on September 30. The reason given was his opposition to the establishment of the Kōain or Asia Development Board—a new central agency apart from the Foreign Ministry for dealing with China. This may well have been the case, although there are indications that the issue involved more than a clash of bureaucratic responsibilities. It may have been forced by the army to provoke Ugaki's resignation and thus thwart his peace negotiations with China; and there is some reason to believe that Ugaki responded decisively with an eye to his political ambitions.[76]

For the post of foreign minister Prime Minister Konoe first considered Saitō Hiroshi, ambassador to the United States; but Saitō was seriously ill and therefore could not fill the position. The matter went to the Five Ministers Conference. Finance Minister Ikeda submitted Arita Hachirō's name. Army Minister Itagaki suggested Matsuoka Yōsuke, but on October 3 Harada Kumao remarked to Konoe, "You don't mean to appoint the likes of Matsuoka as foreign minister!" [77] Another candidate was Shiratori Toshio, who had been appointed ambassador to Italy on September 22. Immediately after Ugaki's resignation the young officials of the Shiratori faction in the Foreign Ministry (said to number about fifty) drafted a jointly signed covenant and asked Konoe to appoint Shiratori to the post. Ugaki referred in his diary to this movement of the "Shiratori faithful." They also worked through Home Minister Yasui Eiji. It is said that on the evening of October 4 Chief Cabinet Secretary Kazami Akira sought Navy Minister Yonai's acceptance of Shiratori as foreign minister and was refused, but this point is not clear. At one time Konoe is said to have been drawn to Shiratori, but ultimately Arita was selected and assumed office on October 29. Ikeda had backed Arita all along, and Harada had suggested Arita to Yonai.[78]

Shiratori himself backed Arita for the position because, he said, Arita was pure, had no private ambitions, and did not make mistakes.[79] As suggested by the exchange of letters between the two previously alluded to, Shiratori seems to have trusted Arita personally despite their disagreements on matters of ideology and policy. Moreover, it would appear that the court was concerned about Shiratori's activities. Ugaki recorded in his diary a visit he made to the imperial palace on September 22 to discuss foreign relations. "The emperor questioned me about relations with Britain, H. H. Kung, and Shiratori." [80]

The appointment of a new foreign minister was not the only personnel change. At the end of Ugaki's term a major shake-up occurred throughout the ministry. Shiratori replaced Hotta Masaaki as ambassador to Italy, taking up his post in December. Yoshida Shigeru was recalled from Britain, where he was replaced by Shigemitsu Mamoru, previously ambassador to the Soviet Union. In turn, Shigemitsu was replaced in Moscow by the then ambassador to Germany, Tōgō Shigenori, whose place in Berlin was assigned, not to a diplomat, but to Attaché Ōshima. The army thought Tōgō unpopular with the Nazis and the German government, and they and the Shiratori faction in the Foreign Ministry wanted Ōshima appointed ambassador.[81] Thus, while adhering to the form of the August 26 decision that the negotiations with Germany should be handled by the Foreign Ministry, the army kept its hand on the reins by having its own General Ōshima appointed by the Foreign Ministry.

The personnel changes, however, did not result in a clear victory for the Axis faction, since Foreign Minister Arita did not behave in the manner the military and the Axis faction in the Foreign Ministry had expected. And Ōshima too began to feel that the negotiations suddenly were no longer proceeding smoothly. As he recalled many years later, "Something seemed to have happened back in Tokyo." [82] Arita had served as adviser to the Foreign Ministry during Ugaki's term and ever since that time had had doubts about the decision of the Five Ministers Conference of August 26. After becoming foreign minister he solicited information from those involved. Ugaki assured him that while the decision had been to strengthen the Anti-Comintern Pact, there had been absolutely no thought of making any country other than the Soviet Union the treaty's target, and that was how it had been reported to the Throne. Konoe, Yonai, and Ikeda confirmed the view that the new treaty was conceived as strengthening the Anti-Comintern Pact aimed at the Soviet Union and was not directed against Britain or France. Arita therefore took a cautious view with regard to the opinions of Army Minister Itagaki.

Meanwhile Ribbentrop, whom Ōshima had informed of the August 26 decision, proposed to Ōshima that, inasmuch as it would take time to achieve agreement in detail on a secret supplementary protocol and in order for the proposed treaty to be rapidly concluded, a public announcement should first be made that the three nations were agreed on the treaty draft. A secret memorandum should then provide that Article 3 of the German draft would come into force after the secret supplementary protocol was agreed upon.[83] Ribbentrop probably also wanted to deal with the situation in Europe, where the atmosphere had become very tense over the Czechoslovakian issue. Hitler and Chamberlain had met at Berchtesgaden, and the Germans wanted the revised pact concluded quickly in order to apply further diplomatic pressure on Britain.

The Army Refuses to Budge

On October 27, with Ōshima in his new post, Germany unofficially submitted a revised draft to him, which he relayed to the Tokyo government on November 1.[84] Ribbentrop had presented the same draft to the Italian government. Mussolini had agreed in principle but asked that, for reasons of domestic politics, adoption be postponed until March of the following year. The new German draft contained certain important revisions of a three-point draft the Germans had shown to Italy prior to the Munich agreement in late September. The new draft read as follows:

Article 1. In the event that one of the contracting parties is faced with diplomatic difficulties with one or several nonsignatory nations, the other contracting parties will meet promptly to discuss joint action to be taken.

Article 2. In the event of a threat to one of the contracting parties by one or several nonsignatory nations, the other contracting parties are obligated to give political, diplomatic, and economic assistance to the aforementioned party in order to eliminate the threat.

Article 3. In the event one of the contracting parties sustains an unprovoked attack by one or several nonsignatory nations, the other contracting parties are obligated to give aid and assistance to the aforementioned party. When a situation arises in which such aid or assistance is required, the three contracting parties will immediately and jointly determine how to carry out this obligation.

Article 4 of the revised German draft was a no-separate-peace requirement which provided:

In the event the three contracting parties are mutually engaged in a war on the basis of Article 3, they will conclude any armistice or peace solely by mutual consent.

Article 5 provided that the treaty should remain in force for ten years and further stipulated:

A year prior to the date of its expiration, if none of the contracting parties desires to discontinue membership, this treaty will remain valid for five additional years, and a similar rule will be observed after this second period.

Finally, the German draft contained the following secret supplementary protocol:

The Tripartite Pact supplementing the Anti-Comintern Pact shall consist of the following:
1. The basic treaties already formulated and signed.
2. Any supplementary agreements made in the future.
The following has been resolved for inclusion in the said supplementary protocol and will become valid for all three nations:

Committees of the related governments or of their defense forces will be organized immediately after the conclusion and publication of the basic treaty to investigate the likelihood of conflict and to discuss in detail the measures that are to be taken to render political, military, and economic assistance in accordance with the articles of the basic treaty.

If a dispute should arise prior to the signing of the supplementary protocol, the contracting parties will meet to discuss joint action to be taken in each case. In all such cases the party concerned must make clear to the other contracting parties, in accordance with their geographical positions, by what methods and to what extent political, military, and economic aid is to be given. Only after this has been agreed to unanimously by the contracting parties will it be adopted by them as the secret supplementary protocol and be signed.[85]

The revised German draft of October 27 contained certain important differences from the Five Ministers Conference decision of August 26. The word "unprovoked," which Tokyo had inserted, was removed from Article 2 and "diplomatic assistance" was added to "political and economic assistance." Assistance was made an obligation in both Articles 2 and 3, and a fourth, no-separate-peace article was inserted.

The basic issue the German draft posed was the identity of the countries against whom it was directed. Who were the "one or several nonsignatory nations" mentioned in the first three articles? On November 11, at the first Five Ministers Conference after Arita had assumed his new post, Itagaki recommended the immediate drafting of a Japanese counterproposal to the German plan. Arita agreed but said that, in order to avoid future misunderstandings, he wished to make clear at this time the nature of the treaty. As he understood it, the treaty was a strengthening of the Anti-Comintern Pact and was aimed at the USSR, not at France or Britain. He asked if this was correct. Ikeda and Yonai immediately said that it was, and Konoe stated that this was how he himself understood it. Only Itagaki was silent. When Arita asked for his opinion, he said he also understood it thus, but in the event that France became communist, the treaty should also apply to France. Arita and the other cabinet officials agreed with this, and the following decision was taken:

1. A tripartite alliance of Japan, Germany, and Italy should immediately be concluded on the basis of the decisions of the Five Ministers Conference of July 19 and August 26, 1938. For this purpose the government should quicky formulate its own draft with reference to the German draft contained in Ōshima's telegram in order to lay the foundations for an alliance.

2. This treaty should be concluded among Japan, Germany, and Italy. Should negotiations be prolonged, however, separate treaties should be concluded between Japan and Germany and between Japan and Italy, which we would expect later to join into a tripartite agreement.

The foreign minister thereupon had the following written into the minutes:

Question: This treaty is directed primarily against the Soviet Union. Nations such as Britain and France will become targets only if they join with the Soviet Union. Nations such as Britain and France alone will not become targets, although of course if France becomes communist, it will become a target of the treaty. Am I correct?

Answer (unanimous): Yes, you are correct.[86]

As far as Arita was concerned, the issue of the treaty's target had been settled and he was "very relieved." [87] Based on this decision, a second Foreign Ministry draft was prepared whose phraseology closely resembled the revised German draft of October 27. This new draft reinserted the word "unprovoked" before "threat" in Article 2. While it retained the German draft's phrase "one or several nonsignatory nations" in Articles 1–3 and accepted Article 1, it changed the word "obligated" (no gimu o yūsu) in the Japanese version of Articles 2 and 3 of the German draft to the somewhat weaker "undertake" (o yakusu) to offer political, diplomatic, and economic assistance in the event of such a threat. Section 1 of the secret supplementary protocol accepted the German no-separate-peace clause and defined the extent of the Japanese commitment to render military assistance as follows:

With respect to the aid and assistance mentioned in Article 3 of the treaty, military aid will be carried out in the event the

Union of Soviet Socialist Republics, alone or in concert with other nonsignatory nations, attacks one of the contracting parties. The concerned allied authorities will meet at once and in advance to decide the method of carrying out military assistance. In the event that the contracting parties engage mutually in a war, an armistice or peace will not be concluded by one of the contracting parties alone.[88]

In reality, events did not develop as Arita had anticipated. An army document on the Five Ministers Conference of November 11 stated: "Although agreement has been reached among the five ministers, the army feels that the phrase 'directed primarily against the Soviet Union' in connection with this treaty means that emphasis is to be placed on giving aid and support against the Soviet Union, not that aid and support against other countries should be excluded." [89] The use of the imprecise word "primarily" in both the August 26 and November 11 decisions was to remain a source of future difficulty. The army's interpretation did influence later developments, but of greater importance at the time was Ambassador Ōshima's response.

Ōshima later claimed that a telegram he received from Arita on November 12 stated that the proposed treaty was directed "primarily against the USSR but secondarily against Britain" and, it was hoped, would solve the current diplomatic impasse; it was thus a diplomatic device designed to kill "three birds with one stone." Ōshima was also to find out the real reason why Italy was stalling action on the pact. Usami Uzuhiko, counselor of embassy in Germany, also acknowledged having received this "three birds with one stone" telegram.[90] But Arita himself denied ever having sent it, and no such telegram is to be found in the archives of the Foreign Ministry. Furthermore, Arita's words and actions at this time raise doubts as to the existence of the telegram. It has been said that the phrase "three birds with one stone" was the wording of Captain Nishi Hisashi, who was then at the German desk, Europe-America Section, of the Army General Staff.[91] Even granting that the phrase was actually used by Arita, Ōshima appears to have taken it out of context.

Arita did send a telegram on either November 17 or 24 which stated: "The proposed treaty is directed mainly at the Soviet Union, but also at Britain and France if they should side with the Soviet Union. It is not aimed at Britain and France by themselves. Of course, if France should become communist, it will become a target." [92] As the contents of this telegram differed from Ōshima's earlier understanding based on the army telegram of August 29, Ōshima protested. He charged that the new decision of the November 11 meeting, that Britain and France would not be targets, contradicted the policy he had received as attaché on August 29. "I cannot understand," he complained, "the alteration of such an important policy as this in a period of two or three months." [93]

The Foreign Ministry thereupon drafted new instructions to the effect that "national policy with regard to this issue has always been limited to anticommunism, and this has not been changed. Even an agreement based on the instructions previously sent to you would have sufficient political impact on Britain and France." These new instructions were discussed at a Five Ministers Conference in early December, when Itagaki went along with Ōshima, stating: "The decision of the Five Ministers Conference of August 26 was to the effect that the main target would be the Soviet Union and secondary targets would be Britain and France. It did not eliminate nations other than the Soviet Union. The decision of the Five Ministers Conference of November 11 was to the same effect." The other four ministers pointed out that he was wrong, but Itagaki held to his own view and the conference did not arrive at a decision that day.[94]

Itagaki's interpretation obviously went too far. This was probably the result of pressure from subordinates concerning the interpretation expressed in the army document on the decision of November 11. In any event, as Arita said, "It became necessary to decide whether we were to change to suit the army the decision already made by the government, or convince the army and have the ambassador in the field correct his explanation to the Germans." [95] It would have been very difficult at this time to convince the army to accept Arita's view. Eventually the five ministers found it difficult to hold their conferences for fear the cabinet might fall, and they were unable to decide on new instructions that year.

As for relations with Italy, the Japanese seem to have been considering the alternative of first concluding a provisional treaty with Germany and then enlarging it to include Italy, probably because Italy wished to delay conclusion of the treaty until the beginning of the following year. Arisue Seizō, army attaché in Italy, implied that for reasons of prestige Italy might not agree to such a procedure, although Mussolini supported the creation of a power bloc based on the combined strength of the three nations.[96] Arisue severely criticized the Foreign Ministry for its telegram to Ōshima, stating:

A fundamental change has been made by the recent Five Ministers Conference, making Britain the target of this treaty only if it joins forces with the Soviet Union. In view of what has transpired in the negotiations thus far, such a drastic change will make it impossible to reach an agreement. All this runs counter to the basic principles decided upon on the basis of the German draft. Please inform me further on this point.[97]

While further instructions to Ōshima were thus held up for lack of a policy decision, the entire cabinet resigned. Konoe had already let it be known at the time of Ugaki's resignation that he too wished to resign, but he had been persuaded to stay on. Domestic and foreign problems had continued to pile up, and on January 3, 1939, the mass resignation occurred. No special reason seems to have provoked it; but at the time of his resignation Konoe issued this statement: "The situation has entered a new stage. The time has come when we must put all of our efforts into the establishment of a new order which will assure the eternal peace of the Orient. I firmly believe that to deal with this new situation, we must plan to revolutionize the hearts of the people by creating a new policy under a new cabinet."[98]

The Hiranuma Cabinet's Decision

On the night of January 4, 1939, when the imperial order for the formation of a new government was issued to Baron Hiranuma

Kiichirō, the prime minister-designate asked Arita to remain in the cabinet as foreign minister. Arita asked Hiranuma's opinion of the plan to strengthen the Anti-Comintern Pact, which was now in troubled waters. How much Hiranuma knew of the situation is not known, but he replied that the treaty's target should be limited to the Soviet Union and should not include Britain and France. He would attempt to deal with the issue on that basis, he indicated, adding that if things did not work out that way, he and Arita should resign together. Arita thereupon consented to remain in his post.[99] But so did Army Minister Itagaki and Navy Minister Yonai, and Konoe himself retained his position as president of the Privy Council while entering the cabinet as minister without portfolio.

After the Hiranuma cabinet had been formed, Germany formally presented a draft treaty to Italy and Japan on January 6. Differences between this official draft and the unofficial German revised draft of October 27 were slight. The word "diplomatic" was dropped from Article 1 and the obligation to give diplomatic assistance removed from Article 2, leaving only the responsibility to give political and economic assistance. To the first sentence of Article 3 was added the obligation to give aid and assistance "by every means available." While the main body of the treaty was essentially unchanged, the secret supplementary protocol was completely revised, as follows:

> 1. For the carrying out of responsibilities resulting from this treaty of alliance, the foreign ministers of the contracting parties or their delegates will form a standing joint committee. After this treaty has come into force, this standing committee of the three foreign ministers will immediately discuss the likelihood of disputes and the nature and extent—according to the geographical position of each contracting party—of political, military, and economic assistance which should be offered. The standing joint committee will then organize standing joint subcommittees of experts, in order to obtain their professional opinions. The organization and activities of each subcommittee will be determined by the standing joint committee of the foreign ministers of the contracting parties.
>
> 2. Immediately after the treaty has come into force, the governments of the contracting parties shall organize standing committees composed of three representatives of the press or other

communications media. The foreign minister or the delegated representative of the foreign minister of each of the three countries shall name one such representative to each committee. There shall be one such three-man committee organized in Berlin, Rome, and Tokyo. In keeping with the spirit and purpose of this agreement, each committee shall be charged with the task of carrying out, by all available means, a campaign through the press and other communications media to enlighten in a positive fashion world public opinion for the protection and benefit of the contracting parties against the hostile activities of other countries.

3. This supplementary protocol is an inseparable part of the treaty and will be considered strictly confidential by the contracting parties.[100]

In deciding on the steps to be taken with regard to this German draft, Arita sought a full exchange of opinions with those persons who favored a stronger alliance, whom he believed were centered in the middle levels of the Army Ministry and the General Staff. On January 11, 13, and 14 he discussed the treaty in the Army Ministry with Kagesa Sadaaki, chief of the Military Affairs Section, and Iwakuro Hideo, a high official of the Military Section; and in the General Staff with Inada Masazumi, chief of the Operations Section, and Tatsumi Eiichi, chief of the Europe-America Section of the Intelligence Division. Arita, as before, thought it undesirable, or at least premature, for Japan to make any nation other than the Soviet Union the target. As a result of these exchanges, Arita reached two decisions: (1) If he accepted as unavoidable the addition of Britain and France as targets of the treaty, the army could be persuaded that Japan would be obligated to give only political and economic assistance to signatory nations; whether or not military assistance was given would be determined by the situation; (2) In the event such a compromise was necessary, he would try to explain to the outside world that the proposed treaty was merely an extension of the Anti-Comintern Pact, so as to mitigate insofar as possible the diplomatic setbacks he expected to result.[101]

At the Five Ministers Conference of January 19 Arita waited for an opportune moment when the army and navy ministers were at odds on the issue and proposed that these two points be added as secret mutual understandings; the other ministers agreed. Immediately thereafter Arita reported to the emperor as follows:

> In revising the principal point of the decision made at the last Five Ministers Conference, Japan's current treaty draft states that countries other than the Soviet Union may become targets whenever the common interests of the allies demand it, even if the subversive activities of the Comintern are not involved. If we are to uphold the principal provision of the earlier decision, our experience indicates that it would reveal distrust of Germany and Italy and would discourage the friendship that has been established between Japan and these countries. Therefore we have adopted the position taken by Germany and Italy, although we will try to minimize as much as possible the disadvantages to Japan, and also to minimize its unfavorable impact by explaining to the outside world that the treaty is merely an extension of the Anti-Comintern Pact. It is Japan's policy not to offer military assistance at present or in the near future should Germany and Italy engage in war against countries other than Russia for any reason other than the subversive activities of the Comintern.[102]

Thus, a basic policy decision was finally reached. Arita felt his position against further compromise would be best transmitted not by telegram but by sending a special mission to achieve understanding on this point. Minister Itō Nobufumi of the Foreign Ministry, Colonel Tatsumi Eiichi of the Army General Staff, and Rear Admiral Abe Katsuo were dispatched to Germany and Italy.[103] Instructions were drawn up, approved by the Five Ministers Conference on January 25, and given to the Itō mission the next day.

The full text of this important document included a draft text of a Treaty of Consultation and Mutual Assistance, as the Japanese government preferred the new agreement to be called in order to emphasize its defensive character, a signed protocol, a secret supplementary protocol, and two secret items of understanding, together with a rationale to guide the negotiations. The full text may be found in Appendix 4. The nub of the issue, which Arita had labored so hard to resolve, was to be found in the secret items of understanding, on which Ōshima and Shiratori were told that agreement was absolutely essential. These items were:

> 1. Concerning Article 3 of the treaty and Item 1 of the secret supplementary protocol [concerning aid and assistance to be offered in the case of unprovoked attack], military assistance will be offered if the Soviet Union should attack one of the contracting parties, whether alone or in concert with other nonsignatory nations.
>
> The above provision does not affect the obligation for the contracting parties to consult and reach agreement concerning military assistance depending upon the situation, even if the Soviet Union is not involved in the attack.
>
> 2. In view of the fact that the treaty and the signed protocol are to be made public, the contracting parties, when required to explain the treaty, will assert in concert that it is an extension of the treaty concluded against the Communist International on November 25, 1936, and that the main purpose of this treaty is defense against nations that pursue subversive activities based upon policies of the Communist International.

Lest there remain any doubt in the minds of Ōshima and Shiratori, the instructions emphasized flatly that, whereas the text of the treaty did not identify or distinguish among the "one or several nonsignatory nations" that the alliance was directed against, it was in fact "directed mainly against the Soviet Union." Therefore, "the military aid obligation is limited to an occasion when the Soviet Union, alone or in concert with other countries, attacks one of the contracting parties." And this item, the instructions underlined, was "for Japan the most important clause." When the Itō mission arrived in Berlin late in February, Itō further emphasized that the military aid obligation was to be assumed only if the Soviet Union were involved, either alone or in concert with another country; if the Soviet Union was not involved, actual military assistance was not to be carried out unless the countries involved were communist.

Uncertain why the mission had been sent and feeling that Germany would not approve of such an agreement, Ōshima put off carrying out his instructions. On March 4 he and Shiratori requested deletion of the secret items of understanding so vital to the Japanese government.[104]

The Foreign Ministry held firm. Insisting that both Germany and Italy could be persuaded to accept an agreement in accordance with its instructions, it sent to the Five Ministers Conference on March 13 a draft of new instructions calling for the previous instructions to be executed immediately. The army and navy ministers, while stressing the absolute necessity of negotiating on the basis of the January 19 decision, felt it would be wise to issue compromise instructions out of deference to the request from the two ambassadors and because Germany and Italy might not accept the Japanese proposal.[105] Arita replied that the policy adopted on January 19 had been "formulated under special circumstances" and that the decision did not allow for any compromise. The army minister persisted. Although the established policy should not be changed, he said, a compromise draft should be drawn up containing technical revisions to meet the wishes of the two nations. Arita completely opposed this suggestion, insisting just as adamantly that no technical corrections were possible. Finally, Prime Minister Hiranuma sought to ease the situation by asking each minister to draft compromise instructions for consideration at the next meeting.

The Foreign Ministry revision of Item 1 of the secret items of understanding continued to insist that a military assistance obligation would be assumed only when the Soviet Union alone or in concert with another country engaged in hostilities, but that Italy might be excused from such an obligation when only the Soviet Union was involved. The navy and army, however, proposed to eliminate the item entirely and to clarify the position of the Japanese government in the detailed agreements concerning the nature and scope of military assistance. The Foreign Ministry was silent on Item 2, and the army suggested only that the treaty be concluded immediately and not officially publicized. The navy suggested that Japan reach an understanding with Italy and Germany that Japan, for its part, would explain the treaty as being directed solely against the Comintern.[106]

The Five Ministers Conference held on March 22 from 8:00 P.M. until 12:30 A.M. was a repetition of earlier meetings and centered around the army's and navy's demands for revised instructions. In the end the foreign minister agreed to a new set of instructions, which were described to Ōshima and Shiratori as a restatement of the points desired in the secret items of understanding with "some slight modification," as follows:

A. It has become clear, after careful study and investigation of the opinions submitted by you concerning the imperial government's draft instructions, that we disagree with you on some serious matters regarding the secret items of understanding. The imperial government has concluded that, from every viewpoint, it is necessary to retain both items and believes that it should be possible to reach an agreement that includes these secret items. Thus, we unfortunately disagree with you, although your opinion may well be the result of having sounded out Germany's and Italy's response to the government's proposal. You believe that our proposal has little chance of being accepted should it be submitted, and that submission in the form desired may significantly offend Germany and Italy so as not only to be detrimental to the conclusion of the treaty but also to affect adversely the currently existing Anti-Comintern Pact. The situation in which Japan finds itself, however, is different from that of either Germany or Italy. During the course of the present conflict with China, friction with nations such as Britain and France has created problems that still remain unsettled. Japan, furthermore, is in the process of improving its military preparedness and of expanding its productive capacity in order to settle the China Incident and to meet further developments in the international situation. Thus, we consider it important to express, frankly and in detail, the position of our empire, our immediate concern being to find a solution to these problems as well as to ascertain the response of Germany and Italy and endeavor, in the course of future negotiations, to find a compromise between our position and theirs.

B. It has been established that the fundamental aim of our empire's present and future policy is to strengthen our relationship with Germany and Italy. Since it is not likely that any change will be made in that policy, it is the sincere wish of our empire that the present treaty be immediately concluded. Therefore, it is far from our intention immediately to abandon the present treaty if the previous instructions are rejected by the concerned countries [i.e., Germany and Italy]. We firmly believe that it would be proper for the government of Imperial Japan to make every effort to bring about the conclusion of this treaty by seeking a compromise with the other side. In the event there is disagreement, the following compromises are suggested for consideration.

1. Concerning Secret Item of Understanding 1.

Plan 1: To revise the clause as follows: Concerning Article 3 of the treaty and Item 1 of the secret supplementary protocol, military aid is to be provided if the Soviet Union, alone or in concert with other nonsignatory nations, should attack one of the contracting parties. "However, Italy is to be excused from this obligation to render military aid when the Soviet Union alone attacks one of the contracting parties."

The preceding clause is not to affect the provision for consultations among the contracting parties concerning military assistance, depending upon the situation, when the Soviet Union is not involved.

Plan 2: To eliminate Item 1 and instead to formulate detailed agreements based upon the following principles: a) if the Soviet Union is involved, it is assumed that military assistance will be given as a matter of course; b) if nations other than the Soviet Union are involved, although it is a basic principle of the treaty to provide military assistance, circumstances make it in fact impossible for the empire to do so at present or in the near future.

2. Concerning Secret Item of Understanding 2. This item is to be eliminated by employing one of the following two plans:

Plan 1: To conclude the treaty as soon as possible, in which case all sections of the treaty must be kept secret.

Plan 2: To make the treaty public. Prior agreement concerning the following statement is required before publication. "Although every section of the treaty is valid, since the real threat to the empire in the current world situation is the subversive activity of the Comintern, the latter constitutes the principal and sole target of the treaty as far as the empire is concerned."

3. The following must be mutually accepted by each nation concerned in some kind of written document, though not in the form of a treaty before the treaty itself is concluded:

  a) Should the second plan concerning Secret Item
1 be accepted: 1) if the Soviet Union is involved, it is
assumed that military assistance will be given as a
matter of course; 2) if nations other than the Soviet
Union are involved, although it is a basic principle of
the treaty to provide military assistance, circumstances make it in fact impossible for the empire to
do so at present or in the near future.

  b) Should the second plan concerning Secret Item
2 be adopted, its attached statement must be agreed
upon.

  C. We appreciate most deeply the efforts that both of you
have made, designed to bring about a prompt and smooth conclusion of the present treaty. We can very well appreciate your
distress at the subsequent negotiations, and we request further
efforts on both your parts, inasmuch as the above is the policy of
the government.[107]

In short, the form outlined in the original instructions might
be modified so that in principle military aid might be given
against Britain and France, but the substance would have to
remain the same. Japan in fact could not obligate itself to give
military aid to its allies under any circumstances other than an
attack by the Soviet Union. The compromise was one of principle but not of substance.

Why had Arita been able to hold firm on the substance?
What were the "special circumstances" to which he had alluded? In the instructions it can be seen that the January 19
decision permitted no alteration. The purpose of the Itō mission, according to Arita, was to explain the delicate situation
that was involved.[108] Even Army Minister Itagaki was placed in
a difficult position at the Five Ministers Conference of March
13, admitting that the January 19 decision could never be altered and hinting at the seriousness of the situation. Why was it
so serious? Apparently because the emperor was involved.

Hiranuma had met with the emperor after the revised instructions were discussed on March 22.[109] The emperor had
asked what action would be taken in the event that Ōshima and
Shiratori did not obey the government's instructions and further
modified the draft. Hiranuma replied that if they took issue with

the government's instructions, they would be recalled or dealt with appropriately, and that it might be necessary to discontinue the negotiations if they made additional changes. On the other hand, he was prepared to set forth a detailed treaty based upon the principle that no "effective military aid" would be available. Responding to a further query from the emperor as to what was meant by "effective military aid," Hiranuma replied that since Japan was allied with Germany and Italy, it would be impossible for Japan to remain neutral in a war between these two nations and other countries. In such circumstances Japan was obliged at a minimum to offer nonmilitary assistance. If military aid were required, Japan could not engage in actual combat, although it might have to consider some kind of demonstration of force, such as the dispatch of warships to check the movement of nations hostile to Germany and Italy. However, it would be entirely impossible for Japan to attack either at Singapore or anywhere in Europe. The emperor requested a document containing responses in writing to his first two questions, whereupon the government submitted to him the following memorandum, dated March 28, 1939, and signed by the five ministers:

> 1. On March 25, 1939 the foreign minister issued new instructions to Ambassadors Ōshima and Shiratori concerning the strengthening of the Anti-Comintern Pact. These modified instructions were issued with special consideration to the ambassadors' requests in spite of the fact that the government's previous instructions had not been carried out. In the light of this situation, should the ambassadors raise objections to the new instructions and fail to act in accordance with them, our government shall take whatever action is necessary to insure the smooth continuation of the negotiations, such as recalling the two ambassadors and appointing other delegates to replace them.
> 2. We shall have to break off negotiations if a compromise cannot be reached with Germany and Italy within the limits of the restrictions imposed in the instructions issued by the foreign minister on January 26 and March 25, 1939.[110]

It was not at all unusual for the emperor from time to time to pose important questions to ministers and to offer suggestions to them; however, it was rather unusual for him to ask for a memorandum signed by all of the ministers concerned. It was customary for the prime minister, officially though privately, to report to the emperor on general developments at the Five Ministers Conference. It was also customary for the foreign minister to report officially to the emperor in private on special foreign policy problems. However, concerning this particular matter of reinforcing cooperation between the three countries, Ugaki and Arita, when each was foreign minister, had reported to the emperor in private every time an important decision was made. Ugaki seems to have obtained the emperor's approval for revising the pact by reassuring him that it would be merely an expression of "benevolent neutrality" on the part of Japan. This presumably meant that if Germany or Italy were engaged in a war with a third power, Japan was obligating itself simply to remain neutral in their favor.[111]

Thus, although the influence exerted by Lord Keeper of the Privy Seal Yuasa Kurahei and others close to the Throne is not known, it seems reasonable to infer that the reason the decision taken by the Five Ministers Conference on January 19 had become inviolable was that it had been given support from within the imperial palace. By taking the unusual step of asking for the signed memorandum of March 28, the emperor made it clear that no further compromise in the government's position could be made.

On March 22, the day after the compromise instructions had been formulated at the Five Ministers Conference, the chief of the Foreign Ministry's Europe-Asia Bureau, Inoue Kōjirō, who was in charge of this issue, submitted a protest to Prime Minister Hiranuma.[112] To approve military assistance against Britain and France "in principle" while insisting on withholding such assistance temporarily, Inoue argued, was a change in policy, and to extend this "temporary" withholding of aid for the entire period of the treaty would cause Japan to lose credit with Germany and Italy. Furthermore, even the granting of only small-scale military assistance to Germany and Italy would obviously be considered a belligerent act, and it would be difficult to be sure that such small-scale assistance would not lead eventually to larger hostilities. In Inoue's view of Ribbentrop's proposals, what Germany wanted was not for Japan to send soldiers to Europe but to attack British and French bases in the Orient in order to destroy their commercial routes from the Far East. Ribbentrop had further stated, said Inoue, that he wished the Japanese navy to check the United States. Thus, small-scale and limited military aid would not be satisfactory. "Ambassador Ōshima, knowing the power of Germany, wants us to unite with Germany as quickly as possible; Ambassador Shiratori believes that the empire's mission is to eliminate British influence from East Asia. It is not unreasonable for Ōshima and Shiratori to be highly cognizant of German and Italian intentions and to disagree with our draft. I have no doubt that both are no less sincere and no less wise than anyone else." After all, Inoue added, Russia was the greatest threat and as much freedom of action as possible should be secured to meet the ever-changing political situation in Europe.

Inoue concluded that further efforts should be made to negotiate on the basis of the government's original instructions. The first and third articles of the treaty, he felt, were sufficiently strong to assure the establishment of a firm triple axis even if the treaty were announced as being only an extension of the Anti-Comintern Pact. Inoue's remarks were very much to the point, particularly in view of the fact that Germany later stressed the obligation to extend military aid against countries other than the Soviet Union. Alterations in the government's original plan had been made at the strong insistence of the army minister; Inoue, Arita, and presumably persons within the imperial court were all against such changes. Significant defects in the decision-making process and the structure of the Japanese government are apparent in this and underline the fact that the strengthening of the Anti-Comintern Pact was more a domestic than an international political issue.[113]

The Army's Intransigence

Regardless of the government's elaborate efforts to clarify its intent, the ambassadors in Berlin and Rome insisted on seeing things their own way. Ōshima still clung to his interpretation of the telegram from the vice minister he had received in response to the German plan taken to Tokyo by Kasahara—that is, that the German plan might be accepted if certain changes in phraseology were made in accordance with the August 26 decision and that, although the Soviet Union was the primary target of the treaty, Britain and France might be included as secondary targets. Much had happened since that telegram. Ōshima had become ambassador and Arita had become foreign minister. The instructions of October had gone far to contradict Ōshima's understanding, particularly with reference to the treaty's target, but he knew little of what was going on in Tokyo. He had received no further government instructions except a warning in December that, since the issue was currently under consideration at home, he should have no further talks on the subject with Foreign Minister Ribbentrop. When he had asked the nature of the question, he had been told only that the problem was the extent of the treaty's applicability.[114]

Consequently, he was hardly prepared for the instructions he received from the Itō mission in February and could not understand how such an important policy could be altered within a few months. How, he wondered, could an alliance that limited its target to the USSR and excluded Britain and France contain anything of significance for Germany? Ribbentrop had always emphasized the inclusion of Britain and France. From Germany's point of view, Ōshima felt, the goal of strengthening the pact was to enable Germany to check French and, more particularly, British moves in order to advance into central Europe.

In the meantime Germany was gradually executing its plans. On September 30, 1938, following the *Anschluss*, Germany obtained Czechoslovakia's Sudetenland by the Munich agreement and finally overran Czechoslovakia on March 15 of the following year. As for Italy, it had expressed its desire to conclude by the end of January an agreement based on the proposal Germany had sent Japan and Italy on January 6. By March, however, Italy had grown suspicious of Japan's intentions and even went so far as to consider a pact with Germany alone.

With the arrival of the new instructions of March 25, Ōshima met with Shiratori in Rome. They understood the new instructions to contain certain basic differences from the plan brought by the Itō mission and interpreted the former to mean that conclusion of the treaty was so absolutely necessary that even though problems were thereby created for the government, certain compromises would be unavoidable.[115] This hardly accorded with the memorandum that had been submitted to the emperor. The two ambassadors cabled Tokyo requesting that the right to choose negotiating procedures be entrusted to them. "Upon consideration of the situation in Germany and Italy," they had decided "to carry out the second plan" on their own.[116] On April 2, ignoring the original instructions, they presented to Germany and Italy Japan's draft of the treaty with the concessions included.

Needless to say, the compromise plans had been designed by the government as possible alternatives if and when Germany and Italy were not willing to accept the original proposals; and in both the original and the compromise instructions the secret items of understanding were most important to the Japanese government. But from the beginning the two ambassadors refused to present the items to Germany and Italy. In this they were obviously acting contrary to their government's instructions, although it could be argued that the prospects for approval of the treaty by Italy and Germany were slim if the items were included and that Japan's relations with both countries might become worse.

Both Germany and Italy accepted almost in their entirety the Japanese treaty proposals presented by the ambassadors. On April 2, however, Foreign Minister Ciano asked whether Japan would participate in hostilities on the side of Germany and Italy if a war should break out in Europe. Ambassador Shiratori, "upon perusal of the new instructions," answered that if Germany and Italy were at war with Britain or France, Japan, in accordance with the terms of the treaty, naturally would join Germany and Italy.[117]

The following day Ribbentrop too asked whether or not he should interpret the proposals to mean that each nation allied by the treaty would be obligated to participate in hostilities in the event that the other allies were involved in hostilities against a nation other than the USSR. Ōshima replied, "Although it is naturally understood that the extent and the method of military assistance will differ depending on the circumstances, your opinion is correct concerning the obligation to participate in hostilities." Ōshima's understanding was as follows:

> After carefully studying the meaning of military assistance in the secret items of understanding contained in the second set of instructions and the meaning of the elimination of point nine of the explanation attached to the instructions carried by the special envoy [Itō], . . . I concluded that in the event a nation other than the USSR is involved, even though, considering various conditions, it is impossible for the empire to offer an effective level of military assistance at present or in the near future, it is clear that Japan is prepared to offer some military assistance, if only to a limited extent.[118]

Ribbentrop opposed Japan's adding a special understanding as to the Japanese explanation of the treaty's goal.

In the course of the negotiations, Ōshima told Ribbentrop of the existence of the secret items of understanding.[119] On April 4, after consulting Hitler, Ribbentrop, recognizing Japan's good faith, expressed Hitler's approval of Japan's proposals in principle but "with various reservations." In the presence of the Italian ambassador, Ribbentrop accepted the text of the treaty, the signed protocol, and the secret supplementary protocol but required that the secret items of understanding be eliminated. The reasons given for this were: (1) that no written statement was necessary regarding military assistance because it was clear from the stipulations in Item 1 of Japan's secret supplementary protocol; and (2) that Germany absolutely could not agree to an explanation to other countries that would decrease the effectiveness of the treaty and would be contrary to its provisions. An even more significant reason, however, was that Germany wanted to leave the matter of the specific responsibility of the allies to later deliberation among them, as provided for in the secret supplementary protocol, for Germany did not want more assistance from Japan than the latter could provide nor did it wish to imply any greater obligation on its own part toward Japan.[120]

Arita wrote that in their statement concerning Japan's obligation to participate in hostilities, "the two ambassadors distorted the instructions of their own ministry and acted in accordance with their own judgment." But in Ōshima's view, "responsibility to participate in hostilities is one thing and actually to participate in hostilities is another. It is a contradiction to conclude a treaty without assuming this responsibility." [121] It may be added that the written opinion of Europe-Asia Bureau Chief Inoue (that the instructions did essentially recognize the obligation to provide military assistance) was not totally groundless, for although Ōshima's and Shiratori's interpretation did not square with that of the government, the government's instructions did contain an ambiguity of which Germany could take advantage.

The ambassadors' explanations to Germany and Italy caused great confusion in Tokyo. The memorandum the five ministers had submitted to the emperor stated that the ambassadors would be recalled if they ignored the compromise proposal and that the negotiations would be discontinued if pressure were exerted upon Japan to alter it. As was made clear in the instructions, the secret items of understanding were of the greatest concern to the government. Without them or a satisfactory substitute, such as was indicated in the revised instructions, there would be no treaty. The government believed that the statement made by the ambassadors went beyond the scope of their instructions. Accordingly, following the Five Ministers Conference on April 8 the emperor called to Arita's attention their possible violation of the imperial prerogative.[122]

The Five Ministers Conference was divided over the ambassadors' statement. One side, headed by Arita, demanded that it be retracted. The other, led by Itagaki, insisted that the Japanese government accept responsibility for the statement even though it went too far, for to demand that it be retracted would only antagonize them. In the end, the ministers acquiesced in the army view and agreed to dispatch ambiguous instructions that would only indirectly nullify the ambassadors' statement.[123] According to these instructions, Japan interpreted the pledge given by the ambassadors to "participate in hostilities" to mean the obligation to give "support" as stated in Article 2 of the proposed treaty. In addition, of the kinds of "aid and assistance" to be given, "military aid" was understood not to be available at present or in the near future. Concerning possible future hostilities, Japan's instructions included the alternative possibilities that Japan might declare war, simply make an announcement, a declaration, or a statement depending on the situation, or offer effective assistance without any prior announcement.[124] Arita himself admitted that the instructions were baffling; but Ōshima and Counselor Usami Uzuhiko, interpreting "participation in hostilities" broadly to include the offer of information, materials, and bases, made strenuous efforts to obtain Germany's approval.[125]

At the Five Ministers Conference on April 14 Arita proposed that the government send a telegram suggesting that, under the circumstances, the negotiations be terminated. Itagaki, visibly upset, strongly opposed the idea, saying, "I wonder if there might not be some other solution." [126] Thus, despite the memorandum submitted to the emperor on March 28, no agreement was reached concerning the problem of discontinuing the negotiations. Recalling the two ambassadors for distorting the government's instructions, Arita tells us, was also "impossible, considering the domestic situation of the time"—a euphemism for the government's inability or unwillingness to go against the army's wishes.[127]

Prevented from terminating the negotiations or recalling the ambassadors, at the Five Ministers Conference on April 21 Arita proposed as a last resort that Prime Minister Hiranuma himself send a cable directly to Hitler and Mussolini to explain frankly and in detail Japan's viewpoint, emphasizing that there was no further chance of a compromise and suggesting that they consider the matter in terms of its political implications; Arita himself would provide a detailed explanation to Ambassador Ott. The rest of the cabinet agreed with this proposal.[128] But when, on April 23, Arita showed the Five Ministers Conference a draft of the cable he proposed the prime minister send, Hiranuma showed little interest and Itagaki demurred, suggesting that Ōshima be given another chance. Arita gave up the plan.[129]

The army, in fact, preferred a different course. It demanded that the secret items of understanding be dropped. The Five Ministers Conference discussed this on April 25, 27, and 28, but no agreement was reached.[130] In the meantime, Ribbentrop decided to visit Italy to discuss the alliance. He wanted first to meet with Ōshima, who requested his government to inform him of its true position. Hiranuma now decided to send a message himself to Hitler and Mussolini. However, there was a fundamental difference between the prime minister's plan and that of the foreign minister. According to Arita:

> My plan was that Japan directly and frankly tell the two leaders about the progress of the negotiations as well as about Japan's position, without using agents who could not be trusted, and thus determine Hitler's and Mussolini's final decision. Prime Minister Hiranuma, in contrast, preferred to convey our government's decision to the ambassadors in order to assist them in their negotiations.[131]

Hiranuma submitted a draft of his message to the Five Ministers Conference on April 28. It included the statement, "Japan is not to maintain a neutral position," to which Arita and Yonai took strong exception.[132] Finally, about May 4, a revised message was sent to Hitler and Mussolini via the German and Italian ambassadors in Japan.[133] This message, which did not include the above statement, read:

> I hereby express Japan's determination to offer to Germany and Italy political and economic aid, as well as military assistance, to the extent possible, even if either Germany or Italy is attacked by one or several countries other than the Soviet Union. However, although Japan is prepared to offer military assistance to Germany and Italy according to the provisions of the said treaty, Japan is not able at present or in the near future to offer an effective level of military assistance to Germany and Italy, considering the empire's present circumstances. Needless to say, however, Japan will do so when conditions make it possible.[134]

The contents of this message were more in accord with Ōshima's ideas than with Arita's, which may be why it has been judged a "decided gain" for the army.[135] This may also explain why Hiranuma had previously sent the contents of the message to the ambassadors not through the Foreign Ministry but via the army.[136]

The following day [137] Ribbentrop, en route to Italy, phoned Ōshima from Munich inquiring whether he could interpret this message to mean that Japan, generally speaking, was ready to assume the status of a belligerent if Germany and Italy were attacked, even though effective military assistance was not available. Ōshima replied in the affirmative.[138] To judge from Ōshima's previous interpretation as well as from Hiranuma's message, this reply was quite reasonable, although his conflict with Arita was thereby aggravated. On April 20, at a party celebrating Hitler's birthday, Ribbentrop had hinted at a possible alliance with the Soviet Union if the negotiations with Japan should fail.[139] The European scene was moving away from Japan, but Japan's Army, Navy, and Foreign ministries were not yet aware of this change.

Sometime in April Germany sent new interpretations of the proposed treaty to Japan. These were as follows: (1) that the treaty was to be a truly defensive pact aiming at peace and not designating any particular country as its target; (2) that the pact was a countermeasure to stop the Comintern's advance, in consideration of the fact that the communist movement, which had originated in the Soviet Union, was a threat to peace; (3) that the pact was not to be concluded in anticipation of an attack by the United States, Britain, or France on any of the allies; and (4) that the provisions of the pact should be adhered to if any of the allies became the target of an unprovoked attack.[140]

The Japanese replied on April 24: (1) that France, Britain, and, if possible, the United States should be excluded as targets of the treaty; (2) that no effective aid was to be offered except in a war declared against the Soviet Union; and (3) that Japan always reserved the right to decide whether to participate in or declare war.[141] This reply showed clearly the differences that existed between Japan and Germany. After receiving it, both Ōshima and Shiratori requested that they be recalled.[142]

Early in May, at the request of Ribbentrop, Counselor Usami and Secretary Takeuchi Ryuji of the Japanese embassy visited Friedrich Gaus, chief of the Treaty Bureau of the German Foreign Office. After several meetings with him the so-called Gaus Plan, which incorporated the Japanese views contained in the secret items of understanding, was drawn up.[143] This plan was prepared in two drafts, but the exact details of each are not known. The first was formulated in the hope that Japan would accept the text without revision, and this appears to have been the draft discussed in subsequent Five Ministers Conferences.[144] Its text included a statement to the effect that the inability to render effective military assistance would not preclude Japan's assuming belligerent status in a war involving Germany or Italy. This section became an issue later, when the army approved it but the navy and, it appears, the Foreign Ministry urged its deletion.[145]

The second draft was agreed to by both Germany and Italy, which had subsequently been consulted. The text introduced at the International Military Tribunal for the Far East did not include the above commitment and therefore is considered to be a second draft. It included the draft of the treaty, the signed protocol, and the secret supplementary protocol as brought by the Itō mission. In addition, it contained the following understanding:

> In the draft Treaty of Consultation and Mutual Assistance between Japan, Italy, and Germany, which is now under negotiation, a new article in the following form should be inserted before the concluding Article 4:
>
> The German government and the Italian government declare in agreement with the Japanese government that the Treaty of Friendship and Alliance between Germany and Italy signed on May 22, 1939, having resulted from the relationship of these two countries as neighbors and from their special position in Europe, will not be affected by the present treaty, and that therefore the present pact shall be applied to the relation between Germany and Italy only insofar as the treaty of May 22, 1939, contains no broader obligations.

The Gaus Plan also included the following explanatory note:

> After the conclusion of the treaty, in the event that there are
> diplomatic inquiries from nonsignatory nations concerning the
> treaty between Germany, Italy, and Japan now under negotia-
> tion, the Japanese government will make oral explanations [146]
> along the following lines:
> 1. This treaty is purely defensive and has no aggressive in-
> tent; rather, its aim is to secure the preservation of peace. This
> treaty consequently is not directed against any country.
> 2. Historically, this treaty originated from the fact that the
> three contracting powers have come together in recent years for
> their common defense against the destructive activities of the
> Comintern. In the present international situation Japan feels
> severely threatened by the machinations of the Communist In-
> ternational. The Japanese government, therefore, views these
> machinations of communism, coming from Soviet Russia, as the
> most serious threat to peace.
> 3. Should one of the participating powers in this pact be at-
> tacked without provocation, the assistance which will be ren-
> dered this country is evident from the text of this treaty. So long
> as third powers do not threaten or attack the contracting powers,
> the obligations provided in this treaty for support and for ren-
> dering aid and assistance shall not be carried out.

Finally, the plan stated:

> On instruction from my government, I ask Your Excellency
> to take note that Japan can carry out the military obligations, ac-
> cepted in Article 3 of this treaty, to render aid and assistance
> only to a limited extent at present and in the immediate future.
> Details of the military assistance to be rendered as future cir-
> cumstances may require shall be reserved for discussions pro-
> vided for in the secret supplementary protocol.[147]

Although the Gaus Plan has the appearance of having been
proposed by Germany, in reality it was Ōshima who suggested it
to Germany.[148] The Japanese army strongly insisted that the
plan be approved and thus found itself in the position of opposing the navy and the Foreign Ministry.[149] At 2:00 P.M. on May 6
Itagaki visited Arita at the latter's official residence to seek
Arita's approval of the Gaus Plan and, without stopping for dinner, argued the matter with him until 9:30 that evening—but in

vain. Reportedly Itagaki called on the navy and finance ministers as well.

The Five Ministers Conference took up the first draft of the Gaus Plan on May 7, but no agreement was reached because of the strong disagreement between the army minister on the one hand and the foreign and navy ministers on the other. It is said that Hiranuma wholeheartedly supported Itagaki. The same conflict arose at a further meeting on May 9, after which, in accordance with Hiranuma's suggestion, it was agreed that the issue should be discussed at another conference, to be held after the army and navy high commands had been consulted.[150]

A memorandum prepared by the army-navy high command on the 15th revealed clearly the differing viewpoints of the two services.[151] Proposed Article 3 concerned the limitations of military assistance to be provided depending on whether the target of the treaty was (a) the Soviet Union only, (b) the Soviet Union assisted by Britain and France, (c) Britain and France assisted by the Soviet Union, or (d) Britain and France alone. In its earlier memorandum the navy had argued that participation in hostilities in the event of (a) or (b) was unavoidable, but that Japan should avoid war as far as possible in the case of (c) and absolutely avoid war in the case of (d). The navy would now participate in situation (c) should such involvement be unavoidable, but it adamantly opposed any responsibility to engage in hostilities in case of (d).

The previous attitude of the army, on the other hand, had been unconditional participation in all instances. Subsequently it altered its position in situation (d) and would admit responsibility for military assistance but refrain from taking military action. More precisely, the army's reasoning was as follows. Were each of the parties to have common boundaries with the Soviet Union, situation (b) or (c), danger of war might be as great on the European as on the Asian front. In that case the likelihood of any of the parties' being called on to fulfill the obligation to render military assistance would seem to be equal. But since only the Japanese empire has a common boundary with the Soviet Union, the danger of its being the object of Soviet attack is actually greater. Therefore the program of mutual obligation under situation (a) actually favors Japan. In situation (d), where the probability of war was great, the balance of obligation would favor Germany and Italy, but this obligation should be reduced. Finally, should situations (a) and (c) occur at the same time, the obligation would be mutual.

The navy refused to accept the army's argument that a mutual obligation existed in situation (a) or when (a) and (c) occurred simultaneously. Concentrating on situations in which Germany and Italy were opposed only by Britain and France, the navy took the cautious position that Japan should be as careful as possible not to become involved in war. Therefore the navy thought Japan should consider Soviet and American positions and other circumstances before making any decision regarding participation. The navy was opposed to an automatic obligation to participate in war without any freedom of choice, since it believed that it was not in Japan's interest to become involved in a European war.

The army, insisting that mutual obligation was the principle of the treaty, acknowledged that Japan would be obliged to participate in an unwanted war. But while it did not anticipate fighting the Soviet Union or any other power at least "for a year or two," it did feel that a tripartite alliance would be immediately useful in the China War for several reasons: (1) It would divert British and American aid from China. (The navy countered that the effect might be just the opposite: British and French aid to Chiang might be increased to check Japan as a member of such an alliance, and settlement of the conflict might be prolonged by involving Russia.) (2) The pact would weaken China's anti-Japanese and procommunist policy. (The navy responded that it was equally possible that China's reaction might be quite the contrary, judging that aid for China from Britain, the United States, and the USSR might be increased.) (3) Conclusion of the pact might mean the imposition of economic sanctions against Japan by Britain, France, and the United States, but it might also mean material aid for Japan from Germany and Italy. (The navy felt no great amount of aid could be expected.) (4) If a new central government were established in China, it would be able to obtain aid from Germany and Italy.

(Again the navy responded that not much could be expected.)

The army insisted that the Gaus Plan corresponded to the principles of the March 25 revised instructions. The navy denied that this was the case as far as the question of belligerent status and the explanatory note were concerned. Under the Gaus Plan, the navy felt, a situation could arise in which Japan would neither use military force nor make a declaration regarding its position, and it would be inappropriate to call this "belligerent status." But the army insisted that a clear distinction should be drawn between the intent to assume a status of belligerency and the actual use of military force. Should the government accept the navy's argument that in the event both were lacking Japan could remain neutral even if military assistance were provided, it would be in the contradictory position of concluding a military alliance from a neutral posture. Therefore, the army averred, the obligation for military assistance should be the same whether war was against Britain and France or against the Soviet Union.

Finally, on May 19 the army and navy reached a joint agreement, as follows:

> Although it is natural for Japan to stand with Germany and Italy in a war against countries other than the Soviet Union, such as Britain and France, the obligation unconditionally to undertake such military action is not accepted. Therefore, the extent and methods of military assistance in a war against Britain and France shall be determined at the time of the conclusion of a detailed agreement and in accordance with the actual situation.[152]

But again the two services did not follow through on measures to implement their joint view.

Meanwhile, Arita had secured the agreement of Navy Minister Yonai to the following propositions: (1) that when Britain and France alone were involved, Japan would remain neutral, and it was therefore necessary to cancel Ōshima's previous statement about Japan's readiness to adopt a status of belligerence even if it were not prepared to extend effective military aid; (2) that the public explanation would not necessarily be confined to questions raised concerning the treaty but would expand upon the principles of the treaty in general and did not necessarily have to be explained orally, and Germany should be so informed.[153] Accordingly, at the Five Ministers Conference on May 20, Arita proposed the retraction of the commitment made by Ōshima to Ribbentrop concerning unconditional Japanese participation in hostilities. Itagaki countered that since that commitment had been simply an expression of the nation's readiness or its determination, it was not necessary to retract it. Yonai equivocated. The commitment was disturbing, he agreed, but it would be difficult to retract. Therefore, he said, it would be best to include some connotation of its retraction in a statement setting forth the reasons for requesting a revision of the first Gaus Plan. Because Hiranuma did not take a position on Yonai's suggestion, the Five Ministers Conference decided to oppose any unconditional obligation to offer military assistance in case of a war in Europe that did not include the Soviet Union. The matter of sending instructions to the ambassadors was left up to Hiranuma and Arita.[154]

The contents of the resulting instructions of May 20 only brought further confusion. In case of a war in Europe not involving the Soviet Union, they read, whether or not Japan participated was "to be decided independently according to the existing situation." [155] Some middle-ranking navy personnel were not satisfied with this phrase and requested that it be revised to read "to be decided in light of the common interests of the three allies." [156] In a letter written on May 22 Ōshima also expressed his dissatisfaction, saying that the phrase was similar to the one in the old instructions brought by Itō. Perhaps this was Arita's intention. Ōshima then went on to complain:

> In reviewing the progress of the negotiations, it can be seen that Japan's lack of determination in the said negotiations has unnecessarily prolonged the matter and has weakened Germany's and Italy's faith in us. Foreign Minister Ribbentrop, as can be seen from my telegrams, has wondered frequently since early this year whether Japan wished not to conclude the treaty or wished to delay the negotiations. In accordance with my instructions set forth in telegrams from the government, I have made great ef-

forts to dissuade him of such feelings, but I must now admit that his suspicions were justified.

By insisting that the secret items of understanding be attached as written documents, he said, the Japanese government had made it apparent that

> . . . as Germany and Italy had both suspected, Japan has attempted to alter or to distort the provisions of the treaty. Although they usually are not concerned with how phrases are written, they do understand the legal implications. A diplomatic strategy that manipulates phraseology in order to disguise its true intentions can result only in failure.[157]

Army records claim that due to some "mistake" in the cabled message Ōshima's statement was rejected after it had actually been approved by the Five Ministers Conference.[158] Hiranuma shifted the blame onto the Foreign Ministry, stating that although he himself had helped in the drafting of the telegram and had signed it when it was brought to him by Treaties Bureau Chief Mitani Takanobu, Mitani had not made the revisions that Hiranuma had ordered.[159]

Even before receiving the instructions of May 20 Shiratori had also protested, charging that the government had in effect delayed the negotiations by persisting with the "two reservations, which have by now already lost their practical significance and value." The German-Italian alliance, he said, represented nothing more than the translation of existing relations between them into treaty form, by which means the two nations hoped to encourage a positive decision by the Japanese government; therefore, reservations which would nullify the effect of the treaty would be difficult for them to accept. He further warned that if Japan were to prolong the negotiations, Germany and Italy would alter their policies. He insisted that such a policy shift would be directed in favor either of Britain and France or of the Soviet Union, "as I have often mentioned." He stated his belief that both possibilities would be disadvantageous to Japan's policy vis-à-vis China. He further suggested the possi-

bility of a peace conference between various European countries and the United States and advised that Japan should seek
allies with this contingency in mind.[160]

Arita tried to clarify the situation by drafting another telegram. The instructions, he contended, contained nothing new.
The same point had been made by Prime Minister Hiranuma. If
Germany and Italy were to fight Britain and France, the instructions would enable Japan to deny its obligation unconditionally
to resort to military force or to declare war. In other words, "if
such a war should arise, whether or not Japan would enter into
hostilities on behalf of Germany and Italy would not be determined until Japan had made its own independent decision." [161]

The draft telegram was sent to Hiranuma by Vice Minister
Sawada Renzō. Hiranuma revised it to incorporate the army's
opinion [162] and proposed to send a telegram approving Ōshima's
statement, which he recognized as having been in conformity
with his own views. Hiranuma declared that the question of
whether Japan could be regarded as a belligerent if it did not
offer any effective military assistance was purely academic and
there was no need to persist in such an argument. Arita, however, rejected the proposed message, and no agreement was
reached about the instructions to be cabled.

The army and navy for the second time were requested to
submit a definitive opinion. They met together for a total of
fourteen hours on May 27 and 28, but so far as the problem of
"participation" was concerned, only a confusing memorandum
that admittedly "avoided contact with the core of the conflict"
resulted.[163] But on May 30 Arita met with the emperor, who
supported the foreign minister and the navy minister and told
Arita that the prime minister should suggest to the army minister that he come to terms with their views.[164]

Finally, on June 2 an agreement was reached. Hiranuma and
Arita added corrections at a Five Ministers Conference on the
3rd, a draft adopting these corrections was accepted the next
day, and the rather lengthy instructions were finally adopted at
a full cabinet meeting on June 5. The principal portions of these
instructions were as follows:

1. In case of a war involving Germany and Italy against the Soviet Union, alone or in concert with other nations, the Empire of Japan shall side with Germany and Italy, shall clearly indicate its intent, and shall also provide military assistance.

2. In case of a war against countries other than the Soviet Union:

a) Japan will support Germany and Italy, not Britain and France.

b) Japan's declaration of intent will be made as stated in Item 1 above. However, in such a situation as might exist before the Soviet Union's attitude has been made clear, and considering the general situation, Japan might not issue a declaration of intent if it is considered beneficial to its allies for Japan to pose a silent threat to deter the participation of countries such as the Soviet Union. Japan will enter into consultations with Germany and Italy concerning a declaration of intent.

c) It has already been stated that the empire, considering the general situation, is unable to provide effective military aid at present or in the near future. Within the category of political and economic support, assistance, and aid of various kinds, Japan will at all times and without fail offer all of these except military action, that is, combat (exchange of fire) and patrolling and blockading with the intent to engage in battle. Concerning military action: 1) it will be employed at the beginning of a war; or 2) it will not be employed at the beginning but will be employed during the course of a war; or 3) it may never be employed at all during the war. Conditions (2) and (3) will hold when it is considered beneficial to its allies for Japan to pose a silent threat and thereby to deter the participation of countries such as the Soviet Union in those cases in which the Soviet Union and other countries have not yet committed themselves; as well as when this seems best in view of the general situation. Japan will consult with Germany and Italy concerning military assistance.

The most crucial issue, namely, whether Japan would participate in or offer military assistance during a war that did not involve the Soviet Union, was still not made clear.[165]

It is said that in a document presented to the Five Ministers Conference on June 6 Arita wrote:

Even were the United States to participate but not the Soviet Union, in light of the general situation Japan might not make any declaration of its intent if it is found that, by posing a silent threat, Japan might benefit its allies through checking certain countries, such as the Soviet Union, from participating. Under such conditions, it is also possible that Japan would not carry out any military action at all.[166]

It is obvious that this kind of ambiguity could never have been accepted by the other side. This memorandum, too, was nothing more than a compromise proposal formulated in the context of domestic politics.

Unreconciled Differences at Home and Abroad

The new draft, the result of tremendous effort, was not accepted by Germany and Italy, as expected. Ciano did not reject the draft outright when Shiratori explained that it indicated "Japan's unwillingness to assume any obligation automatically to participate in a war in which the Soviet Union and the United States assume a neutral posture." However, he left the problem of the reservations to Ribbentrop, who rejected the draft itself.[167] Germany was particularly opposed to having the reservations in written form. Ōshima admitted that, except for the second Gaus Plan, any compromise would be difficult to achieve.[168] At their conference on June 16 Ribbentrop repeatedly insisted that any reservations concerning the extent of the treaty's applicability would decrease its effectiveness. If Japan made reservations so would Germany, and the treaty would become a farce and lose all value. He also stressed that while Japan felt the United States would participate if Japan joined in any war involving Germany and Italy against Britain and France, he believed America would not enter if Japan were to join in from the very beginning. Moreover, Ribbentrop argued, although Japan was emphasizing its relations with the Soviet Union, Britain more than Russia was the obstacle to a solution of the China problem, and if Britain were to participate in a European war against Germany and Italy, Japan would have the most favorable opportunity to oust Britain from the Orient. Next, he objected to reservations by one of the signatories as to its obligations under the pact. As for the explanation to nonsignatory countries, any limitation upon the objectives of the treaty was absolutely to be avoided; and any written demands by Japan, in that they might become known to others, were also to be avoided. Finally, he declared, no treaty at all was better than one which was incomplete. There was no doubt in his mind that, since the three countries shared mutual interests, a satisfactory agreement could be concluded.[169]

Immediately following this meeting Ōshima reported to the government and asked for its decision. It was "utterly fruitless," he said, to carry on negotiations on the basis of the instructions brought by Itō. Was the government prepared at last to give up the written reservations? If not, was it prepared to break off the negotiations?[170]

Ōshima's inquiry brought no reply. A few letters were exchanged by the navy minister and the army minister late in July, but no substantial change resulted. The euphemisms sought so assiduously in Tokyo to paper over the differences between the ministers simply did not meet the desires of Berlin and Rome, and the government was at a loss how to proceed.

As the impasse deepened, public feeling in Japan grew tense. From May on the activities of right wing elements had been increasing. Members of such groups insisted on immediate conclusion of the treaty in accordance with the army's demands. They also invaded the Navy Ministry, denouncing Navy Minister Yonai and Vice Minister Yamamoto Isoroku, who was considered at the forefront of those within the navy opposing the treaty. A stevedore was arrested in Shibaura for carrying dynamite, his arrest revealing a plan to assassinate Yamamoto, Yuasa Kurahei, and Prime Minister Hiranuma. The navy reinforced Yamamoto's police guard, ordered military guards in the ministry to wear swords, and sent a marine platoon to Yokosuka naval base under the command of Aide-de-Camp Sanematsu Yuzuru. Later, when the Imperial Guard Division went to Narashino for exercises, the navy sent stand-by orders to a battalion at Yokosuka in response to rumors that the Imperial Palace Guard Training Troop was planning to attack the Navy Ministry. The combined squadron at Osaka was ordered to proceed to Tokyo, and the Navy Ministry prepared for a possible siege by installing arms, ammunition, provisions, lights, and an independent electric power plant and made preparations for digging wells.[171] It was also reported that assassination plans included, in addition, Imperial Household Minister Matsudaira Tsunco and former finance ministers Yūki Toyotarō and Ikeda Seihin, all of whom were considered pro-British.[172]

Japanese-British relations worsened greatly during this period. When Konoe announced the creation of a New Order in East Asia in a communiqué issued on November 3, 1938, the United States was the first country to express opposition; on January 14, 1939 it joined with Britain and France in a message indicating nonrecognition of the Japanese move. On April 9 Ch'eng Hsi-keng, inspector of maritime customs at Tientsin, was assassinated, and his assassin sought asylum in the British Concession. An extradition demand led to the blockade of the Tientsin Concession by the Japanese army stationed there. In Tokyo, meantime, Arita had been conferring with British Ambassador Craigie, and by July 22 they had reached an agreement on basic principles. On the 26th, however, the United States sent Japan formal notification that nullification of the 1911 Treaty of Commerce and Navigation would become effective six months later, and thereafter Anglo-Japanese tension again increased. The negotiations between Japan and Britain were finally broken off on August 21.

Anti-British activities of the Japanese right wing movement also increased about this time, and it was rumored that right wing groups were receiving financial aid from the army; this could have been true, since civilian right wing groups frequently solicited money from the army. It was also rumored that the Home Ministry Police Bureau had specified that there could be no interference with any lawful movement.[173] The emperor asked Hiranuma whether or not it was possible to stop such anti-British activities. When Hiranuma replied that it would be difficult, the emperor inquired whether it might be possible to disseminate pro-British propaganda. Hiranuma replied only that he would look into it.

The ambassadors' voices became shriller. Shiratori asserted that Britain would seek revenge for Japan's blockade of Tientsin. Foreseeing the outbreak of similar incidents as Japanese policy toward China hardened, he warned, "We must be aware that there is little hope for Japan to resume its former good relations with Britain." Recommending that something be done immediately, he repeated his prediction that if no progress were made on the proposed treaty Germany and Italy might conclude a nonaggression pact with the Soviet Union that would be unfavorable to Japan.[174] Ōshima also reported on the European situation, indicating the essential reasons for Germany's inclusion of Britain and France as targets and maintaining that such an inclusion would not lead to immediate conflict. Furthermore, he felt, Britain and France would be no match for Germany.[175]

The government itself began to tremble. Rumors circulated that Army Minister Itagaki, an active supporter of the proposed treaty, was prepared to resign and thereby bring down the cabinet. On August 4 Home Minister Kido Kōichi asked Itagaki to reconsider.[176] Itagaki, however, had already expressed the opinion that the treaty was vital to block the Soviet Union and to solve in Japan's favor the Nomonhan Incident, a clash with Soviet and Mongolian forces that had begun on May 12 on the borders of Manchukuo.[177]

Heinrich Stahmer, a confidant of Ribbentrop, visited Ōshima on Ribbentrop's behalf on July 24. He stated that there had been no word whatsoever from the Japanese government in the six weeks since June 16, when Ribbentrop had presented Germany's views. Now he had to prepare a report for Hitler's speech at a Nazi Party rally in early September. What was the Japanese government's reply? Ōshima promptly cabled Tokyo, saying, "It is my belief that it would maintain the integrity of Japanese diplomacy frankly to give Germany and Italy reasons, if there are any, for Japan's distress in concluding the treaty and then to break off the negotiations."[178] Ribbentrop himself met with Ōshima on July 28 and expressed his doubts concerning

Japan's intentions. Was Japan stalling? Had Japan's German policies changed as a result of the Japanese-British talks?[179] He was no doubt particularly concerned about establishing Japan's position once and for all, for a German-Soviet nonaggression pact was under negotiation at this time. Shiratori also pressed for an answer. He cabled on August 4: "All the government has to say is 'yes' or 'no.' " [180]

When the five ministers finally met again to discuss the matter on August 8, Itagaki took a very hard stand, demanding the immediate conclusion of the treaty without reservations. The explanation seems to be that just prior to the conference Army Attaché Arisue Seizō returned home from Italy to assume his new post as a section chief in the Military Affairs Bureau of the Army Ministry. His report on conditions in Rome seems to have led on August 3 to an emergency meeting of the three army chiefs—the army minister, the chief of staff, and the inspector general of military education—at which a strong position was decided upon. At the Five Ministers Conference on August 8 Hiranuma cross-examined Itagaki with unusual severity, Arita questioned him from the standpoint of international relations, and Finance Minister Ishiwata Sōtarō asked about the treaty's implications from an economic and financial standpoint. Ishiwata went further to ask Yonai what the chances of victory were if, after conclusion of a tripartite pact, perhaps as much as 80 percent of a war between the allies on one side and Britain, France, the Soviet Union, and the United States on the other would have to be fought by the navy. Yonai replied firmly that there was not a chance of victory.[181] It was also felt that the proposed treaty might only aggravate the world situation and therefore would be disadvantageous to Japan.[182] In the end Hiranuma, Arita, Ishiwata, and Yonai indicated that they were against revising the June 5 decision.

Just before the conference was over, Hiranuma, anxious to prevent an open split in the cabinet, suggested another compromise: although the June 5 decision should be upheld, the foreign minister might propose a revised statement of Japan's reservations, without changing the principles. This greatly disturbed Itagaki, who asked the prime minister if he was implying that the Five Ministers Conference was against a Japanese-German military alliance; but Yonai then called for a postponement of further discussion of the reservations, and the conference was brought to an end.

In the wake of this defeat, on August 10 Itagaki made a final desperate effort. He had Machijiri Kazumotō, chief of the Military Affairs Bureau, convey to Ambassador Ott and Italian Ambassador Giacinto Auriti a personal letter, the surviving summary of which reads as follows:

> The army has made every effort to obtain a favorable decision on the pact at the Five Ministers Conference of August 8, but no progress has been made since Japan's proposal of June 5.
>
> .   .   .   .
>
> The situation is so critical that the army minister will not hesitate to resign as a final measure, which almost definitely will lead to the resignation of Ōshima and Shiratori. The resignations will at first cause a great setback to the pact but will gradually strengthen the foundation in Japan for it. But there is no other way for me to assume responsibility except by resigning. It is planned to execute the foregoing decision by August 15.
>
> .   .   .   .
>
> The cabinet has again upheld the June 5 decision, but the army minister is certain that an immediate conclusion of the treaty is possible if the following mutual concessions can be agreed upon:
>
> Berlin and Rome will tell the Japanese ambassadors that it is possible for them to accept the Japanese proposals of June 5 with the following conditions: 1) that no mental reservations be implied in the text of the treaty by any country; and 2) that Japan will prepare a supplementary oral statement.
>
> If this is done, the Japanese army minister will see that the following are carried out: Concerning (1), Japan will express its acceptance of the above interpretation. Concerning (2), an oral communiqué will be prepared for inclusion in the memorandum concerning the treaty.[183]

Ambassador Ott reported that "Lieutenant-General Machijiri practically begged Germany to accept the foregoing by August 15," and that Machijiri himself was to relay Itagaki's letter to the two ambassadors directly without telling the foreign minister.

But Itagaki did not resign by August 15 and Germany did not accept the conditions. Instead, the long, tortuous negotiations were abruptly terminated by an event that so shocked the Japanese as to end the negotiations and bring down the government in confusion: the signing of the German-Soviet Nonaggression Pact on August 23, 1939.

Throughout this long period Arita thought it would be advantageous for Japan to conclude with Germany a weaker agreement based on anticommunism. Therefore he held out against the stronger reinforced treaty, particularly if it included Britain and France as targets.[184]

Army Minister Itagaki, in contrast, pushed strongly for conclusion of a tripartite pact, although he was sometimes inconsistent in his remarks at the Five Ministers Conference, possibly because of the influence of the middle-level officers behind him. From about February 1939 officers in the Army Ministry (including the vice minister, the chiefs of the Military Affairs Bureau and of the Military and Military Affairs sections, and other high-ranking officials of both sections) and officers in the Army General Staff (including the vice chief of staff, the Intelligence Division chief, and the Planning Section chief) met almost daily at the army minister's official residence to discuss policy.[185] These extraordinary discussions lasted until August and created the heated atmosphere that pervaded the army.

As for the navy, Minister Yonai, Vice Minister Yamamoto, and Naval Affairs Bureau Chief Inoue Shigemi were somewhat more cautious. At one Five Ministers Conference Yonai remarked that there was no possibility of Japan's winning a war if it were against Britain, France, and the United States as well as the Soviet Union. Yonai's caution could be attributed to the fact that at that time the volume of trade with Germany and Italy was not large, while Japan was overhwelmingly dependent on Britain and the United States in its program to mobilize its material resources.

It was the irreconcilability of these views that rendered the negotiations with Germany at this time such an abortive undertaking.

TWO

The Japanese-Soviet Confrontation, 1935-1939
by
Hata Ikuhiko

Translated
with an Introduction by

ALVIN D. COOX

A bamboo curtain masked much of Northeast Asia in the years before the Second World War. For reasons of their own, neither Imperial Japan nor Soviet Russia wanted detailed publicity concerning the confrontation between them. Since the period of the five-year plans and the build-up of the new state of Manchukuo, the 3,000 miles of mainland frontier were coming alive with barbed wire entanglements, pillboxes, observation posts, armed patrols, reconnaissance planes, and gunboats. Affrays broke out incessantly—shootings, kidnappings, hijackings, intrusions. Both sides noted the incidence on fever charts, but few cases could ever be called "solved."

Third powers might fear, expect, or hope for all-out war between the Soviet Union and Japan. There were numerous close calls. Particularly explosive were the crises of 1937–39 on the northern, eastern, and then western borders of Manchuria. This was an extremely dangerous period in Europe too, of course, and observers tended to be diverted by the Nazi and fascist pressures upon Austria, Czechoslovakia, and Poland. One wondered what underlay the meager information filtering from the Far East in the summer of 1938, for instance, when it was reported: "Soviet Hurls Six Divisions and 30 Tanks into Battle with Japanese on Border—Russia Warns that 'Playing with Fire' in Local Clashes May Bring on War." Yet within two weeks nothing more was heard of the hill of Changkufeng. Was it all a figment of superheated journalistic speculation about a nervous frontier that few outsiders had ever seen?

Even more perplexing was the pocket war of 1939 on the Mongolian steppes at Nomonhan, from which sporadic reports emanated of fierce, large-scale fighting between spring and late summer. The respective claims sounded fantastic—hundreds of planes shot down, hundreds of tanks set afire—at obscure dunes that could not easily be located on the best maps. Here again, haze soon obscured the plains, and the outbreak of general war in Europe dispelled further foreign interest. Many dismissed the Soviet-Japanese fighting as mere border skirmishes. How many noticed the Japanese Army Ministry's public admission, in the autumn of 1939, of 17,000 Japanese casualties at Nomonhan alone?

Thus did the situation of ignorance remain until after the Pacific War, when the Soviet prosecutors at the Tokyo trials formally charged Japan with aggression and conspiracy against the USSR—a blanket charge allegedly proved by the affairs at Changkufeng and Nomonhan in 1938–39 in particular. Speaking of Changkufeng (or Lake Khasan, as the Russians preferred to call the locale), the Soviet lawyers contended that "a battle in which participated a [Japanese] division with artillery cannot be considered as a minor frontier incident. . . . It was not a spontaneous clash on the frontier, but an action sanctioned by the [Japanese] Government." According to the Soviet prosecution, "the Japanese warlords, with full approval of the Japanese Government," were responsible for the struggles at Changkufeng and Nomonhan; the former was "in reality an actual war in which artillery, tanks, and air forces participated." It was the "peaceful and democratic" Soviet Union which had borne the brunt of the aggressors' blows, played a decisive role in their defeat, and "saved Mankind from fascist barbarism." [1]

Not unexpectedly, the International Military Tribunal for the Far East, by majority decision, found for the prosecution: The Japanese Army General Staff, the Army Ministry, and the cabinet had deliberately plotted assaults against the peaceloving USSR. Since substantial forces were committed, the operations could not be called mere clashes between border patrols. Japan, in the words of the Tribunal, was guilty of "clear aggression."

The colleagues of the Soviet representatives on the bench could not bring themselves to agree unanimously. Mr. Justice Radhabinod Pal (the member from India), for example, lodged a dissent, in the belief that none of the Soviet-produced evidence supported the charges of preplanned Japanese aggression dating back to the 1920s.[2] "The evidence," wrote Mr. Justice Pal, "does not establish that Japan had any aggressive design against the USSR. No doubt she shared the world dislike of Communism and perhaps this dislike was the most unmerited. Somehow Russia was not considered to be a thoroughly safe neighbor for the rest of the world since her adoption of the Communistic ideology." But prudence in statecraft was an elementary rule, and Japanese preparations in relation to the Soviet Union disclosed nothing more to Pal than "elementary prudence: . . . the whole world suffered from the terror of Communism . . . and Japan only shared this feeling." Even at the time he was writing his dissent (in 1948), Pal noted that the world had "not been able to free its mind of this terror, real or fancied. The whole world was preparing, and is, even now, preparing against the apprehended aggression of Communism and of the Communist state." Concluded Mr. Justice Pal: "I don't see why we should single out Japan's preparation alone as an aggressive one. The border incidents relied on by the Prosecution are mere border incidents. I cannot spell any conspiracy out of them."

Particularly since Japan's reassumption of sovereignty at San Francisco in 1952, a number of us, as individuals, have endeavored to explore the problem from hitherto unavailable documentation, in an effort to provide some balance. But the most concerted task force effort of recent years was mounted by the Nihon Kokusai Seiji Gakkai (Japan Association on International Relations), spearheaded in the Japanese-Soviet phase by Hata Ikuhiko.

In preparing his work on the Japanese-Soviet confrontation of 1935–39, Hata well knew that existing secondary references relied mainly upon official communiqués found in *Pravda*, *Izvestia*, and the Japanese press, or upon passages from the record of proceedings of the International Military Tribunal for the Far East. I can personally attest to the paucity of authentic information. In one case, a veteran correspondent for a leading American newspaper in 1938 described the altitude of Changkufeng heights as 2,000 feet; the correct figure is closer to 500 feet. In another instance, a widely read western commentator on Soviet Russian affairs described the Russo-Japanese fighting of 1939 as the affair at Lake Nomonhan; actually Nomonhan is situated in the arid flatlands beyond the Gobi Desert. More importantly, partisan writers have, without documentation, accused both Japan and the USSR of staging deliberate probes in the period between 1935 and 1939.

Hata therefore turned largely to unpublished documentation in Japanese and to a certain amount of plausible Soviet army materials released since the Second World War. Among the most valuable data uncovered by Hata are archives in the possession of the Foreign Ministry and of the Defense Agency's Office of Military History. He has been able to consult rare unit histories, diaries, and private memoirs. Where imperial army materials could not be found, he has located important contemporary documents recorded by the Japanese Navy General Staff. The validity and value of these primary materials are undeniable. Supplementing the written records, Hata has conducted several interviews with knowledgeable Japanese survivors. Allowing for inevitable memory decay during the past three decades, it is particularly interesting to examine the results of his conversations with former members of the Japanese army who were serving at the operations level of the General Staff in Tokyo between 1937 and 1939.

Hata has produced a concise study that is neither vituperative to the Soviets nor fawning upon the Japanese. His interests are primarily political, diplomatic, and strategic (not tactical), and his broad-view examination takes in the ramifications of Japan's relations with the Axis and with China, as well as with the Soviet Union. With refreshing objectivity and unparalleled entree into Japanese archives dealing with the still delicate subject of Japan's confrontation with Stalinist Russia, he has been able to overcome many of the foes that have plagued Japanese scholars even after censorship was eliminated—the lack of records, the inaccessible documentation, the partisan bias, the absence of detailed probing in depth.

Hata commences with a brief survey of the beginnings of Japanese defense policies against Russia. Contrary to the popular belief that China consistently represented the hypothetical national enemy, he shows that Russia was always the army's main target. He simplifies the complicated features of the various Kwantung Army operational plans, phase by phase, and supplies order-of-battle data and intelligence estimates based upon once-classified Army General Staff sources.

The author next describes the increasingly tense situation along the new Manchukuo-Soviet-Mongolian frontiers in the mid-1930s and indicates the difficulties of achieving rapprochement, indeed coexistence. Until now, few have known the details of the series of incidents that flared between 1934 and 1936, from Hulun Buyr to Lake Khanka: Halhamiao, Hailastyn-gol, Olankhuduk, Tauran, Changlingtzu—all of which are tersely but authoritatively treated here.

Quite rightly, the author enters into greater detail in discussing the Amur (Kanch'atzu) crisis of 1937, which, although far from unknown in general in the West, has largely entered the literature through the filter of Tass releases. In the Amur affair we begin to see the connection between domestic and external events. The influence of jingoistic Kwantung Army autonomy becomes even more apparent. Dissatisfied with the supposedly negative outlook of the high command, local Japanese authorities dared to attack Soviet gunboats in the Amur river. Still, the fact that the central command managed to check the aggressive intent of the Kwantung Army in 1937 engendered an unfortunate sense of humiliation on the part of the field army in Manchuria and was bound to cause serious new dangers afterward.

From the experience at the Amur in 1937 Hata draws some perceptive conclusions. He does not go so far as the demonologists who see a direct connection between the Marco Polo Bridge affair and a supposed Japanese probe of Soviet intentions on the Siberian border; but he does detect the unplanned equivalent of a reconnaissance in force on the eve of the outbreak of the China Incident. Since the Russians backed down so abjectly and completely during the crisis of 1937, the Japanese drew the not-illogical conclusion that the Soviet Union was in a woeful internal state as the result of the bloody purges conducted by Stalin, and consequently was in no real position to interfere with Japanese activities in East Asia. This estimate also exerted a great effect upon Japanese actions at the time of the Changkufeng troubles in 1938. And although Hata does not mention the point, one can be sure that the revelations made by the defecting Commissar Lyushkov in June 1938 only served to reinforce the general impression of Soviet military impotence.[3]

A brink-of-war situation ensued at Changkufeng in July 1938, centering at first on an obscure hillock and a handful of men. Hata devotes about one-third of his study to the Changkufeng Incident. One gets no particular inkling why the Russians chose to appear on the disputed hill at this time, unless it be the desire to distract Japan from the decisive Hankow campaign then in the offing. Certainly there is no suggestion that the Japanese side would have wanted a war with the Soviet Union over trifling Changkufeng at such a crucial time in its own fortunes. On the other hand, Hata is frank enough to discuss the little-known theory of reconnaissance in force propounded by the Army General Staff Operations Section chief, Inada Masazumi. Inada's view was that the Japanese ought to attempt a strictly limited probe designed to reassure the Japanese high command that China could be laid low without the slightest fear of Soviet intervention—the only real threat to Japanese aggression. Inada has described his dangerous theory clearly and effectively; but neither Hata nor I have ever uncovered a living Japanese source of importance who would corroborate its contemporary significance.

Although higher headquarters—the Korea Army staff in Seoul and Imperial Headquarters in Tokyo—steadfastly preached nonenlargement of the Changkufeng affair, from the outset the local Japanese division commander became convinced that forceful measures were imperative. Hata correctly stresses the preemptive aspect and refutes the usual Japanese account of a "counterattack," which one encounters at every level.

After furious night fighting the Japanese drove off the Russian troops by dawn on July 31. Great risks had been taken; indeed, the principles of an imperial order had apparently been challenged. The local Japanese commanders heaved a great sigh when the high command eventually granted ex post facto approval of the action of alleged self-defense.

Would the Russians, who had reacted so meekly to provocation in 1937, want to slink away permanently now that Japanese troops were atop the disputed high ground? One cannot doubt that this was the thought of those Japanese officers who were playing with fire in 1938.

The Russians, however, did not react as expected. Instead the Red Army hurled into action not only regular division after regular division, but several hundred fighters, bombers, tanks, and heavy guns. The escalator had begun to operate. Japan would have to decide whether to ascend or get off. Despite the overt fuming of the sister army in Manchuria, the authorities in Korea and Japan—including the Korea Army, the high command, and the civil government—were all determined to break off the incident at Changkufeng. No divisions were dispatched to reinforce the mauled 19th Division, and no Japanese planes were allowed to fly, although the local forces pleaded for air cover.

In Tokyo the chiefs eventually decided upon a unilateral evacuation of Changkufeng, but the timing was set back by the objections of Operations Section officers on the Army General Staff. Meanwhile, Ambassador Shigemitsu Mamoru, after vexing and difficult negotiations in Moscow, worked out a ceasefire with Commissar Maxim Litvinov. Fighting ended on August 11. Soon afterward the Japanese survivors completely evacuated the disputed area, thereby nullifying whatever tactical success had been achieved by the troops.

Hata calls the whole affair a clear case of Japanese military defeat, in terms of results. He is still not convinced that the Inada concept is not more of a rationalization than a motivation. In any event, he feels that the Changkufeng affair contained very dangerous elements—irresponsible local escalation, uncensured insubordination, and unlearned tactical lessons. The neighboring Kwantung Army, dissatisfied with the handling of the case by the Korea Army and by Tokyo, and still smarting from the "humiliation" of 1937, found expression for its aggressive views in 1939 at Nomonhan.

Half of Hata's work is devoted to the Nomonhan (or Khalkhin-gol) tragedy. Whereas the episode of 1938 centered on an uninhabited hill or hills, the Nomonhan Incident concerned the ownership of some Mongol pastures and the function of a river as the boundary on the trackless steppes. In this sense the affair may have constituted a traditional border dispute, but by August 1939 it was a full-fledged war in all but name.

The fighting began in earnest and most inauspiciously for the Japanese when an entire Japanese cavalry regiment was ambushed and massacred at the end of May. The green Japanese 23rd Division had found that it was not only Outer Mongolian horsemen whom they were encountering but also regular units of the Soviet army and air force committed to the defense of the Mongolian People's Republic by the terms of the underestimated mutual defense pact revealed by Stalin in 1936.

Neither Imperial Headquarters nor the Kwantung Army, at the beginning, seems to have wanted to allow a distraction from presumably more critical concerns, such as the intensifying war in China. In mid-June, however, the affair on the Mongolian border flared again, when enemy defense forces were pushed back on the frontier. Captain Tsuji Masanobu now spearheaded the decision at Kwantung Army headquarters that the enemy must be punished, once and for all. A mighty Japanese ground offensive was planned to clear the enemy from the disputed Nomonhan locale. First, despite the central authorities' known opposition, the Kwantung Army launched an air offensive against bases inside Outer Mongolia. The military success of the raid did not allay Tokyo's wrath, for again local commanders were acting contrary to broad national security policy. A showdown was nearing.

With Soviet air power temporarily immobilized, the Japanese ground offensive went into action at the beginning of July. Japanese infantry spanned the Halha river and invaded Outer Mongolia, but massive formations of Soviet tanks and armored cars forced the Japanese to pull back. Reinforced by heavy artillery, the Japanese attempted a new offensive at the end of July; it, too, was stopped in its tracks by Soviet fire power.

By August 1939 the Soviet Union sensed the need for a

rapid decision. The Russians' major offensive, beginning on August 20 (directed, we now know, by none other than Georgi Zhukov), caught the Japanese forces off balance. By the end of August the Japanese troops had been annihilated. Japanese air supremacy had been lost, and the Soviet mechanized units met little effective opposition. Although the Kwantung Army was still talking about new offensives, Imperial Headquarters would tolerate no further attrition. The field army commander was replaced and his entire staff was transferred.

After much internal disagreement and foot-dragging in Japan, a ceasefire agreement was finally reached in Moscow on September 15 between Ambassador Tōgō Shigenori and Commissar Vyacheslav Molotov. By now war had broken out in Europe and Japanese diplomacy was bewildered. Until the end of the parleys the Japanese attempted to mask their weakness and distress, but the Soviet side was able to achieve its main demands along the disputed frontier lines.

Hata does not hesitate to call the Nomonhan Incident a distinct defeat for Japan, in both military and diplomatic terms. As in the case of Changkufeng, insubordination had been rampant and important lessons ignored. But Nomonhan proved more significant than Changkufeng because a profound sense of defeat was infused in the Japanese military and because subsequent policies toward the USSR were much affected. Without going into details, Hata suggests that Japan found itself at a diplomatic disadvantage because of inability to comprehend and adjust to dynamic European developments. Certainly the Japanese stance was not helped by the feuding between the headstrong Kwantung Army and the central authorities. The Japanese army had once again plunged into the arena of domestic politics and diplomacy.

For their part, the Russians evinced a clearly superior sense of timing. By their finally moderate attitude, in fact, the Soviets could count upon conciliating the Japanese. This was the road that led to the important neutrality pact concluded by Matsuoka Yōsuke in 1941, Hata reminds us. All the while Soviet aid to China never proved decisive, and Japan was free to press westward through the gorges of the Yangtze.

Beyond the preceding considerations, analysis of the period under study reveals a number of facets concerning Japan in the 1930s. Too often in modern Japanese history does one encounter the dichotomy between head and limbs, the attempt by subordinates to usurp the authority of superiors which the Japanese call *gekokujō* and which is best exemplified by the Kwantung Army in Manchuria. One Japanese critic has gone so far as to charge that all staff officers stationed with local armies, from commanders down, meddled in politics; there were numerous cases in which officers hardly twenty years of age manipulated "robot" governors. International repercussions were inevitable. For example, at the end of 1937 a Japanese officer claiming to represent the commander-in-chief at Shanghai conveyed to the British commissioner of international settlement police a memorandum that was so offensive it had to be disavowed by the Japanese authorities. Foreign diplomats were advised that the document had been drawn up by unauthorized junior officers.[4] Soon the nickname "Kwantung Army" came to be applied in Japanese military circles to any expeditionary force that ignored the supreme command's desires.

Many of the Japanese problems in 1937–39 stemmed from the dizzying success achieved in 1931 by the Kwantung Army conspirators. Since the days of Saigō Takamori there had been a saying, "If you win, you're the loyal army; if you lose, you're a rebel army." As a Japanese who had been a colonel during the Nomonhan fighting told me: "Inside the army the feeling had grown that the end justified the means. An atmosphere was engendered whereby one could ignore the high command, as was demonstrated by the locally schemed incidents at Mukden in 1931, Shanghai in 1932, the Marco Polo Bridge in 1937, and Nomonhan in 1939." Japanese army thinking could be summed up in this fashion: If one believed in what was attempted, for the sake of the nation and without personal selfishness, one might oppose even the highest authorities. The latter might be vexed for a while, but later they would be pleased, and one might even end up in Tokyo itself. "Great triumphs," it was argued, "outweigh negligible wrongdoing."

It is true that in 1937 Imperial Headquarters was reconstituted, and the chiefs of the Army and Navy General Staffs were to advise the sovereign on operations and to effect interservice coordination. Nevertheless, army commanders overseas were in the direct chain-of-command line to the Throne. Imperial orders were never issued except at the petition of the chief of the Army General Staff, but it was equally true that army commanders were not liable to direct ordering by the chief of staff himself. This practice was especially visible in 1939. The Kwantung Army commander, an esteemed and senior full general, operated virtually autonomously at critical stages of the Nomonhan Incident—e.g. the "chastisement" of the Outer Mongolians and the aerial offensive against bases inside the Mongolian People's Republic. The honor of the field army, supposedly tarnished in 1937 during the Amur affair, was thereby refurbished—but with dangerous consequences for the country, especially vis-à-vis the Soviet Union.

Much of the difficulty derived from the divorce of civil and military functions in Japan itself. The supreme command prerogative was independent in jurisdiction. Responsibility to the emperor for operational guidance, supreme command, and national defense lay entirely outside the administrative domain of the ministers of state, including those of army and navy. Thus the chiefs of staff of the two services counseled the emperor on operations and strategy, and were privileged to appeal directly to the Throne without encountering the so-called interference of civilian channels of the government, such as the cabinet, the prime minister, or the legislature. As Prince Konoe once confessed, "The fact that the supreme command and state affairs are independent of each other has been a matter of anguish for cabinets from generation to generation. . . . Especially in reference to the problem of the prerogative of the Supreme Command, the government had no power at all to raise its voice. . . . As a matter of course, the Army and Navy said nothing about these matters to the members of the cabinet nor to the premier." Concluded the prince: "While a cabinet member, the war minister was nevertheless independent of the cabinet. . . . The Supreme Command and state affairs were entirely independent. The only connection between them was the minister of war, whose obscure character decided the fate of the cabinet. The latter—the affairs of state, were completely in the hands of the supreme command. And so was the life of the entire nation and diplomacy." [5]

The system of "dual government" often led foreign observers to speak of "two Japans." And in time of crisis the Japanese military was always ready, willing, and able to wreck cabinets and dictate the terms of formation of a new government by resorting to extra-constitutional power over the appointment of service ministers. Such an "invisible government" (to use Maki's apt terminology) [6] constituted a unique military-political structure which placed civil government at the mercy of the military.

During the period of the Japanese-Soviet confrontation of the 1930s we can discern the preceding phenomena in operation. In the Amur episode local units, perhaps trigger-happy, induced a brink-of-war situation until the central authorities in Tokyo enforced their will. Next year the Korea Army handled the Changkufeng fighting prudently and cautiously, under the direction of Imperial Headquarters. Nevertheless a local division commander again brought the nation to the verge of all-out hostilities with the Soviet Union. At the time of the Nomonhan Incident there was a breakdown in the rapport between the authorities in Tokyo and those in Hsinching. The Kwantung Army staff acted irresponsibly; opportunities for *casus belli* presented themselves on more than one occasion to the USSR.

Admittedly the shake-up of the entire Kwantung Army command in September 1939 was unparalleled, but the system of administering military personnel affairs contained grievous elements of foolhardiness, and the junior masters of the art of *geko-kujō* were not permanently removed from the scene. Even the strictly combat experience of 1938–39 was largely ignored by the Japanese. In the face of foes of the caliber of Marshals Blyukher and Zhukov, supported by the most modern tools of war, the Japanese were still extolling the bayonet, human bullets, and hand-to-hand fighting.

Hata has illuminated many hitherto dark nooks of Japanese-Soviet relations. Despite his brevity, the author's account of the

Changkufeng and Nomonhan incidents, in particular, is unmatched. The last word has certainly not been said, but revision or correction of the cruelly partisan Tokyo trials verdict is finally becoming possible, and world history is the richer.

Essay
by
HATA IKUHIKO

From the time of the Russo-Japanese War, Russia constituted the primary hypothetical enemy of the Japanese army. The build-up of the latter's organization, equipment, and training was based upon a hypothetical war against Russia, with Manchuria the battleground. By a twist of fate, the Japanese army ended up in 1937 plunging into all-out hostilities against China, thereby tying down a million men on the Chinese mainland. But storm clouds steeped with the danger of Japanese-Soviet hostilities kept bursting over the Soviet-Manchukuo frontiers to Japan's rear. In particular, the incidents at Changkufeng in 1938 and at Nomonhan in 1939 were large-scale armed clashes entailing the commitment by both sides of forces of strategic-unit size. Both affairs, depending upon their course and circumstances, threatened to bring about the utter collapse of the Japanese effort against China and plunge Japan into the northern war it had long anticipated but for which it was not yet ready.

The origins and significance of this Japanese-Soviet confrontation can best be understood against the background of Japanese strategic thinking and the crescendoing border crises of the mid-1930s.

The Growing Crisis

The Japanese Imperial National Defense Policy (devised in 1907, just after the Russo-Japanese War) fixed upon the United States, Russia, and China as Japan's hypothetical foes. It formu-

This is a translation by Alvin D. Coox of Hata Ikuhiko, "Nitchū sensō no gunji-teki tenkei (1937–1941)," in *Taiheiyō sensō e no michi*, Vol. 4, Part I, Sec. 5, 6, and 7, pp. 73–110, together with footnotes.

lated the basic objectives for the maintenance of armaments, and laid down an annual operations plan, the overall principles for troop use, and the amounts of requisite strength. Although the policy was revised three times (in 1918, 1923, and 1936), except for the addition of Britain to the list of enemies in 1936 there were no major changes in its central characteristics.[1] Japan's hypothetical enemies were split in two: Russia for the army, and the United States for the navy. Although Japan's path of external expansion was aimed at the China mainland, and although it was anticipated that China would be an enemy in case of Japanese hostilities against Russia or the United States, the study of military operations against China itself was neglected. Anti-Chinese operations were assumed to involve only small-scale "political expeditions" for such limited purposes as protecting Japanese residents. The major ground enemy was always assumed to be Russia, and as the years went by, the national defense policy provided various strategies for handling it.

According to the military historian and former chief of the Army General Staff Operations Section, Colonel Hattori Takushirō, the battleground was originally expected to be located inside Manchuria, where Russia's main strength, invading from the Trans-Baikal region, would be sought out and defeated. Concentration was to take place in south Manchuria, and the battle would be fought on the right bank of the Nonni river. With the opening up between 1923 and 1926 of further railways from Ssup'ing to T'aonan and then from T'aonan to Angangch'i, however, the first-stage operational objective was changed to the Tsitsihar plain, and the ultimate objective was moved across the Hsingan range to the Trans-Baikal area. During the early years of Soviet authority, following the collapse of tsarist Russia, concrete battle plans were not developed;[2] but in the Sino-Soviet clash of 1929, when the Soviet Far Eastern forces engaged the troops of Chang Hsueh-liang, the Japanese army was surprised by the Red Army's combat power. Japan sensed danger.

With the Manchurian Incident in 1931, Japan's strategic planning entered a new period. At first the Soviet leaders, preoccupied with their domestic build-up, had adopted a conciliatory policy. They had renounced their rights to the Chinese Eastern Railway and pulled back to the line of the Amur river. When the Manchurian Incident occurred, Soviet strength east of the Urals amounted to a mere 100,000 men, and defense facilities along the frontier were almost nil. With the establishment of Manchukuo, however, the Russians came into direct confrontation with the Kwantung Army, and from around the spring of 1932 they commenced large-scale expansion of their military strength in the Far East (see Table 1). For its part, Japan's military posture in Manchuria did not advance, due to preoccupation with the suppression of banditry. The difference in military strength between the Soviet Far Eastern forces and the Japanese grew ever greater, as may be seen in Table I. In particular, the presence of Soviet transoceanic heavy bombers, which had been moved into the Maritime Province, exerted silent pressure upon Japan. In view of these circumstances and the improvement of the Soviet Union's diplomatic stance in Europe following its entry into the League of Nations and con-

TABLE 1. OPPOSING MILITARY STRENGTHS IN THE FAR EAST, 1932–1939

	Soviet Far Eastern Armies			Kwantung Army			
Year	Infantry Divisions	Number of Aircraft	Total Man-power	Infantry Divisions	Air Regts. (Groups)	Number of Aircraft	Total Man-power
1932	8	200		4	1	30	
1933	8	350		3	3	100	60,000
1934	11	500	230,000	3	3	100	60,000
1935	14	950	240,000	3	3	100	
1936	16–20	1,200	340,000	3	5	180	80,000
1937	20	1,560	370,000	6	5		
1938	24	2,000	450,000	8	12		
1939	30	2,500	570,000	9	18		

Note: The strength of the Soviet Far Eastern forces represents estimates made by the Japanese Army General Staff. The data on Kwantung Army strength are based upon records of the same office. Strengths are given as of the end of the indicated year, except in the case of Soviet Far Eastern strength for 1934, which refers to the situation as of the end of June that year. Throughout the period shown in the table, the Kwantung Army could count upon reinforcement by the two infantry divisions of the Korea Army in case of emergency.

clusion of the Franco-Soviet pact, the Soviet Union from about 1935 dispensed with its earlier policy of retreat and shifted to an aggressive policy of checking Japan. Expressions of this trend were the declaration branding Japan an enemy at the Seventh Comintern Congress in July–August 1935, and the consummation of the mutual assistance pact with the Mongolian People's Republic in March 1936.

In the same year Captain Kōtani Etsuo, then aide to the military attaché in the Soviet Union, obtained intelligence to the effect that the USSR had changed its national defense policy from one-front to two-front operations.[3] At the Communist Party's Central Committee session of January 1937, Marshal M. N. Tukhachevsky spoke in terms that appeared to corroborate Kōtani's information, saying: "Now we are in a position, whenever the government asks, to cope with enemies on both the eastern and western frontiers at any time, using mighty, well-trained, and perfected strength." A rise in the number of border incidents from approximately the end of 1935 seemed to confirm this new stance.

The Japanese army effected a major change in its anti-Soviet operational plans in 1933. As a consequence of the more favorable posture deriving from its occupation of all of Manchuria, the plans now called for launching a fierce offensive eastward against the flank of the Maritime Province, then moving northward through the province, and finally veering westward. The assumed new strength of the Soviet Union, however, caused the Japanese to give up the Trans-Baikal as the ultimate objective. From 1937, operations were to be broken off along the line between Rufrow and the Hsingan mountains; Japan would then go over to a posture of endurance.

Even these more limited plans would require greater strength. The Japanese army estimated that it would be difficult to defeat the Soviet forces in a war unless its relatively weak military strength in Manchuria were to be built up to a minimum of 70–80 percent of the counterpart Soviet Far Eastern armies. Hence, following the appointment of Colonel Ishiwara Kanji as chief of the Operations Section of the Army General Staff in August 1935, major expansion of the forces in Manchuria was begun. The 1936 plans called for six divisions to be stationed in Manchukuo, with two more in Korea, by 1940, while separate plans were made for a great increase in arms and the acceleration of production throughout Japan and Manchukuo.

This program had barely gotten under way when the advent of the conflict with China caused it to bog down. Operational plans for 1937 were roughly adhered to; but with the main strength of the Japanese army being shifted to the China front, the need arose for contingency planning for an anti-Soviet war, should one break out while operations in China were going on. A tentative plan was actually worked into the operations scheme for 1938.[4] By that time the Red Army's positions in the Maritime Province had become so strengthened that a breakthrough along that front was judged to be difficult. Imperial Headquarters and the Kwantung Army began studying an alternate, Operations Plan 8, which called for an offensive westward to Lake Baikal; but in view of the inadequacy of strength and equipment available at the time, this concept was dropped.[5] Despite these circumstances, the Kwantung Army clung tenaciously to the resolute anti-Soviet stance it had held since the Manchurian Incident.

Changes in strength and planning on both sides were accompanied, particularly after 1935, by a rising number of border incidents. There were 152 disputes during the two-and-a-half years between the outbreak of the Manchurian Incident and 1934, but in 1935 the number soared to 136, and in 1936 to 203. By the end of World War II in 1945 the cumulative number of incidents exceeded 1,600.[6]

The border regions were characterized by numerous dense forests, mountains, and deserts. In addition, for many sectors there was uncertainty as to the detailed wording of the various treaties concluded between tsarist Russia and the Ch'ing dynasty. The Japanese General Staff and the Kwantung Army, moreover, interpreted boundaries to favor their own interests. Thus the seeds of dispute could be found in all directions.

The subject of establishing a system for settling these disputes first came up in parleys between Foreign Minister Hirota

Kōki and Soviet Ambassador Constantin Yurenev in June 1935.
The USSR promptly made a proposal, but both the Manchukuo
government and the Kwantung Army opposed it, their contention being that prior boundary demarcation was necessary.
Then, when a dispute occurred at Suifenho that July, the Japanese took the opportunity to suggest the creation of an organization to demarcate the border lines, as a substitute for the Soviet
proposal. But the Russians stood their ground and continued to
argue that provisions dealing with the boundaries already existed in extant pacts, so there was no need to conduct demarcation anew. Since the USSR evinced no enthusiasm, the negotiations did not progress. The three Manchouli conferences, called
to examine various Manchukuo-Mongolia border incidents including the Halhamiao affair, were confronted by the completion of the Soviet-Mongolian mutual assistance treaty as well as
by the Anti-Comintern Pact between Japan and Germany, and
the talks were broken off.[7] So it went until the outbreak of the
Changkufeng Incident in July 1938. The following brief accounts of several of the disputes will illustrate the rising crisis
of this early period.

Halhamiao Incident, January 1935. Although it was assumed in general that the Halha river constituted the border
line in the area of the Hulun Buyr steppes in the northwestern
part of Manchuria, the Outer Mongolians came and went on the
eastern and northern sides of the river. On January 8, 1935,
more than ten Outer Mongolian soldiers penetrated into Manchukuoan territory, occupied Halhamiao, and engaged Manchukuo Army troops, which moved forward on the 24th. On the
26th the Manchukuo government demanded that the Outer
Mongolian forces be withdrawn, but the Outer Mongolian
premier retorted that Halhamiao lay inside MPR territory. Next
day elements of Lieutenant-General Hasunuma Shigeru's Cavalry Group from Hailaerh (Hulun), which had been undertaking
the defense of the region, moved up pursuant to orders from the
Kwantung Army commander. The Outer Mongolian troops
quickly pulled back after they learned that Japanese forces
were arriving, so no combat ensued. The Japanese troops oc-

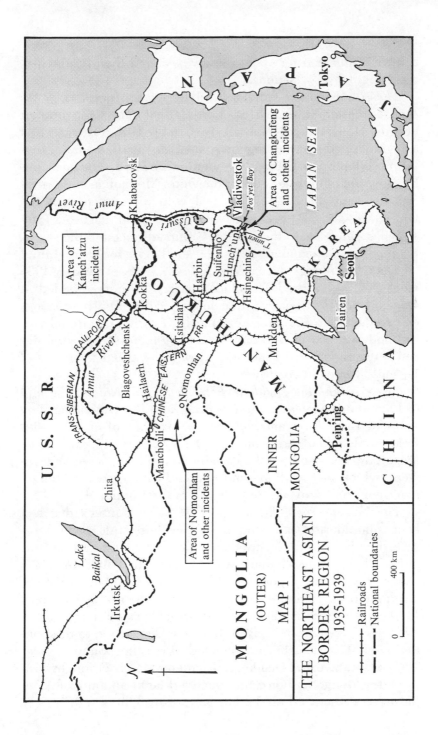

THE NORTHEAST ASIAN
BORDER REGION
1935-1939

MAP I

MONGOLIA
(OUTER)

U. S. S. R.

MANCHUKUO

INNER
MONGOLIA

CHINA

KOREA

JAPAN

Tokyo

JAPAN SEA

Area of Changkufeng
and other incidents

Vladivostok

Pos'yet Bay

Area of Kanch'atzu
incident

Amur River

Khabarovsk

Ussuri R.

Suifenho

Hunch'un

Hsingching

Harbin

Kokka

TRANS-SIBERIAN RAILROAD

Amur River

Blagoveshchensk

Hailaerh

CHINESE EASTERN RR.

Tsitsihar

Manchouli

Nomonhan

Area of Nomonhan
and other incidents

Mukden

Dairen

Seoul

Peiping

Chita

Lake Baikal

Irkutsk

T'umen R.

Railroads
National boundaries

0   400 km

N

cupied Halhamiao for about three weeks and then returned to their original duty stations.[8]

The Hailastyn-gol Incident (Inukai Affair), June 1935. On June 24 Outer Mongolian soldiers dashed across the frontier near the Hailastyn-gol (Holsten river) in the Hulun Buyr district and kidnapped a Kwantung Army surveyor by the name of Inukai, for whom the incident is sometimes named. The Manchukuo government requested that the Outer Mongolian authorities establish a regular agency to deal with disputes or that the Outer Mongolian forces be withdrawn from east of Tamsagbulag. Once again the Cavalry Group advanced to the scene, but it failed to encounter the enemy and before long withdrew.[9]

The Chinch'angkou Incident, January 1936. In January 1936 more than a hundred Manchukuo Army soldiers rebelled at Chinch'angkou in eastern Manchukuo (where the border jogs eastward, about 50 kilometers north of Suifenho-Grodekovo) and fled into Soviet territory. Then they recrossed the frontier and between January 30 and February 1 engaged a small unit of Japanese troops in combat.[10]

The Olankhuduk Incident, February 1936. Around the end of 1935 Outer Mongolian troops came into the Orahodoga area south of Lake Buyr and fomented a number of clashes with local Manchukuo Army forces. On February 12, 1936, the Kwantung Army sent up the Cavalry Group's Sugimoto Detachment, which met artillery- and armored car-supported Mongolian troops and drove them back across the frontier.[11]

The Tauran Incident, March 1936. The troubles that had been smouldering at Hulun Buyr now burst into flame on a scale involving the commitment of both mechanized and air units. Thus, the Kwantung Army, which had discerned the Outer Mongolians' vigorous attitude in the Olankhuduk affair, accelerated preparations designed to deal them a heavy blow. In March the Shibuya Detachment, which was built around the 4th Tank Regiment in Kungchuling, was dispatched to the front line area. The detachment operated along the boundary near Tauran, southwest of Olankhuduk, and on March 31 fought with an Outer Mongolian force that included tanks and aircraft. The Japanese also moved up the Matsumura air fighter unit.[12]

The Changlingtzu Incident, March 1936. The same year on March 25 Japanese army officers reconnoitering in the vicinity of Changlingtzu, 12 kilometers southeast of Hunch'un, were shot at by Russians. Both sides rushed up small units, which engaged each other.[13]

The Kanch'atzu or Amur Incident, June–July 1937. This incident stemmed from a border dispute that occurred at the end of June 1937, just before the outbreak of the Marco Polo Bridge affair, in the vicinity of the islets of Bolshoi and Senufa (Kanch'atzu) in the Kanch'atzu offing of the Amur river southeast of Kokka along the northern border of Manchuria.

For a long time neither Manchukuo nor the USSR had been interested in the ownership of the islets in the Amur river; a difference of opinion appeared only at the time of the consummation of the waterways pact between the Soviet Union and Manchukuo in 1934. In April of that year the USSR announced that it was abrogating the agreement and thereafter began to put pressure upon Japanese and Manchukuoan vessels operating in the channel north of Kanch'atzu island. According to international river law, a river boundary is divided by the midline of the main current; but in this sector the southern channel, in Manchurian territory, was wider, and the Soviet side apparently considered the southern channel to represent the main current.

A small number of Soviet troops landed on the islands on June 19 and abducted or evicted Manchurian gold miners there. At the same time Soviet gunboats engaged elements of the Manchukuo Army. The Japanese General Staff received the report on the incident from the Kwantung Army on June 22 and at first sanctioned a vigorous response by the local authorities. On June 24 the vice chief of staff sent the following instruction: "If territory clearly belonging to Manchukuo has been illegally seized by Soviet troops, we believe that the effects upon our future operations will be serious; consequently we wish you hereafter to take suitable measures to maintain the situation as it has been." [14] Thereupon the Kwantung Army immediately concentrated the 1st (Tokyo) Division (which had been posted in that area since the February 26 mutiny of 1936), together with other elements, in the disputed area. At the same time a strong protest was sent to the Soviet consul in Harbin.

The Soviets, for their part, massed a gunboat unit on the river and gave evidence of mobilizing regular divisions in the Blagoveshchensk area. Consequently, one could envisage the outbreak of large-scale fighting with the Kwantung Army, which was intending to retake the islets. The odds having changed, the General Staff reversed itself, deciding now that "the problem of these islands located so remotely does not warrant risking the national strength." [15] Conferences were held with the Navy and Foreign ministries, and on June 28 a policy of nonenlargement was adopted. The substance of the decision was explained in a telegram sent that day by the navy high command to the naval commander in Manchukuo, which said in part: "Since the resolution of the incident lies in a consistent policy of nonenlargement, even if force is used by local elements of the army it is imperative not to allow matters to spread to the river and air units; this is the opinion jointly held by the navy and the army. . . . Although there are various opinions in the army high command as to the timing and method of recapture by force, it has been decided after careful deliberation for the time being to defer these questions even if such action is to be taken, and first to try diplomatic negotiation." [16] When Major-General Imamura Hitoshi, the Kwantung Army vice chief of staff, arrived in Tokyo the same day, he was told that for the time being the local forces were to suspend their counterattack. The Kwantung Army, however, had already completed concentrating two infantry battalions and one field artillery battalion, all under the command of Major-General Koizumi Kyōji, within the 1st Division at the scene, and at that very moment was pressing forward with preparations to use force. Local units, dissatisfied with the negative attitude of the high command, could not be restrained. On June 29 they arbitrarily bombarded Soviet gunboats on the river, sinking one of them.

In the meantime, diplomatic negotiations in Moscow, conducted by Ambassador Shigemitsu Mamoru and Foreign Commissar Maxim Litvinov, had been limping along. In the early hours of June 28, on the basis of instructions from the Foreign

Ministry, Shigemitsu insisted to Vice Foreign Commissar Boris Stomonyakov that the northern waterway was the main current and that the islets in question had long been recognized as Manchurian territory by both Manchukuo and the Soviet Union, as attested to by the presence of markers. He requested that the Soviet forces withdraw immediately.[17] In reply, the Russians quoted the 1860 Treaty of Peking, contending that both islands belonged to the Soviet side. The next day, however, during talks with Shigemitsu, Litvinov indicated that "apart from the matter of principle, the USSR has no objection to a withdrawal from the disputed points; hence, the Japanese troops should pull out too." [18] But the Japanese stood firm. At a conference of the Japanese army, navy, and foreign ministers on June 30, it was agreed that the Soviet forces must be withdrawn first. With the arbitrary shelling by Japanese forces, the attitude of the USSR stiffened; but eventually, in the course of a meeting between Shigemitsu and Litvinov on the night of July 2, the USSR promised to withdraw from both islets; by the 4th its entire occupying unit had withdrawn to the northern shore. The Kwantung Army also ordered the Japanese units to return to their original garrison stations, whereupon things quieted down again.

The Kanch'atzu Incident was clearly much smaller in scale than the subsequent affairs at Changkufeng and Nomonhan, but it was politically significant. First, regardless of whether the disputed islands belonged to Manchukuo or the USSR, it was a fact that from the middle of the affair the Soviet Union had voluntarily made all of the concessions. Second, inasmuch as the Kanch'atzu Incident broke out accidentally on the eve of Japanese hostilities in China, the clash unexpectedly provided Japan with an opportunity to test Soviet strength. From the engagement the Army General Staff drew the following conclusions:

> 1) The present action was not premeditated on the part of the Soviet government; 2) it represented an arbitrary action by local authorities, in particular the border garrison units and elements of the navy cooperating with them; 3) the Far Eastern Army was obliged to provide instructions after the incident broke out; and

4) therefore, unlike the case of other incidents, there was almost no Soviet press coverage.[19]

In addition, the Kwantung Army reported to Tokyo that a severe purge had been raging inside the Soviet Far Eastern Army at the time and intelligence had been intercepted to the effect that the local division commander had ordered subordinate units not to aggravate the situation; any action was to be undertaken only upon direct instruction from Moscow.[20]

Thus, from the Soviets' conciliatory attitude the Japanese military, and the Kwantung Army in particular, strengthened their impression that the confusion within the USSR, stemming from the purge of the Tukhachevsky faction then in progress, was very serious indeed and meant that the Soviet Union was unable to spare the strength for intervention abroad. Such estimates led the Japanese army to forge ahead with the dispatch of troops to China following the Marco Polo Bridge Incident without worrying about Soviet responses.

Third, the suspension order was issued by the Army General Staff just as local units were about to commence the counterattack. Consequently, the Kwantung Army was pervaded by a sense of humiliation and a feeling that it had suffered a loss of prestige in its command prerogatives toward its subordinate units. The lack of harmony that characterized subsequent relations between the Kwantung Army and the high command in Tokyo constituted a remote cause of the explosion that took place during the Nomonhan Incident.[21]

The Changkufeng Incident, July–August 1938

In July 1938, just as Japan's China Expeditionary Forces were preparing to pour all their strength into the Hankow campaign, a military conflict erupted on the Soviet-Manchukuo frontier as though to check this vast operation. Taking the name of the little hill that served as the focus of the dispute, the Japanese termed the affair the Changkufeng Incident; the Russians called it the Lake Khasan Incident after the little lake lying east of Changkufeng (Zaozernaya) heights. This affray between the Soviets and the Japanese differed from the previous border clashes in that for the first time the fighting was joined by strategic-size military units.

Changkufeng was situated in a low but complicated hilly area where Hunch'un hsien on the southeastern edge of Manchukuo stuck like a tongue into the northeastern part of Korea, between Pos'yet Bay in Soviet territory and the T'umen river. The hill jutted up 149 meters, "a height dotted with short pines and shrubs . . . a clearly defined bald red hillock. . . . Not only could the Japanese railway between Manchukuo and Korea be very clearly seen from here, but the port of Najin could also be observed, more than 18 kilometers away." [22] Due to the complex terrain, there were many places where the frontier was not clear. According to the Hunch'un Protocol concluded in 1886 between the Ch'ing government and Imperial Russia, the only treaty governing the matter, the boundary line was supposed to proceed roughly near the crestline connecting Changkufeng with Shatsaofeng (Bezymyannaya). In practice, however, most of the markers had been lost, and Chinese and Russian maps were not compatible. According to the 1915–20 map put out by the Military Survey Bureau of the Three Northeastern Provinces, for example, the frontier ran somewhat more easterly toward the Soviet side than the line shown by the Hunch'un Protocol. The map published in 1911 by the Russian Army General Staff inclined ever farther to the Soviet side, running east of Lake Khasan.

Both Soviet and Japanese border garrison units had been posted in this area since the days of the Manchurian Incident. Key crestlines on the border were occupied in alternate sequence by the respective sides. For example, both Shuiliufeng, a heights situated on the frontier crestline north of the Changkufeng locale, and Wuchiatzu had been occupied earlier by Japanese troops.[23] There had been a minor affray between small Japanese and Soviet units on the crestline at Shuiliufeng in October 1937, but the Soviet forces had pulled out and the area had reverted to Japanese hands. Changkufeng itself, however, lay at the extreme edge and had been overlooked by both parties.

On July 13, 1938, the Korea Army received a report from the 19th Division, which was under its control,[24] that some forty Soviet soldiers had appeared atop Changkufeng on the 11th and had begun constructing positions.[25] The Korea Army commander, General Koiso Kuniaki, promptly reported to Imperial Headquarters that even if a Soviet border penetration was obvious, this was a critical period, with the projected Hankow operation beginning; hence, the Korea Army's policy was as follows: "At first, reason with the Soviets and directly ask them to withdraw locally"; but "in case they do not accede to our request, then expel their troops east of Lake Khasan, firmly and by force." [26]

Earlier, around July 7, the Kwantung Army had already learned through radio interception that the newly assigned Pos'yet District border garrison unit commander intended to occupy high ground in the vicinity of Changkufeng.[27] Staff officers Tsuji Masanobu, then a captain, and Ōgoshi Kenji were dispatched to the scene by the Kwantung Army to ascertain the Soviet forces' penetration of the border.[28] Thereupon the Kwantung Army adopted a very strong attitude and sent warnings to Imperial Headquarters in Tokyo and to the Korea Army, demanding the use of force. Imperial Headquarters, however, with the agreement of the cabinet and the Army Ministry, inclined to the Korea Army's opinion: the Hankow campaign should not be jeopardized by any adventures against the Soviet Union. It was decided as a first step to seek the withdrawal of the Soviet forces through diplomatic negotiations. Army General Staff officers Lieutenant-Colonel Arisue Yadoru and Major Kōtani Etsuo of the Intelligence Section's Russia desk were sent to the spot on the 15th to transmit the principles of the imperial order issued formally to the Korea Army on July 16, directing it to do no more than concentrate its strength along the local front so as to be able to cope with any emergency.[29]

On the other hand, there were those in Imperial Headquarters who could not reconcile themselves to this decision.

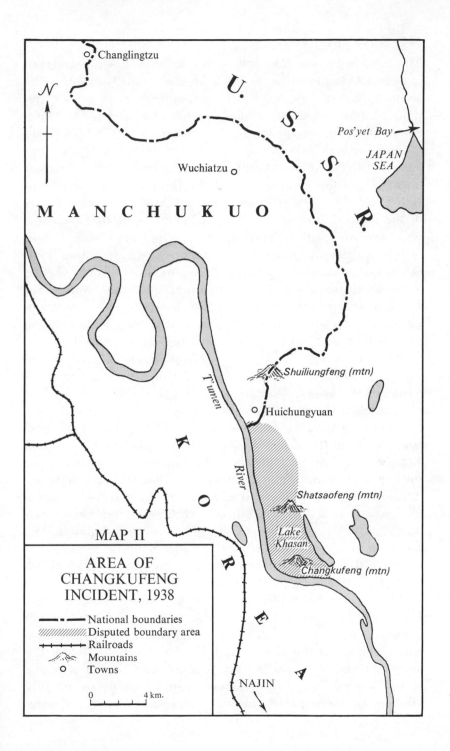

Changlingtzu

U. S. S. R.

Pos'yet Bay

JAPAN
SEA

Wuchiatzu

M A N C H U K U O

Shuiliungfeng (mtn)

Huichungyuan

T'umen

River

Shatsaofeng (mtn)

Lake
Khasan

MAP II

Changkufeng (mtn)

AREA OF
CHANGKUFENG
INCIDENT, 1938

National boundaries
Disputed boundary area
Railroads
Mountains
Towns

K O R E A

NAJIN

0   4 km.

The time had come, they felt, as the Kwantung Army said, not to negotiate but to strike, in the form of a controlled probe. The activists included especially the young officers in the Operations Section, centering around its chief, Colonel Inada Masazumi. Inada succeeded in rallying strong support.[30] Vice Chief of Staff General Tada Hayao had been recommending for some time that the conflict in China should be broken off as soon as possible and the main weight of the Japanese army shifted to confront the Soviets. He joined the activists. Most other heads of the Army Ministry and Army General Staff, Inada recalls, were won over with "surprising ease." The Navy General Staff, which was deeply committed to the operations in China, held out at first, unable to guarantee transportation not only via the Korea Strait but also via the Tsugaru Strait in the event of Soviet-Japanese hostilities. Eventually, however, the navy's opposition was overridden.[31] At the Five Ministers Conference on July 19 Foreign Minister Ugaki Kazushige also opposed the use of force, insisting that it was "not appropriate to give up too soon and to move forces in the midst of diplomatic negotiations." [32] He too was ignored.

Confident that their plans would receive the imperial sanction the next day, the General Staff carefully briefed the new commander of the Korea Army, Lieutenant-General Nakamura Kōtarō, in Tokyo (he had taken over on July 15 as part of the routine annual midsummer command changes). Inada wired Arisue informally in the field while a new emissary, Major Arao Okikatsu, was sent out to provide the new operational guidance.[33] The Korea Army promptly completed deploying its forces, and Lieutenant-General Suetaka Kamezō, commander of the 19th Division, rushed preparations to launch an attack against Changkufeng on the night of July 21.[34]

Meanwhile, Navy Minister Yonai Mitsumasa, Foreign Minister Ugaki, and Lord Keeper of the Privy Seal Yuasa Kurahei conveyed their opposition to these plans to the emperor, who was incensed at the army's high-handed behavior. When the army minister, General Itagaki Seishirō, and the chief of the Army General Staff, Prince Kan'in, went to the palace on July 20 to obtain the imperial sanction for the use of force at Changkufeng and for subsequent mobilization, they were warned by General Usami Oki'ie, the chief aide-de-camp to the emperor, that the emperor unofficially had indicated that he would "not grant sanction, so they need not come." [35] In the end Itagaki was granted audience individually, but when the emperor asked him whether he had coordinated his views with the other ministers and he replied, contrary to the emperor's information, that both the foreign minister and the navy minister had agreed to the use of force, the emperor remarked on the army's "way of doing things" ever since the time of the Mukden and Marco Polo Bridge incidents. He reprimanded Itagaki sternly, saying, "Hereafter, not even a single soldier may be moved without our express orders." [36]

Itagaki withdrew, utterly crestfallen. "I cannot look upon his majesty's countenance again," he groaned. "I want to step down." Next day, however, Prime Minister Konoe went to the palace and smoothed things over, so the army minister and the chief of staff decided to remain in their respective posts.[37]

After hectic conferences on the night of July 20, Operations Section Chief Inada wired Major Arao to suspend the use of force. The tenor of Inada's feelings can be seen in this part of his message:

> . . . there is no prospect of obtaining an imperial order for the use of force. As for the conduct of the Changkufeng Incident hereafter, it is veering toward the following policy: though we shall promote diplomatic negotiations, they will be cut off promptly if there is no hope of success. Have the concentrated forces wait for a while at their present locations, and return the main body to their original positions as soon as possible. The situation has been reversed 180 degrees. *Matters have already progressed beyond the extent of our jurisdiction or initiative. Kindly renovate your thinking and act with prudence under the circumstances.*[38] *

Lieutenant-General Suetaka, unlike the Korea Army's commander and staff officers, was an aggressive personality. He had been bemoaning his bad luck at not being able to participate in

* Hereafter all italics have been added by the author.

the fighting in China and spiritedly looking forward to the commencement of the attack at Changkufeng. Like Arao, he must have been deeply chagrined by the suspension order. Inada opines that these two men "must have felt very close to each other. One cannot pry into their discourse, but it would not be mistaken to surmise that the division commander must have derived some hints from it; and in his mind, whether consciously or not, there must have been a feeling of 'sooner or later' " [39] Arao himself said later that he "did not interpret the fact that the imperial sanction could not be obtained for the use of force to mean the same as an imperial order 'forbidding the use of force.' So far as I was concerned, I ascribed importance to judging how to deal with matters, given the suspension of the use of force." [40] Subsequent events suggest that Suetaka shared Arao's interpretation.

At any rate, Suetaka did not immediately comply with the spirit of the order. On July 21 the 19th Division recommended to the Korea Army that force should be employed "for purposes of nonenlargement," but this was rejected.[41] The same day the division secretly occupied Chiangchünfeng heights 800 meters west of Changkufeng and then asked for ex post facto approval. Although instructed to withdraw, the division eventually prevailed upon the Korea Army to approve the fait accompli. On the 23rd Major Arao reported that the division was still preparing an attack against Changkufeng. These actions brought a new imperial order on the 26th, directing immediate withdrawal. It was not until July 28 that the division finally began to return to its original duty stations, leaving only unit elements forward. This was the situation when new trouble erupted at Shatsaofeng.

About 9:30 A.M. on July 29 several Soviet soldiers crossed the frontier and began to construct positions on the boundary crestline south of Shatsaofeng, about two kilometers north of Changkufeng itself. Division Commander Suetaka had been staying at Kyŏnghŭng with Staff Officer Saitō Toshio, keeping an eye on matters even after division headquarters had been withdrawn to Nanam. Upon receiving this latest report, General

Suetaka, convinced "that his mission called for it," immediately ordered his border garrison unit commander at Chiang-chünfeng, Lieutenant-Colonel Senda Tadasue, to launch an attack. After "repelling the Soviet forces around 3 P.M. with 20 men," the Japanese garrison unit pulled back; but during the evening approximately 80 Soviet soldiers with several tanks advanced onto the same high ground again.[42]

That night General Suetaka reported the outbreak of the "Shatsaofeng Incident"[43] to the Korea Army. The affair, he asserted, "was caused entirely by the enemy's illicit provocation. Hence, I firmly believe that we ought to consider that it has a completely different complexion from the Changkufeng Incident and should be handled separately." To cope with the emergency, Suetaka requested approval for the reconcentration of the units that had been pulled out.[44]

The Korea Army, in reply, agreed tentatively "to treat this affair separately from the Changkufeng Incident" but directed the adoption of a policy of nonenlargement by forbidding pursuit beyond the frontiers.[45] On the afternoon of the 30th Imperial Headquarters in Tokyo also demanded that "the Shatsaofeng affair be handled by adhering to the policy of nonenlargement."[46] Nevertheless General Suetaka, who had been seeking an opportunity to strike at the Russians, acted in collusion with his 75th Infantry Regiment commander, Colonel Satō Kōtoku, who likewise favored the use of force. An attack was arbitrarily planned against the Soviet army positions from Shatsaofeng to Changkufeng for daybreak on July 31. There being no staff officer with them there, Suetaka issued the order simply by scribbling on his personal calling card:

July 30, 5 P.M.

To Colonel Satō:

1) According to Lieutenant-Colonel Senda's report, to the rear of the positions of the enemy who crossed the boundary southwest of Shatsaofeng there were 10–11 tanks and 70–80 infantrymen. They seem to have become active since this morning. 2) You are to deliver a vigorous counterattack . . . once you gather that there is going to be an enemy thrust.

Suetaka[47]

The 19th Division's chief of staff, Colonel Nakamura Yo-shiaki, and Staff Officer Saitō Toshio had been following the Korea Army's policy of nonenlargement of the incident and opposed the division commander's decision. But Suetaka refused to yield, arguing that "the suspension of the offensive by imperial will and this particular situation represent completely different matters. If we do not seize an opportunity such as this to hit the Russians and thus show the power of the imperial army, then the Soviet-Manchukuo border will hereafter be dominated by the Soviet forces, and that will only leave roots of trouble for the future." Reporting was forbidden until the night attack was over lest the army stop it. Thus the offensive was pushed through.[48]

The Satō regiment, with a strength of about 1,600, claimed that "in view of the terrain, in order to sweep out the enemy on the heights southwest of Shatsaofeng, the foe on Changkufeng must be ejected also." [49] Using this as an excuse, the regiment dispatched only one company of the 76th Infantry Regiment, which had been temporarily placed under its control, against Shatsaofeng itself, while turning its main strength, which had already crossed the T'umen river that morning, against Changkufeng; the attack there was begun at 2:15 on the morning of July 31. After engaging in fierce fighting with the Soviet forces, who sent up illuminating shells and laid down withering artillery fire, the Japanese seized Changkufeng crest by 5:15 A.M. and Shatsaofeng by 6 A.M. The Soviet forces were driven off eastward. By noon the battlefield was quiet.

In its report to the high command and the Korea Army headquarters fifteen minutes after its seizure of Changkufeng, the division tried to justify its action by asserting that "since the enemy near Shatsaofeng staged an advance, the Satō unit dealt them a counterattack." Immediately after receiving this report, the Korea Army commander advised the high command that "against the hostile offensive advance and illicit provocation, our front-line units dealt a resolute counterattack." As a consequence, the authorities in Tokyo apparently understood that "on July 29, the night of the 30th, and the morning of the 31st, the Soviet side crossed the border (even that border which they themselves claimed) . . . and made an unlawful assault." [50] The facts, however, seem to be different. Other documentation indicates that the situation near both districts had been quiet after the small fight at Shatsaofeng on the afternoon of the 29th and there was no such thing as a Soviet attack. But "Unit Commander Satō judged that the enemy had an attack in mind . . . and therefore he decided to stage a preventive night assault against the enemy facing him."

Thus it is clear that the actions of Division Commander Suetaka and of Regiment Commander Satō went against the principle of the imperial order. It can be guessed that both officers were well aware of this, too, from the evidence of the Satō regiment's own combat diary which states: "It was a truly awe-inspiring thing, since we have heard that, in accordance with the imperial will, it was decided not to use force against Changkufeng." And according to the memoirs of Division Staff Officer Saitō, when word came from the Korea Army on August 3 that the division's arbitrary night attack had received approval, "tears glistened in the eyes of the division commander at first, and he quickly retired to his room. I too could not control my tears and I sobbed, despite the fact that other people were present."

At Imperial Headquarters in Tokyo the ex post facto account of the night attack brought mixed reactions. But the prevailing feeling was that the front-line division commander's decision, made only after intense pondering, essentially jibed with the intentions of his superiors.[51] After all, the high command itself had privately wished to strike the Soviet forces. But there was the problem of the emperor's views. General Tada, the vice chief of the Army General Staff, went to the imperial villa at Hayama on the 31st, nervously and with every expectation of being reproached. But the arbitrary decision was approved, and Tada came back from Hayama with a beaming countenance.[52]

Since the emperor had given warning, however, against any further aggressive attacks, the Five Ministers Conference the next day (August 1) decided upon the following policy: first, to adhere to the policy of nonenlargement and move matters to diplomatic negotiation as a local problem; second, not to develop military action further as long as the Soviet forces were not provocative; third, in the event that negotiations fell through, to maintain the existing situation in general.[53] In addition, the following instructions were sent out by imperial order No. 163: "The Korea Army commander will, for the time being, occupy approximately the present forward lines in the Chang-kufeng-Shatsaofeng area and will also be on strict guard along the Soviet-Manchukuo frontiers, for which front the army is responsible." Its mission was limited to holding the line, and to reinforce this order new instructions were given the 2nd Air Wing in Hoeryŏng, north Korea, the same day: "Do not engage in combat except in case of self-defense." This had been the policy, but it was restated and, in spite of the subsequent Soviet use of some 150 war planes daily, the repeated requests by local Japanese units for air power were rejected throughout the incident.

The Soviet forces in this area, consisting of the 59th Border Garrison Unit and the 32nd and 40th Divisions under the 39th Infantry Corps, were using the Hsiangshantung district as their forward base.[54] After withdrawing their advance units eastward following the Satō regiment's night attack, they decided to catch the Japanese in a pincers movement, the 32nd Division pushing forward from the northern side of Lake Khasan, while the 40th Division advanced from the southern side. The counterattack began on the night of August 2, with tank and heavy artillery support preceded by air bombings. After furious fighting, during which a Korea Army staff officer, Komatsu Misao, approved, entirely on his own, Suetaka's request on August 2 for air cover of the transportation of concentrating ground units, the Japanese crestline defenders repulsed the first-phase assaults.[55] In accordance with the principles of the decision of August 1, the high command issued strict orders to the Korea Army to hold on, following a policy of nonaggravation and maintaining a strictly defensive stance; in the meantime efforts were made to end the fighting through diplomatic negotiation. But on August 3 Suetaka recommended a flank attack against the Soviet forces by an encirclement movement southward from Huichungyuan, using the 7th Infantry Regiment under Colonel

Ōkido Sanji. Although the Korea Army approved, the Tokyo authorities forbade such action and again ordered that air units must not be committed. Thereafter, the Japanese forces merely defended the crestline, since they were forbidden to take the offensive and could not budge. Vulnerable to Soviet artillery fire and air bombing, their losses mounted steadily.

Within Japanese military circles the idea gained ground that Japan should unilaterally withdraw its troops, inasmuch as the "face" of the local units had been satisfied by the night attack of the 31st, and it was a vital time with the Hankow operation ahead. In the Army Ministry in particular everyone including the vice minister, Lieutenant-General Tōjō Hideki, began to urge withdrawal. Vice Chief of Staff Tada weakened and prepared to issue the order to withdraw when an opportunity should arise during the diplomatic negotiations. The Operations Section under Colonel Inada, however, still clung to its hard attitude and argued that a withdrawal without good reason would serve only to wreck the proud traditions of the imperial army and would have a bad effect upon Soviet-Japanese relations in the future. These conflicting views became entangled with the course of the Shigemitsu-Litvinov parleys of August 4 and 7. No conclusion was reached, and issuance of the official order to withdraw was deferred.

The Soviet side was meanwhile massing its two divisions and on August 6 opened up a second-phase offensive. Among the Japanese troops stubbornly clinging to their hill positions, losses mounted to more than 200 per day. The front-line units clamored for the air force to move in and for a shift to the offensive.[56] Casualties, particularly among the units deployed in the front lines, amounted to 51 percent in the 75th Infantry Regiment and 31 percent in the 76th Regiment. Anxiety sprang up lest the collapse of the 19th Division could not long be checked, even by throwing in Colonel Chō Isamu's 74th Infantry Regiment, the last divisional reserves.[57]

As an emergency measure, Imperial Headquarters transferred the 104th Division, which had been standing by in southern Manchuria under the direct control of the high command, to the Hunch'un district in eastern Manchuria, and on August 9 the division was ordered to assume a position threatening the rear of the Soviet forces. Since the fire power of the artillery directly attached to the 19th Division was weak, consisting only of the 25th Mountain Artillery Regiment under Colonel Tanaka Ryūkichi, steps were taken to send long-range artillery reinforcements from the Kwantung Army in addition to the 15th Heavy Field Artillery Regiment. The Kwantung Army itself pushed forward its main forces to the east Manchurian border in an effort to exert pressure on the USSR.

On August 10 Colonel Terada Masao of the Army General Staff returned from an inspection of the battlefield situation and vigorously expressed his personal opinion that an immediate withdrawal was imperative. Conferences were being held constantly at Imperial Headquarters to study the situation. The general tendency was to sympathize with Colonel Terada's views, but the young officers in the Operations Section put up a stubborn resistance, charging that withdrawal was not proper or that there ought to be a shift to the offensive. Consequently it was decided to wait and see how things went for one more day, but the atmosphere in the Operations Section was "rather gloomy and permeated with a sense of disaster." [58]

At this "eleventh hour" a ceasefire accord was concluded in Moscow. It came as the result of diplomatic negotiations begun on July 15 when the Japanese chargé d'affaires Nishi Haruhiko lodged a protest with Acting Foreign Commissar Stomonyakov against the appearance of Soviet troops on Changkufeng. On July 20 Ambassador Shigemitsu Mamoru hurried back from a trip to Sweden, met with Foreign Commissar Litvinov, and proposed an immediate ceasefire. At this time Litvinov brought out the map attached to the Hunch'un Protocol of 1886 and insisted that this placed Changkufeng in Soviet territory. Shigemitsu refused to look at the map and retorted that settlement of the boundaries was a subject to be discussed by both countries only after a ceasefire agreement had been reached. [59]

After the outbreak of the Shatsaofeng affair Shigemitsu, in accordance with further instructions from the Foreign Ministry, again conferred with Litvinov on August 4 and 7. Litvinov was now prepared to accept the idea of a ceasefire in principle, but

THE JAPANESE-SOVIET CONFRONTATION   153

he still insisted that the Soviet forces had not violated the border. In advancing to Changkufeng they were within their rights, since the Hunch'un Protocol placed the border on the crestline connecting Changkufeng and Shatsaofeng. The ceasefire line, therefore, should be that of July 29, that is, the line of the Soviet advance.

Shigemitsu refused. Even if the Hunch'un Protocol were followed, he argued, Soviet troops had crossed the crestline both at Changkufeng on July 11 and at Shatsaofeng on July 29. In support of the latter charge the Japanese army produced faked photographs of the area, purporting to show Soviet fortifications and corpses at a point "50 meters inside the line." [60] In any event, the Soviet contention concerning the Hunch'un Protocol could not be accepted. Shigemitsu produced other maps at odds with it and insisted that the true boundary was actually east of Lake Khasan. The Soviet forces would have to withdraw, leaving the situation as it was before July 11.

But the situation at the front was not going well for Japan, and the order had already been prepared as early as August 5 for a general withdrawal south of the T'umen river should a ceasefire be unobtainable.[61] Accordingly, on August 10, acting on instructions, Shigemitsu dropped his demand for a Soviet withdrawal. Instead, he offered to have the Japanese forces themselves withdraw one kilometer if the Soviets would agree to a ceasefire. Litvinov agreed, and it was decided that the fighting should end at noon the next day. Then, later the same evening, while the Japanese embassy staff were celebrating the ceasefire with a few drinks, a phone call came from the Soviet Foreign Commissariat. First Secretary Miyagawa Funeo proceeded to the Foreign Commissariat on behalf of the ambassador and was told by Litvinov that it was not necessary for the Japanese troops to pull back one kilometer. The Soviet government preferred the line that both sides were occupying as of midnight on August 10. Shigemitsu surmised that this unexpected compromise must have stemmed from Stalin or the Politburo.[62]

News of the completion of the Moscow agreement came by telegram to the Foreign Ministry in the early hours of August

11. The Japanese high command was delighted. It had been worried about the stipulation of a one kilometer withdrawal, for reasons of "face" affecting the front-line units. Saved from this embarrassment, it decided to withdraw all Japanese forces in a few days. As Inada later recalled, "we didn't have the slightest reluctance about giving up one piddling hill on the border. There was no reason to plant the seeds of future war by continuing forever to confront each other at close range." [63] The Korea Army was ordered to stop the fighting at noon on August 11. Thereupon negotiations concerning local ceasefire arrangements were commenced atop Changkufeng between Colonel Chō Isamu and General Georgi M. Shtern, the chief of staff of the Soviet Far Eastern Army and concurrently commander of the local corps. Agreement was reached that both armies would pull back 80 meters from the peak.[64] In a way, the Changkufeng Incident had been settled.

The 19th Division, made up of foot soldiers and weak artillery, amazed foreigners by its defense against Soviet forces who were more than twice the Japanese in numbers and were supported by a powerful air force, tanks, and artillery. The Japanese troops accomplished the defense of the Hunch'un Protocol "border line" until the very day of the ceasefire; but their losses were appreciable, amounting to 526 killed and 914 wounded, for a total of 1,440; and soon after the ceasefire the Japanese turned the Hunch'un line over to the Soviets and pulled back to the southern banks of the T'umen river. In the 19th Division the casualty rate had reached 21 percent. Soviet losses, according to Tass, were 236 killed and 611 wounded.

The Soviets had won a victory, and they followed up their extensive propaganda surrounding the affair by lauding the exploits of the "heroes of Lake Khasan." [65] At the time, however, in spite of their military adversities and withdrawal, the Japanese did not interpret the outcome of the incident as necessarily constituting a defeat.

Army General Staff Operations Section Chief Inada, who claims to have roused the activists on the staff and in the Army Ministry to consider the use of force, insists that the Changkufeng Incident was not a case of defeat in combat. It was, rather, a limited, strategic "reconnaissance in force" that achieved its purpose quite satisfactorily.[66] "There was a tendency," Inada recalls, for the high command at the time "to hesitate to intensify operations against China because of uneasiness lest the Soviets intervene." If the China War was to be prosecuted with confidence, it was essential to be clear as to Soviet intentions. For this purpose he proposed a "reconnaissance in force" to deal the Soviets a blow at a point where the terrain would make it difficult for the engagement to escalate into major hostilities. Changkufeng was ideally situated. His plan was to commit only the 19th Division; the use of tanks and planes would be avoided insofar as possible, and there would be no pursuit operations across the border. If the Soviet Union intended to intervene in the Sino-Japanese conflict, it could be expected not to limit its response to such an inconvenient point as Changkufeng but rather would broaden the conflict by counterattacking at some other sector on the Manchukuo border.[67] In that case the Hankow campaign would need to be suspended; otherwise it could go ahead. In any event, to keep the strategic probe as limited as possible, operations should be handled directly by Imperial Headquarters in Tokyo rather than by the Korea or Kwantung Army commands, and diplomatic negotiations should be pursued simultaneously.

Although, says Inada, his concept was formally blocked by the emperor on July 20, before it could be initiated, it provided the germ for the activists and was actually put into execution on July 31 when Division Commander Suetaka, who had fathomed the true intentions of Imperial Headquarters, launched the night attack on Changkufeng and Shatsaofeng. Subsequent operations were directed by Imperial Headquarters, and the 19th Division carried out its mission and returned to its original position as expected. The chief difficulty with Inada's explanation is that it remains unclear how many of the activists at headquarters were really motivated by such a scheme at the time. All who were intimately involved in the affair—Hashimoto Gun, Arao Okikatsu, and Imoto Kumao—deny it, Hashimoto's denial being particularly significant, since he was then a major-general, chief of the Operations Division, and therefore Inada's immediate superior.

Foreign Minister Ugaki, for his part, found satisfaction in the fact that the diplomatic service obtained a ceasefire on terms better than had been expected. He credited, first of all, the brave fighting of the troops and the firm resolve of the army. Second, he noted that as the incident continued, world press opinion had become more sympathetic to Japan, and he felt that the attitude of Britain and France, in particular, might have been influential in helping to restrain the USSR. Finally, he thought that the Soviet decision to stop reflected the shakiness of the political situation in the USSR.[68] Ambassador Shigemitsu was especially jubilant over the last-minute offer of the Soviets not to insist that Japanese troops withdraw the one kilometer agreed on. A "diplomatic victory," Shigemitsu hailed it. Inada, however, is not so sure. Judging from the persistence of the Soviet ground assaults on the night of August 10, only hours before the ceasefire, and from the fact that they did finally capture a corner of the southern crest of Changkufeng heights, he suggests that the apparent concession was made in confidence that the Soviet forces would be able that evening to seize the crestline.[69]

Whatever the reasons, Japan was able to avoid charging into a decisive crisis entailing a two-front war against China and the USSR. But what if the Soviet Union had dared to intervene in the Sino-Japanese struggle at that particular point? One may suppose that Japan might not have escaped the danger of losing both Manchuria and Korea, even if the Japanese forces had stopped the Hankow campaign and headed north. In this respect, Japan was playing with fire.

Many of the lessons of the Changkufeng Incident were hardly reflected upon. For instance, although this was the first experience of the Japanese forces with the capabilities of the Soviet military in modern warfare, the Japanese army allowed themselves to be distracted by the limited scope of the fighting, thereby overlooking the superiority of Soviet military production. Japan's supplies in fact were so inadequate that when

Korea Army Staff Officer Iwasaki Tamio, concerned over the Soviet tanks, came to Tokyo and asked for supplies of antitank am-
munitions, he was turned down on the grounds that even the
stocks allocated for November 1938 for the Hankow operation
had already been sent out.[70]

The incident, however, remained as an example that arbitrary action undertaken by a local unit, even when coming close
to violating an imperial order, was accepted without censure.
Still, there was speedy retribution when the Nomonhan Incident broke out, only one year later.

The Nomonhan Incident, May–September 1939

On May 11, 1939, some 70 to 80 Outer Mongolian army troops
dashed across the Halha river in an area 15 kilometers southwest of Nomonhan (in turn, 170 kilometers southwest of the city
of Hailaerh) in the northwest part of Manchukuo and clashed
with the Manchukuo Army garrison there. Thus began what the
Japanese termed the Nomonhan Incident and the Russians
were to call the incident of Khalkhin-gol.[71]

From the historical standpoint, this was an area where the
Mongols of Inner Mongolia and those of Outer Mongolia had
been contending for pastureland since the days of the Ch'ing
dynasty. There was no distinct boundary line. After the Manchurian Incident both Japan and Manchukuo, accepting the
contentions of the Hulun Buyr Mongols, arbitrarily recognized
the natural boundary of the Halha river as the frontier.[72] As we
have seen, from about 1935 frequent clashes occurred with the
Outer Mongolian army. Demarcation of the borders through
diplomatic negotiation was discussed, but the consummation of
the Soviet-Outer Mongolian mutual assistance pact caused
disruption of the parleys. The Nomonhan Incident occurred at a
time when the claims of both parties were far apart.

The Soviet-Outer Mongol side insisted upon a line east of
the Halha. Apart from legal grounds, they cited maps published
by the following agencies: the Chinese Postal Administration,
Peking, 1919; the East Asia Common Script Association, 1932;

the Kwantung Government-General, 1919, 1926, 1934; and the Kwantung Army Staff 1937. At the Tokyo trials it was shown that from 1935 the Kwantung Government-General maps changed the frontier to the line of the Halha river. At the Chita Conference held after the Nomonhan Incident, however, the Japanese submitted 18 different maps indicating that the Halha was the boundary recognized in Chinese Army General Staff maps of 1918.

The report of the incident from Lieutenant-General Komatsubara Michitarō, commander of the 23rd Division stationed at Hailaerh, reached Kwantung Army headquarters on May 13. (See Table 2 for the composition of the Kwantung Army at this time.) Not one of the staff officers had heard of Nomonhan: only with magnifying glasses could they spot the place on the map. Under such circumstances they had difficulty deciding whether it was simply a case where a group of Outer Mongolian cavalrymen had crossed the Halha river to water their horses and then baited the feeble Manchukuo Army, or whether it was a matter

TABLE 2. COMPOSITION OF THE KWANTUNG ARMY AS OF THE END OF APRIL 1939 *

Kwantung Army Headquarters

Third Army (at Mutanchiang):	2nd, 8th, 12th Divisions
	1st, 2nd Border Garrison Units
Fifth Army (at Tungan):	11th Division, 3rd Cavalry Brigade
	3rd, 4th Border Garrison Units
Fourth Army (at Peian):	1st Division
	5th, 6th, 7th Border Garrison Units

4th Division (at Chiamussu)
7th Division (at Tsitsihar)
23rd Division (at Hailaerh):   8th Border Garrison Unit
1st, 2nd, 3rd, 4th, 5th Independent Border Garrison Units
1st Tank Corps (at Kungchuling)
2nd Air Group (at Hsinching)
Kwantung Army Artillery Headquarters
Manchukuo Army (in wartime)
Military Advisers Section
OSS: Harbin Headquarters

* Forces under the Kwantung Army commander. Data revised by translator on basis of Figure 11 in U.S. Army, Office of the Chief of Military History, Japanese Research Division, *The Nomonhan Incident*, Vol. 11, Part 3, Book B (1956).

of reconnaissance fighting directed by Moscow.[73] Certainly nobody judged that the affair would develop into a major clash. After all, Hulun Buyr, the locale that actually became the scene of the battles of Nomonhan, was a vast deserted steppe lying more than 300 kilometers from the rail terminals of both sides, a difficult location for supplying large forces.

Up to this time General Komatsubara had not paid much attention to the usual border trespasses by Outer Mongolian cavalrymen, even when they became particularly active after March and April 1939. But now he decided that the time had come to act. He was motivated no doubt by the new policy of the Kwantung Army. That army had traditionally adopted a vigorous attitude toward border disputes quite unsuited to its real strength; since the time of the Changkufeng Incident it had become more rebellious against the negative attitude of the high command. In April 1939 the Kwantung Army drafted a new operations order entitled "Principles for the Settlement of Soviet-Manchurian Border Disputes"; and on the 25th of that month Kwantung Army Commander Ueda Kenkichi enunciated these principles to a corps commanders' conference. Drawn up by Staff Officer Tsuji Masanobu, who held extremely strong views, the "Principles" stipulated that "the frequent occurrence and enlargement of incidents can be prevented only by resolute and thorough punishment, the fundamental principle being 'neither invade nor allow invasion.' " Illicit actions on the part of the Soviets could not be crushed by following the high command's weak injunctions "not to invade, even if we are invaded." Included were noteworthy sections that completely ignored not only the government but also the attitude of the army high command. For example, the following: "In areas where the border lines are indistinct, the defense commander shall determine a boundary on his own." He was allowed "to invade Soviet territory temporarily, or to decoy Soviet soldiers and get them into Manchukuoan territory." [74] One can surmise that the reason Komatsubara suddenly adopted the concept of striking a blow stemmed from the promulgation of this aggressive policy.

On the night of May 13, in accord with this policy and after eliciting Kwantung Army approval, General Komatsubara dis-

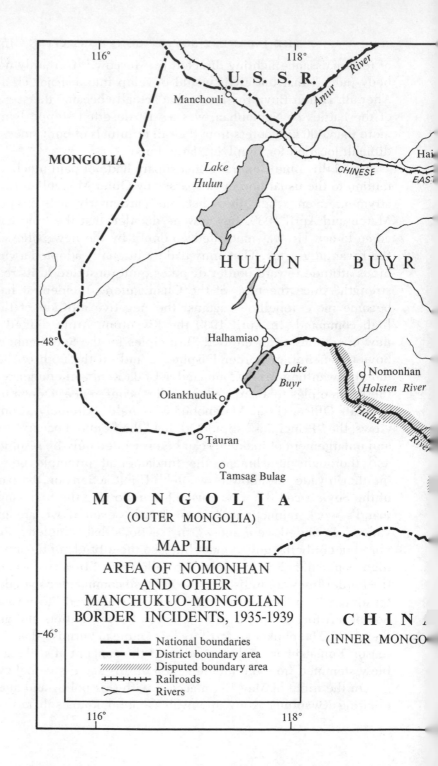

MAP III

AREA OF NOMONHAN
AND OTHER
MANCHUKUO-MONGOLIAN
BORDER INCIDENTS, 1935-1939

- ·—··—··— National boundaries
- — — — — District boundary area
- //////// Disputed boundary area
- +++++++ Railroads
- ⌒⌒ Rivers

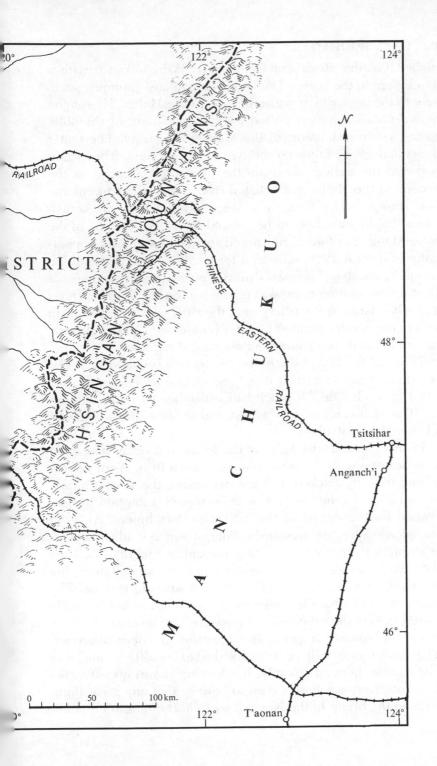

patched Cavalry Regiment Commander Azuma Yaozō with a detachment to the scene. The Outer Mongolians promptly withdrew to the opposite or western shore of the Halha. Thereupon the Azuma detachment pulled back on the night of the 16th, leaving behind elements of the Manchukuo Army. The Outer Mongolian forces followed the Azuma detachment. They again moved to the eastern shore on the 17th, built a bridge at the junction of the Halha and Holsten rivers, and began to enlarge their strength. The Kwantung Army advised General Komatsubara that he ought not to be swayed by every "twitch" of the Outer Mongolian forces; he should seize an appropriate opportunity to destroy them once and for all. But when Colonel Yamagata Takemitsu [75] promptly moved out with a detachment of about a thousand men, he was enveloped on the 28th by Outer Mongolian tanks and artillery near the river crossing. The main body of the cavalry regiment, under Lieutenant-Colonel Azuma, was annihilated; the Yamagata detachment fell back.[76]

Thus did the first phase of the Nomonhan Incident end. The Kwantung Army described it as "one victory for each side, one defeat for each side," [77] but it had really been a one-sided defeat. The Azuma regiment was lost, and remorse ate at the heart of General Komatsubara.

In this phase of the fighting the Kwantung Army had acted in accordance with the principles laid down in its April policy: striking back if attacked, but not expanding the situation, and seeking a local solution. Hence there was no intention to seek revenge for the defeat of the Yamagata detachment. As Tsuji later recalled his feelings at the time, it was not advantageous for strength to be tied up in the Nomonhan vicinity at a time when the Japanese were engaged at home and abroad in coping with the China Incident and the tense situation in Europe. The affair ought to be handled appropriately, of course, but he really wanted to look the other way, if possible, and have no dealings with it.[78] Likewise, Imperial Headquarters in Tokyo observed: "The Soviet side will continually do vexing things, and one must handle them adequately; but looking at various estimates of the situation, we find it hard to believe that any great problem is in the offing in the Nomonhan area. It ought to be rather easy to achieve the objective of chastisement." [79] Headquarters was confident that "the Kwantung Army's intentions at the time of the outbreak of the incident rather clearly coincided with the thinking of the high command." Consequently it decided on a policy of leaving matters for independent handling by the Kwantung Army insofar as possible.[80] And Commander Ueda, expecting the incident to be settled locally, left to inspect the newly-established Fourth Army on the northern front.

It was not until the second phase of the Nomonhan Incident started on June 19 that conflict materialized between the high command in Tokyo and the Kwantung Army concerning the handling of the incident. That morning, the day after Ueda's inspection party had returned to Hsinching, another telegram arrived from 23rd Division Commander Komatsubara, asserting that the Soviet forces in the vicinity of Nomonhan had gradually been built up and on the 18th had driven the Manchukuoan troops back, and that enemy bombers had attacked key strategic points in the rear, at Hailaerh, Aerhshan, and Kanchuerhmiao.[81] Komatsubara indicated that he would like to proceed to punish the enemy again, out of a sense of responsibility for defense. A Kwantung Army staff officers' conference considered the question. The senior staff officer, Colonel Terada Masao, argued that a counterattack should not be considered until such issues with Britain as the Tientsin Concession had been settled; but he was alone in his view, and it was shunted aside by Staff Officers Tsuji Masanobu and Hattori Takushirō who, as advocates of a strong stand, came to formulate the Kwantung Army's policy toward the entire incident.[82] They argued that the affair ought to be judged as a provocation on the part of the Soviet and Mongolian armies. Demonstration of Japan's firm resolve, by dealing out a thorough counterattack, could be expected to alleviate the risk of all-out hostilities.

Accordingly, the Kwantung Army proposed to mass forces close to the maximum. To the entire strength of the 23rd Division and the main body of the 2nd Air Group [83] would be added a detachment commanded by Lieutenant-General Yasuoka Masaomi and built around two regiments of medium and light tanks, one motorized artillery regiment, and one infantry regi-

ment from the 7th Division.[84] Excluding only those forces necessary for the Kwantung Army to defend the other fronts, some
15,000 men were available for commitment, including 13 infantry battalions, 120 antitank guns, around 70 tanks, 400 vehi-
cles, and 180 planes. Somewhat exceeding the Soviet-Mongol
strength on the battlefront, these forces were judged to constitute something resembling "a meat cleaver for slicing up a
chicken." [85]

After the central army authorities were notified of the
Kwantung Army's resolve, a clash of opinion arose between the
Army Ministry and the General Staff, where Major-General Hashimoto Gun continued as chief of the Operations Division and
Colonel Inada Masazumi as chief of the subordinate Operations
Section. The ministry opposed the operation, arguing that it
would be meaningless to pour troops of strategic-unit size into a
trifling border dispute when Japan had to bear the burden of
hostilities in China. The argument of the General Staff was that
the plan should be approved out of respect for the position of
the Kwantung Army commander. Eventually, with the support
of Army Minister Itagaki, the Kwantung Army's plans were approved.[86]

The fact remained, however, that the Kwantung Army included in its counterattack plan an air thrust beyond the border
for which it deliberately evaded eliciting the high command's
prior approval, expecting that Tokyo would be opposed. The
plan called for an attack on Tamsagbulag airfield in Outer
Mongolia. Kwantung Army Commander Ueda had issued instructions to the 2nd Air Group commander on June 23, but to
hide his intentions, particularly from the high command, the
use of telegrams was avoided.[87] The scheduled air assault was
set for a day or two before July 1, when ground operations were
scheduled to begin. The idea was to forestall any action by the
Soviet-Mongol air force. Despite these efforts at secrecy, the
plan leaked out, thanks to Kwantung Army Staff Officer Katakura Tadashi, who visited Tokyo at this time. The Army General Staff was shocked and sent out a telegram saying that
"bombing beyond the frontiers would cause both sides gradually to spread the fighting into Outer Mongolia, and this would

serve also to prolong the incident. Therefore, we are of the opinion that such action would be inappropriate." The Operations desk chief, Lieutenant-Colonel Arisue Yadoru, was promptly dispatched to Manchuria.[88] Learning of this and expecting that Colonel Arisue would bring an official suspension order, Staff Officer Tsuji himself made the decision not to call the attack off but to move it up to June 27. In addition, Kwantung Army Staff Officer Shimanuki Takeji, who went to Tokyo with the attack order, did not deliver it until just after the execution of the air raid, although he had reached the capital the day before.[89]

Thus the air assault was launched with more than 130 planes on the morning of June 27, the day Colonel Arisue arrived in Hsinching. Staff Officer Terada Masao immediately phoned in a report from Hsinching to Tokyo about the "immense combat results" achieved during the air raid on Tamsagbulag: 99 enemy planes were reported shot down and 25 smashed on the ground. But Operations Section Chief Inada, an old classmate of Terada, only roared, "You fool! Combat results—so what?" [90] The high command was furious at the "amoral and devious attitude" of the Kwantung Army. "They had guaranteed not to aggravate matters," said Inada, "yet they went ahead and did it, knowing fully that the high command would have been opposed." [91] Imperial Headquarters Army Order No. 320 was promptly sent to the Kwantung Army directly forbidding attacks on enemy air bases in Outer Mongolia. In addition, the order read, "depending upon the situation, areas where boundaries between neighboring countries and Manchukuo are in dispute and where the use of force is inconvenient need not be defended by force." [92] The vice chief of the Army General Staff, General Nakajima Tetsuzō, went to the palace promptly to render a report to the Throne and was reprimanded sternly by the emperor for the violation of the imperial prerogative of supreme command. The imperial will was unofficially made known to the effect that at least the Kwantung Army commander should be disciplined. Nakajima replied that operations were still going on but promised that censure would be imposed when that phase was concluded.[93]

The Kwantung Army, however, had been offended by what it regarded as Inada's "insolent words." Its staff insisted: "Tremendous combat results were achieved by carrying things out at the risk of our lives. It was also very clear that we were undertaking an act of retaliation. What kind of General Staff ignores the psychology of the front lines and tramples on their feelings?" [94] In fact, the Kwantung Army was so worked up that it sent a telegram to Tokyo asserting, "Although our view seems to differ somewhat from that of headquarters in regard to evaluation and technique on the spot, with respect to the trifling affair in the north kindly set your mind at ease and rely upon our army." [95] The struggle between the high command and the Kwantung Army now entered a critical stage.

Offensive action by the 23rd Division and the Yasuoka detachment commenced on July 1. The ground units were judged to be far stronger than the opposing forces; in addition, the Japanese army controlled the air, the result of hard fighting by the fighter-plane units committed since the end of May as well as the air raid against Tamsagbulag. Staff Officers Tsuji and Hattori had devised a bold operational plan to build a bridge across the Halha river and charge deep into the rear of the enemy positions on the left bank.

The main Japanese infantry force crossed to the left bank of the river as scheduled on the night of July 2 and then pushed southward along the river. There they were attacked by a huge force of several hundred Soviet tanks. By firing their 36 antitank guns and employing Molotov cocktails at close range, the Japanese troops set more than 100 tanks afire; but from the afternoon of the 3rd the battle situation deteriorated. With only one poor bridge, they had no prospects of obtaining adequate supplies of water and ammunition. On the night of the 3rd the Japanese were forced to pull back across the river.[96]

Meanwhile the Yasuoka detachment, which had attacked Soviet-Mongolian positions near the junction of the Halha and Holsten rivers, had had 40 tanks knocked out and had also pulled back. From July 5 the detachment resumed the offensive in conjunction with the main body of the 23rd Division but became bogged down in the face of vigorous fire from heavy artillery and tanks. From the 11th the Japanese forces could do no more than hold their positions, and the remnants of the Yasuoka detachment were withdrawn. The sole mechanized brigade Japan possessed at the time was the 1st Tank Corps, comprising the 3rd and 4th Tank Regiments of the Yasuoka detachment; but its main strength—the Type 89 medium tanks—had thin armor (17 mm.), which was penetrated by the Soviet forces' 47 mm. antitank guns. At the same time, the short-barrelled Japanese 57 mm. cannon had no capability against the Soviet tanks.[97]

The Kwantung Army observed that the reason for defeat in the second-phase fighting derived from misjudgment of the enemy's strength, which was actually one-and-a-half to two times greater than anticipated and particularly from a shortage of artillery. To remedy this situation, Japanese heavy artillery units were brought up, and a new offensive was mounted on July 23. On that and the following day, 86 heavy guns were committed to the fighting, with the intention of overwhelming the Soviet fire power by firing 15,000 shells a day. But the Russians responded with a quantity exceeding that figure, and the Japanese had the fact driven home that they could not match the enemy in matériel and supply.[98] This attack also ended in failure.

The high command in Tokyo now saw that it would be difficult to gain a military victory in the fighting at Nomonhan and inclined toward ending the battle even if concessions had to be made. But the Kwantung Army, insisting that the second-phase fighting represented a "tie" because Soviet losses were also severe, showed a reluctance to yield even one foot.[99]

On July 16 Soviet planes bombed the Nonni bridge at Fulaerhchi, a suburb of Tsitsihar. Although there were no losses, the Kwantung Army was shocked and immediately ordered the institution of combat alert measures and wartime air defense regulations for all units in Manchuria. It also asked Tokyo to rescind its June 29 order forbidding the bombing of bases in Outer Mongolia. But the high command responded coldly, saying that "bombings inside Manchukuo should be and can be endured, in accord with the principles of local settlement." In this view, the bombing of Fulaerhchi was only natural as a retaliation for the Tamsagbulag raid.[100] Consequently, feelings between Tokyo and Hsinching deteriorated steadily.

On July 20 the chief of staff of the Kwantung Army, General Isogai Rensuke, who had been asked to visit Tokyo, was urged, in the presence of military authorities from the vice chief of the Army General Staff down, to end the Nomonhan Incident unilaterally. He was then handed the "Principles for the Settlement of the Nomonhan Incident," a policy that advanced a step beyond the principles of the imperial order of June 29. "In accordance with the policy of localizing the affair," the "Principles" read, "endeavor to terminate the incident by the coming winter at the latest." While holding on to the right bank of the Halha river, the Japanese were to seize an opportunity to enter into diplomatic negotiation. In the event discussions were not successful, forces would be withdrawn with the advent of the winter season to the boundary claimed by the Soviet army. This was now understood to be somewhat east of the right bank.

Operations Division Chief Hashimoto Gun recalls that an argument ensued between himself and General Isogai. Hashimoto contended that since there was more than one boundary in question, it was possible to pull back to the line claimed by the Russians. Isogai stubbornly resisted. Vice Chief of Staff Nakajima tried to tone things down by saying, "Boundary settlements cannot be decided here." But Isogai stuck to his contention that, since the Red Army had no all-out war in mind, localization of the dispute could be expected only if Japan maintained a firm attitude and struck a thorough blow. From the standpoint of the Kwantung Army command, he could not approve a pull-back from the vicinity of the right bank of the Halha river, where the blood of several thousand soldiers had been spilled. Eventually, after arguing, Isogai promised to study the "Principles" and returned with the summary, but the Kwantung Army ignored it.[101] At this point Imperial Headquarters began to feel that if it were to recover control of the Kwantung Army, the leadership of that army would have to be changed.[102]

On July 21, Colonel Doi Akio, military attaché in the Soviet Union, reported to Tokyo that the Russians were sending reinforcements to the Far East in rapid succession. About this time also the Army General Staff Intelligence Division and the Kwantung Army Intelligence Section obtained information to the effect that the Soviet-Mongolian forces would go over to the offensive around the middle of August.[103] But the scale of the Soviets' planned offensive was underestimated. The General Staff Intelligence Division judged that "if it were simply a question of thwarting an enemy offensive, present strength would suffice," and the Operations Division concurred. Doi thought the Japanese should build fortifications east of the Halha and hold on until winter. And the Kwantung Army judged that the fighting at Nomonhan had already passed the peak of intensity and would now settle down into a struggle of endurance. It still wanted the June 29 prohibition of air strikes against targets in Outer Mongolia lifted, however, and when Lieutenant-Colonel Tanikawa Kazuo and Major Shimamura Noriyasu, who went to Manchuria at the end of July, returned to Tokyo, they seemed to have been infected by the atmosphere in the Kwantung Army and urged that permission be given. On August 7 Imperial Headquarters gave its approval.[104] Beyond this, all that was done was to set up a new Sixth Army under Lieutenant-General Ogisu Ryūhei on August 10 to provide unified command; no reinforcements were sent. This misestimate of Soviet strength was the main reason the 23rd Division was dealt a smashing blow in the Soviet offensive, which commenced on August 20 accompanied by a furious artillery bombardment.

The Japanese also suffered at this time from lack of sufficient aerial reconnaissance, which could not be conducted because of continuously bad weather lasting some two weeks. Thus, it was not until around August 27 that they discovered they faced a Soviet force four or five times their own: three infantry divisions and five tank brigades in the front line and two additional divisions in the second line.[105]

Against these forces the Sixth Army undertook a counteroffensive operation on August 24, employing the wounded 23rd Division and the Morita brigade [106] of the 7th Division. As a result of lessons learned during the preceding combat, the Soviet army threw in new types of tanks (replacing gasoline engines with models using crude-oil fuel and covering tank chassis with wire nets). Against these the Japanese rapid-fire guns and incendiary bottles proved utterly ineffective. A tragic struggle developed between "iron and flesh." [107] The Japanese were enveloped by the superior Soviet forces, cut off in many localities, dealt losses approaching annihilation, and obliged to pull back at the end of the month. In addition, the war in the air, in which Japan had held the supremacy at the outset, now gradually inclined to the Soviet side. If the Soviet forces had pressed a pursuit at this time, the Sixth Army would have fallen into uncontrollable confusion; but the Russians halted at the boundary line they had been claiming and began to build positions.[108]

The Kwantung Army then lost its head. It stiffened its resolve for a showdown with the Soviet forces and on August 27 took far-reaching decisions that were incorporated in a paper entitled "Countermeasures to Deal with Changes in the European Situation." [109] Staff Officer Terada promptly communicated the new plan personally to Operations Section Chief Inada, while another staff officer, Isomura Takesuke, was sent to Tokyo to make a formal presentation. The Kwantung Army's plan was to mount a major assault immediately. It would throw into the Sixth Army the 2nd, 4th, 7th, and 8th Divisions, as well as all the heavy artillery and rapid-fire guns in Manchuria. The proposal now was to commit large forces all at once, contrary to the idea of piecemeal employment that one critic called "the chariness of the poor in spending pin money." [110] Since there was still a gap in tank, heavy artillery, and air strength, however, the army judged that it was unable to adopt orthodox tactics. Instead, it proposed to break through the enemy positions in six days of unrelenting night assaults, beginning on September 10.[111] But even this battle was seen only as a prelude to large-scale war with the Soviet Union in the spring. The Kwantung Army's plan, as Terada summarized it for Inada, was "to concentrate four divisions and strike a blow"; but it recognized that with the coming of October, "severe cold will make major operations impossible." Imperial Headquarters should use the winter months so that it would "be prepared to mobilize the entire army to engage in decisive combat" with the Soviet Union in the spring.[112] Terada's letter convinced Tokyo that the time had come for a firm decision.

On August 30 Army General Staff Vice Chief Nakajima flew to Hsinching and delivered Imperial Order No. 343,[113] which stipulated that "the Kwantung Army commander is to hold his position with minimal strength" to "insure a quick end to operations in the Nomonhan area, without enlargement, insofar as possible." By this euphemistic phraseology Imperial Headquarters ordered the suspension of the offensive. But the Kwantung Army was adamant. It would not retreat from its plan to "deal a great blow to the enemy, by concentrating and manifesting maximum strength in a short period, and afterward to withdraw the forces swiftly." In the end Nakajima and an accompanying officer, Lieutenant-Colonel Takatsuki Tamotsu, like Tanikawa and Shimamura a month before, were themselves infected by the atmosphere in Kwantung Army headquarters. They made commitments that seemed to sanction the mounting of the September 10 offensive.[114] At a party given by the army commander that night, talk was open and unreserved. The Kwantung Army was delighted that the conflict with the high command had been completely settled and was certain of victory in its next offensive.

Imperial Headquarters was not at all pleased. When General Nakajima returned to Tokyo, Operations Division Chief Hashimoto expressed the judgment that tanks and artillery were in short supply and that even if the Kwantung Army were reinforced, a target date of September 10 could not be met. Moreover, Third Army Commander Tada Hayao in eastern Manchuria was opposed to a reduction of forces there. Headquarters was also strongly influenced on September 1 by news that the German army had invaded Poland. To cope with further changes in the world situation the Japanese high command saw the necessity, all the more keenly, for ending the Nomonhan Incident. At a conference on the night of September 2 unilateral termination of the incident was decided upon: no ceasefire negotiations, but suspension of the offensive.[115] On September 4 General Nakajima flew back to Hsinching from Tokyo, bearing

Imperial Order No. 349,[116] which stated, in essence, that the offensive planned for September 10 was called off and that the forces must be separated and withdrawn. The Kwantung Army staff officers who met Nakajima blamed him for the change and argued for permission to launch an operation designed at least to retrieve the dead. But Nakajima repeatedly replied, "It is an imperial order," and this time would not give in.[117]

When Kwantung Army Commander Ueda once more asked the chief of the Army General Staff for permission to clean up the battlefield, indicating that if the request were not approved he would respectfully desire removal from his post, he was told on September 6 that the imperial order was to be obeyed; [118] on September 7 he was relieved of command, General Umezu Yoshijirō being appointed the new commander and Lieutenant-General Iimura Yuzuru the new chief of staff.[119] As the battlefield fell silent after August 31, except for the sector south of the Handagal area, the diplomats took over.

The Japanese government, separate from the high command, had been keeping an eye on the Kwantung Army's conduct of the Nomonhan affair.[120] Its concerns were two: first, that the matter should be treated as a local problem between Manchukuo and Outer Mongolia and handled so as not to enlarge it; second, that Japan might acknowledge the existence of the Soviet-Mongolian mutual assistance pact de facto, but it should be careful to take no action that would seem to sanction Soviet influence over Outer Mongolia.

It soon became evident that the incident was being expanded, particularly with the Fulaerhchi bombing episode on July 16. While the Kwantung Army used this occasion to press again for the right to bomb Outer Mongolia, the authorities in Tokyo judged that it would now be advantageous to strive to control the incident as soon as possible. Army Minister Itagaki proposed to Foreign Minister Arita Hachirō that matters be speedily shifted into diplomatic channels.[121] Accordingly, on the 17th the Five Ministers Conference decided that the nonenlargement policy should be retained and diplomatic negotiations opened at an appropriate time.

On the basis of this decision the Foreign Ministry on July 20 instructed Ambassador Tōgō Shigenori in Moscow to seek a suitable opportunity during other conversations, possibly regarding the concessions problem, to indicate Japan's intention of settling the incident, but taking care not to convey the impression that it was overly eager to reach a settlement. At the same time concrete conditions were drafted for a local ceasefire. The preferred plan called for both armies to suspend operations, on the pledge that neither would cross the Halha river. Alternatives, should this plan be unacceptable, provided for a ceasefire in place, as of an agreed-upon time, or for a mutual pull-back by the two sides an equal distance from the ceasefire line, as of an agreed-upon time.[122]

When the Kwantung Army was shown these drafts on July 28, it reacted strongly. In a telegram to Army Vice Chief of Staff Nakajima on July 30 the Kwantung Army chief of staff insisted that the Russians had first to be hit and hit hard. He opposed absolutely any intimation that Japan was contemplating a ceasefire and pointed to a telegram of June 3 from the Army Ministry's Military Affairs Bureau advising that Japan was insisting upon the Halha river as the boundary. It would not be wise now, he argued, to retreat to the alternative proposals. Moreover, according to intelligence reports the Soviets were adopting a firm attitude, so there was no prospect that they would accede to a ceasefire even if it were suggested by the Japanese side; indeed, any such proposal would be exploited for its propaganda value.[123]

The high command hesitated; Ambassador Tōgō waited for the feud between Tokyo and the Kwantung Army to be settled; the negotiations were put off.[124] Then on August 22, while Tōgō was conferring with Vice Foreign Commissar Solomon Lozovsky about the concessions problem, the latter mentioned several times that Russia would like to examine the Nomonhan case if the request were made by the Japanese, making it clear that his government too desired a solution of the incident through diplomatic negotiation. On the 28th, therefore, while the Kwantung Army was planning a major new offensive with four fresh divisions, the Foreign Ministry gave Tōgō instructions to commence discussions without delay.[125] Two days later the Kwantung Army was ordered to desist.

On September 4 and 6 Tōgō was sent increasingly detailed directives, and on September 8, the day following the change in command of the Kwantung Army, he received the final ceasefire plan. It included three alternatives.[126] Plan 1 called for the Nomonhan area to be made into a buffer zone until demarcation of the frontier was effected. Plan 2 provided that neither army should cross the front lines existing in the buffer zone, as of the ceasefire time, until border demarcation was accomplished. Plan 3, representing the maximum concession, proposed that neither army should cross the boundary line claimed by Outer Mongolia until the border was demarcated. Discussions were to be entered as part of a general readjustment of relations, so as to mask Japan's military weakness.

The next day, September 9, Tōgō conferred with Foreign Commissar Vyacheslav M. Molotov and broached the first proposal, prefacing it by saying that the Japanese army was about to unleash a major offensive, in which case a rapprochement between the two countries would become extremely difficult, and suggesting a settlement in order to prevent such a circumstance. Tōgō proposed that a commission to deal with disputes be established, its purpose being to seek a peaceable solution of general frontier issues; that the boundary in the Nomonhan sector be demarcated; and that negotiations for a treaty of commerce be commenced.[127]

On the 10th Molotov presented to Tōgō a proposal that approximated plan 3 of the Japanese: the Russians would agree to the establishment of a border demarcation commission and a body to handle disputes as well as to the working out of a treaty of commerce, but in the Nomonhan area both sides would have to withdraw on the basis of the boundary claimed by the Soviets.[128]

Tōgō conferred again with Molotov on September 14 and submitted his second proposal, which yielded a bit. The next day Molotov accepted this second plan and proposed entrusting the demarcation of the frontier to a commission to be set up in

the near future.[129] The Japanese-Manchukuo forces and the Soviet-Mongolian forces were to suspend all military action at
2 A.M. (Moscow time) on September 16, and both armies were to
hold the lines they occupied as of 1 P.M. (Moscow time) on September 15. For purposes of boundary demarcation a committee
was to be set up, consisting of representatives from the four
countries involved.

The mutual exchange of prisoners was carried out smoothly,
but during the border demarcation conferences held at Chita in
December 1939 and in Harbin in January 1940, the two sides
produced conflicting maps and historical evidence to support
their claims, and no agreement could be reached. Eventually
the problem was shifted to negotiations between Tōgō and
Molotov in Moscow. On July 18, 1940 Japan "endured the un-
endurable" and signed an agreement recognizing essentially
the boundaries claimed by the Soviet side, except that Japan
gained a bit of land in the Aerhshan area southeast of Nomonhan.[130] As the result of Japan's concession the affair was finally
settled.

Although the Nomonhan Incident in many ways resembled
the Changkufeng affair of the year before, it ended in even
greater defeat, both militarily and diplomatically. Not only did
the Nomonhan Incident infect the Japanese military and others
with a profound sense of failure, but it also served as one cause
for the change in subsequent policy toward the Soviet Union.
In this respect, the Nomonhan Incident possessed a far greater
significance.

In its military aspect the Japanese from beginning to end
misjudged Soviet-Mongolian military strength and supply capabilities; and the Kwantung Army sustained a total defeat that
was inexcusable in every respect. Japanese casualties rose to
8,440 killed and 8,766 wounded, for a total exceeding 17,000.
The 23rd Division, in particular, suffered an annihilating blow:
more than 11,000 casualties, or 73 percent of its entire strength.
In all approximately 56,000 Japanese forces were committed;
the overall casualty rates reached 32 percent compared with 17
percent at Liaoyang and 28 percent at Mukden during the
Russo-Japanese War, and only 6 percent for the infantry at Hsu-

chou.[131] Soviet-Mongolian casualties cannot be ascertained, but at the Tokyo trials they were said to have exceeded 9,000. The image of the "invincible Kwantung Army" now underwent a complete reversal. The fact that quite a few unit commanders were discharged for retreating without orders or committed suicide also sullied the "glorious tradition" of the imperial army.[132]

Additionally, the strife that mounted to an emotional conflict between central army authorities and the Kwantung Army caused disunity and confusion in operational guidance and even led to the extraordinary decision to replace key personnel, including the Kwantung Army commander himself and his top-level staff. Yet these measures failed to check the tendency for local forces to try to dominate the central authorities and for staff officers to seek to control their commanders. Not only did this type of insubordination reappear, in more serious form, at the time of the move into northern French Indochina about a year later, but the young staff officers of the Kwantung Army, who were actually responsible for the Nomonhan Incident, were returned to key posts in the high command soon afterward and played an important part in plunging Japan into the Pacific War. Hattori, for example, became an operations staff officer at Imperial Headquarters a year later and in July 1941 was promoted to chief of the Operations Section. That same month Tsuji joined him on the General Staff and became chief of the Operations desk in March 1942. One cannot overlook the fact that this method of administering military personnel affairs "fostered a foolhardiness which, in turn, was to provoke successive disturbances." [133]

Another reason for the defeat was that the study of combat lessons was ignored and material strength was lightly esteemed. The Japanese military retained its fundamental concept: dependence on hand-to-hand fighting.

In its diplomatic aspect also Japan was never able to wrest the initiative from the Soviet Union throughout the entire episode. Many reasons could be adduced. One was certainly that the Foreign Ministry felt compelled to delay opening the negotiations because of the violent clash between the Kwantung Army and the high command, thereby losing valuable time. The

Soviets, on the other hand, carefully coordinated their ceasefire suggestion on August 22 with their military successes and the signing of their Nonaggression Pact with Germany the following day, so that they went into the discussions in a strong bargaining position. Japan, having been itself considering a pact with Germany, was dumbfounded by the international turn of events. On August 28 the Hiranuma cabinet fell. The Abe government replaced it on August 30. Ambassador Tōgō pressed on with the negotiations, but central direction must have been weak, for Abe found no replacement for Foreign Minister Arita until a month later; he himself had to assume the post temporarily in addition to his many other duties. For a while estimates of the situation by the Japanese government and military lost objectivity and disarray grew.

It is also likely that Tōgō's bold front was undermined by Soviet knowledge of Japan's eagerness for a settlement. The details are not clearly ascertainable, but there is evidence that the Japanese army had been covertly fostering, via Ambassador Ōshima Hiroshi in Berlin, a design to achieve a ceasefire through German mediation. It may be this or similar efforts that lay behind David J. Dallin's report that as early as the end of June Italian Foreign Minister Galeazzo Ciano mentioned to the Soviet ambassador the possibility of German mediation. On August 3 Foreign Minister Joachim von Ribbentrop hinted at the same idea to the Soviet ambassador in Berlin, and on the 14th the German ambassador in Moscow, Count Friedrich Werner von der Schulenburg, intimated this to Molotov. At the time of the consummation of the Nonaggression Pact on August 23 the idea was tested out directly on Stalin and Molotov by Ribbentrop, and the Soviet leaders did not oppose it.[134] Ambassador Tōgō too seems to have been involved. His memoirs mention that Schulenburg visited him and advised acceptance of German mediation, but he declined.[135] Tōgō seems also to have reacted negatively when the possibility was raised by Ōshima. There is evidence of similar activities on the part of the Japanese General Staff, via the three German military and naval attachés in Japan, and directed to the German high command.[136] The Soviets not only accomplished the simple termination of the fighting but skillfully timed the conclusion of the negotiations so as to bring about an improvement in their relations with Japan just two days before the Soviet army invaded Poland.

In any event, the Japanese in the end did accept the Soviet Union's demands, and opinion began to grow in military and diplomatic circles that Japan ought to give more attention itself to concluding a nonaggression pact with Russia in order to strengthen its position vis-à-vis Britain. Such a notion appears to have sprung up among the high command, Ambassador Ōshima, and the Kwantung Army soon after the German-Soviet Nonaggression Pact was signed. Ōshima's insistence seems to have been in accord with Ribbentrop's advice, and Ambassador Tōgō later came to agree. According to what Foreign Minister Arita told Harada Kumao, army circles also harbored hopes for an alliance between Japan, Germany, and the Soviet Union, as well as the strengthening of the anti-Comintern alliance.[137] This concept was a by-product of the Nomonhan Incident. It steadily gained support over the following year and eventually served as the foundation of the Japanese-Soviet Neutrality Pact of April 1941.

THREE

The Tripartite Pact
1939-1940
by
Hosoya Chihiro

Translated
with an Introduction by

JAMES WILLIAM MORLEY

Introduction
by
JAMES WILLIAM MORLEY

Coming hard on the heels of the establishment of the Wang Ching-wei regime in China and the Nazi victories over western Europe that spring, the announcement of the signing of the Tripartite Pact in September 1940 was taken by their opponents as sealing an aggressive, unholy alliance of the Nazi Germans, the Italian fascists, and the Japanese militarists to redivide the world. In the months before Pearl Harbor Japanese officials repeatedly denied this. They insisted that the pact was purely defensive. They pointed out that the text explicitly provided for military assistance only in the event that one of the parties was attacked by the United States or another power not then involved in the European war or the Sino-Japanese conflict; and they contended that Japan had retained its freedom of action to judge whether indeed such an "attack" had taken place.

In any event, the Japanese attack on Pearl Harbor and the American declarations of war against both Germany and Japan obviated recourse to the pact, but the controversy over its intent has continued. Once again at the war crimes trials in Tokyo in 1946–48 Japanese officials, some of them now in the prisoners dock, contended that the pact had been purely defensive and that Japan had assumed no automatic obligation to go to war on Germany's behalf. This time a hitherto secret letter (given below as the "First Letter" in Appendix 7) from German Ambassador Ott to Foreign Minister Matsuoka was offered as evidence of the "independence" which the Japanese government claimed to have retained. The Tribunal, however, was unconvinced. It conceded that the pact might have been defensive in form, but it ruled nevertheless that by it the three parties had showed their determination "to support one another in aggressive action whenever such action was considered necessary to the furtherance of their schemes." [1]

But neither the arguments of the defense nor those of the prosecution nor the judgment of the bench have been ultimately convincing. At the time of the trial wartime passions were too high, evidence was too thin, and the involvement of the accused was too personally consequential to permit objective reflection. It has remained, therefore, for scholars later to try to unravel the enigma of the pact. None has been more convincing than Hosoya Chihiro in the essay that follows.

Hosoya is professor of international relations in the Law Faculty of Hitotsubashi University in Tokyo. Respected widely for his careful use of sources and the fairness of his judgments, he has had unusual access to a number of valuable archives that were unavailable at the time of the Tokyo trials and have not been utilized heretofore. They include diaries and official records belonging to former army and navy authorities as well as the Foreign Ministry, and private papers of many participants in the pact proceedings, notably those of the prime minister, Prince Konoe Fumimaro. Hosoya has brought to these new materials a detailed knowledge of Japan's diplomatic history and an intimate sense of the decision-making process within the prewar Japanese government. He is able, therefore, not only to clear the trial record of its sometimes mistaken chronology and identifications but to describe critically important meetings, such as the Ogikubo Conference on July 19, 1940, where Prince Konoe cleared with Tōgō, Matsuoka, and Yoshida the main lines of policy his new cabinet would pursue. He also provides texts and analyses of highly enlightening documents, such as Matsuoka's draft policy of July 30, which enable him to show authoritatively the evolution of the government's thinking and thereby, sometimes by direct statement and sometimes by implication, to throw new light on a number of hitherto perplexing problems.

On Japan's intent in signing the pact, he concludes that Konoe as well as senior Foreign Ministry and navy officials were sincere in not wanting war with the United States. At the same time, especially after Germany's victories in Europe, they were not prepared any more than were the army or the right wing radicals in the media and elsewhere in the bureaucracy to defer to American opposition or possible German greed and let China or the former European colonies in Southeast Asia slip from their grasp. The pact was designed to solve this problem, that is, to confirm Germany's lack of ambition in these areas and, without war but by presenting an appearance of a formidable German-Japanese military combination, to dissuade the United States from pushing its opposition to Japan to a military showdown. It is best explainable, Hosoya implies, not so well in the aggressive-defensive terms so widely used in the interwar years and at the trial as in terms of the postwar concept of deterrence. Deterrence may, of course, be utilized to protect an offensive or a defensive posture. Japan's posture was clearly offensive; but that is not to say that Japan had resolved to go to war with the United States and other western countries at this time. Rather, Japan sought to achieve its offensive or aggressive aims in Asia by deterring its opponents from military intervention, itself not reaching the decision for war with them until a year later when the Hull-Nomura talks had broken down.

There are obvious problems in this explanation. Who spoke for the Japanese government in 1940? The Tokyo Tribunal judged that by then control over policy had clearly passed to the "major war criminals," who had formed a conspiracy to wage aggressive war. These included, in high positions at the time the pact was concluded, three military men: General Hata Shunroku, whose resignation as army minister on July 16, 1940, had set the stage for Konoe's rise to power; General Tōjō Hideki, his successor as army minister in the Konoe cabinet; and General Mutō Akira, chief of the Military Affairs Bureau of the Army Ministry. Three civilians also were particularly pointed out: former Ambassador to Italy Shiratori Toshio, who was appointed adviser to the Foreign Ministry in August 1940; Ōhashi Chūichi, vice foreign minister; and Hoshino Naoki, chief of the Cabinet Planning Board. Evidence that these were the men personally responsible for the Tripartite Pact, however, was highly inconclusive.

Reexamining the trial materials a decade later and supple-

menting them with interviews and particularly the account of
former army Colonel Hattori Takushirō, who as a historian in
General MacArthur's Occupation headquarters was given
access to a broad array of documents seized from the former Imperial Headquarters of Japan,[2] Robert J. C. Butow concluded
that to assign personal responsibility to high Japanese officials
for actions taken under their aegis was to misunderstand the political relationships within the Japanese government.[3] Orthodox
Japanese administrative theory places great emphasis on the
ringisei, a system whereby reports and proposals are expected
to be initiated at the bottom of a bureaucratic pyramid and then
to be pumped upward through the chain of command until,
when they reach the top, they represent the consensus of the institution which the seniors can do little to influence and are expected to represent.[4] Butow builds on this conception to
suggest that the Tripartite Pact was initiated not by those
charged with conspiracy but by a nucleus group of "reformers"
or "renovationists" who were determined by every means to establish Japan's hegemony over the New Order in East Asia. As
section and bureau chiefs at the middle levels of the Army General Staff, they transmitted their proposals to the chief of staff,
who "foisted" them "through the Army Minister and the Chief
of the Military Affairs Bureau [of the Army Ministry] upon the
members of the Cabinet."

Hosoya shows that Butow's contention is not entirely without foundation. By the spring and summer of 1940 a number of
pro-Axis "right wing radicals" were indeed occupying middle-
level positions in the Army General Staff. Two veterans of the
embassies in Berlin and Rome, Karakawa Yasuo and Yamagata
Arimitsu, for example, were chiefs of the Europe-America Section and the German desk respectively, and Usui Shigeki was
chief of the Subversion and Propaganda Section. No doubt they
were among the officers who drafted the army position paper of
July 3, which called on the Japanese government to strengthen
the Axis tie while launching a diplomatic offensive against the
French and Dutch possessions in Southeast Asia, resolving to
attack Singapore and British-held Malaya as well as other areas
if diplomacy failed, and completing preparations for war by

August. They must also have been among the "middle-ranking officers" who, in the name of the chief of staff, persuaded Army Minister Hata to resign, thus bringing down the Yonai cabinet and opening the way for the formation of the Konoe cabinet which they hoped would take up this more aggressive policy.

But Hosoya clearly shows that they did not act alone. They had the encouragement of a pervasive national mood for action and the assurance of strong support from pro-Axis leaders among their peers and their seniors within and outside their chains of command. The Army Ministry, for example, had its own activists at middle levels. Iwakuro Hideo as chief of its Military Affairs Section was one of those who had long called for a surprise attack on Singapore. Such men were linked, moreover, with pro-Axis circles outside, including such influential figures as Asahi editor Ogata Taketora, the publicist Tokutomi Sohō, the maverick Diet member Nakano Seigō, navy Admiral Suetsugu Nobumasa, continental businessman Kuhara Fusanosuke, as well as the former ambassadors to Germany and Italy respectively, Shiratori and Ōshima—in turn linked with the German ambassador Eugen Ott, who had been maneuvering for this moment, with the Japanese press, then panicky lest Japan "miss the bus" in seizing Europe's lost colonies, and with Prince Konoe, prime minister-designate.

Moreover, even this formidable coalition of pro-Axis elements could not unilaterally impose its will. The pact that resulted from Japan's bureaucratic process in September, tied as it was to a secret protocol, differed significantly from the intent of the military radicals. It represented a decision not to go to war—Japan reserved its independence to decide that matter—but to try to persuade the United States to back off and make war unnecessary.

The explanation for this outcome, as Hosoya's essay enables one to see, is that Japanese government in 1940 was no simple dictatorship of the middle-level officers or even of the military as a whole. There has been considerable confusion on this point. We in the West and many Japanese as well have too often found it convenient to describe the decline of the parties, the rise of the military, the growing stridency of national sentiment, and the increasing mobilization of the nation's energies for war by terms growing out of western experience, such as "fascism" or "militarism." But Japan was far less centralized than either of these terms usually implies. Even in the wartime years institutional and factional rivals continued to divide the Japanese government, and conciliation among them was still necessary before major policy could be sanctioned.

In the beginning the army's plan was opposed by both the Foreign Ministry and the navy. The Foreign Ministry did see the need to secure Germany's commitment to give Japan a free hand in Southeast Asia; but in the negotiations among the three ministries from July 12 to 16, for example, Section Chief Andō Yoshirō held out against any commitment to Germany that Japan should go to war on its behalf. When the flamboyant brinksman Matsuoka took over the foreign minister's post a week later he reversed his ministry's position and agreed that a military alliance should be formed. The navy, however, did not give ground so easily. Not that the navy was any less interested in obtaining the resources of the South Seas—it had its own southern expansionists—but a number of its senior officers, especially Admirals Okada Keisuke and Yonai Mitsumasa and Vice Admiral Yoshida Zengo, who served as navy minister until his health broke down on September 3, were too aware of Japan's naval inferiority to be willing to commit Japan to a confrontation with the United States. It was in fact not until the pro-Axis pressure had become intense and a weaker officer, Admiral Oikawa Koshirō, had taken the ministerial post, that the navy finally conceded. Oikawa seems to have acted partly in response to pressure from his own middle echelons and partly out of fear of the hostility that the navy's position was evoking from the army, the rest of the government, and the public. But he did not cave in completely. He exacted a price for the navy's approval of the pact, notably that Japan be compensated by the acquisition of all rights to the former German islands in the mid-Pacific; and he insisted to the end that, whatever the terms in the pact itself about Japan's obligation to go to war on Germany's behalf, it must be absolutely understood that Japan retained the right to decide independently in what circumstances and with what consequences the *casus foederis* could be invoked. It was the essentiality of securing the navy's inclusion in the consensus that explains the apparent contradiction between the pact, which clearly states Japan's obligation to render Germany military assistance against an attack from the United States, and the secret letter from Ott to Matsuoka, exchanged the same day, in which the understandings demanded by the navy are given.

Hosoya's account of how Matsuoka achieved this result is a fascinating story of bureaucratic maneuvering and deliberately fostered misunderstanding. Knowing that his own government was not prepared to propose a military alliance, Matsuoka inveigled the German representatives, Stahmer and Ott, on September 11 to come up with the first hard draft. He then sold this to the Japanese navy with the understanding that a number of provisos, particularly that Japan would retain its independence of action, would be secured. He knew of course that this was not what the German government had in mind, so he did not convey the reservations to Ott and Stahmer until September 19, after he had won Imperial Conference approval from which, he argued, it was impossible to retreat. The German government did indeed object, indicating its displeasure on September 24. Nevertheless, on September 27 when the pact was signed by Ribbentrop and Ciano in Berlin, secret letters containing the essential protocol were signed by Ott and exchanged in Tokyo.

Why this seeming about-face? Why did the Germans finally accept what Johanna Meskill has so aptly termed a "hollow alliance" in which the pledges made in the public text were effectively revoked in the secret protocol? [5] The answer was first suggested to Hosoya when the texts of the protocol were not found in the German archives after the war. It has been confirmed by exhaustive research of the German materials by Theo Sommer.[6] The German government simply did not know what it was getting: Ott signed without authorization and never reported his action.

I had occasion in the summer of 1966 to call on Herr Ott, who was living then in retirement in a modest apartment on Konrad Strasse in Munich. A tall, broad, white-haired man with ruddy complexion and a gentle, gracious manner, he vigorously defended his action of a quarter of a century before. His defense took four lines. The first was that it had been his colleague Stahmer's obligation to inform Berlin, and Stahmer had not done so. "I told Stahmer," he recalled, "that if we went beyond our authority, he would have to present our position to the government in Germany after returning to Berlin. It was Stahmer's duty to take the notes back. I was sure he would do it, of course, but he did not. In March 1941 when I went to Berlin with Matsuoka, I asked Stahmer how the foreign minister had reacted. He answered that he had had no time to discuss it with him. And once during the conversations between Japan and the United States in the middle of 1941 after Matsuoka had returned from Berlin, I mentioned one of the points of this protocol in a telegram to Berlin, but this obviously never reached the eyes of the foreign minister."

Ott's second line of defense was that the protocols were after all in accord with well-known German policy of the time. He cited, for example, the pledge that Germany would accommodate Japan's desire to secure title to the former German colonies in the Pacific. Hitler had several times stated that Germany had no colonial interests in the Far East, he said, so "we felt that this protocol was in line with Hitler's policy." He may also have felt that earlier instructions to press a German-Japanese-Soviet project justified his additional pledge that Germany would "do everything within her power to promote a friendly understanding" between Japan and the Soviet Union. In any event, he said that he personally had shared this objective with Matsuoka and that in fact he had done everything he could to bring it about. "I personally had several talks at that time with Soviet Ambassador Smetanin," he recalled, "a quiet man who was a specialist in fishery. Several times I asked him to improve relations with Japan, but he was rather stubborn and said that 'as long as the Treaty of Portsmouth is valid, there can be no friendly contact between Russia and Japan.' I really tried to bring about more friendly contacts and I especially asked Stahmer when we went back via Moscow to use his stay there to continue trying to improve them. He promised to do so. At

the farewell dinner for Stahmer in Tokyo, Matsuoka also secured Stahmer's promise on this point, but Stahmer did nothing."

Ott's third defense related to the crucial understanding that
Japan should retain its independence of action in spite of the
mutual pledges in the pact. He felt that Matsuoka had "pres-
sured" him by securing the Imperial Conference's agreement to
the protocol on September 19 before asking for the German
government's reaction; and he acknowledged that Ribbentrop's
reply on September 21 contained no approval. But he had
signed anyway, because he felt that he had got "the real commitment of the Japanese government in Article 3. These protocol concessions were simply to facilitate Matsuoka's relations
with various Japanese groups. They did not change the real
facts of the pact."

In any event, Ott concluded, he felt that the situation at the
time within the German government forced him to exercise
some freedom of judgment. A former aide of General von Sch-
leicher, Ott said that he had never quite trusted the Nazis. In
the summer of 1940 Hitler was planning the invasion of Britain
and Ribbentrop wanted the pact, not as "a real political instrument, but as a weapon of propaganda to secure the nonentry
of the United States into the war." But neither one appreciated
the "continental power of the United States" or the depth of its
unwritten commitment to the survival of Britain. They were
fully capable of dropping the pact project in pique over details;
and that, Ott felt, would have been tragic: every effort had to be
made to keep America out of the war. That is why, he recalled,
"I felt entitled to go my own way if the negotiations became difficult."

Matsuoka liked to say that "unless you go into the tiger's
den, you cannot catch the tiger's cub." Great ends do sometimes justify great risks, but history has not dealt kindly with
the Tripartite Pact. True though it seems to be that Matsuoka,
Ott, and others in both governments whose support was cru-
cially important thought of the pact as a diplomatic instrument
to deter war, they were badly mistaken. As subsequent events
revealed, its conclusion served to strengthen the forces for ag-

gressive expansion in both the Axis governments and at the same time to stiffen rather than weaken the resolve of the American government to resist. For all the hollowness of the commitments, the Tripartite Pact did indeed mark another important step on the tragic road to the Pacific War.

Essay
by
HOSOYA CHIHIRO

Japan's Search for an Independent Foreign Policy

On August 23, 1939, the world was shaken by the announcement that Germany had concluded a nonaggression pact with the Soviet Union. Signalizing a drastic change in the international situation, the news of the pact was an especially great shock to the leaders and people of Japan.

At 11 P.M. on the night of August 21 German Foreign Minister Joachim von Ribbentrop had telephoned from Hitler's mountain villa to tell Ōshima Hiroshi, Japan's ambassador to Germany, of the German government's decision. Ōshima had been stunned. He had been negotiating for some time with Germany for the strengthening of the Anti-Comintern Pact of 1936, and the Germans had told him nothing in advance of their about-face. Hurt and angered, he exploded to Ribbentrop: "This action of the German government violates the protocol attached to the Anti-Comintern Pact of 1936. The Japanese government and people will never accept it. The German government must bear the responsibility for any unfortunate results." [1] In spite of the lateness of the hour Ōshima then called on Ernst von Weizsaecker, state secretary in the German Foreign Office, at his private residence and demanded further explanations.[2]

The next evening Ōshima went to the Berlin airport to meet Ribbentrop, who was on his way from Hitler's villa to Moscow to sign the new pact. According to Ōshima, Ribbentrop first expressed his regret that "Germany had been so forced by the

This is a translation by James William Morley of Hosoya Chihiro, "Sangoku dōmei to Nisso chūritsu jōyaku (1931–1941)," in *Taiheiyō sensō e no michi*, Vol. 5, Part II, Sec. 1 and 2, pp. 157–332, together with footnotes.

pressure of circumstances to make a quick decision on the matter of the pact that it had been impossible to consult with Japan beforehand." Ribbentrop explained Germany's action on the ground that "the Anglo-French policy of encirclement against Germany has been so greatly intensified lately in connection with the German-Polish conflict that Germany has been forced to take desperate measures to prepare itself to fight the Anglo-French forces. Since the negotiations for a Japanese-German-Italian tripartite agreement were inconclusive, Germany had no choice but to neutralize the Soviet Union quickly by concluding the Nonaggression Pact."

Ribbentrop urged Japan to cooperate with Germany in its new Soviet policy and went on to suggest the possibility of a three-power alliance. "I, for one," he said, "believe that the best policy for us would be to conclude a Japanese-German-Soviet nonaggression agreement and then move against Britain. During the negotiations for the new pact the Russians repeatedly expressed their desire for a reconciliation with Japan. If Japan desires, Germany is ready to mediate for better Japanese-Soviet relations." Turning to the project Germany had previously been discussing with Japan, the strengthening of the Anti-Comintern Pact, Ribbentrop stated that while "we must end our discussions with Japan regarding an anti-Soviet project, we should still like to draw our two countries together in some other way." [3]

It was extremely difficult for the Japanese leaders and people, with their scant experience of the complexities of power politics, to understand how Germany and the Soviet Union, which had seemed to be ideologically irreconcilable, could suddenly become allies. Moreover, since Japan had been in the process of negotiations with its "ally" (Germany) for a further intensification of the Anti-Comintern Pact, it was only natural that when Germany effected a political rapprochement with the Soviet Union, the very target of their alliance, Japan should regard this as a treacherous and unpardonable act. The German action worried Japan in yet other respects. Japan feared that the new pact might have an adverse effect on the armed conflict it was then engaged in with the Soviet Union in the Nomonhan wilderness near the Manchurian-Mongolian border. In addition, the agreement might make the execution of Japan's China policy more difficult and permit the Soviet Union to apply greater pressure in the east. These concerns naturally aroused suspicion as to Germany's reliability. Clearly the situation demanded that Japan reexamine its foreign policy.

The Hiranuma cabinet decided to terminate all negotiations with Germany for strengthening the Anti-Comintern Pact and to transmit to Germany a statement of Japan's resentment. On August 25 Foreign Minister Arita Hachirō called in Ambassador Eugen Ott in Tokyo and notified him of Japan's decision. The same day Ambassador Ōshima was instructed to convey the same message to the authorities in Berlin.[4] But the Hiranuma cabinet was incapable of dealing with the new situation. With the plea that "there has emerged an intricate and baffling new situation in Europe," it resigned on August 28.

The German-Soviet Nonaggression Pact, which caused the fall of the Hiranuma cabinet, also generated significant changes in the distribution of political power within Japan. In the atmosphere of distrust of Germany that developed, the prestige of pro-Axis elements inevitably fell, and the Axis faction itself began to disintegrate. The army had been its core. Now, with the conclusion of the Nonaggression Pact, the Military Affairs Bureau of the Army Ministry, which had championed the policy of intensifying Japanese-German cooperation, lost its enthusiasm, and for a time sentiment within the ministry made discussion of the tripartite alliance project taboo.[5]

On the other hand, the Anglo-American faction, represented mainly by the imperial court and business circles, found this a golden opportunity to bring about a "drastic reform" of internal politics and to "restore Japan's foreign policy to the correct path." Even some in the army, such as General Hata Shunroku, chief aide-de-camp to His Majesty, welcomed the change, believing that it might offer the possibility of clearing away the dangerous internal political divisions that had been occasioned by the "Anti-Comintern Pact question." [6] Prince Saionji Kimmochi's secretary, Baron Harada Kumao, and his confidant in the business world Koyama Kango tell us that the Anglo-

American faction set about immediately to try to recover political control.[7]

In this general mood of nonconfidence in Germany and with the Axis faction in retreat, a new cabinet was formed on August 30. It was headed by General Abe Nobuyuki and called for "the establishment of an independent foreign policy." The emperor had said, when he summoned Abe to form a cabinet, that the new government should reject the pro-Axis tendency of the past and instead "follow a conciliatory line with regard to Britain and America," [8] and Abe had been impressed by this instruction.

Meanwhile the political situation in Europe was changing rapidly. On September 1 the German army invaded Poland, and on the 3rd the British and French governments declared war against Germany. World War II had finally begun.

On September 4 the new cabinet responded by issuing the following statement: "The empire will not intervene in the war in Europe but will concentrate its efforts upon solving the China Incident." On September 9 Prime Minister Abe elaborated on this decision to the press, explaining that his cabinet would seek to achieve this aim by working chiefly to improve Japan's relations with the United States, Britain, France, and the Soviet Union.[9]

On September 25 Admiral Nomura Kichisaburō was appointed foreign minister. His emergence in this post made the nature of the Abe cabinet's foreign policy still clearer. Nomura had been stationed in the United States for an extended period as naval attaché and had many acquaintances in the upper echelons of American political life. He was known to be pro-American. Furthermore, before his appointment as foreign minister he had been headmaster of the Peer's School, where children of the nobility were educated. This meant that he had close connections with the imperial court and business circles. It was therefore natural that the Anglo-American faction in the court and the business world expected that his appointment as foreign minister would bring about an improvement in Japanese-American relations.

These relations had deteriorated alarmingly. On July 26,

1939, the U.S. government announced its intention to terminate in six months the 1911 Treaty of Commerce and Navigation with Japan. Since the Japanese economy relied increasingly on the United States as the war in China expanded, this news was ominous. The Japanese government felt it absolutely essential to deter America from moving toward a policy of economic sanctions.

On October 4, shortly after Nomura's appointment as foreign minister, a document was completed under the direction of Vice Foreign Minister Tani Masayuki on the basis of an earlier army draft. Entitled "Foreign Policy to be Pursued in Response to the European War," it spelled out concretely the "independent foreign policy" the Abe cabinet had in mind.[10] It first set forth the fundamental policy as follows:

> Japan will maintain an attitude of neutrality toward the European War. It will take advantage of the international situation to concentrate its efforts on settling the China Incident on the basis previously determined. At the same time, it will increase its defensive strength and solidify its financial and economic position, preparing itself to act independently, flexibly, and prudently in the face of any changes in the international situation.

Section 5, the most lengthy item, was devoted to Japan's policy toward the United States. It expressed Japan's readiness to refrain from applying unnecessary pressure on American economic activities in China, promising friendly treatment of American interests in China, protection of American nationals in China, liberalization of restrictions on their business trips, and quick solution of problems pending between the two nations. The document further spoke of a plan to urge the conclusion of a new trade agreement with America, and for this purpose it advocated sending an influential economic mission to the United States. In contrast to its America policy, the proposed policy toward Germany and Italy lacked any positive content. According to the relevant Section 6, "Japan will continue to maintain friendly relations with Germany and Italy as before and will refrain from taking any measures which might create the impression that any estrangement exists."

Having failed to prevent Britain from entering the war, Germany now found less value in an alliance with Japan. Nevertheless, an alliance was still important to Germany as a means of diverting Britain's naval power; furthermore, should Britain institute an economic blockade, Germany would require supplies from the South Seas, and Japan's mediation would be needed. Therefore Germany considered it absolutely essential to continue its positive policy toward Japan so that, by drawing Japan close to the Axis, it might be in a position to renew the negotiations for an alliance at a later time.

It was obvious, however, that after the conclusion of the German-Soviet pact, rapprochement with Japan was no longer possible on the basis of cooperation against communism or the Soviet Union. Consequently, Germany devised a new strategy. It portrayed the reality of international politics as a confrontation or conflict between two groups of nations, one demanding changes in the existing situation and the other seeking to maintain the status quo. Soviet Russia, Japan, and Germany were said to belong to the former group, and Britain and France, the leading nations of the latter group, were posited as the major enemy forces opposing Japan's ambition to establish the New Order. In this manner Germany on the one hand justified its rapprochement with the Soviet Union and, on the other, urged Japan to cooperate fully in its armed conflict with the forces of the Old Order. Furthermore, Germany calculated that the Japanese emotional reaction to the German-Soviet pact, which had its basis in Japan's traditional hostility toward the Soviet Union, would disappear once Japan and the Soviet Union were reconciled. Ribbentrop's idea therefore was to use the reconciliation of Japan and the Soviet Union as a steppingstone for building a political union of the so-called New Order forces: Japan, Germany, Italy, and the Soviet Union.

Ribbentrop and Weizsaecker had made it known to Ambassador Ōshima before the signing of the German-Soviet pact that Germany wanted Japan to improve and consolidate its relations with the Soviet Union and to this end Germany was ready to act as mediator. After his return from Moscow Ribbentrop invited Ōshima to the Supreme Headquarters of the Eastern

Front, on the night of September 5, and explained the German position again.

Japan's fate, he began, was "now as in the past closely bound up with the fate of Germany." Should Germany be defeated, "the Western democracies would quickly form an extensive world coalition which would oppose any expansion by Japan and, in particular, would again wrest from her her position in China." A German victory, on the other hand, would mean that "Japan's position, too, would be definitively assured, assuming that Japan maintained and further strengthened her present relations with Germany." Ribbentrop thus tried to develop the idea that Japan and Germany shared the same destiny. Germany's rapprochement with the Soviet Union, he went on, was likewise in Japan's interest. He assured Ōshima that Germany was "entirely in a position, and on request also prepared, to mediate a settlement between Japan and Russia. If this succeeded, Japan would be able freely to extend her strength in East Asia toward the south . . . the direction in which Japan's vital interests lay." Such a policy, he had emphasized to Stalin, was "fully in harmony" with German-Russian rapprochement. Moreover, close cooperation between Germany, Italy, and Japan, "in conjunction with Japanese-Russian settlement would, in keeping with the world situation, be exclusively directed against England and would thus bring the policy of the three Powers as well as of Russia into a uniform line corresponding to the real interests of all concerned." [11] At Supreme Headquarters on September 20 Ribbentrop and then Hitler himself presented these same views to General Terauchi Hisaichi who, as chief of a Japanese mission to Germany, was then on an inspection tour of the Polish front.[12]

The German government did not fail to make the most of every opportunity to lead Japan's Soviet policy in the direction of conciliation. For this purpose it made special efforts to promote better understanding among Japanese leaders (particularly those in the army) of Germany's war aims against Britain. Ambassador Ott was instructed to try to convince Prince Kan'in Kotohito, chief of the Army General Staff, of the German view and at the same time to take appropriate measures to prevent the Japanese government from recalling Ambassador Ōshima, who had worked most positively for a strengthening of Japanese-German relations.[13]

Throughout the period of the Abe cabinet Ott labored behind the scenes to prevent Japan from deserting the Axis. By encouraging the activities of the Axis faction and utilizing the mass media, he endeavored to influence public opinion in favor of a policy of denunciation of Britain and rapprochement with the Soviet Union.[14] Demoralized by the conclusion of the Nazi-Soviet pact, the strength of the Axis faction in Japan was at a low ebb. Nevertheless, the desire for an alliance with Germany remained firmly rooted in the Army General Staff and among the so-called *kakushin uyoku* or "radical right wing." In the September 1939 issue of the *Bungei shunjū*, for example, Nakano Seigō wrote an article entitled "The Nazi-Soviet Nonaggression Pact and Japan," in which he declared:

> The senile leaders of the Japanese government shamelessly criticize Germany for its conclusion of a nonaggression pact with Soviet Russia. These senile men should be reminded that they are to blame for having missed an opportunity to secure a tripartite pact because of their indecisive attitude. Now these men are about to restore that pro-British diplomacy of coquetry, which seems to have become an ingrained habit of theirs. . . . If Japan is too ashamed to approach Germany now, it can postpone that affair for the time, but it should continue the movement against Britain as scheduled.[15]

Thus the pro-Axis elements sought to use the anti-British movement to bring about a change in Japanese public opinion. All that fall, under the leadership of the "radical right wing" represented by Nakano, Suetsugu Nobumasa, and Hashimoto Kingorō, anti-British activities were stepped up. At the same time a movement urging the conclusion of a Japanese-Soviet nonaggression pact was started.

Despite these activities of the Axis faction in Japan and the diplomatic maneuvers of Germany, the Abe cabinet persisted in its middle-of-the-road policy. Nomura appears to have been guided from the beginning by the policy outline of October 4, which after some revising was formally adopted as the cabinet's "Principles of Foreign Policy" on December 28.[16] Adhering to the negative policy therein stated—namely, that "Japan will refrain from taking any measures which create the impression that any estrangement exists between Japan, Germany, and Italy"—Nomura took no steps toward terminating the Anti-Comintern Pact. On the other hand, he responded coldly to the scheme of a Japanese-German-Soviet entente.

The government's lack of interest in this proposition was shown in its personnel policy. Pro-Axis people were removed from key positions both in the government and in the army, the outstanding example being the recall of Ōshima from Berlin, in spite of Ambassador Ott's efforts to have him remain, and his replacement by the civilian diplomat Kurusu Saburō.[17] In addition, the Japanese government's proposal to postpone the formal signing of the Japanese-German trade pact, scheduled for October 1, was probably not unrelated to its general attitude toward Germany.[18] Finally, in spite of German requests, the Japanese government maintained a strictly neutral posture toward the European war, refraining from taking any measures that might provoke Britain.[19] Thus Japanese-German relations, which had become increasingly closer following the conclusion of the Anti-Comintern Pact, now seemed to have entered a period of freeze.

For a while after the Abe cabinet was formed, Ambassador Ott continued to be optimistic about the future of Japanese-German relations.[20] But the tone of his reports gradually changed and by October began to sound pessimistic. The Anglo-American faction, Ott reported, had finally emerged as victor over the Axis faction in their struggle for leadership in internal politics, and the political influence of the army had been decisively weakened because of its military reverses at Nomonhan and the shock waves produced by the German-Soviet pact. He judged that Germany had no choice but to shelve the Japanese-German alliance project until after Nomura had tried and failed to reach a settlement with the United States.[21]

It was to reaching such a settlement that Nomura's efforts were primarily devoted. Conferences were begun with Ambassador Joseph C. Grew in November. During the talks Nomura expressed Japan's desire to conclude a new trade treaty with the United States or, if that was not possible, even a temporary agreement. He stated that in exchange for a new agreement Japan was ready to respect American interests in China and to reopen the lower reaches of the Yangtze river to the vessels of third powers. But Nomura's overtures for a solution of Japanese-American problems were met by a cool response from the American side. The United States government categorically insisted that the Abe cabinet "was as keen as the army to extend Japanese power over Asia." [22] As long as the United States stood firmly upon this judgment, it was impossible from the outset for it to come to an agreement with Japan on Asian questions. The policy of Secretary Cordell Hull and other high officials of the Department of State at the time was to hold to the basic position of maintaining the principle of the Open Door and to challenge Japan's policy of continental expansion, even resorting to measures of economic pressure if these were required. At the fourth Nomura-Grew conference on December 22, Nomura's proposal for the renewal of the trade agreement was finally rejected.[23]

The failure of the Japanese-American negotiations shattered the hopes placed upon Nomura by business and other leaders of the Anglo-American faction, and criticism of "Nomura's two-faced diplomacy" began to appear in the newspapers. At the same time the Abe cabinet suffered another setback in its handling of the domestic economic problem. Shortages of both electric power and food were growing more and more serious, and prices were rising alarmingly. It seemed inevitable that the cabinet would be compelled to resign by the end of the year.

Ambassador Ott reported to his government on December 31:

> America's attitude brought disappointment to the initially high hopes that were nourished by the calculated optimism of the government. . . . The popular sentiment is conditioned by the foreign trade policy, the deterioration in the food and supply situation resulting from the war with China, specifically by the increase in the price of rice and the failure of the Government in

the distribution of essential goods. . . . Resignation of the Cabinet in the middle of January before the reconvening of the Diet is therefore generally expected. The pro-Anglo-Saxon press also is beginning to abandon the Cabinet. . . . According to recent information, Court circles are trying to prepare a cabinet of national union with the participation of the parties in the Diet in order to forestall any essential change of course.

Ott did not fail, however, to draw his government's attention to the fact that, in spite of the imminent fall of the cabinet, all prerequisites for a revival of the movement to strengthen Japanese-German cooperation were still lacking. "In the opinion of Ambassadors Ōshima and Shiratori, who are working hard for the overthrow of the present Cabinet, two or three transitional cabinets are still necessary to bring about a fundamental change of course." [24]

The Lure of the Southern Advance

On January 16, 1940, a new cabinet headed by Admiral Yonai Mitsumasa was formed. Ever since the issue of strengthening the Anti-Comintern Pact had arisen, Yonai had been regarded as a "most undesirable person" by the Axis faction, particularly by its nucleus, the army. Therefore, when General Sugiyama Gen, a member of the Supreme War Council, and General Hata Shunroku, army minister in the Abe cabinet, both favorites of the army, were bypassed and instead Yonai was appointed prime minister, the Anglo-American faction—especially Lord Privy Seal Yuasa Kurahei and those in court circles who had recommended Yonai to the emperor—showed their resolve to stand up to the army and to block the way to a tripartite alliance. [25]

Prime Minister Yonai selected Arita Hachirō as foreign minister and Ishiwata Sōtarō as chief cabinet secretary. The reappearance of these two men in the cabinet indicated the course its foreign policy would follow, for as members of the Five Ministers Conference under the Hiranuma cabinet both, together with Yonai, had opposed the army-backed proposal to strengthen the Anti-Comintern Pact.

The day the new cabinet was formed, Arita stated in a press conference that it would follow the "independent foreign policy" of its predecessor, continuing the friendly relations with Germany and Italy and "improving as much as possible relations with all other nations so long as they do not conflict with Japan's efforts to establish the New Order in East Asia." [26] Arita was, however, extremely wary of German diplomatic maneuvers apparently aimed at dragging Japan into closer ties with Germany. From 1939 to early 1940 the armed conflict in Europe took on the appearance of a "phony war," and no one could tell what the outcome would be. Under the circumstances, it was not only wise for Japan to wait and see the further development of the war, but also essential for the Yonai cabinet, which still hoped to restore normal economic relations with the United States, not to antagonize it by strengthening relations with Germany.

Arita's cautious attitude toward Germany was revealed in the new cabinet's request to the German government to postpone the congratulatory mission of Karl Edward, Duke of Sachsen-Coburg-Gotha, president of the German Red Cross, who was scheduled to visit Japan in February on the occasion of the celebration of the 2,600th anniversary of the accession of the Emperor Jimmu.[27] Japan's policy toward Germany at this time has been succinctly described by Kurusu Saburō, then ambassador to Germany: "In short, it was negative and passive." [28]

The two main lines of Arita's policy were the improvement of Japan's relations with Britain and the United States and rigorous promotion of the "New Order in East Asia." Ever since November 3, 1938, when he had enunciated the Japanese government's first official statement on the New Order in East Asia, the New Order had become the hallmark of Arita's policy. Needless to say, the idea implied Japan's intention to expel from East Asia the Anglo-American forces that stood for the maintenance of the "Old Order." In this sense, the simultaneous pursuit of the New Order and the improvement of relations with Britain and the United States inevitably involved Arita's diplomacy in self-contradiction.

That phase of his policy which aimed at improving relations

with Britain and the United States was dealt a blow at the start by the *Asama-maru* incident. On January 21 a British battleship intercepted and searched the *Asama-maru*, forcibly removing some twenty German nationals aboard the vessel. This provoked Japanese sensibilities and presented itself as an opportune pretext for arousing the public against Britain. In fact, the mass media succeeded in creating such a strong anti-British popular feeling that Ambassador Grew was led to comment that "the emotional patriotism and chauvinism of the entire country have been let loose." [29] The excited Japanese populace forced the government against its will to take a strong attitude toward Britain, thereby weakening the position of the pro-Anglo-American elements.

In addition, the American government did not greet the new cabinet with any relaxation of its attitude. On January 26 the termination of the Treaty of Commerce finally became effective, and there was no prospect of a new trade agreement to replace it. Not only that, but a bill had been introduced into Congress demanding an embargo on all Japanese trade. While the measure remained unpassed, it was nevertheless clear that U.S. policy toward Japan was gradually moving in the direction of economic sanctions.[30] The American government seemed to have no interest in strengthening the domestic position of the Yonai cabinet so as to improve its relations with Japan.

On March 30, when the Wang Ching-wei regime was established in Nanking, Secretary of State Hull immediately issued a statement denouncing the Japanese action and affirming continued American recognition of the Chiang Kai-shek government as the legitimate government of China.[31] At the same time it was announced that the Export-Import Bank would grant another loan to Chiang's government.[32] The Japanese government's response took the form of a public statement by Suma Yakichirō, chief of the Public Information Division of the Foreign Ministry, who vehemently attacked the Hull statement as "most regrettable." [33] This exchange between the two nations was indicative of the fact that, in spite of the initial high hopes of the Yonai cabinet, relations between Japan and the United States were deteriorating.

Arita's policy was failing, as was inevitable so long as the

United States based its Far Eastern policy on the rejection of Japan's New Order in East Asia. The self-contradictory nature of Arita's diplomacy, which simultaneously aimed at two mutually incompatible targets, was thus exposed.

The deterioration of Japanese-American relations naturally attracted the attention of Germany.[34] At the same time it stimulated the Axis faction in Japan to new activity.

When the Yonai cabinet was formed, Ambassador Ott had reported to his home government that "the strong influence of the anti-reform high finance and Court circles on the new Cabinet is unmistakable" and that the possibility of a change in Japan's foreign policy under this cabinet was very slim. During this period, at least, the German government was not very enthusiastic about cooperating with Japan.[35] The situation as it was did not favor German efforts to draw Japan into an alliance. For that purpose, Germany had to wait for a change in circumstances: either a striking improvement in the European war or a rise in the strength of the political reform movement in Japan.

Nevertheless, Germany was not willing quietly to watch Japan alter its foreign policy in the direction of more concessions to and closer ties with the United States out of the desperate need to improve its economic condition. Furthermore, Germany, because of its own wartime economic need to procure strategic materials, found cooperation with Japan necessary. The German government thereupon sent to Japan an economic mission headed by Emil Helfferich, president of the East Asian Association in Hamburg and Bremen, whose aim was to strengthen economic ties with Japan while keeping Japan away from Britain and the United States. The Helfferich mission arrived in Japan in February and, after extended consultations with various Japanese groups, reported its observations to Berlin. The report urged the German government to make a special effort to restore Japanese confidence in Germany by granting economic advantages.[36] On April 25 the previously postponed friendly mission headed by the Duke of Sachsen-Coburg-Gotha also arrived in Japan.

The Axis faction seemed gradually to regain its ground in 1940. It had been secretly continuing its efforts to create a pro-

German public opinion and to bring about a change in the political situation. Papers in the archives of the Military History Office indicate that at this time such people as Tokutomi Sohō, Nakano Seigō, Suetsugu Nobumasa, and Kuhara Fusanosuke, in addition to Ōshima and Ambassador to Italy Shiratori Toshio, met monthly at the Hoshigaoka Teahouse to discuss the tripartite pact question, after which they expressed their views to Prince Konoe Fumimaro. Within the Army General Staff, even after the conclusion of the Nonaggression Pact, cooperation with the Axis continued to be vigorously advocated by individuals such as Colonel Usui Shigeki, chief of the Subversion and Propaganda Section. In February 1940 the General Staff made a series of personnel charges that were favorable to the movement for closer ties with the Axis; for example, Colonel Karakawa Yasuo, who had actively assisted Ambassador Shiratori in Rome in strengthening cooperation with the Axis, was called home and appointed chief of the Europe-America Section, where Major Yamagata Arimitsu, who had aided Ōshima in Berlin, had been assigned at the end of the previous year as chief of the German desk. These pro-Axis leaders, particularly Ōshima, Usui, and Yamagata, had been continuing their secret activities, in close cooperation with the German embassy, for the conclusion of a tripartite pact.[37] But in spite of the activities of the Axis faction, German diplomatic maneuvers, and the continuing deterioration in Japanese-American relations, it was recognized that a radical change in the European situation would be required before a reorientation in Japan's policy toward Germany could be effected.

The "phony war," wherein the German and Anglo-French armies maintained their battle lines on the western front and avoided full-scale war, was quickly ended by the opening of Germany's campaign in Denmark and Norway on April 9, 1940. On May 10 the German army took the offensive on the western front and, by first invading Holland, Belgium, and Luxembourg, broke through the Maginot Line with its overwhelming mobile power. At the end of the month it launched an annihilation offensive against the British and French forces, achieving a historic victory with the "tragedy of Dunkirk." On June 14 Paris fell, and on June 22 a truce agreement was concluded between Germany and France.

The drastic change in the European situation brought about by the overwhelming victory of Germany had an immediate effect upon the political situation in Japan. First of all, the rising prestige of Germany in the eyes of the Japanese resulted in resurrecting pro-Nazi sentiment from its demise following the conclusion of the Nonaggression Pact. This change in public opinion naturally affected the balance of power between the Anglo-American and Axis factions in Japan. At the same time the "New Political Structure Movement," whose objective was to create a "powerful integrated political system" after the Nazi pattern, suddenly intensified its activities and made a change on the Japanese political scene inevitable. Second, the existence of the French and Dutch colonies in Indochina and the East Indies now swam into the ken of the Japanese people, and a mood to seize the opportunity to advance into Southeast Asia spread to all strata of society.

At a press conference on April 15 Foreign Minister Arita made Japan's special interest in the Dutch East Indies manifest, stating that as the war in Europe progressed, Japan would "follow attentively any development that may affect the status quo in the Netherlands East Indies." [38] On May 17 he instructed Ambassador Kurusu to obtain confirmation from the German government that it would give Japan a free rein in the Netherlands East Indies.[39] After the fall of France Kurusu called on State Secretary Weizsaecker on June 21 and requested German support for Japanese actions in French Indochina, stating that "Japan could not remain disinterested in Indochina." [40]

Thus it was becoming clear that the New Order in East Asia, the mainstay of Arita's diplomacy, included Southeast Asia within its bounds. On June 29 in a radio speech entitled "Japan's Position and the International Situation," Arita expressed his belief in certain principles that might be called an East Asian Monroe Doctrine. This was an open declaration that it was Japan's responsibility "to maintain the coexistence, coprosperity, and security" of all the races in Southeast Asia and that

Japan would deter "European and American nations from disturbing the peace in East Asia." [41]

Thus, in response to the changing situation in Europe the Yonai cabinet began to assume an increasingly positive posture toward a "southern advance," while slackening its efforts to improve relations with the western powers. It should be noted, however, that the cabinet relied exclusively upon diplomacy to achieve its objectives and was inclined to avoid the use of force. The moderation of this southern advance policy was criticized not only within the cabinet by such people as Koiso Kuniaki, minister of overseas affairs,[42] but even more in the army, which represented a more radical view.

Already after the "great victory at Dunkirk" voices were being raised in various quarters in Japan demanding that the government reexamine its policy of noninvolvement in the European war. These voices grew more and more insistent, until the *Ōsaka Mainichi shimbun* declared on June 22 that "the need for a complete renovation of foreign policy has now become an article of national faith." Popular sentiment, afraid that Japan would be left out of the race for the redistribution of colonies, expressed itself in such catch phrases as "don't miss the bus" and supported the rise of the extremists. In this atmosphere the view grew dominant in the army that Japan should endeavor to settle the China Incident speedily by forcing Britain and France to cut off their supply routes to Chungking and should secure the natural resources to the south, even resorting to the use of force if necessary. On May 19 and again early in June the Military Affairs Bureau of the Army Ministry had called for preparations for a drive to the south. At a conference on June 24, Iwakuro Hideo, chief of the ministry's Military Section, reportedly astonished the members of the Army General Staff by suddenly presenting his long-held view of the necessity of a surprise attack on Singapore.[43]

On June 25 Army Minister Hata assembled the staff members of the ministry and exhorted them to "Seize this golden opportunity! Don't let anything stand in the way!" Meanwhile, army authorities were drawing up a basic policy for a Japanese advance to the south, and by June 22 the work had progressed to the point where a policy draft was examined by the responsible persons in the Army Ministry and the Army General Staff. Finally, on July 3, at a conference of the key individuals in the ministry and the General Staff, a final decision was reached on an army draft of a basic national policy,[44] the essential parts of which were as follows:

OUTLINE OF THE MAIN PRINCIPLES
FOR COPING WITH THE CHANGING
WORLD SITUATION

The empire, faced with changes in the world situation, will endeavor to settle the China Incident as quickly as possible, while improving its domestic and foreign position generally, and will seize the most opportune time to solve the problem of the south. If the China Incident cannot be brought to an end completely, the policy toward the south will be determined on the basis of the general situation at home and abroad. In either case, *preparations for war should be completed generally by the target date of the end of August.**

Essential Points

Article 1. In its policy toward the China Incident, Japan will exert every effort to bring about the prompt submission of the Chungking regime and will make special efforts to block acts of assistance by third powers to Chiang Kai-shek.

In foreign policy, emphasis will be placed first on policies toward Germany, Italy, and the Soviet Union, *with the special objectives of strengthening Japan's political solidarity with Germany and Italy and of improving rapidly its relations with Soviet Russia.* As far as the United States is concerned, Japan will keep abreast of changes in the world situation and will avoid creating unnecessary friction, but Japan will not refrain from facing the inevitable aggravations which may result from carrying out whatever policies are deemed necessary for the empire.

1) In regard to French Indochina (Kwangchow Bay included), we shall force it to stop completely all assistance to Chiang Kai-shek and, together with this, force it to shoulder the burden of replenishing our troops and to recognize our rights to

* Hereafter all italics have been added by the author.

the use of airfields and the passage of troops. Should circumstances require it, military force will be used.

2) In regard to Hong Kong, along with the complete closing of the routes for aiding Chiang via Burma, Japan will first of all vigorously launch various operations to eradicate enemy elements in the area. An attack upon Hong Kong will be carried out upon consideration of the general situation and only after Japan has determined to wage war against Britain.

3) In regard to the Dutch East Indies, for the time being Japan will endeavor to secure its vital resources through diplomatic negotiations.

4) In view of the importance of the French possessions in the South Pacific for Japan's national defense, Japan will act speedily to acquire them through diplomatic negotiations (such as purchase), if at all possible.

5) In regard to the foreign concessions in China, in accordance with the various above-mentioned operations, Japan will work to eradicate enemy elements and secure the withdrawal of troops of belligerent countries, and at the same time will induce China [the Wang Ching-wei government] gradually to repossess these areas.

In case of war with Britain, Japan will forcibly seize the British concessions and will endeavor to recover the other concessions by friendly measures if possible.

6) In regard to other areas in the south, Japan will endeavor to lead them by friendly measures to cooperate with Japan's operations.

Article 2. In regard to the use of military force in the south, Japan will decide its time, scope, and method upon consideration of various conditions at home and abroad, especially the state of the China Incident, the European situation, and our war preparedness. *It will attack Hong Kong and the Malay peninsula, restricting insofar as possible its operations to Britain alone. It will endeavor insofar as possible to avoid war with the United States;* however, anticipating that in the end it will resort to the use of force against the United States if the situation requires, Japan will make the necessary military preparations.

In regard to the Dutch East Indies, Japan will endeavor to secure the military resources there by political measures, but it will resort to the use of force if the situation requires.[45]

This "Outline" reflected the army's view that Japan should use force to attempt to expand its influence to the south, firm in the resolve to fight Britain. In addition, in its diplomatic policy it should reject its past policy of neutrality and noninvolvement in the European war and strengthen its alliance with the Axis; at the same time it should adjust its relations with the Soviet Union, adopting a policy of confrontation with the Old Order.

Meanwhile, as already stated, momentum was building up within the Japanese government for the southern advance. In regard to the European war, more emphasis had come to be placed upon a "positive policy of noninvolvement" and upon "moral support" for Germany and Italy as the government began to contemplate a change in its foreign policy. Some attempts were in fact made to approach Germany diplomatically about strengthening the understanding. On June 19, for instance, Ambassador Kurusu called on Dr. Josef Knoll, chief of the Political Affairs Bureau of the German Foreign Office, to mention the desire of Satō Naotake, head of a Japanese mission to Italy, to visit Germany. At the same time he explained that there had been a growing recognition in Japan of the importance of an alliance with Germany, even outside of pro-Axis circles. Japan, he said, was hoping for close economic cooperation with Germany, particularly in the field of heavy industry, and was contemplating a new world order that would divide the world into four major blocs: Germany-Italy, the Soviet Union, Japan-China, and the United States.[46] The new trend in Arita's diplomacy was also expressed by special envoy Satō when he interviewed Foreign Minister Ribbentrop on July 8. Pointing out the close, cooperative, and interdependent relations that had existed between Japan and Germany in the past, Satō asked that Germany give friendly consideration to Japan's efforts to establish the New Order in East Asia.[47]

Thus, as can be seen from the statements of Kurusu and Satō, Arita's diplomacy was aiming at the establishment of the New Order in East Asia and inclining toward a closer alignment with Germany; but a military alliance with Germany was not part of his design. The basic conception of Yonai and Arita seems to have been that Japan must advance toward the south, and for this purpose closer cooperation with Germany would be necessary. On the other hand, it was absolutely imperative to avoid bringing Japan's relations with Britain and the United

States into a state of war by resorting to the use of force for the southern advance or by concluding a military alliance with Germany. Therefore, a dichotomy existed between their policy and that of the army as represented by the "Outline."

Meanwhile the public, which was all in favor of a drive to the south, strongly criticized the government for being lukewarm. On June 25, for instance, the *Hōchi shimbun* carried a lead editorial that declared: "Arita diplomacy stands at a turning point. The pro-Anglo-American-French policy has failed." On July 13 the *Tōkyō Asahi shimbun* asserted that "a drastic change in our empire's diplomacy is inevitable." Germany, Italy, and Japan, it said, "will inevitably establish closer ties to promote their great enterprise of establishing a new world order. . . . The era of 'pallid diplomacy' has ended." On July 14 the *Ōsaka Mainichi shimbun* vigorously tolled the funeral bells for Arita diplomacy, crying, "Now is the time for a drastic change in our foreign policy," and holding up "four targets" for the new policy to aim at: a Japanese-German-Italian alliance, the southern advance, the security of the East Asian sphere, and the abandonment of the pro-Anglo-American diplomacy. On June 18 a People's Roundtable Conference on the Current Situation was set up. The conference aimed at harnessing the energies of the various strata of the nation to bring about the downfall of the Yonai cabinet and the expulsion of the pro-Anglo-American forces from the government. It proclaimed as its political program "the adjustment and reinforcement of the domestic political system" and "the establishment of a strong foreign policy." [48] But it was the army that dealt the Yonai cabinet its fatal blow.

The army had been suspicious of the Yonai cabinet from its inception. It now decided to liquidate the Arita diplomacy, which it felt was not responding to the new developments in the international situation, and, with the support of public opinion, to institute a radical southern advance policy and strengthen the Axis alliance, thereby bringing down the cabinet. To launch its attack, the army seized on Arita's radio speech of June 29, which it criticized as being "contradictory to the policy the cabinet had so far followed and an attempt to forestall the activities of pro-German elements in order to prolong the life of the cabinet." Furthermore, it demanded that Suma Yakichirō, chief of the Public Information Division of the Foreign Ministry, appear at military police headquarters, charging that "he had leaked the original draft of Arita's speech to the *Asahi shimbun* and had made the army's objections public at a press conference." [49]

The army's challenge shook the Yonai cabinet. Then, on July 5 a plot was discovered among certain members of a rightist group known as the Shimpeitai or "Heaven-Sent Soldiers Unit," who sought to murder various pro-Anglo-American officials, senior statesmen, and industrialists. Even though the plot was nipped in the bud, the knowledge of its existence was sufficient to intensify the feeling of political insecurity. On July 4, the day after the decision had been reached on the draft "Outline," the middle-ranking officers who formed the backbone of the Army General Staff presented to Army Minister Hata, in the name of the chief of the General Staff, the following petition:

> It is essential that the empire solve the China Incident as speedily as possible. For this purpose it is urgent that the nation not only strengthen preparedness at home but also cope positively and quickly with the ever-changing international situation. Nevertheless, the policy of the present cabinet is negative and timid, and it is feared that it will adversely affect morale and unity within the army. It is now deemed imperative to set up a powerful cabinet of the entire nation to execute various policies without vacillation. In this connection, we request you, the army minister, to take appropriate action.[50]

On July 8 General Anami Korechika, the vice army minister, visited Marquis Kido Kōichi, lord keeper of the privy seal, and informed him of the army's opinion that "the Yonai cabinet is not suitable for undertaking talks with Germany and Italy," that the cabinet should be replaced, and that the appointment of Prince Konoe Fumimaro as prime minister was desired.[51] Thus, a full-fledged political crisis was induced. On July 16 Army Minister Hata presented his resignation. When the army's Big Three (the army minister, the chief of the Army General Staff, and the inspector-general of military education) decided in conference not to recommend a successor to Hata, the Yonai cabinet was forced to resign.

During the last days of the Yonai cabinet, meetings had been held among the responsible section chiefs of the Army, Navy, and Foreign ministries, who had agreed on a "Proposal for Strengthening Cooperation between Japan, Germany, and Italy." Although this plan did not necessarily reflect the ideas of the key members of the Yonai government, it was significant in that it showed that within the bureaucracy the trend was toward abandoment of so-called "pallid diplomacy," and it pointed the way the succeeding cabinet was to follow.[52]

At the first meeting on July 12, Andō Yoshirō, speaking for the Foreign Ministry as chief of the First (Soviet) Section of its Europe-Asia Bureau, presented a draft. He explained that its object was to have Germany recognize Japan's political and economic leadership in the south as its living-space, while Japan would recognize Germany's political and economic leadership in Europe and Africa as its living-space.

The Foreign Ministry had been prompted to make this proposal by Satō's report on his conference with Ribbentrop on July 8, which had created certain misgivings about Germany's real intentions. As explained in Andō's draft: "In regard to the Dutch East Indies and French Indochina, may it not be Germany's intention to grasp political leadership over these areas, allowing Japan to secure economic interests only? May Germany intend, in other words, not to recognize Japan's political leadership in these regions?" The Foreign Ministry's own assessment of the world situation was that "Germany will certainly conquer Britain, seize hegemony over Europe and Africa, and establish a new order there." Consequently, the ministry felt it imperative to forestall a German move by speedily arranging for the mutual recognition by Japan and Germany of each other's respective new orders and thereby to secure Germany's acknowledgment of Japan's political leadership in the south.

To persuade Germany to agree in its present frame of mind, it was felt essential to offer it some kind of compensation. The compensation the ministry had in mind was for Japan to ease

Germany's burdens in its war with Britain by taking suitable diversionary action in East Asia, such as applying pressure on British interests in the Far East or supporting the independence movements in Burma and India. However, Japan should avoid entering the war at all costs. In short, the strengthened alignment policy the Foreign Ministry had in mind was "to seek the maximum cooperation possible short of involvement in war." This conception was not yet that of a military alliance; but in emphasizing a division of the world into living-spaces and in contemplating a confrontation with the United States, it was significantly different from the "Proposal for Strengthening the Anti-Comintern Pact" approved by the Five Ministers Conference in August 1938.[53]

At the second and final meeting on July 16 the army and navy representatives expressed various opinions about the Foreign Ministry draft; however, both agreed with it in principle and in the end, with slight revisions, the representatives of all three ministries accepted it. Perhaps having in mind the "Outline" adopted by the military authorities on July 3, the army representative stressed that Japan should conduct the negotiations with "the attitude that Japan might engage in a war with Britain independently." [54] But that day the Yonai cabinet resigned. Further discussion of the projected Axis alliance was therefore held over for the next cabinet as its most important task.

Unless You Go Into the Tiger's Den, You Cannot Catch the Tiger's Cub

In December 1936, the month following the conclusion of the Japanese-German Anti-Comintern Pact, Matsuoka Yōsuke, president of the South Manchuria Railway Company, explained the significance of the pact to an audience in the company's Concordia Hall (Kyōwa Kaikan), as follows:

> The present pact has come to replace the Anglo-Japanese alliance as our guidepost. Since we struggle against the Comintern, at present the world's gravest problem, we must struggle with

firm resolution. A half-hearted effort will never do. We must go into the battle assisting and embracing one another. . . . It is a characteristic of the Japanese race that, once we have promised to cooperate, we never look back or enter into an alliance with others. It is for us only to march side by side, resolved to go forward together, even if it means committing "double suicide." [55]

This was a high-sounding speech, characteristic of Matsuoka, playing for the gallery. And it was none other than he who, following the downfall of Yonai, emerged into the limelight on July 22, 1940, as foreign minister in the second Konoe cabinet, calling for an alliance by which "Japan should push boldly forward, hand in hand with Germany," not hesitating to commit "double suicide" with Germany if need be.

Matsuoka knew well the old ministry at Kasumigaseki. As a promising and talented young member of the Chōshū clique led by Yamagata Aritomo, he had spent the first seventeen years of his official career there, devising positive policies for managing affairs on the Asian continent. After World War I his positive continental policy no longer fit the trend of Japanese diplomacy. Moreover, his rustic pose was at odds with the ministry's atmosphere of traditional court diplomacy. He resigned his post to join the South Manchuria Railway Comapany, where he moved into the front line of Japan's continental activities. Matsuoka's return after nineteen years to take over at Kasumigaseki, therefore, indicated that the trend had changed and that a heterodox diplomacy was to replace the orthodoxy of Arita.

Matsuoka apparently was briefed by Ōshima and others on the background of the Axis alliance question. [56] In addition it may be inferred that he knew a lot about the moves inside the army through his connections with officers such as Colonel Usui. The strength of his own interest in the alliance problem is clear from the fact that when the German economic mission came to Japan in February, Matsuoka invited its chief, Emil Helfferich, to his own home for a chat. [57] It seems quite certain, threfore, that when Matsuoka accepted his appointment as foreign minister he knew well that Japan's most pressing foreign policy problem was to decide on its course of action in

regard to the southern advance and the tripartite alliance. Or
may it not be said that he accepted the position of foreign minister with his mind already made up on these questions?

In any case, soon after his appointment as foreign minister
Matsuoka requested Andō Yoshirō, the section chief responsible, to report on the progress of the alliance question. Andō
showed Matsuoka the "Proposal for Strengthening Cooperation
between Japan, Germany, and Italy" that had been agreed to on
July 16. Matsuoka glanced at it and declared, "This won't do."
He thrust it back at Andō, inscribed with his pet phrase,
"Unless you go into the tiger's den, you cannot catch the tiger's
cub." [58] To Matsuoka, a proposal for strengthening the alignment that was based on the principle of seeking "the maximum
cooperation possible short of involvement in war" was insuf-
ficient. Only if Japan and Germany showed their firm resolve
"to go into battle assisting and embracing one another . . . even
if it means committing double suicide," Matsuoka judged,
would Japan be able to achieve the object of the southern advance while at the same time avoiding war with the Anglo-
American forces. "Unless you go into the tiger's den, you cannot catch the tiger's cub" truly expressed Matsuoka's "brink-of-
war diplomacy."

Meanwhile, on July 19, three days before his new cabinet
was formed, Prince Konoe called Lieutenant-General Tōjō
Hideki, Vice Admiral Yoshida Zengo, and Matsuoka, who were
to take the portfolios of army, navy, and foreign minister respectively, to a conference at the Tekigaisō, his villa in the Tokyo
suburb of Ogikubo. Having in mind no doubt the Four Ministers Conference they were all soon to participate in, Konoe
named it the Four Pillars Conference, but it has become known
generally as the Ogikubo Conference. There opinions were exchanged on the important national policies to be promoted by
the new cabinet, including the strengthening of the Axis alignment.

Exactly what went on at this conference has come to be
known in part from the postwar statements of three of the participants; however, these statements are not in complete agree-

ment, and there still remain some unanswered questions. Matsuoka died in 1946, leaving no explanation. Konoe, who took his own life in 1945, did leave a memoir, *Ushinawareshi seiji* (Politics that Failed), published in 1946, in which he said only that "at the time of the formation of my second cabinet, we decided to strengthen our relations with the Axis in accordance with the requests of the army, navy, and foreign ministers. But our policy at the time had not yet developed to the point of a military alliance." [59] Tōjō stated, in an affidavit rebutting the prosecutor's charge at the Tokyo war crimes trials, that it was not true that the conference had "decided on any authoritative foreign policy" but had been merely a discussion concerning the framework of the "Foundations of National Policy" adopted later, including such subjects as "the reform of the national structure to cope with conditions at home and abroad, the need to settle the China Incident, the reorientation of foreign policy, and the strengthening of national defense." According to Tōjō, "only an agreement of opinions" was arrived at during the conference; he did not mention that the problem of strengthening cooperation with the Axis had even been taken up.[60] As for Yoshida, he told Yabe Teiji, who interviewed him while collecting data for a biography of Konoe:

The conference consisted mainly of *extemporaneous free conversation*. Prince Konoe spoke while looking at a memo, but he didn't say anything important, and I have almost forgotten what it was. We did not discuss problems by taking them up item by item as Tōjō implies in his affidavit. . . . Concerning the Axis problem, during the last days of the Yonai cabinet . . . we had *consultations on the exchange of information and the intensification of propaganda in connection with the Anti-Comintern Pact.* The navy was passive in the matter, but a concrete program was drawn up, and the bureau chiefs of the three ministries signed the draft. The draft included measures for increasing cooperation with the Axis and also for a drastic adjustment of relations with the Soviet Union. This program was handed along to the Konoe cabinet before it had been formally decided upon. Since I attended the Ogikubo Conference with this background in mind, I stated there that, *while I agreed with this understanding of the three bureau chiefs, I was not thinking of a tripartite alliance.* This being the case, *there could not have been any items on which agreements were reached at the conference.* We talked for about two hours, dined, and went home.[61]

Is it true that the Ogikubo Conference was, as Yoshida stated, something on the order of extemporaneous conversation, with no understandings reached? Or, as Tōjō stated, was the conference merely a discussion of general problems which would constitute the framework of the "Foundations of National Policy"?

In the Konoe Papers there have survived two documents concerning the Ogikubo Conference. On one a marginal note is written in Matsuoka's hand: "I shall explain this directly to you." The document sets forth basic policies for such problems as global relations, the settlement of the China Incident, and the reorganization of Japan's internal structure. The other is a slight modification of the first, while identical to it in fundamental principles. It contains a marginal note in Konoe's writing: "Decision of the Four Pillars Conference during the formation of the cabinet." Yoshida must have referred to one of these documents when he said that Konoe had spoken from a memo in his hand. It may therefore be concluded that the conference was conducted on the basis of one of these documents, and that it resulted in an agreement among the four concerned which was considered by Konoe to be "a decision." Under the title "Global Policy," Part 2 of the "Decision" contains the following:

1) In order to cope with the drastic changes in the international situation and to establish rapidly the New Order in East Asia, Japan will strengthen the Japanese-German-Italian axis and will execute its major policies so as to coordinate developments in the east with those in the west. The method and timing of strengthening ties with the Axis powers will be determined so as to take advantage of favorable developments in the world situation.

2) Concerning relations with the Soviet Union, Japan will conclude with that country a nonaggression pact to guarantee the boundaries between Japan, Manchukuo, and Mongolia, to remain in effect for a period of five to ten years, and will make

efforts to settle speedily the questions pending between that country and Japan. During the effective period of the proposed nonaggression pact, Japan will strengthen its military preparedness against the Soviet Union so as to be invincible.

3) Japan will take positive measures to draw into the New Order in East Asia the British, French, Dutch, and Portuguese colonies in East Asia and adjacent islands. In connection with the above measures, however, Japan will reject any idea of convening a meeting of powers.

4) While Japan will try to avoid unnecessary conflict with the United States, Japan is firmly resolved to resist armed intervention by the United States related to the establishment of the New Order in East Asia.[62]

As this document shows, the four participants in the Ogikubo Conference did arrive at an agreement on a policy for strengthening the tie with the Axis powers; and although this preceded the formation of the second Konoe cabinet and therefore cannot be said to have been a formal decision on national policy, nevertheless such an agreement among the individuals who were to constitute the Four Ministers Conference is extremely significant in the decision-making process. However, as shown by Yoshida's remarks, the four concerned were not yet agreed, at this point, on the form or strength this tie should have.

Yoshida understood the contents of the policy for strengthening the tie with the Axis exclusively on the basis of the "Proposal for Strengthening Cooperation between Japan, Germany, and Italy" agreed to by the Army, Navy, and Foreign Ministry officials on July 16. Moreover, he seems to have misunderstood the aim of the "Proposal" as "the exchange of information and the intensification of propaganda in connection with the Anti-Comintern Pact." Consequently, before a tripartite military alliance could be concluded, it was to be expected that there would be trouble in the cabinet.

On July 22, the day the Konoe cabinet was instituted, the top leaders of the army and navy held a roundtable conference at the Suikōsha or Navy League. The army was represented by Vice Army Minister Anami Korechika, Chief of the Military Affairs Bureau of the Army Ministry Mutō Akira, Vice Chief of the General Staff Sawada Shigeru, and Chief of the Operations Division of the General Staff Tominaga Kyōji; the navy was represented by Vice Minister Sumiyama Tokutarō, Chief of the Naval Affairs Bureau of the Navy Ministry Abe Katsuo, Vice Chief of the Navy General Staff Kondō Nobutake, Chief of the Operations Division of the Navy General Staff Ugaki Matome. The purpose of the conference was to coordinate the views of the army and navy in preparation for the Imperial Head-quarters–Cabinet Liaison Conference scheduled for July 27.

The views of the two services had already been harmonized on the 15th in consultations among responsible army and navy authorities on the draft, "Outline of the Main Principles for Coping with the Changing World Situation," which was to be taken up at the Liaison Conference. The purpose of the round-table conference, therefore, was to confirm the agreement at the next higher level. One item on the agenda of the conference was "the content and strength of political ties with Germany and Italy." Mutō declared that "if Germany and Italy propose a military alliance, we must accept." Following the same line, Sawada enunciated a Matsuoka-style double-suicide view: "We should resolve to share our fate with Germany and Italy." Thus it became clear that the leaders of the army had already deter-mined on a tripartite military alliance. The navy, on the other hand, reported that it contemplated only one or two amend-ments to the Foreign Ministry's "Proposal for Strengthening Cooperation between Japan, Germany, and Italy" and had in mind no stronger ties than envisaged there. Thus a wide gap between high-level army and navy views concerning the prob-lem of the Axis alliance stood revealed. The discussion ended with the conclusion that "Japan will reconsider the possibility of a military alliance if it should be proposed by Germany and Italy," and the divergence was barely patched over with the statement that for the time being "Japan will proceed to strengthen political ties." [63]

The "Main Principles for Coping with the Changing World Situation" was approved at the Liaison Conference on July 27,[64] and "strengthening political ties with Germany and Italy" was formally adopted as the goal of the new cabinet's foreign policy.

But it should be noted that even at this late date, because of the navy's attitude, the Japanese government was still undecided whether these ties should be developed into a military alliance.

After having obtained the "decision" of the Ogikubo Conference and the approval of the Liaison Conference on the "Main Principles," Matsuoka embarked upon the formulation of a substantive policy draft. On July 30 a document entitled "On Strengthening Cooperation between Japan, Germany, and Italy" was drafted, possibly by someone close to Matsuoka, and became the guiding statement of the Konoe cabinet's policy on this subject.[65]

When we compare this document, which might be called the "Matsuoka Draft," with that adopted by the bureau chiefs of the three ministries on July 16, we find no change in the basic point of mutual recognition and cooperation by Germany and Japan in the establishment of their new orders. However, while there are many points which indicate that a degree of consideration was given to the July 16 draft, there is a clear difference in the content and strength of the proposed alignment. Whereas the July 16 draft aimed at "the maximum cooperation possible short of involvement in war," the Matsuoka Draft stipulated that "in the event that Germany and Italy should express a desire for Japanese military cooperation with them against Britain, Japan will be prepared, in principle, to meet their desire." There is no doubt that the Matsuoka Draft expanded the alignment to the level of "a military alliance against Britain," even though it attempted to avoid assuming the duty of automatic participation in a war by reserving the right of independent decision on the actual use of force. Furthermore, cooperation was extended to apply against the United States, the Matsuoka Draft adding the following new clause: "In the event of a danger of either contracting party entering upon a state of war with the United States, both parties will confer on measures to be taken."

The government having decided on the policy to "strengthen political ties with Germany and Italy" and Matsuoka having obtained a plan for its realization, the time had come for him to begin diplomatic negotiations with Germany. Matsuoka thought the first step would be to feel out German intentions and at the same time to transmit indirectly to Germany Japan's desire for closer ties. The reason for his caution at this time, he later explained to an Imperial Conference, was that he felt it would be an egregious error for Japan to act so impatiently as to allow Germany to detect any weakness in its position, thus putting Japan at a disadvantage during the negotiations.[66]

Japan was no longer as sure of Germany's enthusiasm for an alliance. After the drastic change in the international balance of power brought about by the German military victories, and in view of Hitler's speech on July 19 holding out to the British people the possibility of peace, Japan naturally assumed that Germany would be less interested than it had been a year before. Moreover, Ribbentrop's attitude during his talk with Satō on July 8 seemed to confirm Japanese officials in this feeling.

Under the circumstances, Matsuoka concluded that Japan's best strategy for profitable negotiations would be not to follow meekly the German dictate but "to adopt the attitude that Japan would hold firmly to its independent position, that it had no need to cooperate with Germany and Italy, and that it would join hands with the United States or even dare to save Britain if that were necessary or convenient for its existence and mission." [67]

On August 1 Matsuoka took two important steps. One was to demand of Charles Arsène-Henry, the French ambassador in Tokyo, that transit facilities in northern French Indochina be provided for Japanese troops. The other was to begin "reconnoitering" a tripartite alliance by talking with German Ambassador Ott. Inviting Ott to tea, Matsuoka began by saying: "As you have probably discovered, both the Japanese government and people favor strengthening the Axis, but the cabinet has not yet come to a decision. I cannot persuade Prime Minister Konoe and the other members of the cabinet unless I know at least the outline of Germany's intention or attitude toward this." He was especially anxious to ascertain Germany's attitude on the following three particulars:

  1) Japan intends to establish a New Order in Greater East Asia, based on the ideal of the liberation and freedom, the coex-

istence and coprosperity of all nations and races in that sphere. I believe that Japan can manage by itself in what concerns China, and I do not question Germany about it. But I would like to know what attitude Germany will assume toward the aforesaid Japanese ideal or policy in the South Seas. What does Germany itself want to gain in the South Seas?

2) What does Germany want and what can it do as regards Soviet-Japanese relations?

3) Concerning American-Japanese relations, what is Germany going to do vis-à-vis the United States, and what is it able to do for Japan? [68]

It happened that on that same day Ambassador Kurusu called on State Secretary Weizsaecker in Berlin to obtain the German views in order to give appropriate advice to the new cabinet before it decided on a definite foreign policy. Kurusu attempted to sound out the German attitude on two points: whether Germany still considered an adjustment of Japanese-Soviet relations as important as before, and whether Germany wished the new Japanese cabinet to intensify or diminish its anti-Anglo-Saxon policy.[69] On August 7, having received instructions from Tokyo, Kurusu visited Weizsaecker again, this time to ask for Germany's reaction to Japan's plan to establish the New Order in Greater East Asia.[70]

Ott avoided making any commitment to Matsuoka, and his manner of response gave the impression that Germany had lost its previous enthusiasm for an alliance. Ott expressed strong dissatisfaction at the insulting way the Japanese Foreign Ministry had treated him. He also criticized the Satō mission to Italy, saying, "I am firmly convinced that it has been sent by Japan to alienate Germany from Italy." [71] Similarly in Berlin, during Kurusu's second visit. Weizsaecker carefully refrained from committing himself.[72] Their response must have disappointed Matsuoka, who had expected that the talks would be a first step toward alliance negotiations.

Had the German government no intention whatever, at the time, of concluding a tripartite pact? If it did retain that desire, why had Ott and Weizsaecker responded so coolly? The answer seems in part to be that Germany did not correctly understand Matsuoka's intentions. Ott's report to Berlin of his talk with Matsuoka on August 1 pictured a conference somewhat different from that reported in the Foreign Ministry's summary of the Matsuoka-Ott conversation.

According to Ott, Matsuoka had expressed his readiness to make positive efforts to solve such pending problems between Japan and Germany as economic cooperation and compensation for German economic losses in China and had asked "what attitude Germany could be expected to take in regard to Japan's well-known *economic plans* for Greater East Asia." Ott further reported that at the conclusion of the conversation Matsuoka, referring to Japan's demanding of the French government that it consent to the passage of Japanese troops through northern French Indochina, had stated that he would appreciate it if the German government raised no objections to Japan's demands and used its influence to persuade the French government to accede to them.[73] Weizsaecker was under the impression, following his interview with Kurusu on August 7, that the real aim of the Japanese approach was "to find out Germany's view of these Japanese plans for Greater East Asia." [74] Judging from this evidence, it is safe to say that Germany interpreted Matsuoka's statements to mean that he proposed to continue the former cabinet's policy toward Germany, which had concentrated on obtaining Germany's disinterest concerning French Indochina and the Dutch East Indies. Hence, Germany did not clearly grasp Matsuoka's positive attitude toward an alliance, which entertained even the possibility of concluding a "military alliance against Britain."

Needless to say, Germany's attitude toward Japan at the time was influenced by its great victories in the European war and the consequent change in its international position. After Dunkirk, Germany's military need to have the Japanese fleet check the British forces in East Asia had lessened, and the prospect of a British surrender without German landing operations on British soil was rapidly growing. At the same time, the possibility of American participation in the war was thought to be slight, and Germany may well have feared that an alliance with Japan might have the adverse effect of further inciting the United States.

These changes in Germany's situation not only decreased

the enthusiasm of German advocates of a Japanese alliance, including Foreign Minister Ribbentrop, but also strengthened the position of those opposed to an alliance within the German Foreign Office and elsewhere. Moreover, German dissatisfaction with the Japanese attitude toward economic cooperation had increased since the time of the previous cabinet. Thus, in response to Japan's request for German support on the Indochina question, Emil Wiehl, chief of the Economic Bureau of the Foreign Office, stated in a memorandum of June 20 that "the demand of Japan for a friendly gesture from Germany is somewhat astonishing, in view of the attitude which Japan has adopted during the war in respect of economic relations with Germany." He pointed out that Japan had not cooperated in such matters as the export of soya beans from Manchuria or the shipment of tungsten and tin.[75]

Germany's cold response to the Japanese approach and the following silence must have made Matsuoka impatient. On August 13 he invited Ott to come to see him and, as a device to force Germany to make a decision on the alliance problem, hinted at the possibility of a Japanese-American reconciliation as a result of overtures from the United States:

. . . since the battle in Flanders America has been trying by means of increased threats and enticements to keep Japan away from a rapprochement with the Axis Powers. Thus America on the one side announces the embargo on oil and scrap iron, which in first line is directed against Japan, and on the other indicates readiness to guarantee a larger loan. In principle Japan would not reject the loan, but in no case would she accept thereby any sort of obligations which could hinder her rapprochement with the Axis Powers. The likelihood that the loan will materialize is therefore extremely slight.[76]

On August 23 Ambassador Kurusu was suddenly informed by Ribbentrop that Heinrich Stahmer, promoted to minister plenipotentiary for the occasion, would soon be dispatched to Tokyo.[77] According to Stahmer's affidavit to the Tokyo War Crimes Tribunal, he was instructed by Ribbentrop to perform the following three major tasks: (1) to discover the actual intentions of the Japanese government toward Germany; (2) to open negotiations together with Ambassador Ott should Japan show an inclination to conclude an agreement with Germany; (3) in case approval by Berlin should be needed on any item in the negotiations, to report at once every detail before continuing the negotiations.[78]

The dispatch of Stahmer to Tokyo indicated that the German government had at last begun to respond to Matsuoka's approaches and had decided to enter into negotiations should Japanese intentions to conclude an alliance be confirmed. Three possible explanations may be offered for the revival of German enthusiasm for an alliance with Japan.

The first is that by this time Germany had had to modify its hitherto optimistic expectation of a British surrender. As Hitler's call for peace with Britain on July 19 indicated, the leaders of the German government had expected the British surrender to follow soon after the French. But since May the British people had rallied behind their new prime minister, Winston Churchill, and hardened their resolve to resist. Overcoming the "tragedy of Dunkirk," they intensified their war efforts. On July 22 Lord Halifax rejected Hitler's call to surrender, clearly proclaiming the unwillingness of the British people to conclude a dishonorable peace with Germany and their determination to fight on to victory. On July 16 Hitler had already issued Directive No. 16 concerning landing operations in the British Isles; however, the German navy, which had to face a far superior British navy, hesitated, and the radicals in the army became apprehensive as well. Thus, by the middle of August Hitler had had to scale down his original plans for a grand landing operation and in the end was forced to issue a directive that "the final order will not be given until the situation is clear," indicating the growing doubt in Hitler's mind that a landing operation could succeed.[79] It was only natural that the value of an alliance with Japan grew proportionately as the prospect of a protracted war against Britain loomed larger.

A second possible reason for Germany's renewed interest in an alliance was the weakening of its confidence that the United States would not enter the war. On August 1 Ott told Matsuoka:

As for the American problem, Germany does not think the United States will participate in the war. At this moment I hope you will pay special attention to the fact that Germany does not intend to dispute with America in the future but wants rather to come to a mutual understanding, which is believed to be possible. . . . Germany has collected authentic information about the United States, so the assertion that the Americans are in a high passion to participate in the war is groundless. Recently President Roosevelt has been brought to bay.[80]

Keeping America neutral had been the aim of German diplomacy since the outbreak of the European war. Even after the victory at Dunkirk Germany had been continuing a desperate propaganda war to influence the American public against their government's increase in aid to Britain.[81] Germany's leaders had always to consider relations with Japan in connection with relations with the United States. Meanwhile, in the middle of August two events occurred that impressed the world with the solidarity of the Anglo-Saxon bloc and at the same time crushed Germany's optimistic view of the war against it.

The first event was the announcement on August 17 by President Roosevelt and Canadian Prime Minister Mackenzie King of their agreement at Ogdensburg, N.Y., to establish a joint standing national defense conference for the defense of their two nations. The second was Churchill's announcement on August 20 of the forthcoming lease of bases to the United States in return for fifty American destroyers. Scholars are agreed that these events caused shock and frustration among Nazi leaders, who, as a result, began to contemplate the speedy conclusion of an alliance with Japan in hope of averting the danger of American participation in the war.[82]

A third possible reason for Germany's change of heart was its fear of a Japanese-American rapprochement. Even within the German government there appears to have been a strong tendency to suppose that the primary aim of the Konoe cabinet was the improvement of Japanese-American relations, and consequently to judge that Japan's approach to Germany might be merely a feint to further Japan's negotiations with the United

States.[83] Germany thus was watching very closely for any sign of an improvement in Japanese-American relations. It has been suggested that Ott's telegram of August 15, reporting rumors that Japan was prepared to conclude bilateral treaties with Britain, Holland, and the United States guaranteeing the status quo in Southeast Asia, was particularly influential in Germany's decision to approach Japan.[84]

In any event, the news of Stahmer's visit to Japan encouraged Matsuoka and created tensions within the Japanese government. Even though Japan did not have clear knowledge of the purpose of Stahmer's mission, it was not difficult to surmise that it had something to do with Matsuoka's approach to Germany. Stahmer was known to be a confidant of Ribbentrop who had been engaged in liaison work with the Japanese embassy in Berlin and had visited Japan in the spring of 1940. With the arrival of Kurusu's August 28 report of his talks with Ribbentrop and the August 29 report of Ambassador Tōgō Shigenori in Moscow on his talks there with Stahmer, the Tokyo government gradually concluded that the duties of the Stahmer mission included the strengthening of the alliance between Germany and Japan, and that this time Germany wanted Japan to take the initiative.[85]

The Japanese government had meanwhile continued to deliberate on an appropriate policy. The Matsuoka Draft of July 30, which envisaged a military alliance against Britain, had been presented to the responsible administrative officials of the army and navy for their reaction. The navy expressed the wish to make some amendments to the draft that did not touch upon its essential points, so a conference of army and navy officials was held on August 6. On the 7th the Army Ministry and the Army General Staff accepted the navy's suggestions and approved a new army-navy draft.[86] It was this document, entitled "On Strengthening Cooperation between Japan, Germany, and Italy," dated August 6, which was presented to the Tokyo War Crimes Tribunal.[87]

What draws our attention here is the fact that not only the Foreign Ministry and the army but those within the navy concerned with this matter as well were already inclined to approve a tripartite military alliance against Britain. However, as we have already observed, Navy Minister Yoshida had consistently refused to support such an alliance, and at the conference of army and navy heads on July 22 the top leaders of the navy, including the vice minister, had expressed their disapproval. Clearly there existed a grave difference of opinion between top and middle-ranking officers in the navy. But by the middle of August the idea of a tripartite pact had gained support even among the navy's top leaders, such as Chief of the Naval Affairs Bureau Abe Katsuo, and it was increasingly apparent that Yoshida was becoming isolated. Nevertheless, Yoshida held steadfastly to the views he had expressed when the cabinet was formed. The August 12 entry in the Army General Staff's *Confidential War Diary* reads: "Negotiations with Germany and Italy stalled. Still being studied by the navy minister. Ugh!" [88]

Thus it was the navy, and Yoshida in particular, that continued to prevent the government from coming to a decision.[89] But Stahmer's impending visit required that the impasse be resolved. On August 27 leaders of the Navy Ministry and the Navy General Staff met at the navy minister's official residence to discuss the problem. The conclusion of their conference was a confirmation of the navy's original position that "political ties between Japan, Germany, and Italy will incite the United States," indicating that their attitude toward a tripartite military alliance was still negative.[90] This situation caused Yoshida more and more anguish. He was aware that if he should stubbornly continue to oppose the pact the navy would bear the responsibility for its failure to be concluded, since the Foreign Ministry and the army had already taken up positions in support of it. This would also increase interservice friction with the army. Nor could he ignore the mood of middle-echelon naval officers. At the same time, behind the scenes naval elders such as Okada Keisuke and Yonai Mitsumasa were encouraging Yoshida to continue his opposition to the end.

Yoshida was placed in a terrible dilemma. His health, which had been declining, suddenly gave way, and on September 3, one day before a scheduled Four Ministers Conference, he had to be hospitalized. The following day he resigned his position as navy minister, and on September 5 Admiral Oikawa Koshirō was appointed to replace him. The new navy minister attended the rescheduled Four Ministers Conference the next day.

In contrast to Yoshida, who had been plunged into agony by the news of Stahmer's visit to Japan Foreign Minister Matsuoka had been galvanized into greater action. On August 27 he met former Ambassador Ōshima and asked his advice in preparing for the anticipated negotiations.[91] On August 28 Matsuoka appointed former Ambassador Shiratori and Saitō Yoshie as Foreign Ministry advisers. On September 1 he met with them and with Vice Foreign Minister Ōhashi Chūichi and Europe-Asia Bureau Chief Nishi Haruhiko to examine the August 6 army-navy draft "On Strengthening Cooperation between Japan, Germany, and Italy." [92] As a result, a revised Foreign Ministry draft was prepared for presentation to the Four Ministers Conference under the title "Draft Policy for Negotiating a Military Alliance." [93]

Matsuoka's new plan placed the United States on a level with Britain as the object of the alliance. The army-navy plan of August 6 had included the provision (in Appendix 1, paragraph 5): "In the event of a danger of either contracting party [Japan or Germany and Italy] entering into a state of war with the United States, both parties will confer on measures to be taken." In the new plan this was revised to read: "In the event of a danger of either contracting party entering into a state of war with the United States, the other contracting party will assist that party by all possible means." Thus, the scheme of a military alliance against Britain was expanded by this new plan into a military alliance against Britain and the United States. At the same time, by broadening the circumstances under which Japan might itself decide to take military action against Britain or the United States, the new plan increased the possibility that Japan might be drawn into war.

Why did Matsuoka want to harden the provisions of the alliance against the United States? The answer perhaps lies in the hardening of the attitude of the United States as evident in its measures of economic pressure on Japan following the formation of the Konoe cabinet. On July 25 the American government announced that it would include scrap iron and oil among those items whose exportation required governmental approval. On July 31 it placed an embargo upon aviation gasoline. In the latter part of August Japan intercepted a secret American telegram that hinted a total embargo against Japan was imminent.[94] Moreover, as Britain and France continued to retrench in the Far East, the United States began to oppose more strongly the establishment of Japan's New Order and to take upon itself the role of protector of western interests in the Far East. On August 7 it issued a stern warning against Japan's demand that it be allowed to move troops into northern French Indochina and announced its decision to take over the garrison of the International Concession in Shanghai from Britain, which announced the withdrawal of its forces from China.[95] In response to these American actions, it is likely that Matsuoka, ever a believer in "power politics" and strongly convinced that only a "firm attitude" could prevent a further deterioration of Japanese-American relations, redrafted the alliance proposal, strengthening its anti-American military provision with a view that this would have a deterrent effect on the United States.

On September 5 Matsuoka showed the new Foreign Ministry draft to the army and won its approval.[96] That same day he ordered Vice Minister Ōhashi and his two new advisers Shiratori and Saitō to draft an additional proposal, briefer and less specific than the Foreign Ministry draft. It was called "On Strengthening the Japanese-German-Italian Axis" and read as follows:

> Trends toward the strengthening of cooperation between Japan, Germany, and Italy having lately become very pronounced, it is believed that the time has now arrived for the immediate initiation of conversations among the three countries. Accordingly, it is proposed to begin negotiations with Germany in accordance with the following basic principles:
> 1) To reach a fundamental agreement between the three countries, in order that they shall mutually cooperate by all possible means in the establishment of a New Order in Europe and Asia.

2) To carry out consultations between the three countries in as short a time as possible in regard to the best means of implementing this cooperation.

3) Meanwhile, in a joint declaration of the three countries, to announce publicly the substance of (1) and (2) above.[97]

Matsuoka obviously prepared these documents for submission to the Four Ministers Conference of September 6,[98] but the relationship between them is not clear. It may be that he feared he could not secure the navy's agreement to the detailed military alliance plan but hoped that by the second, more general resolution he could get approval in principle of the policy to strengthen the Axis so as to be able to begin negotiations as soon as Stahmer arrived. On the other hand, it may be that the documents were conceived of as part of one overall plan, the shorter proposal being designed to settle policy for the first stage of the negotiations, and the military alliance plan to stipulate the policy for a second, more concrete stage.

The detailed proceedings of the September 6 Four Ministers Conference are not available, but Army Minister Tōjō, who was one of the participants, later summarized the discussion as follows:

Without prior arrangement or consultation, Foreign Minister Matsuoka suddenly raised the question of strengthening the Japanese-German-Italian axis. He suggested that the three powers cooperate in the establishment of a New Order in Europe and Asia, that they confer as speedily as possible on the best method for doing so, and that they announce their intention publicly. The conference approved.[99]

His statement leaves no doubt but that Matsuoka's brief authorizing resolution was decided upon. This is also confirmed by the fact that the Matsuoka-Stahmer negotiations were indeed begun a few days later. The fate of Matsuoka's Foreign Ministry draft, however, is less certain. It has been assumed hitherto that Matsuoka succeeded in getting it approved as well, including its call for a military alliance against Britain and the United States. Tōjō, however, does not mention it, and Oikawa, in his testimony to the War Crimes Tribunal, seems to deny it:

I had already accepted in general the new policy which was to receive the backing of the combined strength of Germany, Italy, and the Soviet Union, but I feared incurring war with the United States and Britain if we concluded a tripartite alliance with Germany and Italy. I felt, therefore, that *this was a proposal requiring the most careful deliberation before being acted upon*. In particular, I remained *absolutely opposed to accepting the obligation to go to war automatically*.[100]

Moreover, the responsible bureau chiefs in the navy are known not to have given their consent to it immediately but requested that the phrase "military alliance" be deleted from its title, changing it to read "Draft Policy for Negotiating Cooperation between Japan, Germany, and Italy," and that its contents be modified.[101] Consequently, it seems reasonable to conclude that Oikawa withheld his approval of the detailed military alliance plan just as Matsuoka feared he would, thus preventing the conference from voting it, but that all four ministers approved the brief authorizing resolution, so that Matsuoka was able to begin the negotiations with almost no restrictions.

The Matsuoka-Stahmer Negotiations

Stahmer arrived in Tokyo on September 7. The morning of the following day he and Ott visited Ōshima and stressed that for the present Germany was depending upon Japan to take the initiative in the forthcoming talks. Ōshima encouraged Stahmer to meet with Matsuoka soon, saying that the foreign minister had an idea for the conclusion of an alliance. When Ōshima recounted this conversation to Matsuoka that afternoon, Matsuoka is reported to have commented optimistically: "The army is not taking the initiative in this question and neither is the navy, though Navy Minister Oikawa is better than Yoshida. But I'll do it even if it costs me my job, and I'll finish it up in one or two weeks." [102]

The first round of negotiations between Matsuoka and Stahmer took place at the former's private residence in Sendagaya, Tokyo, from September 9 to 12, with Ambassador Ott assisting. The substance of these conversations is known from the summary prepared afterward by Matsuoka and then confirmed by Stahmer.[103]

On the first day of the negotiations Matsuoka expressed his desire to strengthen the alliance of the three powers on the basis of the brief resolution "On Strengthening the Japanese-German-Italian Axis" decided upon at the Four Ministers Conference. Stahmer accepted the first two provisions, saying: "Of course Germany recognizes and respects Japan's political leadership in Greater East Asia. All that we want in these regions is of an economic nature." However, the third provision, calling for a joint declaration, seemed to him inadequate. "A weak, lukewarm attitude or declaration at this juncture," he said, "will only invite derision and danger." He argued that something stronger was needed if the United States was to be deterred from intervening. "What Germany wishes of Japan," he said, "is that Japan shall use every means to restrain the United States, that it shall play the role of preventing the United States from entering the war. . . . Germany believes that it is to the advantage of both our countries to enter into an understanding or agreement whereby both of us will be thoroughly prepared to meet an emergency effectively at any moment. . . . Germany hopes that Japan will size up the situation correctly, realizing the reality and the magnitude of the danger that threatens from the western hemisphere, and will act quickly and decisively to forestall it by reaching an agreement with Germany and Italy that will leave neither the United States nor the rest of the world in doubt."

On the second day of the conversations, September 10, Matsuoka presented a draft of a tripartite treaty as a basis for negotiations, saying that it was no more than tentative. It provided:

1) That Japan shall recognize and respect the leading position of Germany and Italy in the building of the New Order in Europe.

2) That Germany and Italy shall recognize and respect the leading position of Japan in the building of the New Order in Greater East Asia.

3) That Japan, Germany, and Italy shall cooperate with one

another in their efforts based upon the above principles and agree to consult on appropriate and effective means for avoiding or overcoming all obstacles to the achievement of their respective objectives.

4) That Japan, Germany, and Italy believe that they can build a fair and lasting foundation for peace only through the establishment of a new world order in keeping with the changing world situation, and agree to coordinate their respective efforts to this end.[104]

That same day, at the request of the navy, Matsuoka also raised the question of the former German Pacific islands, expressing the desire that those under Japanese mandate should be recognized as Japanese territory without compensation and that the others should be transferred to Japan with compensation. Matsuoka detailed the geographical scope of Greater East Asia, saying, "It will be expanded as the situation develops, but roughly speaking it comprises the whole of East Asia north of Australia and New Zealand." [105]

The private draft Matsuoka had prepared was based on the authorizing resolution "On Strengthening the Japanese-German-Italian Axis" and did not clearly state whether or not the alliance should be strengthened to the level of a military alliance. This point naturally invited German dissatisfaction. On the night of the 10th Ōshima, who had been invited to the German embassy, had the following exchange with Ott and Stahmer:

> Ott: These four articles of the Matsuoka draft are too abstract and therefore not suitable.
> Ōshima: It can be improved if we make Article 3 stronger.
> Ott: Matsuoka does not have that intention.
> Ōshima: Matsuoka could not say anything too definite in the first draft. Why don't you ask for instructions from Ribbentrop?
> Ott: Germany is contemplating a military alliance. Why does Japan not participate in the German-Italian military alliance?
> Ōshima: That is not good. Germany and Italy are neighbors, and they are in the war against Britain. Japan's position is different.
> Stahmer agreed.
> Ōshima: We wish Germany to make a more substantial economic offer.

Ott: Matsuoka talked about a joint declaration to be issued. Why don't you make some gesture to your people at home first?

Ōshima: From the point of view of the international situation, the earlier the better. It can be done right away if we have mutual trust. What shall we do about Italy?

Stahmer: Leave Italy to us.

Ōshima: We would like to have Japan and Germany act as one. What are you going to do about the question of the adjustment of Soviet-Japanese relations?

Stahmer: We would like to promote them positively.

Ott: What do you think about a Japanese-German-Italian-Soviet agreement?

Ōshima: Our alliance will be weakened if we let Soviet Russia join us.

Stahmer agreed.[106]

On September 11 Stahmer and Ott again visited Matsuoka at his private residence and presented their counterproposal to the Matsuoka draft of the previous day. Their intent was to change the character and extent of the proposed alliance into a clearly military one by amending Article 3 as follows:

That Japan, Germany, and Italy shall cooperate with one another in their efforts, based upon the above principles, and *in case one of the three is attacked by a power not presently involved in the European war or the China Incident, the three countries shall aid one another by every means, political, economic, and military.*[107]

Matsuoka agreed to this draft.[108]

Following the agreement between Matsuoka and Stahmer, a Four Ministers Conference was held on September 12. Matsuoka, after explaining the progress of his negotiations with Stahmer, recommended that the Japanese government give its consent to the Stahmer counterproposal, that is, to a mutual assistance treaty whose principal target was the United States. "The army minister agreed," Konoe noted four days later, "but the navy minister wanted to think it over. And that's where the conference ended." [109] The reason for Oikawa's reservation was that the navy still had not reached a final decision on a tripartite military alliance. While it is true that top navy leaders had begun to vacillate, they still thought that before Japan concluded a military alliance, it was absolutely indispensable that Germany at least grant Japan the right of independent decision on whether or not to enter the war, guarantee the transfer to Japan of the former German islands under Japanese mandate, and promise to try to reconcile the Soviet Union with the three cooperating countries.[110] Therefore, before the Japanese cabinet could reach a final decision on the question of a tripartite pact, it was again necessary to take the navy's views into account. On September 13 Matsuoka consulted with Vice Navy Minister Toyoda Teijirō and with the chief of the Intelligence Division of the Navy General Staff Oka Takasumi.[111] In later years Toyoda recalled that when he was first shown Stahmer's counterdraft, he was told that Matsuoka was in a great hurry, that the army had approved, and that the Navy General Staff had not shown any particular opposition.

> When I looked into the draft myself, I found that it required Japan automatically to participate in war on the German side in case a German-American war should break out. I thought that this was not good. I believed that it was absolutely necessary for Japan to decide what it would do on the basis of its own independent judgment, even if an American-German war should begin. So I made revisions at about three places in the draft. The draft then became quite flexible. After that I went to see Matsuoka at his private residence. I entered his house through a back entrance and talked secretly with him in the tea room. When I showed him the navy amendments and expressed our wishes, he agreed to them. Therefore, upon my return from Matsuoka's, I reported to Minister Oikawa and suggested that if our amendments were adopted, he should make the final decision as he saw fit.[112]

We should not understand Toyoda's recollection to mean that Matsuoka agreed to revise the text of the treaty itself but rather to add to it a new supplementary protocol and an exchange of notes. These were to include a stipulation to the effect that the government of each contracting party would independently decide on its participation in a war. In addition, they were to take up the matters of the former German Pacific islands under Japanese mandate and the adjustment of relations between the Soviet Union and Japan. It was with this prior understanding that the navy at last gave its consent to the conclusion of a tripartite military pact, probably at the Four Ministers Conference reconvened at 5 P.M. on September 13,[113] or possibly the following day at the preliminary meeting of the Imperial Headquarters–Cabinet Liaison Conference held to prepare for the Imperial Conference scheduled for September 16.

No record exists of the proceedings of the September 13 Four Ministers Conference; however, a memorandum by Prince Konoe throws some light on the preliminary Liaison Conference of September 14, confirming that the navy's agreement had already been won. This latter meeting was attended by Prime Minister Konoe, Foreign Minister Matsuoka, Vice Foreign Minister Ōhashi, Army Minister Tōjō, Vice Army Minister Anami, Military Affairs Bureau Chief Mutō, Army General Staff Vice Chief Sawada, Navy Minister Oikawa, Vice Navy Minister Toyoda, Naval Affairs Bureau Chief Abe, and Navy General Staff Vice Chief Kondō. Konoe notes:

Kondō, vice chief of the Navy General Staff, who was most outspoken at the conference, said: "The navy is not yet prepared for war against the United States, but preparations will be completed by April of next year. By that time we shall have equipped the vessels already in operation and shall have armed 2.5 million tons of merchant ships. After we have completed this, we will be able to defeat the United States, provided we carry on blitz warfare. If we do not carry on blitz warfare and the United States chooses a protracted war, we will be in great trouble. Furthermore, the United States is rapidly building more vessels, which means that the difference between the American fleet potential and ours will become greater, and Japan will never be able to catch up with it. From that point of view, now is the most advantageous time for Japan to start a war."

Foreign Minister Matsuoka said: "The time has come for Japan to decide upon a clear attitude. Shall we ally ourselves with Germany and Italy, or shall we take the side of Britain and the United States, refusing Germany and Italy? If we leave relations between Japan, Germany, and Italy as indefinite as the Hiranuma cabinet did, by refusing the German proposal, Germany will conquer Britain and, in the worst eventuality, will establish a European federation, come to an agreement with the

United States, and not let Japan lay even one finger on the colonies of Britain, Holland, and other powers in the federation. However, if we do conclude an alliance and if, as a result, the worst happens and we become involved in a war with the United States, our national economy will suffer severely. In order to avoid these difficulties, it would not be totally impossible to ally with Britain and the United States as well as with Germany and Italy. However, to do so we should have to settle the China Incident as the United States tells us, give up our hope for a New Order in East Asia, and obey Anglo-American dictates for at least half a century to come. Would our people accept this? Would the hundred thousand spirits of our dead soldiers be satisfied with this? Furthermore, suppose we did join the United States and Britain. We might then avoid material difficulties for the time being. But remember the treatment we received after the last war. Who knows what bitter pills we should have to swallow this time. And Chiang not only calls for resistance to Japan but daily intensifies his campaigns to insult Japan and boycott Japan. We cannot do anything with half-hearted measures. In short, an alliance with the United States is unthinkable. The only way left is to ally with Germany and Italy."

Navy Minister Oikawa, representing the navy, agreed: "There is no other way," he said, "but I wish the cabinet and particularly the army authorities would give special consideration to naval preparedness." [114]

Lord Privy Seal Kido noted in his diary that same day: "General Tōjō told me confidentially that the army and navy have today come to an understanding on relations with Germany and Italy." [115]

In view of the fact that the navy's opposition to the tripartite military pact had been the greatest internal barrier to its conclusion, the change in the navy's attitude following Oikawa's appointment as navy minister had great consequences. The reasons for this change are still being debated. Former Navy Minister Yoshida said he was "greatly surprised at the sudden change in the navy's attitude." [116] Konoe tells us that he too was puzzled and called in Vice Minister Toyoda to explain. Toyoda is reported to have told him: "To tell the truth, the navy at heart is still opposed to a tripartite pact. However, *the internal political situation of the country no longer allows* the navy to continue its opposition. The navy is therefore forced to agree to it." [117]

The top navy leaders were worried about a political confrontation with the army and wanted to avoid having to accept full responsibility for a failure to conclude a tripartite pact. This must have strongly influenced their decision. Doubtless they remembered vividly the incident of the previous year when the navy had to defend itself against terrorism as a result of the army-navy confrontation over the question of strengthening the Anti-Comintern Pact. But was the "internal political situation of the country" really the ultimate factor that influenced the new naval leaders to agree to the alliance? There is a suspicion that the internal situation in the navy might have been equally important. As already seen, there had been growing inside the Navy Ministry, particularly among middle-echelon officials such as Military Affairs Bureau Chief Abe, a sentiment that favored the alliance in order to advance plans for the drive to the south. May it not be that Oikawa and Toyoda were psychologically more susceptible to this influence than former Navy Minister Yoshida had been? The navy, of course, was still strongly desirous of avoiding an armed clash with the United States; but its psychological resistance to a military pact must have been worn down by Matsuoka's "brink-of-war" logic: war against the United States was inevitable so long as things continued as they were; only by strengthening Japan's power position through a tripartite pact or through a four-power alliance including the Soviet Union could war with the United States be avoided.[118]

As Oikawa later told the War Crimes Tribunal, he had been absolutely opposed to any obligation automatically to go to war. But Matsuoka had convinced him that "Germany not only did not desire Japan to enter the European war at that time but was even more determined than we to keep the United States out of the war." Moreover, Matsuoka reported that "firm understandings had been reached that Germany felt strongly enough to want to cooperate with us on this, that even after the conclusion of the alliance Japan would be free to make its own decision whether or not to enter the war, and that all possible efforts would be made to promote friendly understanding between Japan and the USSR." Therefore, Oikawa concluded, "the navy no longer had any grounds for opposing the proposal. Not only that, but it seemed to me that for the navy to insist stubbornly on its own views (regardless of public opinion, which at that time was turning in favor of the Axis) would lead to a violent internal confrontation. So I told the cabinet that the navy had no alternative to tide us over the current critical situation." [119]

The Conclusion of the Tripartite Pact

Just as the views of the Foreign Ministry, the army, and the navy had been harmonized and a consensus on the Stahmer draft reached between the cabinet and the supreme command, a new draft was sent by Ribbentrop from Berlin. Ott and Stahmer handed it to Matsuoka at his private residence on the night of September 14.[120]

This "first Ribbentrop draft" added to the Stahmer draft two additional articles, numbered five and six, stipulating:

5) That Japan, Germany, and Italy affirm that the above items do not in any way affect the political situation now existing between each of them and the Soviet Union.
6) That Japan, Germany, and Italy will conclude without delay a treaty that will specify the details for implementing the above items.

In addition, Ribbentrop proposed a further change in Article 3. The Stahmer draft, it will be recalled, had strengthened Matsuoka's original mild provision for cooperation by providing for a military alliance in the following terms: "In case one of the three is attacked by a power not presently involved in the European war or the China Incident, the three countries shall aid one another by every means, political, economic, and military." Now Ribbentrop sought to push this commitment one step further by inserting after the word "attacked" the phrase "either openly or in a concealed form." The "concealed" form of attack the Germans had in mind, Stahmer and Ott intimated, included such situations as the appearance of the United States fleet at Singapore or the grant to the United States by the British of bases in the Mediterranean.

These amendments naturally raised problems for Matsuoka. The proposed revision of Article 3 threatened to increase the danger of Japan's involvement in the European war and to circumscribe its freedom of action, which Matsuoka had promised the navy to preserve; but he seems not to have been worried that the Germans would be difficult. The following day he simply handed Ott and Stahmer a counterproposal. It proposed: to delete the phrase Ribbentrop wanted to insert in Article 3; to delete Ribbentrop's proposed Article 6 calling for a detailed treaty and insert it in a secret protocol; and, in addition, to delete Japan's own proposed Article 4, a vague provision for cooperation, and incorporate it into the preamble.[121] In short, he insisted on holding more or less to his original line. He seems to have been optimistic that this would indeed satisfy everyone for, without waiting for a reply from the Germans, he prepared to submit his version for decision the following day to an extraordinary meeting of the cabinet and immediately thereafter to an Imperial Conference.

The cabinet met during the morning and afternoon of September 16. The only extant account is a memorandum by Prime Minister Konoe,[122] who reports that Matsuoka made a long plea for his colleagues to trust him, as follows:

> Japan will obtain the German islands under mandate without compensation and the former German South Sea islands with proper compensation. Moreover, according to Stahmer Germany has plenty of oil. Both Soviet Russia and Rumania are sending oil to Germany, and Germany has more oil than it can use as a result of its occupation of France. So I told Stahmer to have Germany send us about half of it, since Japan is short. Stahmer also said that Germany will work to improve Japanese-Soviet relations. So I asked him to have Germany use its good offices to get the Soviet Union to cede its oil rights in northern Sakhalin to Japan. I even mentioned that Japan would be willing to purchase the oil outright if necessary.

Matsuoka's report was greeted at first by silence but then rallied support from Finance Minister Kawada Isao and Chief of the Cabinet Planning Board Hoshino Naoki. They are quoted as saying:

> The course advocated by the foreign minister will present difficulties, but we should follow it. If we go on as we are now, things will get worse and there will be no way to improve them. On the other hand, if we sign this pact, we may be able to settle the China Incident, and it may be that the United States will change its recent insulting attitude toward us. This isn't very likely to happen, but it is our only chance.

The cabinet is reported to have approved. For some reason the Imperial Conference that was to follow immediately was postponed, but the emperor apparently felt that the die was cast. When told of the proceedings, he is said to have said to Konoe gravely: "Since we have come so far, we cannot turn back. But, Mr. Prime Minister, are you prepared to walk this path with me, sharing my joys and sorrows, wherever it may lead?" [123]

That same day Matsuoka talked again with Ott and Stahmer, informing them orally of the additional understandings Japan would require.[124] On September 19 they were handed written drafts of these items in the form of a secret protocol Matsuoka wished to append to the treaty and two notes he proposed to exchange.[125] The protocol provided:

> I. With a view to determine by consultation with one another the detailed arrangement on the cooperation and mutual assistance between Japan, Germany, and Italy as stipulated in paragraph III of the pact, joint military and naval commissions, preferably one at Tokyo and another at Berlin or Rome, together with a joint economic commission, [shall] forthwith be organized. The composition of the aforesaid commission shall be determined through consultation by the Governments of Japan, Germany, and Italy.
>
> The conclusions of the said commissions shall be submitted to the respective Governments for approval in order to be put in force.
>
> II. Whether or not a contracting party or parties has or have been attacked openly or covertly as stipulated in paragraph III of the pact shall be determined by the respective Governments, and in case the fact of such an attack has been established the measures of mutual assistance of [a] political, economic and mil-

itary nature [to be] adopted by the contracting parties shall be studied and recommended by the aforesaid commissions, subject to approval of the respective Governments.

III. As the cooperation and mutual assistance stipulated in paragraph III of the pact have in view as fundamental aims the efforts to eatablish forthwith a new order in greater East Asia and Europe, to eventuate in a new world order, blessing humanity with a just and equitable peace, Germany and Italy shall, in time of peace or of war, take all possible measures to restrain a third power or powers on the Atlantic with a view to better enabling Japan, Germany, and Italy to accomplish their common aim of establishing a new order in greater East Asia and in the Pacific basin in general.

In the event of Japan being attacked by a power or powers not at present involved in either the European war or the Sino-Japanese conflict referred to in the last part of paragraph III of the present pact, Germany and Italy also undertake to come to Japan's assistance in the Pacific Ocean with all their means and resources.

IV. While Germany and Italy undertake to use their good offices with a view to improve the relations between Japan and the USSR, Japan, Germany, and Italy shall make utmost efforts to induce the USSR to act in accord with the main conceptions of the present pact.

V. The contracting parties undertake to exchange from time to time without delay all useful inventions and devices of war and to supply one another with war equipments, such as aeroplanes, tanks, guns, explosives, etc., which each party may reasonably spare, together with technical skill and men, should they be required. Furthermore, they are prepared to do [their] utmost in furnishing one another with and in aiding one another [to secure] minerals including oil and other materials [and machinery needed] for war industries and various requisites for livelihood.

VI. In conformity with the spirit which prompted the conclusion of the present pact, the Governments of the contracting parties undertake to enter into negotiations without delay, with a view to deciding upon measures of assuring to the other contracting parties or their nationals, in their commercial and industrial activities in the regions where the contracting parties are respectively recognized to have leadership by virtue of paragraph I and II of the present pact, a position which is preponderant in comparison to that of any third power and its nations.

VII. The present protocol shall remain secret and shall not be published.

The first note stated Japan's desire for reassurance that, in case of armed conflict between Japan and Great Britain, Japan might expect assistance "in every possible form." The second note was to set forth Japan's understanding that

> . . . all the former German colonies in the Pacific area should be ceded to Japan, without compensation in the case of the group of islands mandated by Japan and with proper compensation in the case of other mandated islands as well as those actually in [British] possession.
>
> It is understood as [a] matter of course that Japan shall accord a specially favorable Treaty of Peace to the activities of Germany and her nationals in these regions as compared to any other nation or their nationals.

Matsuoka tried to obtain Germany's consent to the supplementary protocol and note by minimizing their significance. "The protocol," he explained, "should not contain any sort of limitations of the obligation of assistance laid down in the pact, but in the interests of quick handling by the Privy Council it should indicate as clearly as possible the advantages for Japan resulting from the pact." [126] He seems to have been successful, as he said, in persuading Stahmer to accept the navy's requirement that Japan retain its freedom to decide independently whether or not it would go to war. This was stipulated in paragraph two of the proposed protocol, and there is no evidence either in the Stahmer-Ott reports to Berlin or in the record kept by Saitō in Tokyo that Stahmer raised any objections.

The German negotiators were not, however, prepared to accept the protocol in its entirety. It seemed to them to be a list of unilateral Japanese demands, particularly in the obligations stipulated in paragraph three. Obligations, they insisted, should be mutual.[127] "At least the outwardly one-sided wording in favor of Japan should be eliminated." [128] But these protests seem not to have been taken very seriously by Matsuoka, who was optimistic that the differences that remained could be resolved with a few minor concessions and a few technical amendments.

Accordingly, on the morning of September 19 an Imperial Conference was held to reach a final decision on the conclusion of the tripartite pact. The participants were: representing the cabinet, Prime Minister Konoe, Foreign Minister Matsuoka, Army Minister Tōjō, Navy Minister Oikawa, Finance Minister Kawada, and Chief of the Cabinet Planning Board Hoshino; representing the General Staffs, Army Chief of Staff Prince Kan'in and Vice Chief Sawada, Navy Chief of Staff Prince Fushimi and Vice Chief Kondō; and Privy Council President Hara Yoshimichi. Following the prime minister's greetings, Matsuoka explained the progress of the negotiations and the gist of the proposed pact. He emphasized that the purpose of the pact was to avoid war by strengthening Japan's power position and thereby deterring the United States from pursuing its policy of pressure against Japan. As he expressed it:

> The fundamental principle in the recent negotiations with Germany is entirely different from that in the days of the Hiranuma cabinet, as can be seen from the fact that Germany has explicitly said that Japan need not participate in the European war. Japan and Germany now have a common aim; namely, Germany wants to prevent American entry into the war, and Japan wants to avoid an armed clash with the United States. . . . Japanese-American relations have now deteriorated to the point where no improvement can be expected through courtesy or a desire for friendship. I rather fear such a weak attitude on Japan's part may only aggravate things. All we can do to improve the situation even a little, or to prevent its further aggravation, is to stand firm. If this is so, then we must confront the United States, strengthening our position by allying firmly with as many countries as possible and making our determination known at home and abroad as quickly as possible. This, I believe, is an urgent diplomatic move.[129]

A question-and-answer period followed Matsuoka's explanations. According to the record of the conference, derived from notes made by Army Vice Chief Sawada,[130] the cabinet members were questioned mainly by Prince Fushimi and Hara, who asked: Is there not a danger that the pact might cause a further deterioration in Japanese-American relations? If the United States should intensify its economic pressure, would Japan not find it difficult to carry on the war because of the lack of essential materials, particularly oil? What effect would the pact have on Japanese-Soviet relations? Has Japan secured the right of independent decision in regard to participation in a war?

Hara expressed his apprehension concerning the effect of the pact on relations with the United States as follows:

> It seems to me that while the United States is playing the self-styled role of watchman in East Asia in place of Britain and is applying pressure upon Japan, still it refrains from extreme measures in order not to force Japan into joining the German-Italian side. However, once this pact is made public and the Japanese attitude becomes clear, the United States will, I am afraid, greatly intensify its pressure upon Japan and increase its aid to Chiang in order to interfere with Japan's prosecution of the war. Furthermore, the United States, which has not declared war against Germany and Italy, will further intensify its economic pressure upon Japan without declaring war. It will apply measures of attrition against Japan by embargoing oil and iron and boycotting Japanese goods, so that Japan will not be able to carry on the war.

The following exchange then took place:

> Matsuoka: America's attitude toward Japan has deteriorated to such a degree that it will not be improved merely by our assuming a pleasing attitude. Only a firm attitude on our part can prevent war with the United States.
>
> Hara: America is a proud nation. I am afraid that a firm attitude on our part may produce an adverse result.
>
> Matsuoka: You have a point there. But Japan is not Spain. It is a powerful nation with a strong naval force in the Far East. The United States may harden its attitude temporarily. But after cool calculation it will return to a quiet attitude. Of course the chances are fifty-fifty whether America's attitude will keep hardening to a critical point or soften again after cool reflection.

Prince Fushimi expressed considerable apprehension concerning the effect of the pact on the resources available to Japan. Hoshino tried to reassure him:

> I do not think other countries will place an embargo upon Japan at the same time the United States does. American economic pressure all along has been directed at vital points that

will hurt Japan without hurting America. Even if the United States further intensifies its economic pressure on Japan in the future, the most effective measures have already been exhausted. Therefore, Japan will not suffer any more than it is at present.

The consensus of the conference on the question of oil was that there was no alternative to securing oil from the Dutch East Indies, in spite of Matsuoka's statement that there was a good possibility of obtaining a considerable amount of oil from the Soviet Union.

> Prince Fushimi: Are we to understand that we have no guarantee on the acquisition of oil? I would also like to add that we cannot rely too much on oil supplies from the Soviet Union, and therefore the only way is to obtain it from the Dutch East Indies. This can be accomplished either peacefully or militarily. The navy strongly hopes it will be accomplished peacefully.
>
> Tōjō: The army pays as much attention to oil as does the navy. The question of oil can be equated with the question of the Dutch East Indies. . . . We have already decided that for the time being we will try to secure essential resources from that region through diplomatic means, but we will resort to the use of force if necessary.

Prince Fushimi then raised a third question: "To what degree will this alliance contribute to the adjustment of Japanese-Soviet relations?" Matsuoka replied:

> We should like Germany to act as mediator in the adjustment of our relations with the Soviet Union. Germany is willing to do this, inasmuch as the adjustment of Japanese-Soviet relations would be to its advantage. Last year at the time of the conclusion of the German-Soviet Nonaggression Pact, the German foreign minister asked Stalin about the future of Japanese-Soviet relations. Stalin answered that if Japan desired peace, then Russia also desired peace; but if Japan wanted war, then Russia also would want war. From this we can assume that the Soviet Union is interested in adjusting its relations with Japan. In fact, Germany considers that it will be able to promote the adjustment quite easily. I suspect that Stahmer had talks with the Russians in Moscow, since he could hardly have kept secret from the Russians his passage through the Soviet Union on his way here. In

any event, I believe we can have high expectations that Germany will use its good offices to adjust our relations with Soviet Russia.

Finally, the following exchange took place concerning Japan's obligation under the fact to enter the war:

> Prince Fushimi: Even if Japan should be compelled to participate in the European war because the United States participates in it, *it is essential for us to choose independently our own time for beginning hostilities*. What assurances does our government have in this regard?
>
> Matsuoka: *It is clear that Japan is obligated automatically to enter the war*. However, the determination of whether or not the United States has participated in the war will be made by consultation among the three countries. A joint army-navy commission will study the appropriate action to be taken and report its recommendation to the respective governments. The final decision will be made by each acting independently.

Thus, Matsuoka explained, while on the one hand Japan was formally accepting the obligation "automatically to enter the war," on the other hand it would be able to choose independently the time and method of fulfilling this obligation.

At the end of the conference the two chiefs of staff and Privy Council President Hara gave their consent to the draft pact. Prince Kan'in expressed the hope that the government would intensify its efforts to adjust relations with the Soviet Union. Prince Fushimi added the recommendation that every measure be taken to avoid war with the United States, that the southward drive be carried out peacefully, avoiding unnecessary friction with third powers, and that guidance and control of the press be strengthened, irresponsible discussion concerning the conclusion of the pact restricted, and harmful activities against Britain and the United States prohibited.

After three hours the Imperial Conference ended. With the affixing of signatures and the granting of imperial approval, the internal process for deciding on the substance of the pact to be sought was concluded. The stage was now set for the final negotiations with Germany that would establish the text to be submitted to the Privy Council. Matsuoka promptly telephoned Ott, suggesting that the language of the pact be English and asking him to secure full powers from Berlin.[131]

Matsuoka must have assumed that he had reached an understanding with Stahmer and Ott on the basic points of the pact and that only technical questions remained. Otherwise it is difficult to see why the Imperial Conference had been called, for he had yet received no reply to his proposed revisions of the first Ribbentrop draft of September 14; nor had there been time for Germany to reply to his proposed supplementary protocol and notes, which had been transmitted formally only on the day of the Imperial Conference. Moreover, negotiations with Italy had still to be initiated. When the second Ribbentrop draft was handed to Japan on September 21, however, it became clear that there existed considerable difference of opinion between the two nations even on the basic points.

Ribbentrop had been conducting negotiations with the Italian government in Rome. Italian Foreign Minister Galeazzo Ciano recorded in his diary on September 19:

> Arrival of von Ribbentrop. He is in good humor. . . . In the car Ribbentrop speaks at once of the surprise in his bag: a military alliance with Japan, to be signed within the next few days at Berlin. . . . He thinks that such a move will have a double advantage: against Russia and against America, which under the threat of the Japanese fleet, will not dare to move.[132]

If it was really Ribbentrop's intention to have the pact function against the Soviet Union, this was contradictory to the statement made by Stahmer and went against the Japanese plan to promote the adjustment of Japanese-Soviet relations through the good offices of Germany. Therefore from the beginning there were serious differences in the intent of the two governments concerning the tripartite pact.

German-Italian negotiations were conducted from September 20 to September 23. Ribbentrop emphasized the effect upon the United States of the alliance with Japan, saying, "If such a world coalition should come into existence by virtue of this pact, the United States would reflect 100 times before par-

ticipating in the war." He also stated that the pact would para-
lyze the United States by strengthening isolationist sentiment
against Roosevelt during the presidential elections. Mussolini
responded with the expectation that the pact would have "the
effect of a bomb" on America and gave it his full support.[133]

The second Ribbentrop draft, which was sent to Tokyo on
September 21, was formulated after Ribbentrop's consultations
with Italy.[134] Ribbentrop proposed to modify Article 3 of his
previous draft, which obligated the signatories to provide mutual assistance in case of attack "either openly or in a concealed
form." The article now stated that the contracting parties were
obliged "to declare war and to assist one another" in case one of
the contracting parties should be the victim of "an act of aggression." The aim of the new German draft was therefore to intensify further the degree of the military alliance between the
three countries. Ribbentrop had Stahmer explain this as follows: "In our opinion an explicit emphasis upon the obligation
to declare war would have a specially strong neutralizing effect
on the United States. The United States would certainly hesitate ten times before entering the war if the pact stated in clear
and impressive terms that America would then automatically be
at war with three great powers."

The new German draft also added to Article 4 a provision
concerning the establishment of the joint military commissions
which Japan had planned to stipulate in the supplementary protocol.[135] The proposed supplementary protocol was not even
mentioned; and the Japanese demand for the right to make an
independent decision concerning participation in the war was
ignored. The navy immediately objected and the pact project
was thrown into crisis.[136]

On the night of September 21, when Matsuoka resumed
talks with Stahmer and Ott, the Germans at once demanded that
the supplementary protocol and notes be eliminated. Matsuoka
refused, but he did present a counterproposal which in effect
constituted a broad concession. He proposed: (1) that the phrase
"to declare war" be deleted from the text of the pact, and that
the proposed joint commissions include economic as well as
military commissions; (2) that the secret supplementary pro-

tocol should remain fundamentally unchanged in content but should take the form of an "exchange of notes" between Japan and Germany only; (3) that the note concerning the islands under mandate be changed in form to an oral statement by the German ambassador and in content to provide that Germany would recognize Japan's continuing possession of those islands under Japanese mandate *with compensation* and would be prepared to confer with Japan in an accommodating spirit concerning the disposal of other former German islands (presumably those in the South Seas mandated to Britain, Australia, and New Zealand).

A new Japanese draft containing these modifications was presented to the German embassy the following day, and that night Matsuoka, Stahmer, and Ott met for the eighth time to effect a compromise between the Japanese and German drafts. During this session agreement was reached on the text of the pact, the note concerning a possible Anglo-Japanese conflict, and an oral statement concerning the mandated islands.[137] Matsuoka accepted the following formulation of Article 3 of the proposed treaty: that Japan, Germany, and Italy "undertake to assist one another with all political economic, and military means when one of the three contracting parties is attacked by a power at present not involved in the European war or in the Sino-Japanese conflict." He also conceded that provision for the joint technical commissions, to be made up of representatives appointed by each of the three governments, should be included as Article 4 of the treaty. And for these concessions Ott and Stahmer gave up their insistence that, should Germany or Italy be attacked, Japan obligate itself specifically to "declare war." But beyond this they would not go.

When Matsuoka pressed the issue of the secret protocol, they offered a compromise note containing the following major points:

> 1) That if Japan, contrary to the peaceful intent of the pact, is attacked by a power not at present a belligerent, Germany will consider it a matter of course to give Japan full support and assist it with all military and economic means.
> 2) That with regard to relations between Japan and the So-

viet Union, Germany will do all in its power to promote friendly understanding and will offer its good offices to this end.

3) That Germany will use its industrial strength as much as possible in favor of Japan in order to facilitate the establishment of a New Order in Greater East Asia.[138]

The effect of the German proposal, while it included certain obligations stipulated in Matsuoka's proposed secret protocol, was to make Germany's obligations milder and vaguer. Furthermore, it did not touch upon the matter of guaranteeing the right of independent decision on participation in the war. Since Japan considered this provision absolutely essential, the following day, September 23, Matsuoka formulated an amendment to the German draft note, reaffirming this right. At the same time he sent through the German embassy a direct oral appeal to Ribbentrop in Berlin, requesting that he accept this amendment and agree additionally that the pact be signed in Tokyo rather than Berlin and that the authorized text of the pact be in the English language.[139]

Ribbentrop is reported to have expressed his displeasure to Mussolini, saying that the Japanese suggestions seemed to him "rather childish." [140] He refused to budge. On September 24 Counselor Erich Boltze of the German embassy called on Matsuoka and delivered his government's oral reply. Germany was weighing the matter of the language of the pact, he said, but it would have to insist that the pact be signed in Berlin, and it would find it difficult to accept the Japanese draft of the note.[141] Thus, the negotiations seemed to be heading for an impasse over Japan's insistence on the right of the independent decision on participation in the war.

In fact, the deadlock was broken that very evening. After lengthy conversation Stahmer and Ott finally gave way, agreeing to the amended version of the note Matsuoka insisted upon. Contrary to the apparent implication of Article 3 of the treaty, which obligated Japan "to assist with all political, economic, and military means" should Germany or Italy be attacked by a new belligerent, such as the United States or the Soviet Union, the note now agreed to reserve to Japan the freedom to decide for itself whether an "attack" had taken place and what effect to give to the recommendations of the joint commissions. The exact text read:

> Conclusions of the technical commissions provided for in Article 4 of the pact should be submitted to the three governments for approval in order to put them into force.
> Needless to say, the question whether an attack within the meaning of Article 3 of the pact has taken place must be determined through joint consultation by the three consulting parties.

It was further agreed that the pact should be signed in Berlin on September 27.[142]

How can one explain this sudden reversal of Germany's position? The answer seems to be that Stahmer and Ott acted on their own authority without instructions from Berlin. They may already have committed themselves to acknowledging Japan's right to decide independently the question of its participation in the war, and they were probably well aware that without a clear statement on this point the Japanese navy would not accept the pact. They had to consider also the position of Matsuoka, who had assured the Imperial Conference that Japan had preserved its freedom of action. One suspects that they acted beyond their authority with a view somehow to bringing the negotiations to a successful conclusion. This suspicion is supported by the fact that for a long time the German government seems not to have known of the existence of the note. In spite of the fact that Stahmer assured Ott when he left Japan for Germany early in October that he would secure Ribbentrop's approval, he did not carry out his promise.[143] Moreover, when Allied investigators searched the archives of the German Foreign Office after the war, no copies were found.

Consequently, from the very beginning there was a grave divergence in understanding between the two countries concerning the basic issue of the pact. The Japanese government thought Germany had acceded fully to Japan's right to decide independently whether or not it would go to war, while the German government assumed that Japan was committed automatically to fight if Germany were attacked. Thus, in spite of the high-sounding outward solidarity of the alliance, its foundation was extremely fragile.

Meanwhile, it was agreed that the place of signature of the pact would be Berlin and the authentic text would be in English. Italy's agreement was received on September 25. On the 26th the Privy Council Investigation Committee held a long meeting to inquire into the treaty. At this late stage, when the basic decision on the conclusion of the pact had already been reached at an Imperial Conference, and when negotiations had been concluded and the signing scheduled for the following day, the privy councillors could hardly be expected to voice opposition, even if some of them might have been apprehensive.[144] Although only General Kawai Misao and Admiral Arima Ryōkitsu spoke in support of the pact, the Investigation Committee approved it unanimously, recommending it that same evening to a plenary meeting of the Privy Council. There too the pact was approved unanimously, although Councillor Ishii Kikujirō expressed the equivocal feelings of many when he said:

> Germany has always been a poor ally. Every country that has concluded an alliance with it has, without exception, suffered unforeseen disasters. . . . However, there have never before been countries whose interests are as similar as those of Japan, Germany, and Italy today. These three countries seem after all to be bound together by some natural force. Therefore, I think the best policy is to conclude this treaty. But we must watch our step closely in carrying it out.[145]

On September 27 the Tripartite Pact was finally signed by Ambassador Kurusu, Foreign Minister Ribbentrop, and Foreign Minister Ciano. At the same time in Tokyo three letters were exchanged between Foreign Minister Matsuoka and Ambassador Ott, and the Tripartite Pact came into effect.

What then was the real intention of the Japanese government, particularly of Matusoka, in concluding the Tripartite Pact? The indictment of the Tokyo War Crimes Tribunal charged that "the Tripartite Pact was concluded as an important step in the Japanese preparation for its military advancement toward Southeast Asia and the South Seas. . . . This fact implied that Japan had the intention of opening war against the United States, if the United States interfered with Japan's achievement of the aim of its aggression." The indictment further alleged that the pact was not defensive but aggressive in nature:

> It is obvious that the three countries were determined to assist one another in their actions whenever they should feel it necessary to take aggressive action in the promotion of their policies. For Japan, which planned to advance southward, the United States was deemed to be the direct barrier, and therefore Matsuoka states that the pact was primarily directed against the United States.[146]

On the other hand, Foreign Ministry advisor Saitō Yoshie, who participated in the alliance negotiations, was indignant at the idea that the pact was construed as a tool of aggression and a measure in preparation for war against the United States. He wrote in his memoir that the pact was a "measure to maintain world peace," its primary objective being the avoidance of war with the United States. He defended Matsuoka as a "peace-lover" and stated that the pact was "no more than a temporary diplomatic scheme to deter the United States from participating in the war" by strengthening Japan's position through an alliance with Germany and Italy.[147]

There is no doubt that both Matsuoka and Konoe desired strongly to avoid an armed clash with the United States. At the same time, it was their common conviction that only by strengthening Japan's international power position would it be possible to mitigate the United States' strong attitude toward Japan and avoid the prospect of war with that country. Konoe told the Privy Council Investigation Committee: "The basic aim of this pact is to avoid war with the United States. However, I think it is necessary for us to display firmness, because if we act humbly, it will only make the United States presumptuous." [148]

As for Matsuoka, he is said to have had a "grand design" to

use the Tripartite Pact as a lever in negotiations with the United States, not only to secure an advantageous solution to various questions pending between the two nations but also to persuade the United States to help in terminating the Sino-Japanese conflict and then to cooperate with Japan in mediating the European war. But even if such a grand design did exist, can the Tripartite Pact be interpreted exclusively as an "alliance for peace"? The record of the Japanese government's deliberations upon the question of the pact from the summer of 1940 on shows that Japan regarded it as a diplomatic prerequisite to the southern advance. The fact that German cooperation was necessary for the drive to the south motivated Japan to strengthen the Axis alliance; and as the American attitude toward Japan hardened, Japanese government leaders decided to conclude the pact to block American armed intervention in Japan's southward move.

Matsuoka must have believed that only a brink-of-war policy, that is, a demonstration of Japan's readiness to go to war if need be, would deter the United States from such intervention. Japan, he hoped, would thereby be able to complete its drive southward and at the same time avoid war with the United States. The outbreak of the Pacific War proved that his view had been wrong. His brink-of-war policy had failed; and it is said that when he was told of the outbreak of the war, Matsuoka shed bitter tears, saying, "The conclusion of the Tripartite Pact was the greatest mistake of my life." [149]

Appendices

Appendix 1
THE JAPANESE-GERMAN ANTI-COMINTERN PACT AND RELATED DOCUMENTS*

PREAMBLE

The government of the German Reich and the government of Imperial Japan, recognizing that the aim of the Communist International, known as the Comintern, is to disintegrate and subdue existing states by all means at its command, convinced that the toleration of interference by the Communist International in the internal affairs of the nations not only endangers their internal peace and social well being but is also a menace to the peace of the world, and desirous of cooperating in the defense against communist subversion, have agreed as follows:

ARTICLE 1

The High Contracting Parties agree to inform one another of the activities of the Communist International, to consult with one another on necessary preventive measures, and to carry these through in close collaboration.

ARTICLE 2

The High Contracting Parties will jointly invite third states whose internal peace is threatened by the subversive activities of the Communist International to adopt defensive measures in the spirit of this agreement or to take part in the present agreement.

ARTICLE 3

The German as well as the Japanese text of the present agreement is to be deemed the original text. It comes into force on the day of signature and shall remain in force for a period of five years. Before the expiration of this period the High Contracting Parties will come to an understanding over the further methods of their cooperation.

* Japan, Foreign Ministry Archives.

Two copies of this document were prepared in Berlin on November 25, 1936.

> Japanese Imperial Envoy Extraordinary and Ambassador Plenipotentiary Viscount Mushakōji Kintomo
>
> German Envoy Extraordinary and Ambassador Plenipotentiary Joachim von Ribbentrop

SUPPLEMENTARY PROTOCOL

On the occasion of the signing today of the agreement against the Communist International, the undersigned plenipotentiaries have agreed as follows:

a) The competent authorities of the two High Contracting Parties will work in close collaboration in matters concerning the exchange of information on the activities of the Communist International as well as in investigatory and defensive measures against the Communist International.

b) The competent authorities of the two High Contracting Parties will within the framework of the existing laws take severe measures against those who at home or abroad are engaged directly or indirectly in the service of the Communist International or promote its subversive activities.

c) In order to facilitate the cooperation among the competent authorities provided for in paragraph (a), a permanent committee will be set up. This committee will consider and discuss further defensive measures necessary for the struggle against the subversive activities of the Communist International.

In Berlin, November 25, 1936.

> [Mushakōji]
> [Ribbentrop]

SECRET SUPPLEMENTARY PROTOCOL

PREAMBLE

The government of the German Reich and the government of Imperial Japan, recognizing that the government of the USSR is working toward a realization of the aims of the Communist International and intends to employ its army for this purpose, and convinced that this fact not only threatens the existence of the High Contracting Parties but is a most serious danger to world peace, in order to safeguard their common interests have agreed as follows:

ARTICLE 1

Should one of the High Contracting Parties become the object of an unprovoked attack or threat of attack by the USSR, the other High Contracting Party obligates itself to take no measures that would tend to ease the situation of the USSR.

Should the situation described in paragraph 1 occur, the High Contracting Parties will immediately consult on measures to safeguard their common interests.

ARTICLE 2

For the duration of the present agreement the High Contracting Parties will conclude no political treaties with the USSR contrary to the spirit of this agreement without mutual consent.

ARTICLE 3

The German as well as the Japanese text of the present agreement is to be deemed the original text. The agreement comes into force simultaneously with the agreement against the Communist International signed today and will remain in force for the same period.

Two copies of this document were prepared in Berlin, November 25, 1936.

[Mushakōji]
[Ribbentrop]

APPENDICES *

Appendix 3: Secret note from Ribbentrop to Mushakōji, Berlin, November 25, 1936:

I have the honor to inform Your Excellency that with the signing today of the Secret Supplementary Protocol to the Anti-Comintern Pact, the German government recognizes that the terms of political treaties, such as the Rapallo Treaty of 1922 and the Neutrality Treaty of 1926 concluded between Germany and the Soviet Union, shall not conflict with the spirit of this pact nor the obligations arising from the pact, inasmuch as the circumstances in which this pact is to be en-

---

* Appendices 1 and 2 are not extant in the Foreign Ministry Archives; the German texts may be found in Theo Sommer, *Deutschland und Japan zwischen den Mächten, 1935–1940* (Tübingen, 1962), pp. 495–96. Appendices 3 and 4 are in the Foreign Ministry Archives; the latter, being simply an acknowledgment from Mushakōji to Ribbentrop of receipt of Appendix 3, is omitted here.

forced would render them null and void. I beg to avail myself of this opportunity to submit my highest respect and courtesy to Your Excellency.

Appendix 4: (omitted)

ARTICLE OF UNDERSTANDING FOR INSURING THE SECRECY OF THE SECRET SUPPLEMENTARY PROTOCOL OF THE ANTI-COMINTERN PACT AND ITS APPENDICES

Both High Contracting Parties agree to keep secret the Supplementary Protocol of the Anti-Comintern Pact as well as the four appendices.

When it is thought advantageous for both High Contracting Parties to inform a third nation of the contents of the Secret Supplementary Protocol, it shall be accomplished only by mutual agreement.

In Berlin, November 25, 1936.

[Mushakōji]
[Ribbentrop]

ADDITIONAL CORRESPONDENCE

Mushakōji to Ribbentrop, Berlin, October 23, 1936:

I have the honor to inform you that I have today sent to Foreign Minister Arita the enclosed telegram together with copies of our correspondence. Once again I avail myself of the opportunity to express my highest esteem to Your Excellency.

[Enclosure: Mushakōji to Arita]

I am convinced, as a result of consultations with Ambassador Ribbentrop in connection with Appendices 3 and 4 of the Secret Supplementary Protocol of the Anti-Comintern Pact, that the spirit of this pact will provide the sole basis for future German policy toward the Soviet Union. I have shown this telegram to Ambassador Ribbentrop and received his concurrence.

Ribbentrop to Mushakōji, Berlin, October 23, 1936:

I have the honor to inform you that I received your letter dated the 23rd of this month. I am happy to concur with the contents of your letter and with your telegram to Foreign Minister Arita, a copy of which was enclosed with your letter to me. I beg to avail myself of this opportunity to express my highest esteem and courtesy to Your Excellency.

Appendix 2
PROCLAMATIONS
OF THE JAPANESE AND GERMAN GOVERNMENTS
ANNOUNCING THE SIGNING OF
THE ANTI-COMINTERN PACT,
NOVEMBER 25, 1936 *

PROCLAMATION OF THE JAPANESE GOVERNMENT

The Comintern, which has its headquarters in Moscow, has as its goal the destruction of the internal stability of many nations in order to promote world revolution. Last summer at its Seventh Congress it decided to seek the creation of a united front with the Second International in order to oppose fascism and imperialism, thereby clarifying the fact that its activities would be directed against Japan, Germany, Poland, and other countries. Thus it aimed at opposing Japan through assistance to the Chinese communist army.

The Comintern's activities became even more cunning and dangerous after the Seventh Congress. Everyone should be alarmed by the Comintern's interference in the domestic affairs of other nations and by the profound threat it poses to domestic tranquility and world peace, as evidenced by its activities in the Spanish Civil War. At the very least, those countries which protested the activities of the Seventh Congress should recognize the dangers posed by the Comintern's activities.

Red aggression in the Orient has been especially concentrated in China proper as well as in Outer Mongolia and Sinkiang. China has been badly ravaged by the communist armies, and Comintern activity has increased substantially since the Seventh Congress. In Manchuria the Comintern seized the leadership of the Chinese communist provincial committees, sought to increase the number of local cells, contacted rebel elements, sent Red partisans into many areas, and engaged in other secret activities.

In our own country ultraleftist activities seemed to be declining after the Manchurian Incident, but after the Comintern Congress the communist movement became more active, sought to organize a united front, and thereby attempted to gain control over all leftist movements. Our imperial government has vigorously pursued a consistent policy of opposition to all communist activities in order to defend our polity and

* Japan, Foreign Ministry Archives.

our nation and to maintain peace in Asia. Nonetheless, it has now become necessary to engage in stricter defensive measures to confront the Comintern's increased threat.

Moreover, international cooperation is necessary to counter the Comintern, which is international in its organization and activities. Because Germany has pursued an actively anticommunist policy since Hitler came to power in 1933 and because the Comintern has decided to make Japan and Germany its principal targets, the two countries have adopted a similar stance vis-à-vis the Comintern.

Our imperial government has today signed a pact with Germany which is the first step in our effort to strengthen our defense. This pact provides for mutual assistance against the subversive activities of the Comintern, for the exchange of information about the Comintern's activities, for consultation and enforcement of joint defensive measures, and for the enlistment as members of the pact of other nations threatened by the Comintern. A separate agreement provides for specific measures to implement the pact.

Our imperial government desires only to perfect its defense against any future Comintern threat and seeks the cooperation of as many nations as possible. Our sole purpose is defense against the Comintern; no special, hidden agreement exists, nor is there any intent to form a separate international bloc. It goes without saying that this pact is not directed against any particular country such as the Soviet Union.

PROCLAMATION OF THE GERMAN GOVERNMENT

Japan and Germany have been united in the firm determination not to submit to any aggression by the Red Comintern. This pact is strictly defensive in spirit, as is made clear in the invitation for other nations to join; it is not directed against any particular country; and its sole objective is to oppose any revolutionary or provocative activities of the Comintern.

Despite Germany's and Japan's open-mindedness toward the Comintern, the Comintern has defiantly persisted in attempts to foment revolutions and thus create chaos in the world. The Comintern poses a grave threat to the civilized world and attempts to destroy the holy system of the private ownership of property. It has therefore become our right as well as our political and moral duty to defend ourselves.

Germany and its people have established a firm defense against bolshevist encroachments. Since Hitler assumed leadership, the Comintern has sought by every means to regain the ground it has lost in Germany. The Comintern has fomented hatred against Germany throughout the world and has tried to prejudice the people of other countries against the Germans.

Has it not actually tried to destroy Germany with an anti-Nazi crusade? Germany has been able to defend its borders with a strong army, and by criticizing the Comintern at the Nuremberg rally was able to thwart its plan to annihilate our nation.

Though its efforts to subvert our country have been thwarted, should we not have learned a lesson from the Comintern's planned subversion of Spain, namely, how necessary it is to resist communist aggression? Today, Germany and Japan, both civilized nations, have signed this pact to smash the vicious plots of the Comintern; undoubtedly the pact will contribute to world peace.

Appendix 3
THE ARMY'S HOPES
REGARDING CURRENT FOREIGN POLICIES
JULY 3, 1938 *

I. GENERAL FOREIGN POLICY

Policy
1. By strengthening the anti-Comintern axis and disposing of the China Incident decisively, to win de facto recognition by the Powers of our China Policy and persuade them to cooperate in the construction of a new China in accord with our wishes; to win their support for our posture; and by so doing to bring about a resolution of the Incident quickly and smoothly and also contribute to the success of the empire's foreign policy after the Incident has been settled.
2. To coordinate all diplomatic and economic activities on the principle of "national policies first."

Details
1. Diplomatic efforts should concentrate on the following:
   a) Strengthening of the anti-Comintern axis.
   b) Adopting positive measures to persuade the Soviet Union not to participate in the China Incident (there is no change in the fundamental policy of discouraging the Soviet Union's aggressive intentions toward East Asia).
   c) Inducing Britain to abandon its policy of supporting Chiang Kai-shek.
   d) Persuading the United States at the very least to retain a neutral attitude, if possible to adopt a pro-Japanese attitude, and especially to strengthen friendly economic relations.
2. The importation of arms into China should be stopped by diplomatic means as well as by military force.
3. The rights of the Powers in China should be respected so long as they do not interfere with the principles below. At the same time we welcome the participation of third countries friendly to Japan in the economic development of the new China.

* Originally taken from the Konoe Papers, this document is now published in *Gendai shi shiryō 9: Nitchū sensō 2* (Source Materials on Contemporary History, 9: Sino-Japanese War, 2) pp. 263–65.

a) The Empire of Japan will assist the new China in the determination of all financial and economic policies, including matters relating to currency, customs, and customs rates; these are to be observed by third powers.
b) In north China and eastern Mongolia [Mōkyō] the empire will assume actual control over the development of national defense resources.
c) In central China, usually in cooperation with the Powers, the empire will engage in industrial development projects.
d) In areas other than those specified in the two preceding items, the empire generally will acknowledge existing industrial development projects.
e) Trade with China, in principle, will be based on free competition.
f) No concessions granted by the Chiang regime since the beginning of the Incident will be approved.
4. Amicable mediation efforts by third powers should not be rejected so long as they do not contradict established policies concerned with solution of the Incident.
5. Intervention by third nations should be decisively blocked.
6. The empire should establish an effective propaganda organ to enable third powers to understand the true intention of the empire, to reverse quickly their pro-Chiang Kai-shek attitudes, and to create a worldwide anticommunist sentiment. For this purpose, the government should consider the employment of suitable persons from outside the government.

II. OPERATIONS TO STRENGTHEN THE ANTI-COMINTERN AXIS

Policy
1. To strengthen political relations between Japan, Germany, and Italy.
2. To strengthen economic cooperation of Japan and Manchukuo with Germany and Italy.
3. To endeavor to persuade needed countries to join the Anti-Comintern Pact. In particular, the adherence of Manchukuo should be brought about as quickly as possible.

Details
1. The policy for the strengthening of political relations between Japan, Germany, and Italy should be as follows: Separate, secret agreements should be concluded with Germany, expanding the

spirit of the Anti-Comintern Pact so as to convert it into an anti-Soviet military alliance; and with Italy, so that it can serve mainly for the purpose of blocking Britain.

2. In general, the following should be considered for strengthening economic cooperation between Japan and Manchukuo on the one hand and Germany and Italy on the other:

   a) Promotion of a trade agreement and general economic cooperation between Japan and Manchukuo, and Germany and Italy.

   b) Devising suitable measures to meet the demand for an expansion of industrial facilities, particularly machine tool production.

   c) Cooperation in the economic development of Manchukuo and China and, if necessary, granting economic privileges to Germany and Italy in China.

   d) Taking up the question of returning to Germany its former colonies in the Pacific in order to strengthen Japan's relations with Germany, particularly in the realm of economic cooperation.

3. Efforts should be made to persuade countries such as Poland and Rumania to join the Anti-Comintern Pact as soon as possible.

4. Efforts should be devoted to creating a worldwide anticommunist sentiment.

III. OPERATIONS VIS-À-VIS THE SOVIET UNION

Policy
To conduct various operations so as effectively to discourage the USSR from participating in the China Incident.

Details
1. Our national strength should be increased, the economic development of China and Manchukuo should be hastened, and our forces in Manchukuo should be enlarged so as to maintain and increase our strength vis-à-vis the Soviet Union.

2. Propaganda should be disseminated in Britain, the United States, and France, telling the truth about the Soviet Union and its untrustworthy behavior, so as to discredit and isolate it internationally.

3. Direct relations with the USSR should be conducted fairly and firmly, with particular attention to insuring that the Soviet Union adheres to the letter of existing treaties.

4. Soviet schemes in China and its illegal activities vis-à-vis Japan and Manchukuo should be publicized in order to arouse domestic public opinion.

5. A nonaggression treaty between Japan and the USSR should not be concluded.

IV. OPERATIONS VIS-À-VIS BRITAIN

Policy
To bring about British understanding of Japan's firm and fair attitude and adjust Anglo-Japanese economic relations in China, thereby causing Britain promptly to abandon its policy of support for Chiang Kai-shek.

Details
1. Britain should be convinced that prolongation of the China Incident is disadvantageous to its Far Eastern policy; and to the extent that Britain accepts Japan's policy for solving the Incident, friendly consideration should be given to British rights in south-central China.
2. Special care should be taken regarding measures that concern British rights in China, and unnecessary friction should be avoided.
3. Our diplomatic, economic, and propaganda agencies in the British bloc should be coordinated and improved. Japanese behavior, both public and private, toward Britain should be restrained, so as to convince Britain of Japan's good faith and ability to accomplish its policies in China.

V. OPERATIONS VIS-À-VIS THE UNITED STATES

Policy
To persuade the United States at the very least to retain its neutral attitude during the period of the Incident and if possible adopt a pro-Japanese attitude, and especially to strengthen friendly economic relations.

Details
1. Efforts should be made to correct Japan's image by disseminating appropriate propaganda, especially by presenting the facts about the actual situation.
2. Every possible effort should be made to insure the security of American rights in China.
3. In addition, all other available action should be taken to strengthen friendly economic ties, especially to promote trade and to secure the introduction of American capital, for example:
   a) Strengthening trade with the United States in order to secure the resources needed for total mobilization.
   b) Establishing credit in the United States to meet the demand for an expansion of production, particularly of the machine industry.
   c) Cooperating in the economic development of Manchukuo and

China and, if necessary, granting economic privileges to the United States in China.

d) Adjusting Japanese-American relations by diplomatic negotiation whenever necessary for the attainment of the present policy.

VI. OPERATIONS VIS-À-VIS FRANCE

Policy

To persuade France to abandon its policy of support for Chiang Kai-shek, particularly to discontinue supplying arms to China.

Appendix 4
INSTRUCTIONS
TO THE JAPANESE AMBASSADORS
IN BERLIN AND ROME
CONCERNING THE CONCLUSION
BY JAPAN, GERMANY, AND ITALY
OF A TREATY OF CONSULTATION
AND MUTUAL ASSISTANCE
JANUARY 25, 1939 *

From: Foreign Minister Arita Hachirō
To: Special Plenipotentiary to Italy, Ambassador Shiratori Toshio, and Special Plenipotentiary to Germany, Ambassador Ōshima Hiroshi, instructions concerning the conclusion by Japan, Germany, and Italy of a Treaty of Consultation and Mutual Assistance

1. At the Five Ministers Conference held on August 26 of last year [1938], it was decided that the strengthening of the Anti-Comintern Pact should be based on the principle that the new treaty would be merely an extension of the pact, that it therefore should not depart from the principles of the Anti-Comintern Pact, and that the new treaty was not to be directed against countries such as Britain and France unless the Soviet Union were involved. In order for the Empire of Japan to establish its position as a stable power in East Asia and in order to carry out smoothly Japan's conception of its New Order in East Asia, it is extremely important that Japan avoid involvement in European problems not directly relevant to Japan, and that Japan avoid such situations as would result in making enemies of nations such as Britain and the United States. Therefore, it has been decided that the strengthening of cooperation between Japan, Germany, and Italy should remain limited for a time to anticommunism and that conclusion of a full treaty of alliance would be inadvisable for the empire.

2. Since we were unable to convey the decision of the Five Minis-

---

* Harada Kumao, *Saionji kō to seikyoku: bekkan* (Prince Saionji and the Political Situation: Supplementary Volume), pp. 368–77. Certain naval sources contain slight variations from Harada's published version, which has been followed here.

ters Conference clearly to our representatives abroad, Germany and Italy have not proposed a three-power treaty. While there was some difficulty for our government in altering the decision of the Five Ministers Conference, it has been decided that it would not be appropriate to insist on our previous decision, because we were responsible for Germany's and Italy's misunderstanding of Japan's policy. The ministers concerned met on the 19th of this month to consider the question and agreed upon the government's policy as described in Attachment A. On the basis of that policy statement, the Japanese government draft of the proposed treaty is included in Attachment B.

3. The Japanese draft is a compromise designed to be as advantageous to Japan as possible, while incorporating the import of the German and Italian drafts by including as targets third countries not related to the subversive activities of the Comintern. At the same time, in order to minimize its adverse impact on third countries, Japan will explain to the outside world that the new treaty will be no more than a strengthening of the Anti-Comintern Pact. Please understand that for many reasons the decision in Attachment A is not to be amended. Therefore, I hope you understand this latter point and will negotiate with Germany and Italy according to the attached documents.

4. The present Japanese-German Anti-Comintern Pact was concluded on the basis of pursuing an anti-Comintern policy on the one hand and maintaining joint pressure on the USSR on the other. In practice it has been used to solve various problems arising between the two countries regardless of the literal text of the treaty; and the participation of Italy will greatly strengthen this feature.

It goes without saying that the importance of this kind of treaty is not in what is written in the documents but rather in the closer political relations between the allied states that will be promoted by the conclusion of the treaty. Already the Anti-Comintern Pact has enabled all three countries—Japan, Germany, and Italy—to influence third countries politically and to check them considerably. Therefore, it is my firm belief that although outwardly the present treaty is to be strengthened only concerning anticommunism, in actual practice it can exert considerable political pressure on Britain and France.

It is not difficult to imagine that Germany and Italy will hesitate to consent to a draft that camouflages the new agreement as an anti-Comintern pact, for by giving the treaty the appearance of an alliance, they seem to be thinking of using it for their diplomatic maneuvering in Europe. Since we can all fully anticipate future political moves in the practical application of the treaty, I believe it will be possible to convince them if the proper method of explanation is selected and the right efforts are made.

5. Details of the agreement in Attachment B are described separately, as follows:

a) The secret items of understanding are absolutely essential to our government; although they are in the form of an understanding, we attach to them a weight equal to that of the protocol.

b) We plan to publish the present treaty after consultation with Germany and Italy and after carefully considering the domestic as well as the international situation from our own standpoint. As you know, Japan is presently negotiating with the USSR for the conclusion of a fisheries treaty; in view of our experience when concluding the existing Anti-Comintern Pact, I think it is best that this pact with Germany and Italy be published only after the formal or tentative conclusion of the fisheries treaty, or after such negotiations prove to be fruitless. Further instructions on this point will follow.

ATTACHMENT A
GUIDELINES FOR THE TRIPARTITE PACT

1. Target: The Soviet Union is the main target. Other countries may become targets should the situation so require.

2. Military assistance: Will be offered as a matter of course if the target is the Soviet Union. Whether or not and to what extent it should be offered when other countries are involved will depend on the situation.

3. Time of conclusion: As soon as possible.

4. Time of announcement: Proper timing will be determined after consultation.

5. Valid period: Five years.

6. Explanation to other countries: Explain that it is aimed at the Comintern.

ATTACHMENT B
TREATY OF CONSULTATION AND MUTUAL ASSISTANCE BETWEEN JAPAN, ITALY, AND GERMANY (draft)

The governments of Imperial Japan, Italy, and Germany,

In view of the fact that friendly relations between the three nations have been further promoted since the conclusion of the treaty against the Communist International on November 25, 1936, and believing that the international activities of the Communist International are a threat to peace in Europe and Asia, and having decided to strengthen their defense against communist subversion in Europe and Asia and to protect the mutual interests of the three contracting parties, according to the spirit of the previously mentioned pact, have agreed that:

Article 1. In the event that one of the contracting parties is faced with difficulty because of the attitude of one or several nonsignatory nations, the contracting parties will meet promptly to discuss joint action to be taken.

Article 2. In the event that one of the contracting parties sustains an unprovoked attack by one or several nonsignatory nations, the other contracting parties will offer aid and assistance. The three parties will meet promptly to consult and reach agreement concerning those measures necessary to carry out their obligations.

Article 3. The Japanese, Italian, and German texts of the present agreement will be considered the original text.

This treaty will remain valid for five years from the date of its signing. At a propitious time prior to the expiration of the treaty the contracting parties will come to an agreement concerning future cooperation among them. The undersigned, in witness of the above, and with the authority given to them by their governments, sign this treaty. On the _____ day of _____, _____. Three copies of the text are prepared.

Signed Protocol

On this day, _____, in signing this agreement, the undersigned plenipotentiaries have unanimously agreed to the following:

1. With respect to Articles 2 and 3 of this treaty, in view of the provisions of the second item of the protocol agreed to between Japan and Manchukuo on September 15, 1932, any attack or threat against Manchukuo will be regarded as an attack or threat against Japan.

2. With respect to the second clause of Article 4 of this treaty, should aid or assistance based upon Articles 2 and 3 of this treaty be extended at the time of the expiration of this treaty, the treaty will remain in effect until the situation requiring such aid or assistance has ended.

On the _____ day of _____, _____.

Secret Supplementary Protocol

On this day, _____, in signing this treaty, the undersigned plenipotentiaries have agreed to the following:

1. Concerning Articles 2 and 3 of this treaty, as soon as possible after the implementation of this treaty, concerned authorities of the three countries will meet to discuss possible areas of trouble and the kind of aid or assistance each contracting party, according to its geographical position, should offer to the others in each instance.

2. Should the contracting parties be jointly engaged in war, a truce or peace treaty is not to be concluded by one of the contracting parties alone.

3. The contracting parties will not be bound by responsibilities created by existing agreements with nonsignatory states requiring obligations that conflict with the foregoing items of this treaty.

4. This secret supplementary protocol will not be made public or made known to other countries without the unanimous consent of the contracting parties.

5. This secret supplementary protocol is an inseparable part of this treaty and of the signed protocol and will be valid for the same period.

Secret Items of Understanding

On this day, _____, in signing this treaty, the undersigned plenipotentiaries have agreed to the following:

1. Concerning Article 3 of the treaty and Item 1 of the secret supplementary protocol, military assistance will be offered if the Soviet Union should attack one of the contracting parties, whether alone or in concert with other nonsignatory nations.

The above provision does not affect the obligation for the contracting parties to consult and reach agreement concerning military assistance depending upon the situation, even if the Soviet Union is not involved in the attack.

2. In view of the fact that the treaty and the signed protocol are to be made public, the contracting parties, when required to explain the treaty, will assert in concert that it is an extension of the treaty concluded against the Communist International on November 25, 1936, and that the main purpose of this treaty is defense against nations that pursue subversive activities based upon policies of the Communist International.

On the _____ day of _____, _____.

ATTACHMENT C

Explanatory Note Concerning the
Imperial Japanese Government Draft

1. Name of the treaty: Believing it best to assert that the treaty is defensive in nature, it has been decided to call it a Treaty of Consultation and Mutual Assistance.

2. The preamble:

a) The German draft has been amended with respect to the conditions of ratification. It is Japan's policy that the treaty will become valid at the time of signing, for the reason mentioned in item 6(b) below. Therefore, instead of stating that the chiefs of state "have appointed . . . plenipotentiaries," the Japanese draft, following the example of the Anti-Comintern Pact, adopts the statement, "The [three] governments . . . have agreed that. . . ."

b) The German draft and the Japanese draft are essentially the same as far as the second phrase is concerned. The former uses the expression "Anti-Comintern Pact," whereas the latter uses "treaty against the Communist International."

c) "The Comintern's activities" in the German draft has been amended in the Japanese draft to "the international activities of the Communist International."

d) There is an important difference between the German and the Japanese drafts in respect to the fourth phrase. The German draft, adopting the Italian amendment, declares that the purpose of the treaty is "to conclude a treaty of alliance for the protection of the mutual interests of the three nations in Europe and Asia." The Japanese draft states that the treaty's goal is "to strengthen their defense against communist subversion in Europe and Asia and to protect the mutual interests of the three contracting parties, according to the spirit of" the Anti-Comintern Pact. In other words, the Japanese draft holds to the position that the present treaty is merely an extension of the Anti-Comintern Pact and therefore, although the treaty text is applicable to countries other than the USSR, on the surface it is primarily concerned with anticommunism. It can be anticipated that Germany and Italy will submit objections; but as explained in item 9(b) of this attachment concerning Item 2 of the secret items of understanding, which deals with the matter of public announcement and explanation, Japan will stick to this draft.

3. Article 1: The German and Japanese drafts are the same.

4. Article 2: The German draft says simply, "In the event . . . is threatened," whereas the Japanese draft says, "In the event . . . sustains an unprovoked attack," to clarify that the intent is always defensive.

5. Article 3:

a) The German and Japanese drafts are the same, except that the former says "by every means available." The expression is eliminated in the Japanese draft because, although at first glance it seems to strengthen the meaning of the article, whether aid is "available" or not depends upon the judgment of the party offering such aid, and thus it could be interpreted as limiting it. We therefore decided that a general statement of responsibility was sufficient.

b) The German and Japanese drafts are the same in principle as regards the second clause, which requires discussion of the measures needed to meet the responsibility created by the first clause. However, the German draft uses the expression "jointly agree" instead of "consult and reach agreement." The Japanese draft uses the word "consult" in order to indicate that the three countries will meet "promptly" and reach a decision. This item is also in a sense a camouflage of the statement in the first item of the secret protocol that support, aid, or assistance, and the method by which they will be offered, must be discussed prior to a decision's being made.

6. Article 4:

a) The German draft states in Article 5 that the treaty is to be valid for ten years, with provision for renewal for another five years unless, one year prior to the date of expiration, one of the contracting parties indicates its wish to terminate the treaty. However, considering the present world situation, the ten-year period is too long. The Japanese draft, following the Anti-Comintern Pact, proposes a five-year period and requires agreement concerning the future prior to the date of expiration.

b) The German draft containing provision for ratification seems advantageous for Japan in that the signing may be more quickly effected and in that it provides for a regular procedure for ratification. However, because Germany and Italy are interested primarily in the political effect which will result from publication of the treaty, it is possible that final ratification may be delayed, thereby creating a disadvantageous situation for Japan. Therefore, for various reasons it is our decision that the treaty must become effective on the day it is signed.

In view of such matters as the fisheries negotiations, Japan desires to submit a special proposal concerning the time its conclusion is to be made public. It is possible that the contents of the treaty might be leaked to outsiders should publication be delayed. Therefore, it would be best to have it made public immediately after signing; furthermore, in estimating the time required for ratification procedures in Japan, we believe it should be submitted for imperial approval before its signing. In other respects the text should follow that of the Anti-Comintern Pact as much as possible.

7. The signed protocol:

a) In view of the fact that any attack or threat by the Soviet Union against the Japanese empire will most likely occur in the area between the Soviet Union and Manchukuo, the provisions in Item 1 have been submitted to avoid future misunderstanding.

b) In view of the provision in the secret supplementary protocol that a separate peace treaty is not to be concluded by a single contracting party, the provisions in Item 2 have been submitted to cover situations other than those created by war.

c) This signed protocol is to be published simultaneously with the treaty. However, if Germany or Italy wants to include other items in the signed protocol respecting, for example, a problem similar to the relationship between Japan and Manchukuo in Item 1, they should not be refused. Each proposal submitted by Germany or Italy shall be considered according to its particular merit.

This signed protocol is also intended to camouflage to some degree the existence of the secret protocol.

8. The secret supplementary protocol:

a) Item 1 is essentially the same as the German draft in that it states that once the treaty has been ratified, concerned officials of the three countries will hold prior consultations regarding the political and economic assistance provided under Article 2 and the aid and assistance provided under Article 3. However, Japan's policy is that the obligation to provide military assistance is applicable only if the Soviet Union alone or in concert with other countries should attack one of the contracting parties. This point is clarified in item 9(a) below concerning the secret items of understanding.

The German draft calls for the establishment of a standing committee composed of foreign ministers or their representatives. However, the Japanese foreign minister is generally unavailable, and doubts will arise as to the qualifications and authority of Japan's representative. Japan would always have a representative while Germany and Italy would be represented by their foreign ministers. Thus, on matters other than the execution of the treaty, particularly those requiring quick action, there is the danger that Japan might be manipulated by Germany and Italy. Therefore, Japan considers consultation among concerned authorities to be sufficient. Having a domestic situation different from that of Germany or Italy, Japan also considers it difficult and unnecessary to require the establishment of a committee in charge of controlling information.

b) The German draft provides that Item 2 be published in the text of the treaty. If primary attention is given to the propaganda value of the treaty, its main effect will be to demonstrate the power of the three nations by making other countries expect them jointly to fight a war. However, since Japan's view is that the treaty is defensive, on the surface, a text that positively anticipates a war is inadvisable. Hence our decision is to retain such a text in the secret protocol, in order to maintain on the surface the treaty's defensive nature.

The German draft states "a war fought jointly . . . in accordance with the treaty," whereas Japan's draft says simply "jointly engaged in war." It has been so changed, not for any particularly significant reason but rather because a jointly fought war may be possible as an indirect consequence even if the Soviet Union is not involved, although only a war with the Soviet Union could be anticipated as a direct consequence of the treaty.

c) Item 3 is provided because of the Italian-Soviet and the German-Soviet neutrality treaties, the Rapallo Treaty, etc., and is based on the same principle as the supplementary protocol of the Anti-Comintern Pact.

d) Items 4 and 5 do not require special explanation, but we considered it appropriate to include them.

9. The secret items of understanding:

a) The first clause of Item 1 clarifies that the military aid obligation is limited to an occasion when the Soviet Union, alone or in concert with other countries, attacks one of the contracting parties. It is for Japan the most important clause.

This item has a two-fold significance. First, although in concluding this treaty Japan asserts that it must be directed mainly against the Soviet Union, because of the nature of the treaty no clause of the treaty distinguishes between the Soviet Union and other countries. Therefore, although Articles 1 and 2 of the treaty are applicable to countries such as Britain and France, when aid and assistance are to be provided under Article 3 Japan restricts the military aid obligation to occasions when the Soviet Union, alone or in concert with other countries, is a belligerent.

Second, in its draft Germany seems fundamentally concerned with the impact on the world of the treaty's publication and less with the import of the treaty itself. In other words, the first German draft included in the text to be made public the obligation to give aid, yet the secret protocol established the principle that such an obligation would not begin until agreed upon by the committee. In the latest German draft this point has been revised, but it also includes a ratification clause. Thus there seems to be a great difference between what Germany and Japan expect from a tripartite pact. Japan believes it necessary to obtain a commitment to military assistance if the Soviet Union is involved. Therefore, in conjunction with our first point under item 9(a), we believe this item to be absolutely necessary. It is not difficult to anticipate objections from Germany and Italy to including this item, but since Japan has decided on a policy of not assuming an obligation of military aid, we must not conclude the treaty without clearly informing Germany and Italy of our position. Some may also argue that this point can be left for consultation among concerned government authorities, as anticipated in Item 1 of the secret protocol. However, this is obviously impossible, because detailed agreement cannot be reached without clear stipulation in the treaty text. Without this understanding, Germany and Italy will make many different requests of Japan. However, Japan admits that there would be room for reconsideration should, for example, Italy refuse to assume any obligation of military assistance if the Soviet Union alone initiates hostilities. The second clause was drafted specifically to clarify the position that military assistance may be offered, depending upon the situation, even if the Soviet Union is not involved.

b) Item 2 is as important for Japan as Item 1. Since Japan initially wanted to conclude a German-Italian-Japanese treaty as an extension of the Anti-Comintern Pact but has now decided to sign a treaty that also includes countries other than the Soviet Union as targets, Japan must explain to the outside world that the treaty is an extension of the pact in order not to arouse unnecessarily countries such as Britain, the United States, and France. This is also why in the preamble the purpose of the treaty is limited to defense against the Comintern. Germany and Italy will oppose this item, but even though its objective is limited to anticommunism, as the earlier pact has shown, it will have an impact on Britain, France, etc., sufficient for our purposes. Japan does not wish to go further to make countries such as Britain and France clear targets. It should not be impossible to convince Germany and Italy on this point.

Appendix 5
THE MATSUOKA DRAFT POLICY
"ON STRENGTHENING COOPERATION
BETWEEN JAPAN, GERMANY, AND ITALY"
JULY 30, 1940 *

I. POLICY

Japan, Germany, and Italy, recognizing that they stand on common ground in regard to the construction of a New World Order, will arrive at a mutual understanding concerning support for the establishment and administration of their living spheres and will cooperate in their policies toward the Soviet Union and the United States.

II. BASIC PRINCIPLES

A. Japan, Germany, and Italy will arrive at a fundamental understanding on the basis of the above-mentioned policy (see Appendix 1).
Note: On the basis of this fundamental understanding, such further agreements as may be necessary will be concluded between Japan, Germany, and Italy or separately between Japan and Germany or Japan and Italy.
B. Japan, Germany, and Italy will, in accordance with the above-mentioned fundamental understanding, speedily arrive at an additional understanding with respect to their mutual support and cooperation concerning the China Incident and the European war, with which they are respectively confronted (see Appendix 2).
C. The above understandings will be reached as follows:
1. The negotiations under paragraph A and paragraph B above will be conducted in accordance with the Essentials for Strengthening Cooperation between Japan, Germany, and Italy in Appendix 3, and on the basis of the Main Principles Governing Negotiations in Appendix 4.

* Prepared under Matsuoka's direction for the guidance of the Konoe cabinet following the Ogikubo Conference of July 19 and the Imperial Headquarters–Cabinet Liaison Conference of July 27. The text in Japanese, entitled "Nichi-Doku-I teikei kyōka ni kansuru ken," is in a file entitled "Nichi-Doku-I dō-mei jōyaku kankei ikken" (Documents Relating to the Treaty of Alliance between Japan, Germany, and Italy), in the Japanese Foreign Ministry Archives.

2. The negotiations under paragraph A above will be conducted at Berlin and Rome.

3. The negotiations under paragraph B above will be proposed along with paragraph A above at Berlin and Rome, but the actual negotiations will be conducted in Tokyo.

D. The understandings mentioned above need not necessarily take the form of agreements, but if Germany and Italy so desire, there is no objection to the conclusion of agreements.

Appendix 1: Terms of the Political Understanding Which Is to Form the Basis for Strengthening Cooperation between Japan, Germany, and Italy

1) Japan, Germany, and Italy, recognizing that they stand on common ground in regard to the construction of a New World Order, whose realization is the goal of their present efforts, will mutually cooperate for the creation and improvement of world peace with justice.

2) Japan, Germany, and Italy, in order to establish a New World Order, will mutually respect the living sphere Japan is planning in East Asia, including the South Seas, and the living sphere Germany and Italy are planning in Europe and Africa, and will cooperate for the construction of the New Orders in the said regions.

3) Japan, Germany, and Italy will mutually effect close economic cooperation.

With this end in view, they will carry out a preferential mutual interchange of material resources and techniques existing in their respective living spheres and will also accord favorable consideration to the other parties' economic activities in their respective living spheres.

4) Japan, Germany, and Italy will cooperate in maintaining peace with the Soviet Union and in inducing the Soviet Union to bring its policy into line with the common interests of the contracting parties. In addition, they will confer on measures to be taken in the event of a danger of either Japan or Germany and Italy entering into a state of war with the Soviet Union.

5) Japan, Germany, and Italy will mutually cooperate in order not to allow the United States to interfere in regions other than the American continent and also in order to safeguard the political and economic interests of both contracting parties vis-à-vis the United States. Further, in the event of a danger of either contracting party entering into a state of war with the United States, both parties will confer on measures to be taken.

Japan, Germany, and Italy will cooperate closely in their policies toward Central and South America.

Note: Paragraphs 4 and 5 will be treated as confidential.

Appendix 2: Terms of Understanding between Japan, Germany, and
Italy Concerning Mutual Assistance and Cooperation in
Regard to the European War and the China Incident

1) Japan, Germany, and Italy, in settling the China Incident and the
European war, by which the contracting parties respectively are now
confronted, and considering the fact that Britain is the major enemy of
both, will effect mutual support and cooperation as follows:

   a) Japan will:
   1. Facilitate insofar as possible the desires of Germany and Italy
      in regard to the acquisition of resources existing in East Asia,
      including the South Seas; and
   2. Cooperate insofar as possible in intensifying the pressure on
      Britain in East Asia, including the South Seas, and in facilitat-
      ing the prosecution of the war by Germany and Italy against
      Britain.
   b) Germany and Italy will:
   1. Cooperate insofar as possible in supplying such machinery
      and offering such technical assistance as Japan may desire;
      and
   2. Cooperate with Japan in the settlement of the China In-
      cident.

Note: This understanding will be treated as confidential.

Appendix 3: Essentials for Strengthening Cooperation between Japan,
Germany, and Italy

1) Concerning Japan's living sphere for the construction of the New
Order in East Asia:

   a) The sphere to be envisaged in the course of negotiations with
   Germany and Italy as Japan's living sphere for the construction of a
   New Order in East Asia will comprise:

   The former German islands under mandate, French Indochina,
   the Pacific islands, Thailand, British Malaya, British North Bor-
   neo, the Dutch East Indies, Burma, Australia, New Zealand, and
   India, with Japan, Manchuria, and China as the backbone.

   It is understood, however, that the South Seas region which Japan
   will indicate in conducting negotiations with Germany and Italy
   will be the region from Burma eastward, and from the Dutch East
   Indies and New Caledonia northward. Concerning Australia, New
   Zealand, and India, Japan will endeavor to have its desires prevail
   in these regions (see sections e and f below).

   b) Japan will take measures to bring under its control the former
   German islands in the Pacific under mandate to Britain and France
   in view of their strategic importance in the event of war against the
   United States.

c) The goal for the Dutch East Indies is to have it become independent, but at least for the time being it will be placed under Japan's political influence. Should German proposals be at variance with the above, recognition of Japan's political leadership in the Dutch East Indies should still be obtained by allowing Germany preferential access to the natural resources existing in that country and by guaranteeing the continuance of existing German economic undertakings there as well as by negotiations of a political nature on other matters in general.

d) The same principles as in section b above will be followed with respect to French Indochina.

e) Although Australia and New Zealand are somewhat distant from the other regions, it is nevertheless true that Japan has interests in this area, and consequently Japan does not want these countries to become territories of or come under the administration of any country outside East Asia.

f) Needless to say, Japan has interests in India; but with respect to Japan's cooperation vis-à-vis the Soviet Union, there is room for further consideration with respect to western India.

2) Concerning economic cooperation between Japan, Germany, and Italy:

a) With regard to trade, Japan will supply Germany and Italy with Japanese, Manchurian, and Chinese agricultural, forest, and marine products and will also cooperate in supplying Germany and Italy with special mineral products, rubber, and other articles from China, French Indochina, and the Dutch East Indies. Germany and Italy, for their part, will supply Japan with such technical assistance, aircraft, machinery, chemical products, etc. as may be required by Japan.

(Insertion: With regard to mutual economic activities, Japan recognizes, especially in China and Manchuria, that Germany and Italy have a preferential position and will permit their technology and equipment to come in.)

b) For the above-mentioned purposes, there will be separately concluded an economic agreement, a trade agreement, and a payments agreement.

3) Concerning Japan's attitude toward cooperation between Japan, Germany, and Italy in their policies toward the Soviet Union and the United States:

Being destined to be the leader of East Asia in the postwar New Order, wherein it is anticipated that the world will be divided into the four great spheres of East Asia, the Soviet Union, Europe, and the American continent, Japan will cooperate closely with Germany and Italy, who will constitute the guiding forces in Europe, so as to:

a) Restrain the Soviet Union on the east and the west and, in-

ducing the Soviet Union to align its policies with the common interests of Japan, Germany, and Italy, endeavor to direct the Soviet
sphere of influence into areas where there will be little direct conflict with the interests of Japan, Germany, and Italy, for example
toward the Persian Gulf, and which will contribute to the attainment of Japan's aspirations. Further, Japan will make use of the important immigrational and economic footholds that Germany and
Italy presently have in South America to carry out its future policies
toward the United States.

4) Concerning Japan's attitude toward cooperation between Japan,
Germany, and Italy in their policies toward Britain:

a) Japan will, in the construction of its New Order in East Asia,
take measures to eliminate British political interests from East Asia,
including the South Seas.

Such measures are intended to weaken Britain's position. The
facts show that the policy Japan is currently pursuing toward Britain in China has had a consistently good effect on the war situation
in Europe.

b) With a view to furthering its cooperation with Germany and
Italy in their prosecution of the war against Britain, Japan will spare
no effort to cooperate with Germany and Italy in their efforts to
secure the natural resources existing in East Asia, including the
South Seas. Further, Japan will to a greater degree cooperate with
Germany and Italy in the war against Britain, with respect to the
elimination of British interests in East Asia, anti-British demon-
strations and propaganda, the support of independence movements
in the colonies and dependencies of Britain, and other matters.

c) In the event that Japan should come to use force against Britain in order to achieve the end stipulated in section (a) above, the
timing thereof will be conditioned by: 1) the extent to which a settlement has been reached in the China Incident, 2) the degree of
Japan's military preparedness, and 3) the situation vis-à-vis the adjustment of relations with the Soviet Union and the United States.

In the event that Germany and Italy should express a desire for
Japanese military cooperation against Britain, Japan is prepared as a
matter of principle to meet that desire. As to timing, however, Japan
will decide independently in accordance with the above-mentioned
conditions.

Appendix 4: Main Principles Governing Negotiations

1) In order to strengthen cooperation between Japan, Germany, and
Italy, Japan should not miss the present opportunity wherein Germany
and Italy are concentrating all their forces to defeat Britain. If Japan
were to start negotiations after the victory of Germany and Italy has

become certain, not only would the negotiations have much less effect, but there is danger that the attitude of Germany, which has considerable ambitions in the South Seas, might also change for the worse.

Negotiations for this understanding will be conducted separately with Germany and Italy. However, in the event that Germany and Italy desire that the negotiations be carried out among all three countries, Japan will meet their desire.

2) The understanding with respect to our mutual assistance and cooperation in the European war and the China Incident will be suggested at the same time as the above-mentioned fundamental understanding when we propose the strengthening of cooperation with Germany and Italy. While the discussions concerning the details of cooperation in the European war and the China Incident will be conducted in Tokyo, the two above-mentioned understandings must be considered inseparable.

3) The principal purpose of the negotiations under Appendix 1, paragraph 2, which is designed to have Germany and Italy recognize and respect Japan's living sphere in East Asia, including the South Seas, is to obtain overall recognition of Japan's position of political leadership in the whole of East Asia, including the South Seas. However, should Germany and Italy be inclined to make any reservations in regard to any of the designated areas, Japan will attempt to persuade them by conducting concrete negotiations on each area, bearing in mind the provision in Appendix 3, paragraph 1, sections b through f.

4) Concerning Appendix 3, paragraph 4, section c, in the event that Germany and Italy raise the question of Japanese military cooperation against Britain, Japan will reply that it is prepared as a matter of principle to meet their desire. With respect to the use of armed force, since the outbreak of hostilities depends on certain conditions, Japan must decide independently the timing of its participation in the war. In the event that Germany seeks the above-mentioned military cooperation, efforts will be made to secure Germany's understanding of Japan's position on this point and at the same time to persuade Germany and Italy to aid in the elimination of those conditions that would restrict Japanese military action against Britain.

Appendix 6

COMPARISON OF REVISED PROVISIONS OF DRAFT POLICY PAPERS FOR STRENGTHENING TIES BETWEEN JAPAN, GERMANY, AND ITALY [1]

The Matsuoka Draft, July 30, 1940 [2]	*The Army-Navy Draft, August 6, 1940* [3]	*The Foreign Ministry Draft, September 4, 1940* [4]
Appendix 1, paragraph 4: "In addition, they will confer on measures to be taken in the event of a danger of either Japan or Germany and Italy entering into a state of war with the Soviet Union."	Same	To original sentence add: ". . . if in the course of negotiations with Germany and Italy it turns out that such desire is entertained by those two countries."

[1] Only significant revisions are listed; slight changes of wording, changes in alphabetical or numerical designations of provisions, etc. are ignored. A verbatim textual comparison is in Nihon Kokusai Seiji Gakkai Taiheiyō Sensō Gen'in Kenkyūbu (Japan Association on International Relations, Study Group on the Causes of the Pacific War), *Taiheiyō sensō e no michi: Bekkan shiryō hen* (The Road to the Pacific War: Supplementary Volume of Documents), pp. 329–32.

[2] For complete text, see Appendix 5.

[3] Revision of the Matsuoka Draft of July 30, approved by responsible army and navy authorities on August 6, 1940. The text in Japanese, entitled "Nichi-Doku-I teikei kyōka ni kansuru ken" (On Strengthening Cooperation between Japan, Germany, and Italy), is in Japan, Foreign Ministry, "Nichi-Doku-I sangoku jōyaku" (The Tripartite Pact), pp. 9–29, in JFM Archives.

[4] Revision of the army-navy draft of August 6, prepared by officials of the Foreign Ministry close to Matsuoka for the Four Ministers Conference of September 6. The text in Japanese, entitled "Gunji dōmei kōshō ni kansuru hōshin an" (Draft Policy for Negotiating a Military Alliance), is in *ibid*.

The Matsuoka Draft, July 30, 1940 [2]	*The Army-Navy Draft, August 6, 1940* [3]	*The Foreign Ministry Draft, September 4, 1940* [4]
Appendix 1, paragraph 5: "Japan, Germany, and Italy will mutually cooperate in order not to allow the United States to interfere in regions other than the American continent and also in order to safeguard the political and economic interests of both contracting parties vis-à-vis the United States. Further, in the event of a danger of either contracting party entering into a state of war with the United States, both parties will confer on measures to be taken."	Same	Replace "the American continent" with "the western hemisphere and the United States' possessions"; and replace "both parties will confer on measures to be taken" with "the other contracting party will assist that party by all possible means."
Appendix 1, paragraph 5, note: "Paragraphs 4 and 5 will be treated as confidential."	Revise as follows: "The understanding will be treated as confidential."	Restore original sentence
Appendix 2, paragraph 1, first sentence: "Japan, Germany, and Italy, in settling the China Incident and the European war, by which the contracting parties respectively are now confronted, and considering the fact that Britain is the major enemy of both,	Delete: "and considering the fact that Britain is the major enemy of both."	Same

will effect mutual support and cooperation as follows:"		
Appendix 2, paragraph 1, section b-2: "Cooperate with Japan in the settlement of the China Incident."	Same	Replace with: "Render as much political and economic cooperation as possible in the settlement of the China Incident."
Appendix 3, paragraph 1, section a: "Concerning Australia, New Zealand, and India, Japan will endeavor to have its desires prevail in these regions (see sections e and f below)."	Same	Replace with: "It is further understood tentatively that India may be recognized as being in the living sphere of the Soviet Union."
Appendix 3, paragraph 1, section b: "Japan will take measures to bring under its control the former German islands in the Pacific under mandate to Britain and France in view of their strategic importance in the event of war against the United States."	Add: "Japan will take measures to annex the former German islands under its mandate and . . ."	Delete entire section
Appendix 3, paragraph 1, section c: "The goal for the Dutch East Indies is to have it become independent, but at least for the time being it will be placed under Japan's political influence. Should German proposals	Same	Replace "political influence" with "political and economic predominance"; replace "political leadership" with "predominant position"; insert "goods and" before "natural resources."

The Matsuoka Draft, July 30, 1940 [2]	*The Army-Navy Draft, August 6, 1940* [3]	*The Foreign Ministry Draft, September 4, 1940* [4]
be at variance with the above, recognition of Japan's political leadership in the Dutch East Indies should still be obtained by allowing Germany preferential access to the natural resources existing in that country and by guaranteeing the continuance of existing German economic undertakings there as well as by negotiations of a political nature on other matters in general."		
Appendix 3, paragraph 1, section 3: "Although Australia and New Zealand are somewhat distant from the other regions, it is nevertheless true that Japan has interests in this area, and consequently Japan does not want these countries to become territories of or come under the administration of any country outside East Asia."	Same	Delete entire section

Appendix 3, paragraph 1, section f:

"Needless to say, Japan has interests in India; but with respect to Japan's cooperation vis-à-vis the Soviet Union there is room for further consideration with respect to western India."

Replace with: "Policy concerning India should conform generally with that under section e above."

Appendix 3, paragraph 2, section a, last sentence:

"With regard to mutual economic activities, Japan recognizes, especially in China and Manchuria, that Germany and Italy have a preferential position and will permit their technology and equipment to come in."

Revise as follows: "With regard to mutual economic activities, Japan will, especially in China and Manchuria, accord to Germany and Italy de facto preferential treatment and will permit . . ."

Appendix 3, paragraph 3, section a:

"Restrain the Soviet Union on the east and the west and, inducing the Soviet Union to align its policies with the common interests of Japan, Germany, and Italy, endeavor to direct the Soviet sphere of influence into areas where there will be little direct conflict with the interests of Japan, Germany, and Italy, for example toward the Persian Gulf, and which will contribute to the attainment of Japan's aspirations."

Same

Delete entire section, but see phrase added under paragraph 3, section a.

Same

Add the following: ". . . it being also possible that, in case of need, a Soviet advance toward India may have to be recognized."

The Matsuoka Draft, *July 30, 1940* [2]	*The Army-Navy Draft,* *August 6, 1940* [3]	*The Foreign Ministry Draft,* *September 4, 1940* [4]
Appendix 3, paragraph 3:	Add the following section b: "While peaceful means will be adhered to insofar as possible in dealing with the United States, Japan will, through political and economic cooperation with Germany and Italy in East Asia and Europe, endeavor to create a situation in which it can bring pressure to bear on the United States as occasion may require and thereby cause that nation to assist in the attainment of Japan's aspirations."	Same
Appendix 3, paragraph 4, section a: "Japan will, in the construction of its New Order in East Asia, take measures to eliminate British political interests from East Asia, including the South Seas."	Same	Insert "and economic" before "interests."
Appendix 3, paragraph 4, section b: "With a view to furthering its cooperation with Germany and Italy in their prosecution of the war against	Same	Insert "goods and" before "natural resources."

Britain, Japan will spare no effort to cooperate with Germany and Italy in their efforts to secure the natural resources existing in East Asia, including the South Seas."

Appendix 3, paragraph 4, section c:
"In the event that Japan should come to use force against Britain in order to achieve the end stipulated in section a above, the timing thereof will be conditioned by: 1) the extent to which a settlement has been reached in the China Incident, 2) the degree of Japan's military preparedness, and 3) the situation vis-à-vis the Soviet Union and the United States.

"In the event that Germany and Italy should express a desire for Japanese military cooperation against Britain, Japan is prepared as a matter of principle to meet that desire. As to timing, however, Japan will decide independently in accordance with the above-mentioned conditions."

Revise as follows: "Concerning the possible use of armed force against Britain, Japan will decide independently in accordance with the following principles: 1) In the event that a favorable settlement of the China Incident should be near, it would be a good time to use force insofar as the general domestic and foreign situation permitted. 2) In the event that the China Incident should remain unsettled, Japan will take measures short of war. However, if the domestic and foreign situations take a decidedly favorable turn, Japan will resort to armed force. 3) The 'domestic and foreign situation' signifies the situation including the China Incident, that is, the European situation, especially the state of our relations with the Soviet Union, the attitude of the United States toward Japan, our preparedness for war, etc."

Redesignate as paragraph 5; same text except for item 2, revised as follows: "In the event that the China Incident should remain unsettled, Japan will as a matter of principle take measures short of war. However, if the domestic and foreign situations take a decidedly favorable turn, or if it is deemed that, irrespective of whether or not our preparations are complete, the development of the international situation permits of no further delay, Japan will resort to force."

The Matsuoka Draft, *July 30, 1940* [2]	*The Army-Navy Draft,* *August 6, 1940* [3]	*The Foreign Ministry Draft,* *September 4, 1940* [4]
Appendix 4, paragraphs 1 and 2:	Same	Deleted entirely
Appendix 4, paragraph 3: "The principal purpose of the negotiations under Appendix 1, paragraph 2, which is designed to have Germany and Italy recognize and respect Japan's living sphere in East Asia, including the South Seas, is to obtain overall recognition of Japan's position of political leadership in the whole of East Asia, including the South Seas."	Same	Replace "political leadership" with "predominant position."
Appendix 4, paragraph 4: ". . . in the event that Germany and Italy raise the question of Japanese military cooperation against Britain, Japan will reply that it is prepared as a matter of principle to meet their desire. . . . In the event that Germany seeks the above-mentioned military cooperation, efforts will be	Substantially the same	Replace "Britain" in both instances with "Britain and the United States."

made to secure Germany's understanding of Japan's position on this point and at the same time to persuade Germany and Italy to aid in the elimination of those conditions that would restrict Japanese military action against Britain."

Appendix 7
THE TRIPARTITE ALLIANCE
OF GERMANY, ITALY, AND JAPAN
AND ACCOMPANYING NOTES,
SEPTEMBER 27, 1940 *

The Governments of Germany, Italy, and Japan, considering it as the condition precedent of any lasting peace that all nations of the world be given each its own proper place, have decided to stand by and co-operate with one another in regard to their efforts in Greater East Asia and the regions of Europe respectively wherein it is their prime purpose to establish and maintain a new order of things calculated to promote mutual prosperity and welfare of the peoples concerned.

Furthermore it is the desire of the three Governments to extend co-operation to such nations in other spheres of the world as may be inclined to put forth endeavours along lines similar to their own, in order that their ultimate aspirations for world peace may thus be realized. Accordingly the Governments of Germany, Italy, and Japan have agreed as follows:

ARTICLE 1

Japan recognizes and respects the leadership of Germany and Italy in the establishment of a new order in Europe.

ARTICLE 2

Germany and Italy recognize and respect the leadership of Japan in the establishment of a new order in Greater East Asia.

ARTICLE 3

Germany, Italy, and Japan agree to co-operate in their efforts on the aforesaid lines. They further undertake to assist one another with all

* This official English language text is from *Documents on German Foreign Policy, 1918–1945,* Series D (1937–45), Vol. 11, pp. 204–5. An identical version, except for the order of names of the three countries, is in Saitō Yoshie, "Nichi-Doku-I jōyaku teiketsu yōroku" (Summary Record of the Conclusion of the Tripartite Pact), in JFM Archives.

political, economic, and military means when one of the three Contracting Parties is attacked by a power at present not involved in the European war or in the Sino-Japanese conflict.

ARTICLE 4

With a view to implementing the present Pact, Joint Technical Commissions, the members of which are to be appointed by the respective Governments of Germany, Italy, and Japan, will meet without delay.

ARTICLE 5

Germany, Italy, and Japan affirm that the aforesaid terms do not in any way affect the political status which exists at present as between each of the three Contracting Parties and Soviet Russia.

ARTICLE 6

The present Pact shall come into effect immediately upon signature and shall remain in force for ten years from the date of its coming into force.

At proper time before the expiration of the said term the High Contracting Parties shall, at the request of any one of them, enter into negotiations for its renewal.

In faith whereof, the Undersigned, duly authorized by their respective Governments, have signed this Pact and have affixed hereto their Seals.

Done in triplicate at Berlin, the 27th day of September 1940—in the XVIII year of the Fascist Era—, corresponding to the 27th day of the 9th month of the 15th year of Showa.

> Joachim v. Ribbentrop
> Ciano
> Kurusu

FIRST LETTER FROM THE GERMAN AMBASSADOR TO THE JAPANESE FOREIGN MINISTER *

Strictly Confidential
No. g.1000   Tokyo, September 27, 1940
Excellency: At the moment when our conversations on the Tripartite Pact, begun on the 9th of this month in Tokyo, are about to con-

---

* This letter is a translation of the original German from the files of the Japanese Foreign Ministry submitted as Exhibit 555A to the International Military Tribunal for the Far East, reproduced in *Documents on German Foreign Policy,*

clude successfully, it is Minister Stahmer's and my sincere desire to express to Your Excellency our deepest appreciation for the decisive part which you have played throughout in a most generous and accommodating spirit. We would like also to take this opportunity to state once more in this letter some of the most important points touched upon in our conversations.

The German Government is convinced that the contracting parties are about to enter a new and decisive phase of world history in which it will be their task to assume the leadership in the establishment of a new order in Greater East Asia and Europe respectively.

The fact that for a long time the interests of the contracting parties will be the same, together with their unlimited confidence in each other, forms the secure foundation for the Pact.

The German Government is firmly convinced that the technical details concerning the execution of the Pact can be settled without difficulties; it would not be in keeping with the far-reaching importance of the Pact, and would also not be practically possible, to try to regulate at the present time all the individual cases which may sometime come up. These questions can only be settled, instance by instance, in a spirit of intimate cooperation.

Conclusions of the Technical Commissions, provided for in article 4 of the Pact, should be submitted to the three Governments for approval in order to be put into force.

Needless to say, the question, whether an attack within the meaning of article 3 of the Pact has taken place, must be determined through joint consultation of the three contracting parties.

If Japan, contrary to the peaceful intent of the Pact, be attacked by a power so far not engaged in the European War or the China conflict, Germany will consider it a matter of course to give Japan full support and assist her with all military and economic means.

With regard to the relations between Japan and Soviet Russia, Germany will do everything within her power to promote a friendly understanding and will at any time offer her good offices to this end.

Germany will use her industrial strength and her other technical and material resources as far as possible in favor of Japan in order both to facilitate the establishment of a new order in Greater East Asia and to enable her to be better prepared for any emergency. Germany and Japan will further undertake to aid each other in procuring in every possible way necessary raw materials and minerals including oil.

1918–1945, Series D (1937–45), Vol. 11, pp. 205–7. No copy has been found in the German Foreign Office Archives. Another version, slightly different in wording but identical in substance, is given in Saitō Yoshie, "Nichi-Doku-I jōyaku teiketsu yōroku" (Summary Record of the Conclusion of the Tripartite Pact), in JFM Archives.

The German Foreign Minister is firmly convinced that, if Italy's assistance and cooperation are sought in reference to the matters above enumerated, she will of course act in concord with Germany and Japan.

I have the honor to submit these statements to Your Excellency as the views of the German Foreign Minister conveyed personally by his special delegate, Minister Stahmer, and repeated also in instructions to me from my Government.

I avail myself of this opportunity to renew to Your Excellency the assurance of my highest consideration.

Ott

FIRST LETTER FROM THE JAPANESE FOREIGN MINISTER TO THE GERMAN AMBASSADOR IN TOKYO *

Tokyo, September 27, 1940

Excellency: I have the honor to acknowledge receipt of Your Excellency's letter (No. g.1000) of this date and I feel happy to take note of the contents therein.

I avail myself of this opportunity to assure Your Excellency the highest consideration.

Matsuoka

SECOND LETTER FROM THE JAPANESE FOREIGN MINISTER TO THE GERMAN AMBASSADOR IN TOKYO †

Tokyo, September 27, 1940

Excellency: I have the honor to inform Your Excellency that, the Japanese Government earnestly share the hope with the Governments of Germany and Italy that the present European War will remain lim-

---

* Saito Yoshie, "Nichi-Doku-I jōyaku teiketsu yōroku" (Summary Record of the Conclusion of the Tripartite Pact), in JFM Archives.

† The agreed English text, reproduced as an enclosure in the second letter from the German ambassador to the Japanese foreign minister (see below) in *Documents on German Foreign Policy, 1918–1945*, Series D (1937–45), Vol. 11, p. 207, using a document from the files of the Japanese Foreign Ministry, submitted as Exhibit 555B to the International Military Tribunal for the Far East. No copy has been found in the German Foreign Office Archives. An identical version is in Saitō Yoshie, "Nichi-Doku-I jōyaku teiketsu yōroku" (Summary Record of the Conclusion of the Tripartite Pact), in JFM Archives.

ited as far as possible in its sphere and scope and will come to a speedy conclusion and that they shall on their part spare no effort in that direction.

However, the conditions actually prevailing in Greater East Asia and elsewhere do not permit the Japanese Government to rest assured in the present circumstances that there is no danger whatever of an armed conflict taking place between Japan and Great Britain, and accordingly they desire to call the attention of the German Government to such a possibility and to state that they feel confident that Germany will do its utmost to aid Japan in such an eventuality with all means in its power.

I avail myself of this opportunity to assure Your Excellency of my highest consideration.

Matsuoka

SECOND LETTER FROM THE GERMAN AMBASSADOR
TO THE JAPANESE FOREIGN MINISTER *

Strictly Confidential
No. g.1001   Tokyo, September 27, 1940

Excellency: I have the honor to acknowledge receipt of Your Excellency's second letter Jyo-ni Nr. 133 of this date with contents as follows:

"I have the honor to inform Your Excellency that the Japanese Government earnestly share the hope with the Governments of Germany and Italy that the present European War will remain limited as far as possible in its sphere and scope and will come to a speedy conclusion and that they shall on their part spare no effort in that direction.

"However, the conditions actually prevailing in Greater East Asia and elsewhere do not permit the Japanese Government to rest assured in the present circumstances that there is no danger whatever of an armed conflict taking place between Japan and Great Britain, and accordingly they desire to call attention of the German Government to

---

* See preceding note on source of text. An identical version, except for a slight change of wording in the final sentence, is in Saitō Yoshie, "Nichi-Doku-I jōyaku teiketsu yōroku" (Summary Record of the Conclusion of the Tripartite Pact), in JFM Archives.

such a possibility and to state that they feel confident that Germany will do their utmost to aid Japan in such eventuality with all means in their power."

I take this occasion to note the contents of Your Excellency's letter.

Accept, Mr. Minister, the renewed assurance of my highest consideration.

Ott

THIRD LETTER FROM THE JAPANESE FOREIGN MINISTER TO THE GERMAN AMBASSADOR IN TOKYO *

Tokyo, September 27, 1940

Excellency: I have the honor to ask Your Excellency to confirm the following oral declaration which was made by Your Excellency on behalf of the German Government:

"The German Government agree that the former German Colonies actually under Japan's Mandate in the South Seas shall remain in Japan's possession, it being understood that Germany be in a way compensated therefor. In regard to other former Colonies in the South Seas, they shall be restored automatically to Germany upon conclusion of peace ending the present European War. Afterwards the German Government would be prepared to confer, in an accommodating spirit, with the Japanese Government with a view to disposing of them as far as possible in Japan's favour against compensation."

I avail myself of this opportunity to renew to Your Excellency the highest consideration.

Matsuoka

* This letter is a translation of the original German from the files of the Japanese Foreign Ministry submitted as Exhibit 556 to the International Military Tribunal for the Far East and reproduced in *Documents on German Foreign Policy, 1918–1945*, Series D (1937–45), Vol. 11, p. 208, fn. 2. No copy has been found in the German Foreign Office Archives. An identical version is in Saitō Yoshie, "Nichi-Doku-I jōyaku teiketsu yōroku" (Summary Record of the Conclusion of the Tripartite Pact), in JFM Archives.

THIRD LETTER FROM THE GERMAN AMBASSADOR
TO THE JAPANESE FOREIGN MINISTER *

Strictly Confidential
No. g.1002   Tokyo, September 27, 1940

Excellency: I have the honor to acknowledge receipt of Your Excellency's letter Jyo-ni Nr. 134 of this date and to confirm the oral declaration reproduced in it which I made concerning the former German colonies in the South Seas.

I avail myself of this opportunity to assure Your Excellency once more of my highest consideration.

Ott

* This letter is a translation of the original German from the files of the Japanese Foreign Ministry submitted as Exhibit 555C to the International Military Tribunal for the Far East and reproduced in *Documents on German Foreign Policy, 1918–1945*, Series D (1937–45), Vol. 11, p. 208. No copy has been found in the German Foreign Office Archives. Another version, slightly different in wording but identical in substance, is given in Saitō Yoshie, "Nichi-Doku-I jōyaku teiketsu yōroku" (Summary Record of the Conclusion of the Tripartite Pact), in JFM Archives.

Notes

Full English-language titles, publication information, and
Japanese characters may be found in the bibliography.

ONE

The Anti-Comintern Pact

Introduction

1. Comments (freely translated) made by Ōshima Hiroshi during an interview at his home in Chigasaki, November 12, 1966.

2. See, for example, Frank William Iklé, *German-Japanese Relations;* Johanna Margarete Menzel Meskill, *Hitler and Japan;* Ernst L. Presseisen, *Germany and Japan;* and Theo Sommer, *Deutschland und Japan zwischen den Mächten.*

3. Ōshima interview, November 12, 1966. I am convinced of the truth of these assertions. Ōshima spoke frankly and freely; he was eighty years old; he had spent ten years in prison for his role as an important leader on Japan's road to the Pacific War. There was little reason for him to be disingenuous.

4. Note Ōhata's extensive discussion of this point. The story was reconfirmed by Ōshima during my interview with him.

5. Private interview on November 5, 1966, with a retired official of the Japanese Foreign Ministry who had been stationed in the Japanese embassy in Berlin during the 1930s and belonged to the anti-mainstream group.

6. These are dealt with in detail by Presseisen and Sommer.

Essay

1. For further details see Vols. 1 and 2 of Nihon Kokusai Seiji Gakkai Taiheiyō Sensō Gen'in Kenkyūbu (Japan Association on International Relations, Study Group on the Causes of the Pacific War), *Taiheiyō sensō e no michi* (The Road to the Pacific War) (hereafter cited as *TSM*).

2. There are numerous studies of Japanese fascism. To mention only a few: Tanaka Sōgorō, *Nihon fashizumu shi* (History of Japanese Fascism); Maejima Shōzō, *Nihon fashizumu to Gikai* (Japanese Fascism and the Diet); and Hata Ikuhiko, ed., *Gun fashizumu undō shi* (History of the Military-Fascist Movement). An extensive bibliography is to be found in the August and September 1953 issues of *Shisō* as well as in the volume edited by Hata.

3. Keishichō-shi Hensan Iinkai (Metropolitan Police Board History Editorial Committee), *Keishichō shi I: Shōwa zempan* (History of the Metropolitan Police Board, I: The Early Shōwa Era), p. 336.

4. *Ibid.*, pp. 347ff.

5. This pamphlet is reprinted in Hata, *Gun fashizumu*, pp. 253ff.

6. Shigemitsu Mamoru, *Gaikō kaisōroku* (Diplomatic Reminiscences), pp. 168–71; Obata Yūkichi Denki Kankōkai, ed., *Obata Yūkichi*, pp. 384, 402; Arita Hachirō, *Bakahachi to hito wa yū: gaikōkan no kaisō* (People Call Me "Hachi the Fool": Memoirs of a Diplomat), p. 62.

7. Ernst L. Presseisen, *Germany and Japan*, pp. 34–35.

8. According to Chief Secretary of Embassy Shichida Kigen, in *Obata Yūkichi*, p. 377.

9. Ōshima Hiroshi Interrogation, in Kyokutō Kokusai Gunji Saiban Kōhan Kiroku (Records of the International Military Tribunal for the Far East), Exhibit 477, in Japan, Justice Ministry, War Crimes Materials Office (hereafter cited as IMTFE Records). German information about the Soviet Union was excellent at that time, and the Japanese army was anxious to obtain access to it.

10. Interviews with Ōshima Hiroshi, November 14, 1959, and March 10, 1962.

11. Wakamatsu Tadaichi Affidavit, IMTFE Records, Exhibit 3492.

12. Ōshima denied having discussed this matter with Inoue (interview, March 10, 1962). In addition to this interview and that of November 14, 1959, further material is contained in notes in the possession of Hasegawa Shin'ichi, former secretary to Matsuoka Yōsuke, taken during an interview with Ōshima on December 14, 1955, entitled "Bōkyō kyōtei oyobi Nichi-Doku-I sangoku dōmei teiketsu ni itaru jijō ni kansuru kaisō" (Recollections of the Negotiations for the Anti-Comintern Pact and the Tripartite Pact) (hereafter cited as Ōshima, "Recollections of the Negotiations").

13. Japan, Foreign Ministry (hereafter JFM), "Nichi-Doku-I bōkyō kyōtei kankei ikken" (Documents Relating to the Anti-Comintern Pact), in JFM Archives (hereafter cited as JFM, Anti-Comintern Pact Documents); and the Ōshima interviews cited above.

14. Arita Hachirō, *Hito no me no chiri o miru: gaikō mondai kaikoroku* (Beholding the Mote in Other Men's Eyes: Memoirs of Diplomatic Problems), p. 275; and Arita, *Bakahachi*, p. 74.

15. Tōgō Shigenori, *Jidai no ichi-men* (One View of an Era), p. 96.

16. Arita, *Hito no me no chiri o miru*, p. 277; and *Bakahachi*, p. 76; Tōgō, p. 96; and JFM, Anti-Comintern Pact Documents.

17. Harada Kumao, *Saionji kō to seikyoku* (Prince Saionji and the Political Situation), Vol. 5, pp. 114–15 (entry of July 19, 1935).

18. Ōhata Tokushirō, "Dai-ichiji sekai taisen go no Doku-So kankei to kyōchō gaikō no seiritsu" (Post-World War I German-Soviet Diplomatic Relations and the Establishment of Cooperative Diplomacy), *Shikan*, No. 62 (July 1961), pp. 47–63.

19. Yamaji Akira Affidavit, IMTFE Records, Exhibit 3615; JFM, "Nichi-Doku seiji kyōtei teiketsu mondai" (Conclusion of the Japanese-German Political Pact), IMTFE Records, Exhibit 3267; and Presseisen, p. 102.

20. See Appendix 1 for full text of the pact and related documents. The name "Anti-Comintern Pact" is said to have been suggested by Hans von Raumer, who conducted the negotiations with Ōshima. JFM, "Nichi-Doku kan ni okeru kōshō, keii" (The Japanese-German Negotiations, Particulars), in JFM Archives (hereafter cited as JFM, Particulars).

21. Harada, Vol. 5, pp. 192–93, 198.

22. The prime minister's and foreign minister's testimony before the Privy Council Investigation Committee is in IMTFE Records, No. 219; the committee's report is in IMTFE Records, Exhibit 479; and the report submitted by Arai Kentarō, chairman of the committee, is in IMTFE Records, Exhibit 484.

23. See Appendix 2 for the full text of the Japanese and German proclamations.

24. W. G. Krivitsky, *I Was Stalin's Agent*, pp. 37–38; and JFM, Particulars.

25. Jane Degras, ed., *Soviet Documents on Foreign Policy*, Vol. 3, pp. 220–26; and newspaper and other accounts in Presseisen, pp. 111–18.

26. JFM, "Shōwa jūichi-nendō shitsumu hōkoku" (Annual Report, 1936), IMTFE Records, Defense Document 1425, not admitted as evidence.

27. *Ibid.* The Keelung Incident took place in early October while the British fleet was at the port of Keelung in Taiwan. On October 20 Britain revoked the commercial treaty between Japan and India and on the 27th postponed the fleet's visit to Japan.

28. IMTFE Records, Defense Document 1424, not admitted as evidence; Horinouchi Kensuke Affidavit, IMTFE Records, Defense Document 2147, not admitted as evidence; "Kyokutō Gunji Saiban ni okeru Hirota Kōki bengo kankei shiryō kōkyoshō sono ta" (Materials for the Defense of Hirota Kōki at the International Military Tribunal: Affidavits, etc.), which includes the oral testimony of Yamaguchi Iwao, in Shidehara Heiwa Bunkō (Shidehara Peace Collection).

29. Telegram from Ambassador Sugimura to Foreign Minister Arita, November 18, 1936, IMTFE Records, Exhibit 2615.

30. Telegram from Sugimura to Arita, November 28, 1936, IMTFE Records, Exhibit 2616.

31. Italy announced its official recognition of Manchukuo on November 29, 1937. Ichimata Masao, "Manshū teikoku no kokusaihō-jō no chii" (Manchukuo's Position under International Law), *Waseda hōgaku*, Vol. 21 (1946), p. 13.

32. Telegram from Ambassador Sugimura to Foreign Minister Satō Naotake, May 25, 1937, IMTFE Records, Exhibit 2618.

33. JFM, Anti-Comintern Pact Documents.

34. *Ibid.*

35. JFM, Particulars.

36. Yosano Shigeru, "Bōkyō kyōtei yori sangoku dōmei teiketsu ni itaru keii" (From the Anti-Comintern Pact to the Conclusion of the Tripartite Pact), in "Kyokutō Gunji Saiban ni okeru Hirota hikoku bengo kankei shiryō (Morishima chōsho)" (IMTFE, Materials Related to the Defense of Hirota Kōki: Morishima Gorō Testimony) in Shidehara Heiwa Bunkō (hereafter cited as Yosano Statement).

37. JFM, Particulars.

38. Kurt Bloch, *German Interests and Policies in the Far East*, pp. 32–36. See also Presseisen, pp. 124–26.

39. *Ibid.*, pp. 41, 50.

40. International Military Tribunal, *Trial of the Major War Criminals*, Vol. 34, pp. 734–38, 740–43.

41. *Ibid.*, Vol. 25, pp. 402–13; U.S., Department of State, *Documents on German Foreign Policy, 1918–1945*, Series D (1937–45), Vol. 1, pp. 29–39 (hereafter cited as *DGFP*).

42. Joachim von Ribbentrop, *Zwischen London und Moskau*, pp. 98–100; Frank William Iklé, *German-Japanese Relations*, pp. 77ff; Presseisen, pp. 276ff.

43. Ribbentrop, p. 116; *DGFP*, Vol. 1, pp. 162–68.

44. JFM, Europe-Asia Bureau, "Bōkyō sūjiku kyōka mondai keika oboe" (Memorandum on Strengthening the Anti-Comintern Axis), in *Gendai shi shiryō 10: Nitchū sensō 3* (Source Materials on Contemporary History, 10: Sino-Japanese War, 3) (hereafter *GS 10*), p. 166 (hereafter cited as JFM, Axis memorandum).

45. Japan, Army Ministry (hereafter JAM), Military Affairs Section, "Nichi-Doku-I 'sangoku kyōtei' mondai no keii" (Particulars Concern-

ing the Question of a "Tripartite Pact"), January 9, 1939, in *GS 10*, p. 153 (hereafter cited as JAM, Particulars 1).

46. *GS 10*, p. 173.

47. JFM, Axis memorandum, p. 167; Ōshima interviews, November 14, 1959 and March 10, 1962; and Ōshima, "Recollections of the Negotiations."

48. Ugaki Kazushige, *Ugaki Kazushige nikki* (Diary of Ugaki Kazushige), Vol. 2, pp. 1240–41 (hereafter cited as *Ugaki Diary*); also in Ugaki Kazushige, *Shōrai seidan* (Interview with Ugaki), edited by Kamata Sawaichirō, p. 269.

49. *Ibid.*, pp. 260–68.

50. *GS 10*, pp. 351–54.

51. Unofficial talks between Ugaki and Craigie concerning British rights in China were held during the summer and fall of 1938. The Japanese army objected strongly to these talks.

52. *TSM: Bekkan shiryō hen* (Supplementary Volume of Documents), pp. 262–63; also summarized in Yabe Teiji, ed., *Konoe Fumimaro*, Vol. 1, pp. 529–30. On August 3, 1938, Itagaki told Navy Minister Yonai Mitsumasa that the purpose of strengthening the Anti-Comintern Pact was to cooperate with Germany against the Soviet Union and with Italy against Britain. Yonai objected, saying that this would not solve the China problem but would only have the opposite effect of alienating the United States and Britain. See Ogata Taketora, *Ichi gunjin no shōgai: kaisō no Yonai Mitsumasa* (The Life of an Admiral: Reminiscences of Yonai Mitsumasa), pp. 40ff; Ōhata Tokushirō, "Nichi-Doku kankei no ichi kōsatsu" (A Study of Japanese-German Relations), *Shikan*, Vol. 45, pp. 50–51; and Kurihara Ken, *Tennō: Shōwa shi oboegaki* (The Emperor: A Note on the History of the Shōwa Period), pp. 120–21.

53. *GS 10*, p. 172.

54. *Ibid.*, pp. 172–73.

55. *Ibid.*, pp. 173–74.

56. Yosano Statement.

57. JFM, Axis memorandum, p. 167.

58. JAM, Particulars 1, p. 153; interview with Yokoi Tadao, July 8, 1961.

59. JAM, Particulars 1, p. 153; Yabe, Vol. 1, p. 595.

60. JFM, Axis memorandum, pp. 167–68; also *GS 10*, pp. 177–78.

61. JFM, Anti-Comintern Pact Documents; and Yosano Statement. See

also Takagi Sōkichi, "Nichi-Doku-I gunji dōmei seiritsu no keii" (Particulars of the Conclusion of the Military Alliance between Japan, Germany, and Italy), *Sekai*, No. 59 (November 1950), p. 75; Hayashi Shigeru, "Nichi-Doku-I sangoku dōmei seiritsu no keii" (Particulars Concerning the Conclusion of the Tripartite Pact), *Shakai kagaku kenkyū*, Vol. 4, No. 2 (April 1948), p. 10; and Harada, Vol. 7, p. 193. The revised draft prepared overnight probably related only to the preamble.

62. *GS 10*, pp. 178–79.

63. *Ibid.*, pp. 168–69. Presumably the "conditions" referred to in point 1 were the changes incorporated in the Foreign Ministry draft of August 12. Those mentioned in point 3 were detailed in telegrams of August 31 from Ugaki to Tōgō in Berlin; see notes 69–70 below.

64. JAM, Particulars 1 (p. 154), for example, says: "The concerned officials of the Army, Navy, and Foreign ministries view this agreement as being aimed at Britain and France as well as the Soviet Union (in spite of the fact that there is a difference of opinion between the Foreign Ministry on the one hand and the Navy and Army ministries on the other concerning the military support mentioned in Article 3). It is understood that the preamble is agreed upon by the various ministers as a kind of 'camouflage,' drawn up in consideration of relations with Britain and the United States."

65. JFM, *Nihon gaikō nempyō narabi ni shuyō bunsho* (Chronology and Major Documents of Japanese Foreign Relations), Vol. 2, pp. 391–92; *GS 10*, pp. 179–80.

66. Ōshima, "Recollections of the Negotiations."

67. Ōshima Hiroshi Affidavit, IMTFE Records, Exhibit 3509; Kasahara Yukio Affidavit, IMTFE Records, Exhibit 3493.

68. Ōshima, "Recollections of the Negotiations." For Kasahara's understanding, see his affidavit, cited above; for Ikeda Seihin's view of the conference, see Yosano Shigeru, "Zoruge jiken no zengo" (At the Time of the Sorge Incident), *Yomiuri hyōron*, December 1950, p. 35.

69. Ugaki to Tōgō, telegram 326, August 31, 1938, *GS 10*, pp. 180–81.

70. Ugaki to Tōgō, telegram 328, August 31, 1938, *ibid.*, p. 181.

71. JAM, Particulars 1, p. 154.

72. *Ibid.*, p. 155; *GS 10*, pp. 182–83.

73. *Ibid.*, pp. 183–85; Harada, *Bekkan* (Supplementary Volume), pp. 361–64.

74. *GS 10*, p. 187; Harada, *Bekkan*, p. 364.

75. *GS 10*, p. 183.

76. Yabe, Vol. 1, pp. 545–53.

77. Harada, Vol. 7, p. 139.

78. Harada refers frequently to the movement among young Foreign Ministry officials in support of Shiratori for foreign minister. See, for example, *ibid.*, p. 142. On Yonai's opposition, see Yabe, Vol. 1, p. 557.

79. *Ibid.*, p. 557; interview with Takase Jirō, December 2, 1961.

80. *Ugaki Diary*, Vol. 2, p. 1261.

81. Harada, Vol. 7, p. 18; Ugaki Kazushige, "Rōhei no jukkai" (Recollections of an Old Soldier), *Yomiuri hyōron*, October 1950, p. 77; Arita, *Bakahachi*, p. 20; Ueda Toshio, "Nichi-Doku-I sangoku dōmei" (The Tripartite Pact), in Nihon Gaikō Gakkai (Association for the Study of Japanese Diplomacy), *Taiheiyō sensō gen'in ron* (The Origins of the Pacific War), p. 283. See also Tōgō Shigenori Affidavit, IMTFE Records, Exhibit 3614; Masatani Tadashi Affidavit, IMTFE Records, Exhibit 3620.

82. Ōshima interviews, November 14, 1959, and March 10, 1962; Ōshima, "Recollections of the Negotiations."

83. JFM, Axis memorandum, p. 170.

84. On the proposal of November 1, see Takagi, p. 82; also Ōshima Affidavit, Exhibit 3509.

85. *GS 10*, pp. 188–89; see also JAM, Particulars 1, p. 155. For the German original, see Theo Sommer, *Deutschland und Japan zwischen den Mächten*, pp. 501–2.

86. *GS 10*, pp. 189–90; see also JAM, Particulars 1, p. 155; Harada, *Bekkan*, p. 365.

87. JFM, Anti-Comintern Pact Documents, special file marked "Bōkyō kyōtei kyōka mondai" (The Question of Strengthening the Anti-Comintern Pact) (hereafter cited as JFM, File on Strengthening the Anti-Comintern Pact) contains "Iwauru bōkyō kyōtei kyōka mondai ni kansuru zen Arita gaimudaijin shuki" (Memorandum by Former Foreign Minister Arita on Strengthening the Anti-Comintern Pact) (hereafter cited as Arita Memorandum), to which comments have been added by the Ōshima defense at the Tokyo trials.

88. *GS 10*, pp. 190–91.

89. JAM, Particulars 1, p. 155.

90. Ōshima to Arita, May 22, 1939, in *GS 10*, p. 312; JFM, *Nihon gaikō nempyō*, Vol. 2, p. 409. See also Ōshima Hiroshi Affidavit, IMTFE Records, Exhibit 3508; Usami Uzuhiko Affidavit, IMTFE Records, Exhibit 3494.

91. Memorandum by Yosano Shigeru, in JFM, Anti-Comintern Pact Documents.

92. *Ibid.* The telegram is dated November 24, but according to Arita it was sent on November 17.

93. Ōshima to Arita, received December 6, 1938, *GS 10,* p. 193.

94. Arita Memorandum; Arita, *Hito no me no chiri o miru,* pp. 8, 10; Ōshima Affidavit, Exhibit 3508.

95. It was only when Kasahara returned to Japan that the government became aware that Ōshima had proposed to Germany an alliance similar to that envisaged by Itagaki.

96. JFM, File on Strengthening the Anti-Comintern Pact. At the time of the Munich talks the Germans had presented to Italy a proposed treaty to strengthen the Anti-Comintern Pact. On October 27, when Ribbentrop was in Rome, he showed Mussolini the draft treaty and discussed Italy's entry into the pact. Mussolini agreed in principle but, according to Arisue, found it difficult to accept the draft at that time and therefore sought postponement of the treaty until he could obtain national support for it. Toward the end of the year Ribbentrop asked Ōshima to encourage Italy to join, and in mid-December, after obtaining the permission of the Foreign Ministry, Ōshima went to Rome to discuss the issue with Mussolini. Mussolini was still hesitant, hoping to pick a time when the alliance would be welcomed by the Italian people, so he withheld an affirmative answer. By January he was eager to conclude the alliance. *Ibid.*

97. Arisue Seizō to Vice Chief of General Staff, telegram 372, December 1, 1938, *GS 10,* p. 194; see also Arisue to Vice Chief, telegram 382, December 16, 1938, *ibid.,* p. 195.

98. Yabe, Vol. 1, p. 627.

99. Arita Memorandum; Arita, *Hito no me no chiri o miru,* pp. 11–12; Harada, Vol. 7, p. 258.

100. For texts of the draft, see *GS 10,* pp. 202–3; Harada, *Bekkan,* pp. 365–67; Sommer, pp. 504–5; Mario Toscano, *Le origini diplomatiche del patto d'acciaio,* pp. 103–5; Royal Institute of International Affairs, *Documents on International Affairs, 1939–1946,* Vol. 1, pp. 152–53, contains only the secret supplementary protocol. See also F. C. Jones, *Japan's New Order in East Asia,* pp. 110–11. According to the Arita Memorandum, an unofficial proposal was made in December 1938.

101. Arita Memorandum; Arita, *Hito no me no chiri o miru,* pp. 12–14; Yabe, Vol. 2, pp. 18–19.

102. JFM, *Nihon gaikō nempyō,* Vol. 2, p. 408; *GS 10,* pp. 210–11.

103. Arita Memorandum; Arita, *Hito no me no chiri o miru,* pp. 12–14;

Yabe, Vol. 2, pp. 18–19. The navy agreed to the strengthening of the Anti-Comintern Pact on the following grounds: (1) to strengthen cooperation with Germany alone was dangerous because it might encourage the army to engage in a blitz-type war with the Soviet Union; (2) to limit the pact's target to the Soviet Union ran counter to the objective of strengthening naval preparations vis-à-vis Britain and the United States; (3) a policy of accommodation with Britain, France, and the United States had been proved ineffective in the China conflict. Harada, Vol. 7, pp. 268–69.

104. Ōshima Affidavit, Exhibit 3509; Ōshima Hiroshi Interrogation, IMTFE Records, Exhibit 497; Usami Affidavit; Kawabe Torashirō Affidavit, IMTFE Records, Exhibit 349; and Arita Memorandum.

105. Compromise instructions were apparently demanded by certain naval leaders, largely from the middle echelons and not including top officials such as Navy Minister Yonai. Arita Memorandum.

106. Harada, *Bekkan*, pp. 367–68. For details of the discussions among the Army, Navy, and Foreign ministries concerning the secret items of understanding, see *GS 10*, pp. 226–35.

107. Arita Memorandum; Arita, *Bakahachi*, pp. 15–16 (Arita, p. 95, dates this conference on March 10); Takagi, p. 77. For the draft, see Harada, *Bekkan*, pp. 376–77, where the compromise plan is dated March 24; and *GS 10*, pp. 235–36.

108. Arita Memorandum.

109. Harada, Vol. 7, pp. 325–26.

110. A copy of this is in JFM, File on Strengthening the Anti-Comintern Pact; see also Harada, Vol. 7, p. 326.

111. From documents in Japan, National Defense Agency, Military History Office (hereafter JDA Archives).

112. JFM, File on Strengthening the Anti-Comintern Pact.

113. See, for example, Yale Candee Maxon, *Control of Japanese Foreign Policy*, pp. 136–39.

114. Ōshima to Arita, May 22, 1939, as cited in note 90.

115. Arita Memorandum.

116. JAM, Military Affairs Section, "Sangoku kyōtei no keii" (Particulars Concerning the Tripartite Pact), May 27, 1939, in *GS 10*, p. 157 (hereafter cited as JAM, Particulars 2).

117. *Ibid.*; Arita Memorandum. Shiratori's telegram is in *GS 10*, p. 242; and Harada, *Bekkan*, pp. 379–80.

118. Ōshima to Arita, telegram 344, April 11, 1939, *GS 10*, pp. 252–53; see also JAM, Particulars 2, p. 157.

119. Arita Memorandum; see also Ōshima to Arita, telegram 315, April 4, 1939, *GS 10*, p. 244.

120. Ōshima to Arita, telegram 324, April 11, 1939, *GS 10*, pp. 246–47; JAM, Particulars 2, p. 158; Ōshima Hiroshi Affidavit, IMTFE Records, Exhibit 3510.

121. See Ōshima defense annotations on the Arita Memorandum.

122. Harada, Vol. 7, pp. 335–36.

123. Arita, *Hito no me no chiri o miru*, pp. 327–28.

124. Arita to Ōshima, telegram 214, April 8, 1939, *GS 10*, pp. 250–51; Arita Memorandum; JAM, Particulars 2, p. 158.

125. Ōshima Affidavit, Exhibit 3510; Usami Affidavit.

126. Arita Memorandum.

127. *Ibid.*

128. *Ibid.;* Arita, *Bakahachi*, pp. 99–100.

129. *GS 10*, pp. 259–60.

130. *Ibid.*, pp. 260–62; Arita Memorandum; Arita, *Hito no me no chiri o miru*, p. 21; Harada, Vol. 7, pp. 344–45.

131. Arita Memorandum.

132. *GS 10*, p. 262.

133. JFM, File on Strengthening the Anti-Comintern Pact, says May 4; Arita Memorandum gives May 5. On the communiqué, see Iklé, pp. 105–6. According to Harada (Vol. 7, p. 347), Prime Minister Hiranuma argued for a statement declaring explicitly that Japan did not want to remain neutral; Arita and Yonai, however, considered this too dangerous, preferring the expression "benevolent neutrality."

134. Hiranuma's message is in IMTFE Records, Exhibit 503; and in *GS 10*, pp. 268–69; the draft submitted to the Five Ministers Conference on April 28 with French translation is in *ibid.*, pp. 262–64.

135. Iklé, p. 102.

136. Arita, *Hito no me no chiri o miru*, p. 22; Yosano, "Zoruge jiken," p. 37; interview with Yosano Shigeru, January 27, 1962. For a discussion of this episode, see Iklé, pp. 101–6.

137. JAM, Particulars 2, p. 159, says it was May 5; according to other sources it was the 6th.

138. Ōshima to Arita, telegram 411, May 6, 1939, *GS 10*, p. 269; JAM, Particulars 2, p. 159; Harada, Vol. 7, p. 353.

139. Ōshima to Arita, telegrams 369–70, April 21, 1939, *GS 10*, pp. 257–58.

140. Report from the Italian ambassador to Germany, April 25, 1939, *Documents on International Affairs*, Vol. 1, p. 156. Prior to this Ribbentrop and Ōshima were reported to have asked Italy to tell Shiratori that: (1) Italy agreed in principle with the Japanese plan; (2) the pact was to be valid for a period of ten years; and (3) the treaty was merely defensive so far as Britain and France were concerned and was not directed against any particular country. Ribbentrop also wanted to convey to Japan Italy's view that any nonsignatory nation that attacked one of the signatories would be regarded as the enemy of all the signatory powers. *Ibid.*, p. 155.

141. Quoted in telegram from the Italian ambassador in Berlin, cited in note 140. This may be the cable Arita described as "an instruction I sent out in full knowledge that it would be a futile effort." Arita, *Hito no me no chiri o miru*, p. 21.

142. *Ibid.*; Ōshima and Shiratori to Arita, telegram 375, April 24, 1939, *GS 10*, p. 260. Ōshima is said to have frequently expressed a desire to resign, but he has denied this.

143. Ōshima Interrogation, Exhibit 497; Ōshima Affidavit, Exhibit 3508; Usami Affidavit; see also the telegram from the German Foreign Office to Ambassador Ott, May 15, 1939, IMTFE Records, Exhibit 2619.

144. JAM, Particulars 2, p. 159; minutes of these conferences are in *GS 10*, pp. 270–76.

145. For the navy's objection, see the Navy Ministry paper in *ibid.*, pp. 163–65.

146. Ōshima defense annotations on the Arita Memorandum as well as navy sources indicate that Germany feared Japan might leak the proposed secret clauses to Britain if they were stated in written form.

147. IMTFE Records, Exhibit 2619. The translation here is based upon the official translation contained in the IMTFE transcript, pp. 22548–50.

148. Ōshima interview, November 14, 1959; Presseisen, p. 207.

149. JAM, Particulars 2, p. 159; see also *ibid.*, p. 164.

150. Arita Memorandum; see minutes cited in note 144.

151. *GS 10*, pp. 286–90.

152. *Ibid.*, p. 300.

153. Arita Memorandum.

154. According to JAM, Particulars 2 (p. 159), the Five Ministers Conference was held on the 20th and decided that delivery of the instructions would be left to the prime minister and the foreign minister. The

Arita Memorandum says the instructions were issued in keeping with a Five Ministers Conference decision of the 20th, but according to *GS 10*, pp. 300–2, the decision was reached at a meeting on the 19th.

155. Arita to Ōshima, telegram 297, May 20, 1939, *ibid.*, p. 301.

156. JFM, "Gogatsu jūkunichi no Goshōkaigi kettei ni kansuru kaigungawa no shuchō" (Opinion of the Navy Concerning the Five Ministers Conference Decision of May 19), in *GS 10*, pp. 301–2.

157. Ōshima to Arita, May 22, 1939, in JFM, *Nihon gaikō nempyō*, Vol, 2, pp. 408–12; also in *GS 10*, pp. 311–15. See JAM, Particulars 2, p. 160, for a report that Ōshima and Shiratori, in protest against the instructions of May 20, demanded that they be recalled.

158. JAM, Particulars 2, p. 159.

159. See JFM, "Gogatsu jūkunichi no Gōshokaigi kettei," p. 302. According to documents in the JDA Archives, the Five Ministers Conference on May 20 accepted the clauses agreed upon by the army and the navy but left delivery of the instructions to the foreign minister. When Army Minister Itagaki saw the draft the next day, however, he discovered that it still contained the clause providing that Japan's entry into hostilities would be independently determined by the situation at the time, and he therefore demanded that it be revised. At Arita's suggestion he submitted an amended draft to Navy Minister Yonai, who refused to approve it until Hiranuma threatened to resign, whereupon Yonai agreed to reconsider his stand. The instructions were delivered to Ōshima without Itagaki's knowledge and made it impossible for the ambassadors to continue the negotiations, whereupon they submitted their resignations. JAM, Particulars 2, and JFM, "Gogatsu jūkunichi no Gōshokaigi kettei," likewise disagree concerning Itagaki's objection.

160. Shiratori to Arita, telegram 139, May 20, 1939, *GS 10*, pp. 302–4.

161. Arita's original draft and Hiranuma's modifications are in *ibid.*, pp. 309–10.

162. The army expressed satisfaction with Hiranuma's version. See JAM, Particulars 2, p. 160.

163. *GS 10*, pp. 316–17.

164. JDA Archives.

165. The text of the instructions to Ōshima and Shiratori of May 5, 1939, is in *GS 10*, pp. 320–21. Summaries are in Ogata, pp. 54–55; Yabe, Vol. 2, pp. 21–22; Takagi, p. 81.

166. Arita Memorandum; also *GS 10*, pp. 321–22.

167. Shiratori to Arita, telegram 158, June 11, 1939, *ibid.*, p. 322; see also Ogata, p. 56.

168. Ōshima to Arita, telegram 548, June 16, 1939, *GS 10*, p. 326; see also telegram 547, June 16, 1939, *ibid.*, pp. 324, 326.

169. Ōshima to Arita, telegram 554, June 17, 1939, *ibid.*, pp. 326–27.

170. Telegram 551, June 16, 1939, *ibid.*, p. 326; Iklé, pp. 120ff.

171. Interview with Sanematsu Yuzuru, July 12, 1961.

172. Harada, Vol. 8, p. 21.

173. *Ibid.*, pp. 15–16.

174. Shiratori to Arita, telegram 192, July 11, 1939, and telegrams 199 and 200, July 13, 1939, *GS 10*, pp. 328–31.

175. Ōshima to Arita, telegram 658, July 18, 1939, in JFM Archives, "Sangokudōmei kōshō shiryō" (Materials Relating to the Negotiation of the Tripartite Pact) (hereafter cited as JFM, Tripartite Pact Documents).

176. Kido Kōichi, *Kido Kōichi nikki* (Diary of Kido Kōichi), Vol. 2, p. 737.

177. Takagi, p. 81.

178. Ōshima to Arita, telegram 724, July 25, 1939, in JFM, Tripartite Pact Documents.

179. Ōshima to Arita, telegram 763, July 29, 1939, *ibid.*

180. Shiratori to Arita, telegram 224, August 4, 1939, *ibid.*

181. *GS 10*, p. 336; Ogata, pp. 57–58.

182. JAM, "Nichi-Doku-I sangoku kyōtci mondai no kcii" (Particulars Concerning the Question of a Tripartite Pact), August 30, 1939, in *GS 10*, p. 360.

183. The Arita Memorandum dates the letter August 11. A telegram from Ambassador Ott of the 11th reports it as the 10th (in JFM, Tripartite Pact Documents).

184. Memorandum by Arita, in JFM, Anti-Comintern Pact Documents.

185. JDA Archives. According to Sanematsu Yuzuru (interview, July 12, 1961), after each Five Ministers Conference Yonai would consult with the vice navy minister, the vice chief of the Navy General Staff, and the chief of the Navy Ministry's Naval Affairs Bureau. Problems relating to the strengthening of the Anti-Comintern Pact had been a constant topic of discussion since November 1938 in conferences among top army officials at the official residence of the army minister. See Horiba Kazuo, *Shina jihen sensō shidō shi* (A History of Military Strategy during the China War), Vol. 1, pp. 282–83.

TWO

The Japanese-Soviet Confrontation,
1935–1939

Introduction

1. Summation by Prosecutor Vasiliev, in International Military Tribunal for the Far East (hereafter IMTFE), Transcript of Proceedings, H/2,
February 17, 1948.

2. Judgment of the Honorable Mr. Justice Pal, Member from India, in
IMTFE, Indictment, Part 4, "Overall Conspiracy, Aggression against
the Soviet Union," Appendix A, Section 8.

3. Akamatsu Yūsuke, *Shōwa jūsan-nen no kokusai jōsei* (The International Scene, 1938), pp. 332–40.

4. U.S., Department of State, *Foreign Relations of the United States:
Diplomatic Papers, 1937,* Vol. 3, pp. 756, 760.

5. "Konoye Memoirs," IMTFE, No. 3, pp. 73–76.

6. John M. Maki, *Japanese Militarism,* pp. 170–72.

Essay

1. Hayashi Saburō, *Taiheiyō sensō rikusen gaishi* (History of
Ground Campaigns in the Pacific War), pp. 2–3; translated into English
and annotated by Alvin D. Coox as *Kōgun: The Japanese Army in the
Pacific War,* pp. 2–3.

2. Hattori, Takushirō, "Manshū ni taisuru yōhei-teki kansatsu" (A
Study of Tactics in Manchuria), in Japan, National Defense Agency,
Military History Office (hereafter JDA Archives).

3. *Ibid.*

4. JDA Archives.

5. Hattori, "Manshū ni taisuru yōhei-teki kansatsu."

6. Japan, Foreign Ministry (hereafter JFM), Archives.

7. JFM, *Nisso kōshō shi* (A History of Japanese-Soviet Relations),
pp. 331–44.

8. JDA Archives.

9. *Ibid.*

10. Akamatsu Yūsuke, *Shōwa jūichi-nen no kokusai jōsei* (The International Scene, 1936), p. 16.

11. JDA Archives.

12. *Ibid.*

13. Akamatsu, *Shōwa jūichi-nen,* p. 21.

14. JDA Archives.

15. Confirmed in an estimate drafted on June 30, 1937, in JDA Archives.

16. Japan, Navy General Staff (hereafter NGS), Second Division, "Kanchāzu jiken keika gaiyō" (Summary of the Kanch'atzu Incident), copy in JDA Archives.

17. Shigemitsu to Hirota, telegram 528, June 29, 1937, in JFM Archives.

18. Shigemitsu to Hirota, telegram 530, June 29, 1937, in JFM Archives.

19. NGS Archives.

20. Kwantung Army, Staff Section, to Foreign Ministry, telegram 783, July 2, 1937, in NGS Archives.

21. Tsuji Masanobu, *Nomonhan,* p. 36.

22. Affidavit of General Nakamura Kōtarō, commander of the Korea Army from July 1938 to July 1941, in Kyokutō Kokusai Gunji Saiban Kōhan Kiroku (Records of the International Military Tribunal for the Far East), Defense Document 1223, in Japan, Justice Ministry, War Crimes Materials Office (hereafter cited as IMTFE Records).

23. Inada Masazumi, "Soren kyokutō gun to no taiketsu" (Confrontation with the Soviet Far Eastern Army), *Bessatsu Chisei 5: himerareta Shōwa shi,* December 1956, pp. 276–77. From March 1938 to October 1939 Inada held the post of chief of the Operations Section of the Army General Staff, with the rank of colonel.

24. The southern part of the Hunch'un district lay within Manchukuo territory, but for reasons of convenience the Korea Army rather than the Kwantung Army was responsible for the defense of the area.

25. Inada (p. 278) gives July 6 as the date the Soviet soldiers first appeared atop Changkufeng. JDA materials mention July 9, but the contemporary official report says July 11.

26. Korea Army Commander to Vice Chief of Army General Staff, telegram 913, July 13, 1938, in *Gendai shi shiryō 10: Nitchū sensō 3* (Source Materials on Contemporary History, 10: Sino-Japanese War, 3), p. 4 (hereafter cited as *GS 10*).

27. JDA Archives.

28. Translator's note: Tsuji is often mentioned as visiting the Changkufeng locale at this time, but Ōgoshi once told me he did not recall that Tsuji actually made it to the front in July 1938.

29. Japan, Army General Staff, "Chōkohō jiken shori yōkō" (Principles for Handling the Changkufeng Incident), July 14, 1938, in JDA Archives; and Imperial Headquarters, Army Order 154, July 16, 1938, *ibid.*, published in *GS 10*, p. 4.

30. Inada, "Soren kyokutō gun," p. 280.

31. The navy, still anxious about contingencies, tightened its guard in the Korea Strait and secretly studied a plan for staging a surprise attack against the naval base at Vladivostok, employing one air group built around two aircraft carriers. JDA Archives.

32. JDA Archives.

33. JDA Archives, published in *GS 10*, p. 10; also Inada, "Soren kyokutō gun," pp. 280–81.

34. JDA Archives, published in *GS 10*, p. 10.

35. Harada Kumao, *Saionji kō to seikyoku* (Prince Saionji and the Political Situation), Vol. 7, p. 50.

36. Translator's note: Other highly authoritative information indicates that old Prince Kan'in also was received separately by the emperor and that he blundered in his presentation to the Throne.

37. Harada, Vol. 7, pp. 51–52.

38. JDA Archives.

39. Inada, "Soren kyokutō gun," pp. 281–82.

40. Interview with Arao Okikatsu, December 18, 1955.

41. JDA Archives, published in *GS 10*, p. 12.

42. JDA Archives; also *GS 10*, p. 17.

43. JDA Archives. This is what Division Commander Suetaka deliberately labeled the clash, but the emperor used the term "Changkufeng Incident," it is said, so Suetaka's appellation was abandoned.

44. Division Commander Suetaka to Korea Army Commander, telegram sent 8:37 P.M., July 29, 1938, *GS 10*, pp. 18–19.

45. Korea Army Commander to Chief of Army General Staff, telegram sent 1:25 A.M., July 30, 1938, and telegram 77 to Division Commander, sent 1:20 A.M., July 30, 1938, in JDA Archives, published in *GS 10*, pp. 19–20.

46. Vice Chief of Army General Staff to Korea Army Commander,

Army General Staff telegram 284, sent 4:50 P.M., July 30, 1938, in JDA Archives, published in GS 10, p. 20.

47. JDA Archives.

48. Recollections of Saitō Toshio, in "Oetsu kyoki" (Sobbing and Weeping), Dōkiseikai shi, March 1958.

49. JDA Archives.

50. Vice Army Minister to Korea Army Chief of Staff, secret telegram 134, August 1, 1938, in JDA Archives, published in GS 10, pp. 21–22.

51. Inada, "Soren kyokutō gun," p. 283.

52. Ibid.

53. See note 50.

54. "Khasan," in Bol'shaia sovetskaia entsiklopediia (The Great Soviet Encyclopedia), Vol. 46, p. 90.

55. JDA Archives, published in GS 10, p. 23.

56. JDA Archives, published in GS 10, p. 37.

57. Inada, "Soren kyokutō gun," p. 284.

58. JDA Archives.

59. Shigemitsu Mamoru, Gaikō kaisōroku (Diplomatic Reminiscences), p. 216. See also the English version, Japan and Her Destiny: My Struggle for Peace, translated by Oswald White and edited by F. S. G. Piggott, pp. 158–59.

60. JDA Archives.

61. Imperial Order 172 was issued on August 11. JDA Archives.

62. Shigemitsu, Gaikō kaisōroku, pp. 219–20; Japan and Her Destiny, pp. 159–60.

63. Inada, "Soren kyokutō gun," p. 285.

64. JDA Archives.

65. The Soviets seem from the outset to have had confidence in the outcome of the fighting. They announced the progress of events from an early period and publicized them widely. At the time of the Nomonhan Incident, in contrast, strict press control was instituted. Interview with Doi Akio, military attaché in the Soviet Union from 1938 to 1940, on December 16, 1961.

66. Inada, "Soren kyokutō gun," p. 285.

67. Interview with Inada Masazumi, March 2, 1962.

68. Ugaki Kazushige, Ugaki Kazushige nikki (Diary of Ugaki Kazushige), Vol. 2, pp. 1257–58 (entry for August 13, 1938).

69. Shigemitsu, *Gaikō kaisōroku*, p. 220; Inada, "Soren kyokutō gun," p. 284.

70. JDA Archives.

71. The author has followed the account given in Japan, Imperial Headquarters, Army Division, "Nomonhan jiken keika no gaiyō," (Summary of the Nomonhan Incident), November 6, 1939, in JDA Archives. At least two other versions exist. Tsuji Masanobu, in *Nomonhan*, asserts that "approximately 700 Outer Mongolian soldiers pushed across the Halha river west of Nomonhan on the morning of the 12th." According to IMTFE materials, the Soviet side contended that 300 Japanese-Manchukuo army troops crossed the frontier east of the Halha at about 6 o'clock on May 11.

72. JDA Archives.

73. Tsuji, p. 67.

74. Kwantung Army Operations Order 1488, in JDA Archives, published in *GS 10*, pp. 106–7.

75. Translator's note: Yamagata was commander of the 64th Infantry Regiment belonging to the 23rd Division.

76. Tsuji, pp. 78ff.

77. *Ibid.*, p. 98.

78. *Ibid.*, p. 97.

79. Inada Masazumi, "Kaisōroku" (Reminiscences), October 1939, in JDA Archives.

80. "Nakajima Tetsuzō chūjō kaisōroku" (Reminiscences of Lieutenant-General Nakajima Tetsuzō), 1939, in JDA Archives.

81. Tsuji, p. 97.

82. *Ibid.*, p. 98.

83. Translator's note: The 2nd Air Group was commanded by Lieutenant-General Giga Tetsuji.

84. Translator's note: This was the 26th Infantry Regiment of Colonel Sumi Shin'ichirō.

85. Kwantung Army Headquarters, First Section, "Nomonhan jiken: kimitsu sakusen nisshi" (Confidential Diary of Kwantung Army Operations during the Nomonhan Incident), Vol. 1, in *GS 10*, pp. 71–149. Soviet data indicate that the Soviet-Mongolian strength consisted of 12,541 men, 139 heavy machine guns, 86 light guns, 23 antitank guns, 186 tanks, and 266 armored cars. G. N. Sevost'yanov, "Voennoe i diplomaticheskoe porazhenie Yaponii v period sobytii u reki Khalkhin-gol" (Japan's Military and Diplomatic Defeat at the Time of the Khalkhin-gol Incident), *Voprosy istorii*, No. 8 (August 1957), p. 66.

86. Inada, "Soren kyokutō gun," p. 289.

87. Tsuji, p. 112.

88. Vice Chief of Army General Staff to Kwantung Army Chief of Staff, telegram of June 24, 1939, in JDA Archives.

89. Tsuji, p. 112.

90. *Ibid.*, p. 119.

91. Inada, "Soren kyokutō gun," p. 290.

92. JDA Archives.

93. Hata Shunroku, "Nikki, Shōwa yo-nen jūgatsu shichinichi kara Shōwa nijū-nen sangatsu nijūhachinichi" (Diary, October 7, 1929–March 28, 1945), in JDA Archives.

94. Tsuji, p. 119.

95. Kwantung Army Chief of Staff to Vice Chief of Army General Staff, telegram of June 27, 1939, in JDA Archives.

96. Tsuji, pp. 133ff.

97. Hattori, "Manshū ni taisuru yōhei-teki kansatsu."

98. JDA Archives.

99. Tsuji, p. 156.

100. Vice Chief of Army General Staff to Kwantung Army Chief of Staff, telegram of July 16, 1939, in JDA Archives.

101. Tsuji, p. 168.

102. Inada, "Soren kyokutō gun," p. 293.

103. "Nomonhan jiken kankei tsuzuri" (Nomonhan Incident Files), in JDA Archives.

104. Tsuji, p. 172.

105. *Ibid.*, p. 206. According to Sevost'yanov (p. 78), the Soviet forces included: the 82nd, 36th, and 57th Divisions; the 6th and 11th Tank Brigades; the 7th and 8th Motorized Brigades; the 601st Independent Infantry Regiment; and the 6th and 8th Mongolian Cavalry Divisions.

106. Translator's note: This was the infantry brigade commanded by Major-General Morita Norimasa, not to be confused with the 71st Infantry Regiment (23rd Division) commanded for a time by Colonel Morita Tōru.

107. Yamanaka Minetarō, *Tetsu to niku* (Iron and Flesh).

108. Inada, "Soren kyokutō gun," p. 295. This is confirmed by the local Soviet commander, Major-General Bykov, who testified at the Tokyo trials that "it was quite possible for us to have pushed to Hailaerh without incurring resistance after the defeat of the Japanese field

forces, but we conducted no pursuit beyond the frontier." Shinsō Henshū Kyoku, ed., *Nihon no tai-So imbō* (Japanese Plots against the USSR), p. 148.

109. *GS 10*, pp. 133–34.

110. Tsuji, p. 215.

111. *Ibid.*, p. 217.

112. Inada, "Soren kyokutō gun," p. 296.

113. *GS 10*, p. 141.

114. Tsuji, p. 222.

115. JDA Archives.

116. *GS 10*, p. 142.

117. Tsuji, p. 225.

118. Chief of Army General Staff to Ueda, telegram 330, September 6, 1939, *GS 10*, p. 146.

119. The bitterness of personal relations can be seen in Inada's insistence in the September 6 message: "It is imperative that you report the measures you have taken with respect to the execution of the above-mentioned." (*Ibid.*) This made Tsuji furious: "Is this the way of a man who wears the same uniform?"

120. JFM, *Nisso kōshō shi*, p. 519.

121. Harada, Vol. 8, p. 24.

122. JFM, *Nisso kōshō shi*, pp. 519–20; see also Vice Chief of Army General Staff to Kwantung Army Chief of Staff, telegram 19, July 28, 1939, *GS 10*, p. 123.

123. Kwantung Army Chief of Staff to Vice Chief of Army General Staff, telegram 468, July 30, 1939, *GS 10*, pp. 123–24.

124. Nishi Haruhiko, "Kanzen gunshuku e no michi" (The Path to Total Disarmament), *Ekonomisuto*, December 26, 1961, pp. 120–22. Nishi served as counselor of embassy in Moscow from December 1936 to June 1939, when he was reassigned to Tokyo as chief of the Foreign Ministry's Europe-America Bureau, where he supervised matters relating to the settlement of the incident. See his autobiography, *Kaisō no Nihon Gaikō* (Diplomatic Memoirs), pp. 91–96.

125. JFM, *Nisso kōshō shi*, p. 520.

126. *Ibid.*, pp. 521–22.

127. *Ibid.*, p. 522.

128. *Ibid.*

129. *Ibid.*

130. *Ibid.,* p. 536.

131. JDA Archives.

132. For example, 23rd Division Cavalry Regiment Commander Ioki Eiichi committed suicide prior to being court-martialed for an unauthorized retreat. Colonel Sakai Mikio, commander of the 72nd Regiment, also committed suicide upon receiving orders for his replacement. Heavy Artillery Regiment Commander Colonel Takatsukasa Shinki was retired for having abandoned guns. Not a few others were also charged with lack of "fighting spirit." See Tsuji.

133. Hayashi, *Taiheiyō sensō rikusen gaishi,* p. 26; *Kōgun,* p. 17.

134. David J. Dallin, *Soviet Russia and the Far East,* p. 43.

135. Tōgō does not say when, but this may have been in September. Tōgō Shigenori, *Jidai no ichi-men* (One View of an Era), p. 129.

136. Interview with Hattori Toyohiko, former Japanese naval attaché in Germany, on May 8, 1961.

137. Harada, Vol. 8, p. 79.

THREE

The Tripartite Pact, 1939–1940

Introduction

1. *Judgment of the International Military Tribunal for the Far East,* November 1948, p. 518.

2. Hattori Takushirō, *Dai Tōa sensō zenshi* (A History of the Greater East Asia War), Vol. 1, pp. 48–71.

3. Robert J. C. Butow, *Tojo and the Coming of the War,* pp. 142–66.

4. For a description of this system, see Tsuji Kioaki, *Nihon kanryosei no kenkyū,* pp. 155–72.

5. Johanna Margarete Menzel Meskill, *Hitler and Japan: The Hollow Alliance.*

6. Theo Sommer, *Deutschland und Japan zwischen den Mächten,* pp. 436–46.

Essay

1. Ōshima to Arita, telegram 824, August 22, 1939, in Japan, Foreign Ministry (hereafter JFM), Archives, "Sangoku dōmei kōshō shiryō" (Materials Relating to the Negotiation of the Tripartite Pact) (hereafter cited as JFM, Tripartite Pact Documents).

2. Ernst von Weizsaecker, *Memoirs*, p. 201.

3. Ōshima to Arita, telegram 832, August 23, 1939, JFM, Tripartite Pact Documents.

4. Arita to Ōshima, telegram of August 25, 1939, *ibid.*

5. Interview with Iwakuro Hideo, at this time chief of the Military Section of the Army Ministry, February 4, 1961.

6. Hata Shunroku, "Nikki, Shōwa yo-nen jūgatsu shichinichi kara Shōwa nijū-nen sangatsu nijūhachinichi" (Diary, October 7, 1939–March 28, 1945), in Japan, National Defense Agency, Military History Office (hereafter JDA Archives). Hata was appointed army minister in the new cabinet.

7. Harada Kumao, *Saionji kō to seikyoku* (Prince Saionji and the Political Situation), Vol. 8, p. 57; Koyama Kango, *Koyama Kango nikki* (Diary of Koyama Kango), pp. 223, 230. Koyama, a Diet member, formerly president of the Jiji Press and at this time director of the Meiji Life Insurance Company, was a leading pro-Anglo-American businessman closely related to Prince Saionji, whom he had served as secretary at the Versailles Peace Conference.

8. Kido Kōichi, *Kido Kōichi nikki* (Diary of Kido Kōichi), Vol. 2, p. 743 (entry of August 28, 1939) (hereafter cited as *Kido Diary*); and Kiba Kōsuke, ed., *Nomura Kichisaburō*, pp. 388–90.

9. *Asahi shimbun*, September 10, 1939.

10. In the Konoe Papers.

11. Ōshima to Abe, telegram 945, September 7, 1939, in JFM, Tripartite Pact Documents. The proceedings of the conversations were also telegraphed to Ambassador Ott on September 9. See also Ribbentrop to Ott, telegram 335, September 9, 1939, in U.S., Department of State, *Documents on German Foreign Policy, 1918–1945*, Series D (1937–45), Vol. 8, pp. 36–38 (hereafter cited as *DGFP*); and Kyokutō Kokusai Gunji Saiban Kōhan Kiroku (Records of the International Military Tribunal for the Far East), Exhibit 507, in Japan, Justice Ministry (hereafter JJM), War Crimes Materials Office (hereafter cited as IMTFE Records).

12. *DGFP*, Vol. 8, pp. 131–33; and IMTFE Records, Exhibit 509.

13. Ribbentrop to Ott, telegram of September 9, 1939, IMTFE Records, Exhibit 507.

14. The *Kokumin shimbun* seems to have had particularly close connections with the Axis faction. See Ernst L. Presseisen, *Germany and Japan*, p. 231.

15. *Bungei shunjū*, special edition, September 1939, pp. 4–9.

16. Text in JFM, *Nihon gaikō nempyō narabi ni shuyō bunsho* (Chronology and Major Documents of Japanese Foreign Relations), Vol. 2, pp. 421–24.

17. Ott to German Foreign Office, telegram of September 16, 1939, *DGFP*, Vol. 8, p. 74.

18. Ott to German Foreign Office, telegram of September 8, 1939, *ibid.*, pp. 26–27.

19. *Ibid.*, pp. 490–93; Presseisen, p. 233.

20. Ott to German Foreign Office, telegrams of September 8 and 20, 1939, *DGFP*, Vol. 8, pp. 28–29, 75–76.

21. Ott to German Foreign Office, telegrams of October 5 and 7, 1939, *ibid.*, pp. 216–17, 237–38.

22. Herbert Feis, *The Road to Pearl Harbor*, p. 44.

23. *Ibid.*; and the official Japanese memorandum of the fourth talk between Grew and Nomura on a new commercial treaty, December 22, 1939, in JFM, *Nihon gaikō nempyō*, Vol. 2, pp. 18–21.

24. Ott to German Foreign Office, telegram of December 31, 1939, *DGFP*, Vol. 8, pp. 585–86.

25. Ogata Taketora, *Ichi gunjin no shōgai: kaisō no Yonai Mitsumasa* (The Life of an Admiral: Reminiscences of Yonai Mitsumasa), pp. 63–65.

26. *Asahi shimbun*, January 17, 1940.

27. Ott to German Foreign Office, telegram of January 20, 1940, IMTFE Records, Exhibit 3503A; Frank William Iklé, *German-Japanese Relations*, p. 148.

28. *Kurusu Saburō, Hōmatsu no sanjūgo-nen* (Vain Endeavor), p. 35.

29. Joseph C. Grew, *Ten Years in Japan*, p. 313.

30. Feis, p. 50.

31. U.S., Department of State, *Papers Relating to the Foreign Relations of the United States: Japan, 1931–1941*, Vol. 2, pp. 59–60 (hereafter cited as *FR, Japan*).

32. Feis, p. 51.

33. Text in JFM, *Nihon gaikō nempyō*, Vol. 2, pp. 425–26.

34. Ott to German Foreign Office, telegram of March 23, 1940, IMTFE Records, Exhibit 514.

35. Ott to German Foreign Office, telegram of January 17, 1940, *DGFP*, Vol. 8, pp. 676–77; and Presseisen, pp. 234–35.

36. Helfferich to German Foreign Office, telegram of March 1, 1940, *DGFP*, Vol. 8, p. 820; Ott to German Foreign Office, telegram of March 2, 1940, *ibid.*, pp. 835–37.

37. JDA Archives.

38. Text in JFM, *Nihon gaikō nempyō*, Vol. 2, p. 426; Ott to German Foreign Office, telegram of April 15, 1940, *DGFP*, Vol. 9, pp. 175–76.

39. Weizsaecker memorandum, May 17, 1940, *ibid.*, pp. 360–62.

40. Weizsaecker memorandum, June 21, 1940, *ibid.*, pp. 642–43; Ott to German Foreign Office, telegram of June 19, 1940, *ibid.*, pp. 617–18.

41. Text in JFM, *Nihon gaikō nempyō*, Vol. 2, pp. 433–34.

42. *Ōsaka Mainichi shimbun*, June 22, 1940.

43. Tanemura Sakō, *Daihon'ei kimitsu nisshi* (Confidential Record of the Imperial Headquarters), pp. 15–16; and Japan, Army General Staff, "Daihon'ei kimitsu sensō nisshi" (Confidential War Diary of the Imperial Headquarters), JDA Archives (hereafter cited as AGS, *Confidential War Diary*).

44. *Ibid.*; and Tanemura, p. 17.

45. The original army draft, together with explanations by Colonel Usui Shigeki, changes desired by Captain Ōno Takeji of the Navy General Staff War Guidance Section, and the views of Navy General Staff Operations Division Chief Ugaki Matome, expressed at an army-navy conference at Navy General Staff headquarters on the morning of July 4, are preserved in the archives of the Navy General Staff held by the Shiryō Chōsakai (Documentary Research Society) and have been published in Nihon Kokusai Seiji Gakkai Taiheiyō Sensō Gen'in Kenkyūbu (Japan Association in International Relations, Study Group on the Causes of the Pacific War), *Taiheiyō sensō e no michi: Bekkan shiryō hen* (The Road to the Pacific War: Supplementary Volume of Documents), pp. 316–18 (hereafter cited as *TSM: Bekkan*). Article 3 is omitted here.

46. Knoll memorandum, June 20, 1940, *DGFP*, Vol. 9, pp. 634–36; IMTFE Records, Exhibit 522. Individuals such as Ayukawa Gisuke and Kobayashi Ichizō in the business world advocated closer economic cooperation with Germany.

47. Schmitt memorandum, July 9, 1940, *DGFP*, Vol. 10, pp. 162–67; and IMTFE Records, Exhibit 524.

48. *Ibid.*, Exhibit 3830.

49. Ott to German Foreign Office, telegram of July 3, 1940, *ibid.*, Exhibit 531; Harada, Vol. 8, pp. 277–80.

50. Hata, "Nikki," published in *TSM: Bekkan*, p. 315.

51. *Kido Diary*, Vol. 2, p. 801 (entry of July 8, 1940); Harada, Vol. 8, p. 284.

52. For the draft "Proposal for Strengthening Cooperation between Japan, Germany, and Italy," see JFM, *Nihon gaikō nempyō*, Vol. 2, pp. 434–35.

53. See *Gendai shi shiryō 10: Nitchū sensō 3* (Source Materials on Contemporary History, 10: Sino-Japanese War, 3), p. 179 (hereafter cited as *GS 10*); for this first meeting see IMTFE Records, Exhibit 527. Hiranuma Kiichirō recalled that the alliance question in the days of the Hiranuma cabinet had been differently motivated; it was ideological and irrational. Hiranuma Kiichirō, *Kaikoroku* (Memoirs), pp. 246–53.

54. The original draft of the "Proposal for Strengthening Cooperation between Japan, Germany, and Italy" was modified as a result of the conferences among responsible administrative officials. For the modified draft, see IMTFE Records, Exhibit 527; for the proceedings of the conference of July 16, see *ibid.*, Exhibit 528.

55. Matsuoka Yōsuke, *Nichi-Doku bōkyō kyōtei no igi* (The Significance of the Anti-Comintern Pact), pp. 47–48.

56. Interviews with Ōshima Hiroshi, November 14, 1959, and March 10, 1962.

57. *Ibid.*

58. Kurihara Ken, *Tennō: Shōwa shi oboegaki* (The Emperor: A Note on the History of the Shōwa Period), p. 145; interview with Andō Yoshirō, November 14, 1961.

59. Konoe Fumimaro, *Ushinawareshi seiji* (Politics that Failed), p. 30.

60. Asahi Shimbu Hōtei Kishadan, *Tōkyō saiban: Tōjō jimmon roku* (The Tokyo Military Tribunal: Record of the Tōjō Trial), pp. 24–25.

61. Yabe Teiji, ed., *Konoe Fumimaro*, Vol. 2, pp. 120–21.

62. Konoe Papers, published in *TSM: Bekkan*, pp. 319–20.

63. Japan, Navy Ministry, "Sekai jōsei no suii ni tomonau jikyoku shori yōkō tsuzuri" (File on the Main Principles for Coping with the

Changing World Situation), in JDA Archives; see also *TSM: Bekkan,* pp. 325–29.

64. The text of the Liaison Conference decision has been published in *ibid.*, pp. 322–25.

65. See Appendix 5 for full text.

66. Matsuoka's explanation at the Imperial Conference of September 19, 1940. See the Foreign Ministry study, "Nichi-Doku-I sangoku jōyaku" (The Tripartite Pact), pp. 197–98, in JFM Archives (hereafter cited as JFM, Tripartite Pact Study).

67. *Ibid.*

68. JFM, Europe-Asia Bureau, "Matsuoka gaishō to Otto taishi to no kaidan yōryō" (Summary of the Matsuoka-Ott Conversation), August, 2, 1940, presented to the IMTFE as Exhibit 544, in JFM Archives (hereafter cited as JFM, Matsuoka-Ott Conversation).

69. Weizsaecker memorandum, August 1, 1940, *DGFP*, Vol. 10, pp. 391–92; IMTFE Records, Exhibit 542.

70. Weizsaecker memorandum, August 7, 1940, *DGFP*, Vol. 10, pp. 432–33; IMTFE Records, Exhibit 544.

71. JFM, Matsuoka-Ott Conversation.

72. Weizsaecker memoranda, August 1 and 7, 1940.

73. Ott to German Foreign Office, telegram of August 2, 1940, *DGFP*, Vol. 10, pp. 393–95; Iklé, p. 166.

74. Weizsaecker memorandum, August 7, 1940.

75. Wiehl memorandum, June 20, 1940, *DGFP*, Vol. 9, pp. 633–34; anonymous memorandum, July 26, 1940, *ibid.*, Vol. 10, pp. 324–25; H. L. Trefousse, *Germany and American Neutrality*, p. 69.

76. Ott to German Foreign Office, telegram of August 14, 1940, *DGFP*, Vol. 9, pp. 476–77.

77. Saitō Yoshie, "Nichi-Doku-I jōyaku teiketsu yōroku" (Summary Record of the Conclusion of the Tripartite Pact), compiled by Saitō after the conclusion of the pact, in JFM Archives (hereafter cited as Saitō, "Tripartite Pact Record").

78. Heinrich Stahmer Affidavit, IMTFE Records, Exhibit 2744.

79. William L. Shirer, *The Rise and Fall of the Third Reich*, pp. 746–74.

80. JFM, Matsuoka-Ott Conversation.

81. Trefousse, pp. 38–59.

82. *Ibid.*, p. 69; Presseisen, pp. 253–54; William L. Langer and S. Everett Gleason, *The Undeclared War,* p. 24.

83. Stahmer Affidavit.

84. Iklé, p. 168.

85. Saitō, "Tripartite Pact Record."

86. AGS, *Confidential War Diary.*

87. See Appendix 6 for a comparison of the Matsuoka Draft and this army-navy draft.

88. AGS, *Confidential War Diary.*

89. The August 20 entry in the diary kept by Colonel Takashima Tatsuhiko, a member of the staff of the Army War College, records: "Internal situation; army and navy oppose each other on German-Italian question; foreign minister has revealed his true colors." JDA Archives.

90. JJM, War Crimes Materials Office; Takagi Sōkichi, "Nichi-Doku-I gunji dōmei seiritsu no keii" (Particulars of the Conclusion of the Military Alliance between Japan, Germany, and Italy), *Sekai,* No. 59 (November 1950), p. 85. See also the reference materials prepared on August 27 by the Navy Division of Imperial Headquarters, and the related memorandum prepared by the Army and Navy divisions on August 28, in *TSM: Bekkan,* pp. 325–29.

91. Nakamura Garō, "Gyōmu nisshi" (Office Diary), in JDA Archives.

92. Saitō, "Tripartite Pact Record," states that the consultations were held on August 31; according to Matsuoka, "Shitsumu nisshi" (Office Diary), JFM Archives, September 1 is correct.

93. See Appendix 6 for revised provisions in this Foreign Ministry draft.

94. Ohashi Chūichi, *Taiheiyō sensō yuraiki* (Origins of the Pacific War), p. 54; interview with Ohashi Chūichi, September 30, 1961.

95. *FR, Japan,* Vol. 2, pp. 111–12.

96. AGS, *Confidential War Diary.*

97. Identical texts of the authorizing resolution are given in *ibid.* and in JFM, Tripartite Pact Study, pp. 7–8.

98. It has been generally believed that the draft of the authorizing resolution was examined at a Four Ministers Conference on September 4. However, following the resignation of Navy Minister Yoshida and his replacement by Oikawa as explained above, the conference was postponed to September 6. "Konoe shitsumu nisshi" (Konoe Office Diary), in the Konoe Papers.

99. Asahi, *Tōjō jimmon roku*, pp. 30–31.

100. Oikawa Koshirō Affidavit, IMTFE Records, Defense Document 1664.

101. For instance, the navy demanded deletion of the clause "or if it is deemed that, irrespective of whether or not our preparations are complete, the development of the international situation permits of no further delay" (Appendix 3, section b, paragraph 5). Saitō, "Tripartite Pact Record."

102. Nakamura, "Gyōmu nisshi."

103. "Kaidan yōshi" (Summary of Conversations), in JFM, Tripartite Pact Study, pp. 31, 43–49 (hereafter cited as JFM, Matsuoka-Stahmer Conversations); and Matsuoka, "Shitsumu nisshi"; the summary has been published in *TSM: Bekkan*, pp. 334–36.

104. JFM, Matsuoka-Stahmer Conversations, pp. 33–35.

105. Saitō, "Tripartite Pact Record."

106. Nakamura, "Gyōmu nisshi."

107. JFM, Matsuoka-Stahmer Conversations, pp. 37–39.

108. Saitō, "Tripartite Pact Record."

109. Memorandum in Konoe Papers, published in *TSM: Bekkan*, pp. 332–33.

110. Statement by Toyoda Teijirō, December 1957, in JDA Archives.

111. *Ibid.;* Takagi, p. 86.

112. Toyoda statement.

113. "Konoe shitsumu nisshi."

114. Konoe Papers, published in *TSM: Bekkan*, p. 333.

115. *Kido Diary*, Vol. 2, p. 822 (entry of September 14, 1940).

116. Yabe, Vol. 2, p. 151.

117. Konoe Fumimaro, *Heiwa e no doryoku* (My Struggle for Peace), p. 31.

118. Interview with Miyo Kazunari, former member of the Operations Section of the Navy General Staff, December 10, 1960.

119. Oikawa Affidavit.

120. JFM, Tripartite Pact Study, pp. 51–53.

121. Saitō, "Tripartite Pact Record."

122. Konoe Papers, published in *TSM: Bekkan*, p. 333; Yabe, p. 156.

123. Konoe Papers, published in *TSM: Bekkan*, p. 333; Harada, Vol. 8, p. 347.

124. Saitō, "Tripartite Pact Record."

125. *Ibid.;* and JFM, Tripartite Pact Study, pp. 1–2. For the supplementary protocol and the notes exchanged, see Saitō, "Tripartite Pact Record"; and *DGFP,* Vol. 11, p. 123. (Translator's note: The Japanese and German versions have been compared; since the latter has been found faithful, it is followed here for convenience of reference, except that garbled material has been corrected by the Japanese version.)

126. Stahmer and Ott to Ribbentrop, telegram of September 20, 1940, *ibid.,* p. 133.

127. Stahmer and Ott to Ribbentrop, telegrams of September 19 and 20, 1940, *ibid.,* pp. 123, 132.

128. Saitō, "Tripartite Pact Record."

129. JFM, Tripartite Pact Study, pp. 195–205.

130. Sawada Shigeru, "Gozen kaigi gijiroku" (Proceedings of Imperial Conferences), in JDA Archives, published in *TSM: Bekkan,* pp. 337–42.

131. Stahmer and Ott to Ribbentrop, telegram of September 20, 1940.

132. Galeazzo Ciano, *The Ciano Diaries, 1939–1943,* edited by Hugh Gibson, p. 293.

133. Elizabeth Wiskemann, *The Rome-Berlin Axis,* p. 227; Iklé, pp. 175–76; Presseisen, p. 262.

134. Saitō, "Tripartite Pact Record."

135. JFM, Tripartite Pact Study, pp. 77–79.

136. Saitō, "Tripartite Pact Record."

137. *Ibid.;* JFM, Tripartite Pact Study, pp. 2, 85–92; Stahmer and Ott to Ribbentrop, telegram of September 21, 1940, *DGFP,* Vol. 11, p. 142. Stahmer and Ott reported in this telegram that elimination of the secret supplementary protocol and the exchange of notes would be possible.

138. JFM, Tripartite Pact Study, pp. 101–3; Saitō, "Tripartite Pact Record."

139. JFM, Tripartite Pact Study, p. 103; Saitō "Tripartite Pact Record."

140. Presseisen, p. 262; Iklé, p. 177.

141. JFM, Tripartite Pact Study, p. 3.

142. *Ibid.,* pp. 3–4; Saitō, "Tripartite Pact Record."

143. "Interrogation of General Eugen Ott," IMTFE, *Interrogation of Japanese Prisoners*, cited in Presseisen, p. 263.

144. Fukai Eigo, *Sūmitsuin jūyō oboegaki* (Notes on Important Sessions of the Privy Council), p. 96.

145. JFM, Tripartite Pact Study, pp. 207–46; Fukai, pp. 69–98.

146. Mainichi Shimbunsha, *Tōkyō saiban hanketsu* (Judgment of the Tokyo Military Tribunal), p. 133.

147. Saitō Yoshie, *Azamukareta rekishi: Matsuoka to sangoku dōmei no rimen* (History Deceived: The Inside Story of Matsuoka and the Tripartite Pact). This book was written to defend Matsuoka's position. Matsuoka's desire for peace is emphasized also in Ōhashi, pp. 69–71.

148. JFM, Tripartite Pact Study, p. 228.

149. Saitō, *Azamukareta rekishi*, p. 5.

Glossary

Abe Genki　　　　　　安部源基
Abe Katsuo　　　　　　阿部勝雄
Abe Nobuyuki　　　　　阿部信行
Aikawa Katsuroku　　　相川勝六
Anami Korechika　　　　阿南惟幾
Andō Yoshirō　　　　　安東義良
Aoki Kazuo　　　　　　青木一男
Aoki Morio　　　　　　青木盛夫
Arai Kentarō　　　　　荒井賢太郎
Araki Sadao　　　　　　荒木貞夫
Arao Okikatsu　　　　　荒尾興功
Arima Ryōkitsu　　　　有馬良橘
Arisue Seizō　　　　　有末精三
Arisue Yadoru　　　　　有末次
Arita Hachirō　　　　　有田八郎
Ayukawa Gisuke (Yoshisuke)
　　　　　　　　　　　鮎川義介
Azuma Yaozō　　　　　東八百蔵
Chang Hsueh-liang　　　張学良
Chang Tso-lin　　　　　張作霖
Ch'eng Hsi-keng　　　　程錫庚
Chiang Kai-shek (Chieh-shih)
　　　　　　　　　　　蔣介石
Chō Isamu　　　　　　長勇
Doi Akio　　　　　　　土居明夫
Furuuchi Hiroo　　　　古内廣雄
Fushimi Hiroyasu (Prince)
　　　　　　　　　　　伏見宮博恭
Giga Tetsuji　　　　　儀峨徹二
Gotō Fumio　　　　　　後藤文夫

Hamaguchi Osachi (Yūkō)
　　　　　　　　　　　浜口雄幸
Hara Yoshimichi　　　　原嘉道
Harada Kumao　　　　　原田熊雄
Hashimoto Gun　　　　橋本群
Hashimoto Kingorō　　　橋本欣五郎
Hasunuma Shigeru　　　蓮沼蕃
Hata Shunroku　　　　　畑俊六
Hattori Takushirō　　　服部卓四郎
Hattori Toyohiko　　　　服部豊彦
Hayashi Senjūrō　　　　林銑十郎
Hiranuma Kiichirō　　　平沼騏一郎
Hirota Kōki　　　　　廣田弘毅
Horinouchi Kensuke　　　堀内謙介
Hoshino Naoki　　　　　星野直樹
Hotta Masaaki　　　　　堀田正昭
Iimura Yuzuru　　　　　飯村穣
Ikeda Seihin　　　　　池田成彬
Imamura Hitoshi　　　　今村均
Imoto Kumao　　　　　井本熊男
Inada Masazumi　　　　稲田正純
Ino Hiroya (Sekiya)　　井野碩哉
Inoue Kōjirō　　　　　井上庚二郎
Ioki Eiichi　　　　　　井置栄一
Ishiguro Tadaatsu　　　石黒忠篤
Ishii Kikujirō　　　　　石井菊次郎
Ishiwara Kanji　　　　石原莞爾
Isogai Rensuke　　　　磯谷廉介
Isomura Takesuke (Takeakira)
　　　　　　　　　　　磯村武亮

Itagaki Seishirō 板垣征四郎
Iwakuro Hideo (Takeo) 岩畔豪雄
Iwasaki Tamio 岩崎民男
Kagami Kenkichi 各務謙吉
Kagesa Sadaaki 影佐禎昭
Kai Fumihiko 甲斐文比古
Kan'in Kotohito (Prince)
　　　　　　　　関院宮載仁
Karakawa Yasuo 唐川安夫
Karasawa Toshiki (Shunki)
　　　　　　　　唐沢俊樹
Kasahara Yukio 笠原幸雄
Katakura Tadashi 片倉衷
Kawada Isao (Retsu) 河田烈
Kawai Misao 河合操
Kaya Okinori 賀屋興宣
Kazami Akira 風見章
Kido Kōichi 木戸幸一
Kikuchi Takeo 菊地武夫
Kishi Nobusuke 岸信介
Kobayashi Ichizō 小林一三
Koiso Kuniaki 小磯国昭
Koizumi Kyōji 小泉恭次
Kojima Hideo 小島秀雄
Komatsu Misao 小林己三雄
Komatsubara Michitarō
　　　　　　　　小松原道太郎
Kondō Nobutake 近藤信竹
Konoe Fumimaro 近衛文麿
Kōtani Etsuo 甲谷悦雄
Koyama Kango 小山完吾
Kuhara Fusanosuke 久原房之助
Kurihara Tadashi (Sho) 栗原正
Kurusu Saburō 来栖三郎
Machijiri Kazumoto (Ryōki)
　　　　　　　　町尻量基
Masuda Kaneshichi 増田甲子七
Matsudaira Tsuneo 松平恒雄

Matsuoka Yōsuke 松岡洋右
Mihara Eijirō 三原英次郎
Minobe Tatsukichi 美濃部達吉
Mitani Takanobu 三谷隆信
Miyagawa Funeo 宮川船夫
Miyo Kazunari 三代一就
Mori Kaku (Tsutomu) 森恪
Morishima Gorō 守島伍郎
Morita Norimasa 森田範正
Morita Tōru 森田徹
Mushakōji Kintomo 武者小路公共
Mutō Akira 武藤章
Nakagawa Tōru 中川融
Nakajima Tetsuzō 中島鉄蔵
Nakamura Keinoshin 中村峯太郎
Nakamura Kōtarō 中村敬之進
Nakamura Yoshiaki 中村美明
Nakano Seigō 中野正剛
Nimiya Takeo 仁宮武夫
Nishi Haruhiko 西春彦
Nishi Hisashi 西久
Nomura Kichisaburō 野村吉三郎
Obata Yūkichi 小幡酉吉
Ogisu Ryūhei (Rippei) 荻洲立兵
Ōgoshi Kenji 大越兼二
Ōhashi Chūichi 大橋忠一
Oikawa Koshirō 及川古志郎
Oka Takasumi 岡敬純
Okabe Nagakage 岡部長景
Okada Keisuke 岡田啓介
Okamura Yasuji 岡村寧次
Ōkido Sanji 大城戸三治
Okumura Kiwao 奥村喜和男
Ōno Takeji 大野竹二
Ōshima Hiroshi 大島浩
Ōta Kōzō 太田耕造
Saionji Kimmochi 西園寺公望
Saitō Hiroshi 斎藤博

Saitō Toshio	斉藤敏雄	Tanaka Giichi	田中義一
Saitō Yoshie	斉藤良衛	Tanaka Ryūkichi	田中隆吉
Sakai Mikio	酒井美喜雄	Tani Masayuki	谷正之
Sakai Tadamasa (Chūsei)		Tanikawa Kazuo	谷川一男
	酒井忠正	Tatsumi Eiichi	辰己栄一
Sanematsu Yuzuru	実松譲	Terada Masao	寺田雅雄
Satō Kōtoku	佐藤幸徳	Terauchi Hisaichi (Juichi)	
Satō Naotake	佐藤尚武		寺内寿一
Sawada Renzō	沢田廉三	Tōgō Shigenori	東郷茂徳
Sawada Shigeru	沢田茂	Tōjō Hideki	東条英機
Senda Tadasue	千田貞季	Tōkō Takezō	東光武三
Sengoku Kōtarō	千石興太郎	Tokutomi Sohō	徳富蘇峰
Shichida Kigen	七田基玄	Tominaga Kyōji	富永恭次
Shigemasa Seishi (Masanori)		Tomita Kenji	富田健治
	重政誠之	Toyoda Teijirō	豊田貞次郎
Shigemitsu Mamoru	重光葵	Tsuji Masanobu	辻政信
Shimamura Noriyasu	島村矩康	Uchida Yasuya (Kōsai)	内田康哉
Shimanuki Takeji	島貫武治	Ueda Kenkichi	植田謙吉
Shiratori Toshio	白鳥敏夫	Ugaki Kazushige (Kazunari)	
Suetaka Kamezō	毛高亀蔵		宇垣一成
Suetsugu Nobumasa	末次信正	Ugaki Matome	宇垣纒
Sugimura Yōtarō	杉村陽太郎	Umezu Yoshijirō	梅津美治郎
Sugiyama Gen (Hajime)	杉山元	Usami Oki'ie	宇佐見興屋
Suma Yakichirō	須磨弥吉郎	Usami Uzuhiko	宇佐美珍彦
Sumi Shin'ichirō	須美新一郎	Ushiba Nobuhiko	牛場信彦
Sumiyama Tokutarō	住山徳太郎	Usui Shigeki	臼井茂樹
Suzuki Teiichi	鈴木貞一	Wada Hiroo	和田博雄
Tada Hayao (Shun)	多田駿	Wakamatsu Tadaichi	若松只一
Takagi Hiroichi (Kōichi)		Wakatsuki Reijirō	若槻礼次郎
	高木廣	Wang Ching-wei	汪精衛
Takahashi Korekiyo	高橋是清	Yamada Tatsuo (Takio)	山田竜雄
Takase Jirō	高瀬侍郎	Yamada Yoshitarō	山田芳太郎
Takashima Tatsuhiko	高嶋辰彦	Yamagata Arimitsu	山県有光
Takatsukasa Shinki	鷹司信熙	Yamagata Aritomo	山県有朋
Takatsuki Tamotsu	高月保	Yamagata Takemitsu	山県武光
Takeuchi Kakichi	竹内可吉	Yamaguchi Iwao (Hisao)	山口巌
Takeuchi Kakuji	竹内賀久治	Yamaji Akira	山路章
Takeuchi Ryūji	武内竜次	Yamamoto Isoroku	山本五十六

Yamawaki Masataka	山脇正隆	Yoshida Zengo	吉田善吾
Yasui Eiji	安井英二	Yoshinaka Kazutarō	芳仲和太郎
Yasuoka Masaomi	安岡正臣	Yoshino Shinji	吉野信次
Yokoi Tadao	横井忠雄	Yoshioka Yayoi	吉岡弥生
Yonai Mitsumasa	米内光政	Yuasa Kurahei	湯浅倉平
Yosano Shigeru	与謝野秀	Yūki Toyotarō	結城豊太郎
Yoshida Shigeru	吉田茂		

Bibliography

I. Archives

Note: Major documents and other archival sources cited in the notes are listed separately in section III below.

Japan, Foreign Ministry Archives. Cited as JFM Archives.

The following collections of documents are noteworthy:

"Bōkyō kyōtei kyōka mondai" 防共協定強化問題 (The Question of Strengthening the Anti-Comintern Pact), a special file contained in JFM, Anti-Comintern Pact Documents below. Cited as JFM, File on Strengthening the Anti-Comintern Pact.

"Nichi-Doku-I bōkyō kyōtei kankei ikken" 日独伊防共協定関係一件 (Documents Relating to the Anti-Comintern Pact). Cited as JFM, Anti-Comintern Pact Documents.

"Nichi-Doku-I dōmei jōyaku kankei ikken" 日独伊同盟条約関係一件 (Documents Relating to the Treaty of Alliance between Japan, Germany, and Italy).

"Nichi-Doku-I sangoku jōyaku kakushu ambun sakusei oyobi kokunai tetsuzuki keika gaiyō" 日独伊三国条約各種案文作成及び国内手続経過概要 (Outline of the Framing of Various Drafts of the Tripartite Pact and the Domestic Procedures), prepared by the Treaties Bureau, October 1940.

"Sangoku dōmei kōshō shiryō" 三国同盟交渉資料 (Materials Relating to the Negotiation of the Tripartite Pact). Cited as JFM, Tripartite Pact Documents.

Japan, Justice Ministry, War Crimes Materials Office.

These archives contain the Kyokutō Kokusai Gunji Saiban Kōhan Kiroku 極東国際軍事裁判公判記録 (Records of the International Military Tribunal for the Far East). Cited as IMTFE Records.

Japan, National Defense Agency, Military History Office. Cited as JDA Archives.

Japan, Navy General Staff Archives, held by the Shiryō Chōsakai 史料調査会 (Documentary Research Society), Tokyo. Cited as NGS Archives.

Papers of Konoe Fumimaro, held in the Yōmei Bunko 陽明文庫, the private library of the Konoe family, Kyoto.

Shidehara Heiwa Bunko 幣原平和文庫 (Shidehara Peace Collection), National Diet Library, Tokyo.

This collection contains "Kyokutō Gunji Saiban ni okeru Hirota hikoku bengo kankei shiryō: kōkyoshō sono ta" 極東軍事裁判における 広田 被告弁護関係資料 (口供書その他) (Materials for the Defense of Hirota Kōki at the International Military Tribunal: Affidavits, etc.).

II. Interviews

Andō Yoshirō 安東義良, former chief of the European Section, Europe-America Bureau, Foreign Ministry. November 14, 1961.

Arao Okikatsu 荒尾興功, member of the Operations Section, Army General Staff, April 1938–September 1940. December 18, 1955.

Doi Akio 土居明夫, military attaché in the Soviet Union, January 1938–March 1940. December 16, 1961.

Hattori Toyohiko 服部豊彦, former naval attaché in Germany. May 8, 1961.

Inada Masazumi 稲田正純, chief of the Operations Section, Army General Staff, March 1938–October 1939. March 2, 1962.

Iwakuro Hideo 岩畔豪雄, former chief of the Military Section, Army Ministry. February 4, 1961.

Miyo Kazunari 三代一就, former member of the Operations Section, Navy General Staff. December 10, 1960.

Ōhashi Chūichi 大橋忠一, former vice foreign minister. September 30, 1961.

Ōshima Hiroshi 大島浩, military attaché in Germany, 1934–October 1938; ambassador to Germany, October 1938–October 1939. November 14, 1959 and March 10, 1962.

Sanematsu Yuzuru 実松譲, former secretary to Navy Minister Yonai, July 12, 1961.

Takase Jirō 高瀬侍郎 , former Foreign Ministry official, December 2, 1961.

Yokoi Tadao 横井忠雄 , former naval attaché in Germany. July 8, 1961.

Yosano Shigeru 与謝野秀 , former official of the Europe-Asia Bureau, Foreign Ministry. January 27, 1962.

III. Published Works and Major Unpublished Documents Cited

Akamatsu Yūsuke 赤松祐之 . *Shōwa jūichi-nen no kokusai jōsei* 昭和十一年の国際情勢 (The International Scene, 1936). Tokyo, Nihon Kokusai Kyōkai, 1938.

———. *Shōwa jūsan-nen no kokusai jōsei* 昭和十三年の国際情勢 (The International Scene, 1938). Tokyo, Nihon Kokusai Kyōkai, 1939.

Arita Hachirō 有田八郎 . *Bakahachi to hito wa yū: gaikōkan no kaisō* 馬鹿八と人はいう外交官の回想 (People Call Me "Hachi the Fool": Memoirs of a Diplomat). Tokyo, Kōwasha, 1959.

———. *Hito no me no chiri o miru: gaikō mondai kaikoroku* 人の目の塵を見る:外交問題回顧録 (Beholding the Mote in Other Men's Eyes: Memoirs of Diplomatic Problems). Tokyo, Kōdansha, 1948.

———. "Iwauru bōkyō kyōtei kyōka mondai ni kansuru zen Arita gaimudaijin shuki" 所謂防共協定強化問題ニ関スル前有田外務大臣手記 (Memorandum by Former Foreign Minister Arita on Strengthening the Anti-Comintern Pact), in JFM, Anti-Comintern Pact Documents. Cited as Arita Memorandum.

Asahi Shimbun Hōtei Kishadan 朝日新聞法廷記者団 . *Tōkyō saiban: Tōjō jimmon roku* 東京裁判東条尋問録 (The Tokyo Military Tribunal: Record of the Tōjō Trial). Tokyo, Nyūsusha, 1949.

Bloch, Kurt. *German Interests and Policies in the Far East.* New York, Institute of Pacific Relations, 1940.

Butow, Robert J. C. *Tojo and the Coming of the War.* Princeton, Princeton University Press, 1961.

Ciano, Galeazzo. *The Ciano Diaries, 1939–1943.* Edited by Hugh Gibson. Garden City, N.Y., Doubleday, 1946.

Dallin, David J. *Soviet Russia and the Far East.* New Haven, Yale University Press, 1948.

Degras, Jane, ed. *Soviet Documents on Foreign Policy*, Vol. 3. London, Oxford University Press, 1953.

Feis, Herbert. *The Road to Pearl Harbor: The Coming of the War between the United States and Japan*. Princeton, Princeton University Press, 1950.

Fukai Eigo 深井英五. *Sūmitsuin jūyō giji oboegaki* 極密院重要議事覧書 (Notes on Important Sessions of the Privy Council). Tokyo, Iwanami Shoten, 1953.

Gendai shi shiryō 9: Nitchū sensō 2 現代史資料 9. 日中戦争 2 (Source Materials on Contemporary History, 9: Sino-Japanese War, 2). Tokyo, Misuzu Shobō, 1964.

Gendai shi shiryō 10: Nitchū sensō 3 現代史資料 10. 日中戦争 3 (Source Materials on Contemporary History, 10: Sino-Japanese War, 3). Tokyo, Misuzu Shobō, 1964. Cited as *GS 10*.

Grew, Joseph C. *Ten Years in Japan*. New York, Simon and Schuster, 1944.

Harada Kumao 原田熊雄. *Saionji kō to seikyoku* 西園寺公と政局 (Prince Saionji and the Political Situation). 8 vols. and supplementary vol. of documents: *Bekkan*. Tokyo, Iwanami Shoten, 1950–52, 1956.

Hata Ikuhiko 秦 郁彦. *Gun fashizumu undō shi* 軍ファシズム運動史 (History of the Military-Fascist Movement). Tokyo, Kawade Shobō Shinsha, 1962.

Hata Shunroku 畑 俊六. "Nikki, Shōwa yo-nen jūgatsu shichinichi kara Shōwa nijū-nen sangatsu nijūhachinichi" 日記 昭和四年三月七日から 昭和二十年三月二十八日 (Diary, October 7, 1929–March 28, 1945), in JDA Archives.

Hattori Takushirō 服部卓四郎. *Dai Tōa sensō zenshi* 大東亜戦争全史 (A History of the Greater East Asia War). 4 vols. Tokyo, Masu Shobō, 1953.

——. "Manshū ni taisuru yōhei-teki kansatsu" 満州に対する用兵的観察 (A Study of Tactics in Manchuria), in JDA Archives.

Hayashi Saburō 林三郎. *Kōgun: The Japanese Army in the Pacific War*. Translated and annotated by Alvin D. Coox. Quantico, Va., Marine Corps Assn., 1959.

——. *Taiheiyō sensō rikusen gaishi* 太平洋戦争陸戦概史 (History of Ground Campaigns in the Pacific War). Tokyo, Iwanami, 1951.

Hayashi Shigeru 林 茂 "Nichi-Doku-I sangoku dōmei seiritsu no keii" 日独伊三国同盟成立の経緯 (Particulars Concerning the Conclusion of the Tripartite Pact), *Shakai kagaku kenkyū*, Vol. 4, No. 2 (April 1948).

Hiranuma Kiichirō 平沼騏一郎 . *Kaikoroku* 回顧録 (Memoirs). Tokyo, Hiranuma Kiichirō Kaikoroku Hensan Iinkai, 1955.

Horiba Kazuo 堀場一雄 . *Shina jihen sensō shidō shi* 支那事変戦争指導史 (A History of Military Strategy during the China War). 2 vols. Tokyo, Jiji Tsūshinsha, 1962.

Ichimata Masao 一又正雄 . "Manshū teikoku no kokusaihō-jō no chii" 満州帝国の国際法上の地位 (Manchukuo's Position under International Law). *Waseda hōgaku*, Vol. 21 (1946).

Iklé, Frank William. *German-Japanese Relations, 1936–1940*. New York, Bookman Associates, 1956.

Inada Masazumi 稲田正純 . "Kaisōroku" 回想録 (Reminiscences), October 1939, in JDA Archives.

——. "Soren kyokutō gun to no taiketsu" ソ連極東軍との対決 (Confrontation with the Soviet Far Eastern Army), *Bessatsu Chisei 5: himerareta Shōwa shi*, December 1956.

International Military Tribunal. *Trial of the Major War Criminals*. Nuremberg, Secretariat of the Tribunal, 1947–49.

Japan, Army General Staff. "Chōkohō jiken shori yōkō" 張鼓峰事件処理要綱 (Principles for Handling the Changkufeng Incident), July 14, 1938, in JDA Archives.

——, War Guidance Office. "Daihon'ei kimitsu sensō nisshi" 大本営機密戦争日誌 (Confidential War Diary of the Imperial Headquarters), 1938–45, in JDA Archives. Cited as AGS, *Confidential War Diary*.

Japan, Army Ministry, Military Affairs Section. "Nichi-Doku-I 'sangoku kyōtei' mondai no keii" 日独伊三国協定問題の経緯 (Particulars Concerning the Question of a "Tripartite Pact"), January 9, 1939, in *Gendai shi shiryō 10*, pp. 153–56. Cited as JAM, *Particulars 1*.

——. "Nichi-Doku-I sangoku kyōtei mondai no keii" 日独伊三国協定問題の経緯 (Particulars Concerning the Question of a Tripartite Pact), August 30, 1939, in *Gendai shi shiryō 10*, pp. 358–61.

——. "Sangoku kyōtei no keii" 三国協定の経緯 (Particulars Concerning the Tripartite Pact), May 27, 1939, in *Gendai shi shiryō 10*, pp. 156–60. Cited as JAM, Particulars 2.

Japan, Foreign Ministry, Europe-Asia Bureau. "Bōkyō sūjiku kyōka mondai keika oboe" 防共枢軸強化問題経過覚 (Memorandum on Strengthening the Anti-Comintern Axis), in *Gendai shi shiryō 10*, pp. 166–71. Cited as JFM, Axis memorandum.

——. "Gogatsu jūkunichi no Goshōkaigi kettei ni kansuru kaigungawa no shuchō" 五月十九日の五相会議決定に関する海軍側の主張 (Opinion of the Navy Concerning the Five Ministers Conference Decision of May 19), in *Gendai shi shiryō 10*, pp. 301–2.

——. "Kaidan yōshi" 会談要旨 (Summary of Conversations), compiled by Matsuoka Yōsuke, in JFM, Tripartite Pact Study, published in *TSM: Bekkan*, pp. 334–36. Cited as JFM, Matsuoka-Stahmer Conversations.

——. "Matsuoka gaishō to Otto taishi to no kaidan yōryō" 松岡外相とオット大使との会談要領 (Summary of the Matsuoka-Ott Conversations), August 2, 1940, presented to the International Military Tribunal for the Far East as Exhibit 544, in JFM Archives. Cited as JFM, Matsuoka-Ott Conversation.

——. "Nichi-Doku-I sangoku jōyaku" 日独伊三国条約 (The Tripartite Pact), in JFM Archives. Cited as JFM, Tripartite Pact Study.

——. "Nichi-Doku kan ni okeru kōshō, keii" 日独間における交渉経緯 (The Japanese-German Negotiations, Particulars), in JFM Archives. Cited as JFM, Particulars.

——. *Nihon gaikō nempyō narabi ni shuyō bunsho* 日本外交年表並主要文書 (Chronology and Major Documents of Japanese Foreign Relations). 2 vols. Tokyo, Hara Shobō, 1965; first published in 1955.

——. *Nisso kōshō shi* 日ソ交渉史 (A History of Japanese-Soviet Relations). Tokyo, Gannandō, 1969; originally issued in 1942.

Japan, Imperial Headquarters, Army Division. "Nomonhan jiken keika no gaiyō" ノモンハン事件経過の概要 (Summary of the Nomonhan Incident), November 6, 1939, in JDA Archives.

Japan, Navy General Staff, Second Division. "Kanch'atsu jiken keika gaiyō" カンチャーズ事件経過概要 (Summary of the Kanchāzu Incident), copy in JDA Archives, original in NGS Archives.

Jones, F. C. *Japan's New Order in East Asia: Its Rise and Fall.* London, Oxford University Press, 1954.

Keishichō-shi Hensan Iinkai 警視庁史編纂委員会 (Metropolitan Police Board History Editorial Committee). *Keishichō shi I: Shōwa zempan* 警視庁史 I 昭和前編 (History of the Metropolitan Police Board, I: The Early Shōwa Era). Tokyo, Keishichō-shi Hensan Iinkai, 1959.

"Khasan," in *Bol'shaia sovetskaia entsiklopediia* (The Great Soviet Encyclopedia), Vol. 46, p. 90. Moscow, 1957.

Kiba Kōsuke, 木場浩介, ed. *Nomura Kichisaburō* 野村吉三郎. Tokyo, Nomura Kichisaburō Denki Kankōkai, 1961.

Kido Kōichi 木戸幸一. *Kido Kōichi nikki* 木戸幸一日記 (Diary of Kido Kōichi). 2 vols. Tokyo, Tōkyō Daigaku Shuppankai, 1966. Cited as *Kido Diary.*

Konoe Fumimaro 近衛文麿. *Heiwa e no doryoku* 平和への努力 (My Struggle for Peace). Tokyo, Nihon Dempō Tsūshinsha, 1946.

——. "Konoe shitsumu nisshi" 近衛執務日誌 (Konoe Office Diary), in Konoe Papers.

——. "Konoye Memoirs," International Military Tribunal for the Far East, No. 3.

——. *Ushinawareshi seiji* 失われし政治 (Politics that Failed). Tokyo, Asahi Shimbunsha, 1946.

Koyama Kango 小山完吾. *Koyama Kango nikki* 小山完吾日記 (Diary of Koyama Kango). Tokyo, Keio Tsūshin, 1955.

Krivitsky, W. G. *I Was Stalin's Agent.* London, Hamilton, 1939.

Kurihara Ken 栗原健. *Tennō: Shōwa shi oboegaki* 天皇 昭和史覚書 (The Emperor: A Note on the History of the Shōwa Period). Tokyo, Yūshindō, 1955.

Kurusu Saburō 来栖三郎. *Hōmatsu no sanjūgo-nen* 泡沫の三十五年 (Vain Endeavor). Tokyo, Bunka Shoin, 1948.

Kwantung Army Headquarters, First Section. "Nomonhan jiken: kimitsu sakusen nisshi" ノモンハン事件機密作戦日誌 (Confidential Diary of Kwantung Army Operations during the Nomonhan Incident), Vol. 1, in *Gendai shi shiryō 10,* pp. 71–149.

Langer, William L., and S. Everett Gleason. *The Undeclared War, 1940–1941.* New York, Harper, 1953.

Maejima Shōzō 前島省三. *Nihon fashizumu to Gikai* 日本ファシズムと議会 (Japanese Fascism and the Diet). Kyoto, Hōritsubunkasha, 1956.

Mainichi Shimbunsha. 毎日新聞社. *Tōkyō saiban hanketsu* 東京裁 判判決(Judgment of the Tokyo Military Tribunal). Tokyo, Mainichi Shimbunsha, 1949.

Maki, John M. *Japanese Militarism: Its Cause and Cure.* New York, Knopf, 1945.

Matsuoka Yōsuke 松岡洋右. *Nichi-Doku bōkyō kyō tei no igi* 日独防共協 定の意義(The Significance of the Japanese-German Anti-Comintern Pact). Tokyo, Daiichi Shuppansha, 1937.

——. "Shitsumu nisshi" 執務日誌(Office Diary), in JFM Archives.

Maxon, Yale Candee. *Control of Japanese Foreign Policy: A Study of Civil-Military Rivalry, 1930–1945.* Berkeley and Los Angeles, University of California Press, 1957.

Meskill, Johanna Margarete Menzel. *Hitler and Japan: The Hollow Alliance.* New York, Atherton, 1966.

"Nakajima Tetsuzō chūjō kaisōroku" 中島鉄蔵中将回想録 (Reminiscences of Lieutenant-General Nakajima Tetsuzō), 1939, in JDA Archives.

Nakamura Garō 中村雅郎. "Gyōmu nisshi" 業務日誌(Office Diary), June 1, 1940–December 31, 1943, in JDA Archives.

Nihon Kokusai Seiji Gakkai Taiheiyō Sensō Gen'in Kenkyūbu 日本国際政治学会太平洋戦争原因研究部 (Japan Association on International Relations, Study Group on the Causes of the Pacific War), *Taiheiyō sensō e no michi* 太平洋戦争への道(The Road to the Pacific War). 7 vols. and supplementary vol. of documents: *Bekkan shiryō hen.* Tokyo, Asahi Shimbunsha, 1962–63. Cited as *TSM.*

Nishi Haruhiko 西 春彦. *Kaisō no Nihon gaikō* 回想の日本外交(Diplomatic Memoirs). Tokyo, Iwanami Shoten, 1965.

——. "Kanzen gunshuku e no michi" 完全軍縮への道 (The Path to Total Disarmament), *Ekonomisuto,* December 26, 1961.

Obata Yūkichi Denki Kankōkai 小幡酉吉傳記刊行会, ed. *Obata Yūkichi.* Tokyo, Obata Yūkichi Denki Kankōkai, 1957.

Ogata Taketora 緒方竹虎. *Ichi gunjin no shōgai: kaisō no Yonai Mitsumasa* 一軍人の生涯:回想の米内光政 (The Life of an Admiral:

Reminiscences of Yonai Mitsumasa). Tokyo, Bungei Shunjū Shinsha, 1955.

Ōhashi Chūichi 大橋忠一. *Taiheiyō sensō yuraiki* 太平洋戦争由来記 (Origins of the Pacific War). Tokyo, Kaname Shobō, 1952.

Ōhata Tokushirō 大畑馬四郎. "Dai-ichiji sekai taisen go no Doku-So kankei to kyōchō gaikō no seiritsu" 第一次世界大戦後の独ソ関係と協調外交の成立 (Post-World War I German-Soviet Diplomatic Relations and the Establishment of Cooperative Diplomacy), *Shikan*, No. 62 (July 1961).

———. "Nichi-Doku kankei no ichi kōsatsu" 日独関係の一考察 (A Study of Japanese-German Relations), *Shikan*, Vols. 45 (September 1955), 46 (March 1956), and 47 (September 1956).

Ōshima Hiroshi 大島浩. "Bōkyō kyōtei oyobi Nichi-Doku-I sangoku dōmei teiketsu ni itaru jijō ni kansuru kaisō' 防共協定及び日独伊三国同盟締結に至る事情に関する回想 (Recollections of the Negotiations for the Anti-Comintern Pact and the Tripartite Pact), notes in the possession of Hasegawa Shin'ichi 長谷川進一, former secretary to Foreign Minister Matsuoka, based on an interview of December 14, 1955. Cited as Ōshima, "Recollections of the Negotiations."

Presseisen, Ernst L. *Germany and Japan: A Study in Totalitarian Diplomacy, 1933–1941*. The Hague, Martinus Nijhoff, 1958.

Ribbentrop, Joachim von. *Zwischen London und Moskau*. Leoni am Starnberger See, Druffel Verlag, 1953.

Royal Institute on International Affairs. *Documents on International Affairs, 1939–1946*, Vol. 1. London, Oxford University Press, 1951.

Saitō Toshio 斉藤敏雄. "Oetsu kyoki" 嗚咽獻欷 (Sobbing and Weeping), *Dōkiseikai shi*, March 1958.

Saitō Yoshie 斉藤良衛. *Azamukareta rekishi: Matsuoka to sangoku dōmei no rimen* 欺かれた歴史 松岡と三国同盟の裏面 (History Deceived: The Inside Story of Matsuoka and the Tripartite Pact). Tokyo, Yomiuri Shimbunsha, 1955.

———. "Nichi-Doku-I Dōmei jōyaku teiketsu yōroku" 日独伊同盟条約締結摘録 (Summary Record of the Conclusion of the Tripartite Pact), in JFM Archives. Cited as Saitō, "Tripartite Pact Record."

Sawada Shigeru 沢田茂. "Gozen kaigi gijiroku" 御前会議議

事錄 (Proceedings of Imperial Conferences), in JDA Archives, published in *TSM: Bekkan*, pp. 337–42.

Sevost'yanov, G. N. "Voennoe i diplomaticheskoe porazhenie Yaponii v period sobytii u reki Khalkin-gol" (Japan's Military and Diplomatic Defeat at the Time of the Khalkin-gol Incident), *Voprosy istorii*, No. 8 (August 1957).

Shigemitsu Mamoru 重光 葵. *Gaikō kaisōroku* 外交回想錄 (Diplomatic Reminiscences). Tokyo, Mainichi Shimbunsha, 1953.

——. *Japan and Her Destiny: My Struggle for Peace*. Translated by Oswald White and edited by F. S. G. Piggott. New York, E. P. Dutton, 1958.

Shinsō Henshū Kyoku 真相編集局, ed. *Nihon no tai-So imbō* 日本．対ソ陰謀(Japanese Plots against the USSR). Tokyo, Shinsō Jimminsha, 1948.

Shirer, William L. *The Rise and Fall of the Third Reich*. New York, Simon and Schuster, 1960.

Sommer, Theo. *Deutschland und Japan zwischen den Mächten, 1935–1940: vom Antikominternpakt zum Dreimächtepakt*. Tubingen, JCB Mohr (Paul Siebeck), 1962.

Takagi Sōkichi 高木惣吉. "Nichi-Doku-I gunji dōmei seiritsu no keii" 日独伊軍事同盟成立・経緯 (Particulars of the Conclusion of the Military Alliance between Japan, Germany, and Italy), *Sekai*, No. 59 (November 1950).

Takashima Tatsuhiko 高島辰彦. "Nisshi" 日誌 (Diary), in JDA Archives.

Tanaka Sōgorō 田中惣五郎. *Nihon fashizumu shi* 日本ファシズム史(History of Japanese Fascism). Tokyo, Kawade Shobō Shinsha, 1960.

Tanemura Sakō 種村佐孝. *Daihon'ei kimitsu nisshi* 大本営機密日誌 (Confidential Record of the Imperial Headquarters). Tokyo, Daiyamondosha, 1952.

Tōgō Shigenori 東郷茂徳. *Jidai no ichi-men* 時代の一面 (One View of an Era). Tokyo, Kaizōsha, 1952.

Toscano, Mario. *Le origini diplomatiche del patto d'acciaio* (The Diplomatic Origins of the Pact of Steel). 2nd rev. ed., Florence, Sansoni, 1956.

Trefousse, H. L. *Germany and American Neutrality, 1939–1941*. New York, Bookman Associates, 1951.

Tsuji Kiyoaki 辻 清明. *Nihon kanryōsei no kenkyū* 日本官僚制の研究(A

study of Japanese bureaucracy). Tokyo, Tōkyō Daigaku Shuppankai, 1969.

Tsuji Masanobu 辻 政信. *Nomonhan* モンハン. Tokyo, Tōa Shobō, 1950.

Ueda Toshio 植田捷雄. "Nichi-Doku-I sangoku dōmei" 日独伊三国同盟 (The Tripartite Pact), in Nihon Gaikō Gakkai 日本外交学会 (Association for the Study of Japanese Diplomacy), ed. *Taiheiyō sensō gen'in ron* 太平洋戦争原因論 (The Origins of the Pacific War). Tokyo, Shimbun Gakkansha, 1953.

Ugaki Kazushige 宇垣一成. "Rōhei no jukkai" 老兵の述懐 (Recollections of an Old Soldier), *Yomiuri hyōron*, October 1950.

——. *Shōrai seidan* 松籟清談 (Interview with Ugaki). Edited by Kamata Sawaichirō 鎌田沢一郎. Tokyo, Bungei Shunjū *Shinsha*, 1951.

——. *Ugaki Kazushige nikki* 宇垣一成日記 (Diary of Ugaki Kazushige). Edited by Tsunoda Jun 角田順. 3 vols. Tokyo, Misuzu Shobō, 1968–71.

U.S., Department of State. *Documents on German Foreign Policy, 1918–1945, from the Archives of the German Foreign Ministry*, Series D (1937–1945), Vols. 1 (1949), 8 (1954), 9 (1956), 10 (1954), 11 (1960). Washington D.C., U.S. Government Printing Office. Cited as *DGFP*.

——. *Foreign Relations of the United States: Diplomatic Papers, 1937*, Vol. 3. Washington D.C., U.S. Government Printing Office, 1954.

——. *Papers Relating to the Foreign Relations of the United States: Japan, 1931–1941*. 2 vols. Washington D.C., U.S. Government Printing Office, 1943. Cited as *FR, Japan*.

Weizsaecker, Ernst von. *Memoirs*. Chicago, H. Regnery, 1951.

Wiskemann, Elizabeth. *The Rome-Berlin Axis: A History of the Relations between Hitler and Mussolini*. New York, Oxford University Press, 1949.

Yabe Teiji 矢部貞治, ed. *Konoe Fumimaro* 近衛文麿. 2 vols. Tokyo, Kobundo, 1952.

Yamanaka Minetarō 山中峰太郎. *Tetsu to niku* 鉄と肉 (Iron and Flesh). Tokyo, Seibundō Shinkosha, 1940.

Yosano Shigeru 与謝野 秀 "Bōkyō kyōtei yori sangoku dōmei teiketsu ni itaru keii" 防共協定ヨリ三国同盟締結ニ至ル経緯 (From the Anti-

Comintern Pact to the Conclusion of the Tripartite Pact), in "Kyokutō Gunji Saiban ni okeru Hirota hikoku bengo kankei shiryō (Morishima chōsho)" 極東軍事裁判に於ける広田被告弁護関係資料（守島調書）(International Military Tribunal for the Far East, Materials Related to the Defense of Hirota Kōki: Morishima Gorō Testimony), in Shidehara Heiwa Bunkō. Cited as Yosano Statement.

——. "Zoruge jiken no zengo" ゾルゲ事件の前後 (At the Time of the Sorge Incident), *Yomiuri hyōron*, December 1950.

Contributors

HANS H. BAERWALD is professor of political science at the University of California, Los Angeles. Born in Tokyo in 1927, he received his doctorate from Berkeley in 1956 and has spent many years in Japan, most recently as director of the Study Center of the University of California in Tokyo. His professional interests have been focused on practical politics and parliamentary government, his writings including *The American Republic: Its Government and Politics* (with Peter H. Odegard, 1964 and rev. ed. with William Havard, 1969), *The Purge of Japanese Leaders under the Occupation* (1959), and "The Japanese Communist Party—Yoyogi and Its Rivals," in R. A. Scalapino, ed., *The Communist Revolution in Asia* (1969).

ALVIN D. COOX is professor of history and director of the Center for Asian Studies at San Diego State University. He was born in 1924, received his B.A. from New York University in 1945 and his Ph.D. from Harvard University in 1951. A specialist in Japanese military history, he has served as: senior historian in the Operations Research Office of Johns Hopkins University; historian in the Japanese Research Division of the U.S. Army, Japan; and managing editor of *Orient/West* magazine in Tokyo. His principal works include *Kōgun: the Japanese Army in the Pacific War* (with Hayashi Saburō) (1959), *The Year of the Tiger* (1964), *The Japanese Image* (coedited with Maurice Schneps) (2 vols., 1965, 1966), *Japan: The Final Agony* (1970), and most recently, *Tojo* (1974).

HATA IKUHIKO, chief historian of the Japan Finance Ministry, was born in 1932. After graduating from Tokyo University in 1956 he studied at both Harvard and Columbia Universities. Combining public service and academic interests, he has served in Japan's Economic Planning Agency and Defense Agency and as professor at the National Defense College. His principal writings include *Nitchū sensōshi* (A history of the Japanese–Chinese war, 1931–1941) (1961), *Gun fashizumu undōshi* (A history of the Japanese military fascist movement) (1962), and, in English, *Reality and Illusion: The Hidden Crisis between Japan and the U.S.S.R., 1932–1934* (1967). He is currently supervising the writing of an official history of Japan's immediate postwar fiscal policy.

HOSOYA CHIHIRO is professor of international relations, Faculty of Law, Hitotsubashi University in Tokyo. He is also vice president of the Japan Association of International Relations and chairman of the editorial committee of *Nihon gaikō bunsho*, the Foreign Ministry's official series of historical documents on Japanese foreign policy. He was born in 1920 and graduated from Tokyo University in 1951, and since receiving the Ph.D. from Kyoto University in 1961 has carried on research at a number of centers abroad. A specialist in diplomatic history and decision-making, he has published in both Japanese and English, including most recently *Roshia kakumei to Nihon* (The Russian revolution and Japan) (1972). He is coeditor and coauthor of *Nichi-Bei kankeishi, 1931–1941* (4 vols., 1971–72) and he contributed to the English version, *Pearl Harbor as History: Japanese–American Relations, 1931–1941* (1973), which was edited by Dorothy Borg and Shumpei Okamoto.

JAMES WILLIAM MORLEY is professor of government at Columbia University. Born in 1921, he received his B.A. from Harvard College in 1942 and his Ph.D. from Columbia University in 1954. A member and former director of the East Asian Institute, Columbia University, he has served as special assistant to the American ambassador in Tokyo and as consultant to the U.S. Department of State. He has most recently edited and contributed to *Dilemmas of Growth in Prewar Japan* (1971), *Forecast for Japan: Security in the 1970s* (1972), *Prologue to the Future: The United States and Japan in the Postindustrial Age* (1974), and *Japan's Foreign Relations, 1868–1941: A Research Guide* (1974).

ŌHATA TOKUSHIRŌ, professor of diplomatic history at Waseda University, Tokyo, was born in 1929, received his undergraduate and graduate education at Waseda, and joined the faculty in 1956. He is an authority on Japan's foreign relations and is well known for his manual of diplomatic history, *Gaikōshi teiyō* (1964, rev. ed. 1972), which he coauthored with Iriye Keishirō. His other works include *Kokusai kankyō to Nihon gaikō* (The international environment and Japan's diplomatic history) (1966), and most recently, *Nihon gaikōshi* (A history of Japan's diplomacy) (1974).

Index

Studies of The East Asian Institute

The Ladder of Success in Imperial China, by Ping-ti Ho. New York: Columbia University Press, 1962.

The Chinese Inflation, 1937–1949, by Shun-hsin Chou. New York: Columbia University Press, 1963.

Reformer in Modern China: Chang Chien, 1853–1926, by Samuel Chu. New York: Columbia University Press, 1965.

Research in Japanese Sources: A Guide, by Herschel Webb with the assistance of Marleigh Ryan. New York: Columbia University Press, 1965.

Society and Education in Japan, by Herbert Passin. New York: Bureau of Publications, Teachers College, Columbia University, 1965.

Agricultural Production and Economic Development in Japan, 1873–1922, by James I. Nakamura. Princeton: Princteon University Press, 1966.

Japan's First Modern Novel: Ukigumo of Futabatei Shimei, by Marleigh Ryan. New York: Columbia University Press, 1967.

The Korean Communist Movement, 1918–1948, by Dae-Sook Suh. Princeton: Princeton University Press, 1967.

The First Vietnam Crisis, by Melvin Gurtov. New York: Columbia University Press, 1967.

Cadres, Bureaucracy, and Political Power in Communist China, by A. Doak Barnett. New York: Columbia University Press, 1967.

The Japanese Imperial Institution in the Tokugawa Period, by Herschel Webb. New York: Columbia University Press, 1968.

Higher Education and Business Recruitment in Japan, by Koya Azumi. New York: Teachers College Press, Columbia University, 1969.

The Communists and Chinese Peasant Rebellions: A Study in the Rewriting of Chinese History, by James P. Harrison, Jr. New York: Atheneum, 1969.

How the Conservatives Rule Japan, by Nathaniel B. Thayer. Princeton: Princeton University Press, 1969.

Aspects of Chinese Education, edited by C. T. Hu. New York: Teachers College Press, Columbia University, 1970.

Documents of Korean Communism, 1918–1948, by Dae-Sook Suh. Princeton: Princeton University Press, 1970.

Japanese Education: A Bibliography of Materials in the English Language, by Herbert Passin. New York: Teachers College Press, Columbia University, 1970.

Economic Development and the Labor Market in Japan, by Koji Taira. New York: Columbia University Press, 1970.

The Japanese Oligarchy and the Russo-Japanese War, by Shumpei Okamoto. New York: Columbia University Press, 1970.

Imperial Restoration in Medieval Japan, by H. Paul Varley. New York: Columbia University Press, 1971.

Japan's Postwar Defense Policy, 1947–1968, by Martin E. Weinstein. New York: Columbia University Press, 1971.

Election Campaigning Japanese Style, by Gerald L. Curtis. New York: Columbia University Press, 1971.

China and Russia: The "Great Game," by O. Edmund Clubb. New York: Columbia University Press, 1971.

Money and Monetary Policy in Communist China, by Katharine Huang Hsiao. New York: Columbia University Press, 1971.

The District Magistrate in Late Imperial China, by John R. Watt. New York: Columbia University Press, 1972.

Law and Policy in China's Foreign Relations: A Study of Attitudes and Practice, by James C. Hsiung. New York: Columbia University Press, 1972.

Pearl Harbor as History: Japanese-American Relations, 1931–1941, edited by Dorothy Borg and Shumpei Okamoto, with the assistance of Dale K. A. Finlayson. New York: Columbia University Press, 1973.

Japanese Culture: A Short History, by H. Paul Varley. New York: Praeger, 1973.

Doctors in Politics: The Political Life of the Japan Medical Association, by William E. Steslicke. New York: Praeger, 1973.

The Japan Teachers Union: A Radical Interest Group in Japanese Politics, by Donald Ray Thurston. Princeton: Princeton University Press, 1973.

Japan's Foreign Policy, 1868–1941: A Research Guide, edited by James William Morley. New York: Columbia University Press, 1974.

Palace and Politics in Prewar Japan, by David Anson Titus. New York: Columbia University Press, 1974.

The Idea of China: Essays in Geographic Myth and Theory, by Andrew March. Devon, England: David and Charles, 1974.

Origins of the Cultural Revolution, by Roderick MacFarquhar. New York: Columbia University Press, 1974.

Shiba Kokan: Artist, Innovator, and Pioneer in the Westernization of Japan, by Calvin L. French. Tokyo: Weatherhill, 1974.

Insei: Abdicated Sovereigns in the Politics of Late Heian Japan, by G. Cameron Hurst. New York: Columbia University Press, 1975.

Embassy at War, by Harold Joyce Noble. Edited with an introduction by Frank Baldwin, Jr. Seattle: University of Washington Press, 1975.

Rebels and Bureaucrats: China's December 9ers, by John Israel and Donald W. Klein. Berkeley: University of California Press, 1975.

Deterrent Diplomacy, edited by James William Morley. New York: Columbia University Press, 1976.

House United, House Divided: The Chinese Family in Taiwan, by Myron L. Cohen. New York: Columbia University Press, 1976.

Escape from Predicament: Neo-Confucianism and China's Evolving Political Culture, by Thomas A. Metzger. New York: Columbia University Press, 1976.